entencing

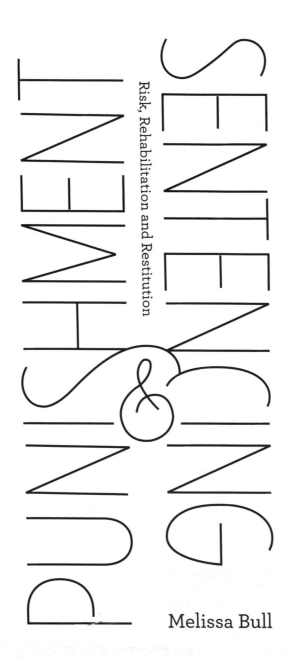

SENTENCING & PUNISHMENT

Risk, Rehabilitation and Restitution

Melissa Bull

OXFORD
UNIVERSITY PRESS
AUSTRALIA & NEW ZEALAND

OXFORD
UNIVERSITY PRESS
AUSTRALIA & NEW ZEALAND

253 Normanby Road, South Melbourne, Victoria 3205, Australia

Oxford University Press is a department of the University of Oxford.
It furthers the University's objective of excellence in research,
scholarship, and education by publishing worldwide in

Oxford New York

Auckland Cape Town Dar es Salaam Hong Kong Karachi
Kuala Lumpur Madrid Melbourne Mexico City Nairobi
New Delhi Shanghai Taipei Toronto

With offices in

Argentina Austria Brazil Chile Czech Republic France Greece
Guatemala Hungary Italy Japan Poland Portugal Singapore
South Korea Switzerland Thailand Turkey Ukraine Vietnam

OXFORD is a trademark of Oxford University Press
in the UK and in certain other countries

National Library of Australia Cataloguing-in-Publication entry

Bull, Melissa.
Punishment and sentencing: risk, rehabilitation and restitution / Melissa Bull.

9780195561081 (pbk)

Includes index.
Bibliography.

Punishment.
Sentences (Criminal procedure)
Criminals—Rehabilitation.
Alternatives to imprisonment.
Restitution.

345.077

Edited by Jocelyn Hargrave
Cover designed by Elizabeth Smith
Text designed by Leigh Ashforth
Typeset by diacriTech, Chennai, India
Proofread by Elaine Cochrane
Indexed by Karen Gillen
Printed in China by Sheck Wah Tong Printing Press Ltd

CONTENTS

PART 1: INTRODUCTION   1

CHAPTER 1: It's not just about the prison   3

Introduction   3
Colonial Australia: A prison without walls   4
The birth of Australian prisons   7
Australia's carceral archipelago   10
An 'other' history of Australian punishment: First contact   13
More contemporary alternatives to prison   15
Conclusion: Where to from here?   18

CHAPTER 2: Principles and practices of punishment and sentencing   23

Introduction   23
Bentham's utilitarianism and the end of transportation   24
Punishment and reform: Offenders as broken machines   26
Incapacitation   29
Just deserts and retribution   32
Managerialism   35
Restorative justice and communitarianism   37
Other innovations in justice   40
Conclusion   43

CHAPTER 3: Some social perspectives on punishment   45

Introduction   45
Durkheim   46
Critical theory: Marxism, feminism and post-colonialism   48
Foucault   52
Risk   55
Elias   58
Conclusion   61

CONTENTS

PART 2: RISK   63

CHAPTER 4: Child sexual offences and community notification   65

Introduction   65

The problem: Child sex offending   66

Responding to sexual violence offences against children   69

Australian responses to child sex offending   70

Penological principles: The utility of incapacitation?   77

Thinking theoretically: Civilising vengeance   80

Conclusion   83

CHAPTER 5: Terrorism: Risk, retaliation and preventive detention   85

Introduction   85

The problem of terrorism   86

Causes and responses   87

Responding to terrorism in Australia   88

Penological principles: Pre-emptive prevention   100

Thinking theoretically: Risk and retaliation   102

Conclusion   106

PART 3: REHABILITATION   109

CHAPTER 6: Drug courts: Clinic or panopticon?   111

Introduction   111

Alternative strategies in the unwinnable 'war on drugs'   112

The Australian alliance   114

Penological principles: Just treatment or preventive punishment?   118

Thinking theoretically: The panopticon and beyond   120

Conclusion   127

CHAPTER 7: Indigenous justice and the decolonisation of punishment   129

Introduction   129

Indigenous people in the criminal justice system   130

Indigenous justice programs   139

Indigenous courts and circle sentencing courts   142

Penological principles: The politics of partnership   145

Thinking theoretically: The decolonisation of justice?   147

Conclusion   150

CHAPTER 8: Responding to domestic violence: Special pleas and specialist courts   153

Introduction   153

The problem with domestic violence   154

Responding to women as offenders: Battered women's syndrome   156

Responding to women as victims: Domestic violence courts and programs for men   160

Penological principles: Punishment and protection   167

Thinking theoretically: Feminism and its discontents   170

Conclusion   171

PART 4: RESTITUTION   173

CHAPTER 9: Youth justice and group conferencing: Restoration and restitution   175

Introduction   175

A brief history of responses to young offenders   176

Australia as a leader in restorative justice and youth justice conferencing   178

Penological principles: Restoration or restitution   184

Thinking theoretically: YJCs as rituals of responsibilisation   191

Conclusion   196

CONTENTS

CHAPTER 10: From fines to forfeiture   199

Introduction   199
The problem of hooning   200
Penalties for traffic offences   202
Penological principles: Managerialism, deterrence and incapacitation   211
Thinking theoretically: Justifying draconian penalty   215
Conclusion   218

CHAPTER 11: The three Rs of the penological
triangle   221

Introduction   221
Risk   221
Rehabilitation   224
Restitution   227
Punishment and sentencing: The prison and beyond   229

BIBLIOGRAPHY   235

INDEX   255

Introduction

1

It's not just about the prison

INTRODUCTION

This book is about punishment in Australia. It provides an overview of the ways of thinking, social institutions and practices that have shaped sentencing and punishment in this country at different times. Here the term *sentencing* is not used in the narrow legal sense; instead, it refers more generally to decision-making processes involved in responding to offenders. *Punishment* is also defined more broadly, allowing us to consider the various ways in which the criminal justice system responds to those who break the law. The discussion of sentencing and punishment throughout this book is both descriptive and analytical, providing information across a range of areas, locating current practice in a broad context and raising important questions about how we understand and engage these processes today.

Most Australian texts on this topic begin with some discussion of transportation and the convict experience during the early years of settlement. This is an important place to start. As Mark Finnane points out, '[this] nation-state's origins were an experiment in punishment. Before the penitentiary there was transportation … No history of punishment in Australia after the convict era can proceed without acknowledging the significance of this experiment in penal systems' (1997, p. 1). However, much of this literature is not so much concerned with the transportation of convicts as punishment as 'issues of national identity and moral worth' (Finnane 1997, p. 3). Australian histories generally fail to locate the convict system within the boarder history of punishment and rarely extend beyond a history of imprisonment (Garton 1996). Few have sought to investigate the variety of punishments for criminal offences or the changing patterns in their use.

Imprisonment both in colonial and contemporary Australia was and remains far from universal as a form of punishment. This is something that is not widely acknowledged. At the beginning of the twenty-first century, popular opinion in Australia regularly identifies imprisoning offenders as the logical response to lawbreaking (Hogg and Brown 1998). Many people believe that prison is an archetypal form of punishment that has a very long history. Contrary to this view, in Australia and elsewhere, imprisonment as a form of punishment is a relatively recent practice. Admittedly, there have been societies that have used the detention of people at different points in history, but the purpose and the effect of such practices within the specific social and historical context of the time make these distinctive societal phenomena. Even in the contemporary global context, imprisonment specifically, and punishment as a set of broader social practices, varies significantly according to cultural contexts (O'Toole 2006). With this in mind, it is worth beginning by asking what types of punishment existed in colonial Australia and what legacy might they have for sentencing and corrections today?

This first chapter begins by addressing these questions. It traces the development of punishment in Australia, highlighting the diversity of practices and ends that have made up penality: 'the complex of ideas (about proper punishment, about effective punishment), institutions (laws, policies and practices, agencies and buildings), and relationships (who has the power to say who is punished, whose ideas count, what is the relationship of those who punish and are punished to the rest of society) involved in the punishment of offenders' (Hudson 2003a, pp. 6–7). Sketching the historical and social context of Australian penality makes it clear that while imprisonment has made, and continues to make, a significant contribution to the domain of criminal justice, there is much more to it. In short, to fully appreciate the scope and complexity of punishment and sentencing, we need to look beyond the prison. We should also remember that it is not a question of either/or. There is a tendency in both popular and specialist debates to imagine a complete dichotomy between imprisonment and 'freedom': that release from imprisonment under some form of supervisory order, such as parole or licence, is portrayed as 'being free', on 'early release', no longer subject to punishment (Brown 1998). This privileges imprisonment as the only 'real' punishment. Instead, it is important to acknowledge and engage with the connections between prison and non-custodial or post-prison orders. All such orders are sentences: periods of supervision that are served in varied settings and under varied conditions, not the either/or of incarceration or freedom. As David Brown suggests, the crucial question is 'not one of regulation versus non-regulation—but, rather, one of the specific nature of regulatory conditions' (Garland and Young 1983, p. 33 in Brown 1998, p. 382).

The chapter concludes by outlining the intellectual framework for this book, which allows us to survey this broader horizon, which includes more contemporary and 'innovative' programs of punishment and sentencing in this country.

COLONIAL AUSTRALIA: A PRISON WITHOUT WALLS

In the early eighteenth century the most common sentence imposed on offenders in Britain was transportation. Offenders were initially sent to America, but the American War of Independence marked the end of this arrangement in 1776 (O'Toole 2006). Old sailing ships known as hulks were then used to house the resulting overflow from England's prisons on the Thames River. Provision was made for the construction of two new prisons—penitentiaries— but delays linked to concerns about the high cost of construction put pressure on the use of hulks. The decision in 1786 to found a settlement in Botany Bay made transportation to Australia an option. Transportation was an attractive solution (Finnane 1997): it provided an alternative to the death penalty at a time when an alternative was sought; removing large numbers of offenders from local communities acted as a safety valve in societies that were under significant pressure from expanding populations; and sending convicts on an uncertain voyage to an indeterminate fate in a remote place like Botany Bay seemed like a weighty deterrent. However, transportation was more than the removal of the unwanted and dangerous: its punishment rationale was linked to imperial objectives at the time. According to Finnane (1997, see also Braithwaite 1999a; Hirst 1983; O'Toole 2006), whether the settlement at Botany Bay was primarily a solution to the pressing problems of overcrowded hulks or a means to secure strategic advantage in the South Seas remains a matter of debate. Nevertheless, in the broader context of the expansion of Europe, transportation of large numbers of convicts to Australia was made possible by the idea of the British Empire and was part of its consolidation (Finnane 1997; Pratt 1991).

Australia was colonised initially as an open jail. The First Fleet was dispatched in 1787. It was made up of eleven ships and around 1350 people, including approximately 750 convicts. It arrived to establish Australia's first penal settlement at Port Jackson in January 1788. This was the beginning of the era of convict transportation, which ended when the last convict ship sailed up the Swan River in Western Australia in 1868. During the intervening eighty years, 160 000 male and female prisoners landed in Australia from Great Britain (mostly from England) and Ireland. Some 1321 convicts came to Australia from places other than this. Most of the convicts transported to Australia arrived in the 1820s and 1830s. About half—approximately 72 500 men and 11 500 women—were landed in New South Wales, 66 500 went to Van Diemen's Land and nearly 10 000 went to Western Australia, which succeeded the other colonies as the main destination for transported convicts during the 1850s and 1860s. Smaller numbers were landed directly at penal stations on Norfolk Island and at Moreton Bay and Port Phillip during the declining years of transportation to the eastern mainland colonies (Finnane 1997; O'Toole 2006).

Penal settlements are often cited in descriptions of the brutality of the convict system. In the first three decades, flogging was the principal form of punishment. There is evidence of high rates of flogging at different times and places in the penal colonies (Finnane 1997). Women and men were whipped until restrictions on the punishment of women, which prohibited flogging, were introduced in 1817. According to Braithwaite (1999a), while the floggings were often brutal, they could mostly be avoided by sticking to the rules—after all, the convicts were in an open prison where 'the lash had to do the work of the walls, the warders and the punishment cells' (Hirst 1983, p. 68). Unlike the American colonies and some work environments in England, flogging in Australia was not a punishment that could be given indiscriminately by a private master. It was a legal punishment that resulted from hearing a charge against the convict defendant (Braithwaite 1999a; Finnane 1997; Hirst 1983). Australian masters of convicts had to send them to a hearing before a magistrate before the lash could be administered by a constable.

English prisoners did not enjoy these rights. Some historians argue that, in many respects, the adversity of male convicts in Australia was less than that of employed men in England. The convicts worked shorter hours, were better fed, better housed, better clothed and had better access to medical care than free English workers. Australian convicts had a right to hold property and sue to protect it, to sell part of their labour on the free market, to appear as witnesses in court cases, and to write petitions to a governor who mostly treated them seriously. Convicts could and did press charges against their masters for ill treatment or exploitation (Hirst 1983, pp. 109–11).

For early governors of the colony, the primary objective was to get their convict population to be willing workers. In their view the best way to do this was to institutionalise just treatment. According to Governor Lachlan Macquarie, for example, transportation was punishment; after surviving the ordeal of the journey, it was up to individuals to work hard and re-establish their lives. He provided convicts with the chance to earn a reprieve and re-establish citizenship (O'Toole 2006); he offered a system of assignment, tickets-of-leave and land grants to the emancipated, as well as their appointment to positions of trust. Upon arrival in Australia, most convicts could expect to be assigned to work for a master. This usually meant a private landowner, but for many it also meant working as domestic servants in towns or for the government. About one in every ten convicts was kept by the government to labour on public works projects. The principle of the assignment system was to disperse convicts in various locations throughout the colony, keeping them in working contact with the settler population. The system taught them practical skills, encouraged independence and brought rewards for the completion of their work (Braithwaite 1999a). Having a convict placed completely under the control of a free settler put the onus on the settler to ensure they got the best out of the individual. Convicts were paid modestly at government-regulated rates for this work. In addition, once convicts completed their assigned work or assigned hours, they had a right to work at market rates for other masters. In conditions of acute labour shortage, many masters secured the best convicts by offering them side payments (Hirst 1983).

Responsible conduct on assignment would entitle convicts to a ticket-of-leave, which enabled them to work for whoever they chose. There were only three constraints on behaviour: convicts were confined to a specified district, they had to report regularly to the local authority, and the ticket-of-leave could be revoked. Pardons were widely granted to well-behaved, highly productive convicts. In New South Wales, certificates of freedom were issued to convicts who were pardoned or who had served their terms. This was necessary in a convict society where sometimes emancipists needed to prove they were free. The certificate established that the holder was 'restored to all the rights and privileges of free subjects' (Hirst 1983, p. 108). This was another example of colonial law bestowing more full rights on ex-convicts than English law of the time, where even a pardon was not sufficient to restore certain rights to the ex-offender. Emancipated convicts were given substantial free grants of land, animals, tools and seeds, sufficient for them to become economically viable settlers. Many became large landholders. They became masters of convicts on assignment themselves. By the late 1820s ex-convicts were masters of the majority of convicts on assignment, owned over half the wealth of the colony and three-quarters of the land (Hirst 1983, p. 81). Men were given 50 acres if they had a wife to support and 30 acres if they were single; they received another 10 acres for each child. The policy was intended to encourage marriage as part of the strategy of reform. There is no evidence that women were given land. Women were denied economic security by any route other than marriage (Braithwaite 1999a).

THE BIRTH OF AUSTRALIAN PRISONS

Governor Macquarie administered the colony of New South Wales primarily as a place of settlement, in which a large labour force of convicts provided a key resource for development. His project of building a new society conflicted with the penal objectives expected by the British criminal justice system. The relative freedoms of the convicts under the system of assignment and government service allowed too much liberty to those who were supposed to be undergoing a severe punishment. As the colony became better established, there was growing uncertainty in England about what transportation actually meant once the convict had arrived in New South Wales. This was a threat to the integrity of the British criminal justice system. In 1819 Commissioner John Thomas Bigge was therefore given the task of examining the efficiency and effectiveness of the penal colonies as a jail. He aimed to reinstitute the certainty of punishment and reduce the living standards of convicts. The removal of the convict through transportation from Great Britain or Ireland was no longer the penalty; rather, the circumstances of bondage in Australia were to be harsh enough that no one could regard transportation as a ticket to a better life (Finnane 1997, p. 11).

Convicts were subjected to a stricter regime of control. Transportation without the visible punishment of hard labour was not punishment enough. Between 1820 and 1840, convict labour was organised to explicitly express the colony's penal character. The hardest convicts were subject to secondary punishment in specifically designated remote penal settlements, like Norfolk Island, Port Arthur and Moreton Bay. The less reliable were sentenced to lengthy service in government-run penal labour gangs, whose task was the building of roads, bridges and ports, thereby providing infrastructure for a growing economy. Government work gangs were extremely harsh. In 1826 Governor Darling developed the chain-gang system. Prisoners worked in heavy chains, including a neck collar, and were locked up at night in cramped 'prison boxes' mounted on wheels and placed at the work site (O'Toole 2006).

Norfolk Island

Before the First Fleet sailed to found a convict settlement in New South Wales, final instructions received by Governor Arthur Phillip, received less than three weeks before sailing, included the colonisation of Norfolk Island to prevent it falling into the hands of France, whose naval leaders were showing interest in the Pacific. Upon arrival at Port Jackson in January 1788, Phillip ordered Lieutenant Philip Gidley King to lead a small party of convicts and free men to take control of the island and prepare for its commercial development. On 6 March 1788 they landed on Norfolk Island. More convicts were sent and the island was seen as a farm, supplying Sydney with grain and vegetables during its early years of near starvation (Clark 1980). However, the crops often failed and the lack of a natural safe harbour hindered communication and the transport of supplies and produce. Impeding starvation in Sydney led to a greater movement of convicts and marines to Norfolk Island in March 1790 on HMS *Sirius*. This attempt turned to disaster when *Sirius* was wrecked and although there was no loss of life, some stores were destroyed and the ship's crew was marooned for ten months (Tench 2006). Despite this setback, the settlement grew slowly as more convicts were sent from Sydney; many chose to remain as settlers when their sentences expired. By 1792, the population had grown to more than 1000. In 1794 King first suggested the closure of Norfolk Island as a penal settlement because it was too remote and difficult for shipping and too costly to maintain. By 1803 the Secretary of State, Lord Robert Hobart, called for the removal of part of the Norfolk Island military establishment, settlers and convicts to Van Diemen's Land due to its great expense and the communication difficulties between Norfolk Island and Sydney. This was achieved rather slowly: the last settlers left on 15 February 1814. From that day until 6 June 1825, the island was abandoned.

In 1824 the British government instructed Thomas Brisbane, then Governor of New South Wales, to occupy Norfolk Island as a place to send the worst convicts. While its remoteness was seen previously as a disadvantage, it was now considered an asset for secondary punishment through the detention of those who had committed further crimes since arriving in New South Wales. Brisbane assured his masters that those sent to Norfolk Island would be excluded from any hope of return. Governor Ralph Darling, who succeeded Brisbane, was even more severe; for him, Norfolk Island was held out as a place of the most extreme punishment, only short of death.

The harshness of the penal colony was demonstrated by repeated mutinies in 1826, 1834 and 1846. Following a convict mutiny in 1835, Father William Ullathorne, Vicar General of Sydney, visited Norfolk Island to comfort the mutineers sentenced to execution. He found it 'the most heartrending scene that I ever witnessed'. Having the duty of informing the prisoners as to who was reprieved and who was to die, he was shocked to record as 'a literal fact that each man who heard his reprieve wept bitterly, and that each man who heard of his condemnation to death went down on his knees with dry eyes, and thanked

God' (Ullathorne 1941, p. 100). In 1846 a report by magistrate Robert Pringle Stuart provided an account of the scarcity and poor quality of food, inadequacy of housing, torture and incessant flogging, insubordination of convicts, and corruption of overseers.

A few convicts left a written record of their experience. Their descriptions of living and working conditions, food and housing, and the punishments given for seemingly trivial offences are extreme (see Hazzard 1984; Hughes 1988). They describe a settlement devoid of all human decency and under the iron rule of tyrannical and autocratic commandants. The actions of most of the commandants were reported to be excessively harsh. The exception was Captain Alexander Maconochie who arrived in 1840. He concluded that brutality would breed defiance. He attempted to apply his own theories of penal reform, providing incentives as well as punishment (O'Toole 2006). His methods were criticised as being too lenient and he was replaced in 1844. His successors, Joseph Child and John Price, quickly returned the settlement to harsh rule. This second penal settlement began to be wound down after 1847. The entire settlement was closed down in 1956. The New South Wales government gave the expense of maintaining it as the reason for its closure.

In England the anticipated prisons were eventually built and the penitentiary became dominant in the 1840s as a new form of punishment. The proportion of convicted felons who were sentenced to transportation dropped from three in five to less than one in five. The penitentiary aimed to reform the incarcerated prisoner through a regime of silence, separation from the social world of crime and offending, and contemplation of one's faults. The coincidence of the program of prison building in Great Britain, together with opposition to transportation as an uncertain punishment and growing colonial resistance, ended transportation to New South Wales in 1840; Tasmania, in 1853; and Western Australia, in 1868. By the 1830s the growth of free immigration to New South Wales provided a more reliable and less costly means of supplying labour and meeting imperial needs; thus the punishment rhetoric that had been used to justify transportation had shifted its focus towards the prison (Finnane 1997, p. 13). At times, however, principle and pragmatism came into conflict in both imperial and colonial decisions on transportation. For example, in 1849 while one group of colonists in Sydney were forcefully resisting the offloading of a shipment of convicts, another group at Fremantle, in Western Australia, were calling for them because they would address the labour needs of the newer, still struggling colony (Finnane 1997).

In the nineteenth century the foundations of the physical infrastructure of Australia's prison system were laid. By the mid-century, cities began to develop in each of the colonies and the makeshift prisons, watch houses and stockades that initially served these settlements were no longer adequate. A significant commitment to prison building across the country lasted from 1850 to 1880.

In most Australian states for the first half of the twentieth century, the prison assumed a very low profile. (The reasons for this are considered in more detail below.) History repeated itself 100 years after the first prison-building boom and the 1980s saw the beginnings of a second extensive program of construction. In the last two decades of the twentieth century, new prisons were built in most states to replace the 100-year-old prisons that had come to house more than half of all prisoners until the late 1980s.

From colonisation until the end of the twentieth century, Australia was unique because punishment began and remained entirely the responsibility of the state. The 1990s saw the beginnings of a rival model (O'Toole 2006). The growing influence of neoliberal political rationalities promoted the sale of government assets and the entry of the private sector into competition with the government services. For the first time in this country's history, privately run prisons became a reality. Moyle (2000) explains, that along with ageing prison infrastructure, the catalyst for Australia's first private prison, Borallon in Queensland in 1989, was the idea that market forces generated by the profit motive would ensure greater efficiencies and superior performance than the public sector had been able to achieve. Throughout the 1990s other states—New South Wales, South Australia and Victoria—followed suit. State governments purchased prison management and programs that were provided by private companies. The overall responsibility for the correctional system, however, stayed in government hands. By the end of the twentieth century, there were almost 200 privately managed prisons in the world, holding 140 000 prisoners (Austin and Coventry 2001). Australia had the greatest proportion of prisoners under private management (18.8 per cent) of any country in the world. By 2004 there were 124 custodial facilities in Australia. They included eighty-one government-operated and seven privately operated prisons (in five jurisdictions—New South Wales, Victoria, Queensland, Western Australia and South Australia), four government-operated and five privately operated community custodial facilities (Commonwealth of Australia 2004). In 2009 custodial facilities totalled 119: eighty-seven government-operated prisons, seven privately operated prisons, three government-operated community custodial facilities, eight periodic detention centres and fourteen twenty-four-hour court cell complexes (Commonwealth of Australia 2009).

AUSTRALIA'S CARCERAL ARCHIPELAGO

Michel Foucault's (1977) book *Discipline and Punish: The Birth of the Prison* describes how prisons became the preferred form of punishment in the nineteenth century, and how the techniques of the penal system extended beyond the walls of the institution itself. He called this expansion of disciplinary control the 'carceral archipelago'. Explaining that '[w]e have seen that, in penal justice, the prison transformed the punitive procedure into a penitentiary technique; the carceral archipelago transported this technique from penal institutions to the entire social body' (Foucault 1977, p. 289). The history of imprisonment in Australia includes a range of institutions and regimes that have come under the prison's umbrella or have been linked to it in some way (Finnane 1997). Stephen Garton's (1982; 1986) work shows how seeing the prison in isolation overlooks the complexity of the processes of institutionalisation that made up Australia's early criminal justice system. He links a decline in prison admissions in the late nineteenth century with the introduction of fine payment systems and first offenders legislations, and maps the diversion of other traditional prison populations—such as those then described as lunatics[1], drunkards, prostitutes and juveniles—to other medicalised institutional spaces. In the 1880s the largest number of convictions and imprisonments were for offences 'against good order'. Drunkenness accounted for between 60 and 70 per cent of all male imprisonments, and prostitution-related offences were between 80 and 90 per cent of all female imprisonments. Sentences as such were minor. Approximately 70 per cent of all persons imprisoned had sentences of less than one month (Garton 1982). Garton describes how an increase in admissions to prison in the early 1890s prompted a reassessment of the function and aims of criminal incarceration. A constant theme in the debates was whether the purpose of imprisonment was deterrence or rehabilitation. The initial response was to stress the deterrent role of prison, but in 1894 such views increasingly came under attack. A range of groups—including those concerned with the welfare of imprisoned women and children—called for reform in the prison system.

The successful introduction of a program of rehabilitation was linked to reforms that narrowed the definition of who should be in prison. Captain Frederick Neitenstein—Comptroller-General of Prisons in New South Wales from 1895 until 1909—considered it essential that 'first offenders, old feeble vagrants, diseased and friendless incapables, inebriates, lunatics and juveniles' be kept out of prison (Garton 1982, p. 99). He argued that such categories of prisoner formed a large part of the prison population. These groups required a specialised treatment that prison was not designed to provide; those who were considered 'criminals', however, would benefit from a more extensive period of prison treatment. He supported a series of reforms designed to prevent some people from reaching prison and to ensure that others were detained for longer periods. The initial focus of change was on first offenders who might be ruined by the stigma of criminality. *The First Offenders Act 1894* provided for suspended sentences for those convicted of summary offences who had never been convicted before. They were placed on bonds and were to report to the police regularly. The large proportion of persons convicted for summary offences, and subsequently imprisoned for the non-payment of fines, was a serious strain on the resources

---

1 Lunacy Acts 1878 and 1898.

of the prison system: they accounted for between 65 and 75 per cent of all imprisonments. In the 1890s *The Justice Fines Act 1899* addressed this problem by allowing the payment of fines by instalment, and permitting those of limited means to graduate their payments. Alternatively, prisoners could undertake to pay off the debt through work in prison. This latter provision resulted in almost 25 per cent of those imprisoned for the non-payment of fines gaining substantial remissions of sentence between 1900 and 1920.

The Inebriates Act 1901 and *Amendment Acts 1909* and *1912* established a number of separate institutions for the treatment of inebriates. People in prison who were certified as habitual drunkards could be detained for a maximum of twelve months, treatment. *The Prisoners Detention Act 1908* provided for the incarceration of any prisoner found to have venereal disease in a locked hospital for a maximum of nine months. Juveniles were considered a major problem for the prison system. Despite the availability of juvenile reformatories and a boarding-out system run by the State Children's Relief Board, during the 1880s prisons received 8586 boys and 2617 girls under the age of twenty. Reformers proposed a completely separate system of juvenile justice made up of a children's court, parole and probation systems attached to that court, the extension of boarding out for many juveniles and the retention of reformatories only for special cases, such as 'mental defectives'. A Children's Court was established in New South Wales in 1905 (Garton 1982).

This shift in punishment should not only be described in terms of strategies of decarceration, or diversion from prison. The same logic — the system should not needlessly aggravate a breakdown in offenders' social relationships with their dependent families or their capacity to continue useful and self-supporting labour — that justified part payment of fines, or probation for first offenders, also justified the introduction of indefinite sentences and the de facto introduction of parole (Finnane 1997, p. 163). In *The Habitual Criminal Act 1905* introduced a system of indeterminate sentencing in New South Wales to resolve the problem of habitual offenders serving endless short sentences and being returned to the community only to recommit the same offences. Society would both be protected from repeat offenders and receive rehabilitated citizens back into itself at a future stage. The idea of conditional release for such prisoners appealed to early twentieth-century reforms and prison administrators. Parole was introduced incrementally and more through policy than legislation. In New South Wales the release-on-licence system was amended in 1908 so that even prisoners released as a result of remission of sentence were required to report to police regularly and be of good behaviour; previously these prisoners had been released unconditionally. The conditions of release could go well beyond the requirement of good behaviour. In Tasmania, for example, the administration of ticket-of-leave, and later of parole, provides evidence of cases in which very specific residential or behavioural conditions were imposed; for instance, release for a woman could be conditional on marriage to an 'appropriate' man (Finnane 1997, p. 163).

AN 'OTHER' HISTORY OF AUSTRALIAN PUNISHMENT: FIRST CONTACT

From the foundation of a British penal colony in New South Wales in 1788, the official position of the imperial government was that Aboriginal people were British subjects *protected* and bound by British laws then applicable in the new colony. But as Russell Hogg (2001) explains, this relationship was not really feasible as long as such laws did not recognise and safeguard traditional rights to land. There could be no meaningful protection against settler violence when the law effectively sanctioned dispossession and punished Aboriginal resistance and retaliation, especially when settler occupation ran well ahead of effective civil authority in many parts of the new colony. The history of warfare and violence on the frontier in the nineteenth century is well documented. Intermittent warfare, 'punitive expeditions', and other forms of extrajudicial violence were common, persisting into the twentieth century in some parts of Australia (Edney 2002).

So far we have seen how at the close of the transportation era, for the settlers at least, punishment in the colonies shifted away from a reliance on corporal and capital measures and the use of places of secondary transportation to a commitment to the penitentiary and confinement in cells. This was not the case for everyone. From the mid-nineteenth century, official reservations were expressed regarding the appropriateness of imprisonment as a punishment for Aboriginal people. For example, an 1887 Queensland report on prisons concluded that imprisonment had no meaning for Aboriginal people, while Western Australia introduced a system of racial classification by establishing an Aboriginal prison on Rottnest Island (Finnane and McGuire 2001) and 'native cells' and 'compounds' in some jails in the north of the state (Roebourne). These measures did not mitigate the harshness of incarceration for Aboriginal prisoners, who were separated not only from the settler community but also, more importantly, from their own kin and land.

In contrast to the changes in punishment aimed at the settler population and trends in punishment in England, bodily punishments and restraints continued to be used for Aboriginal people in many places as an alternative to confinement. Historical evidence indicates that flogging, the use of neck chains and the tying or chaining to trees were commonplace methods that prevailed well into the first half of the twentieth century in central and northern Australia (McGrath 1995, pp. 34–7). This treatment reflected particular cultural attitudes towards Aboriginal people (especially those of full decent) who were thought to be, by nature, inferior, uncultivated, slaves to their passions and therefore subject to methods of disciplinary control then thought appropriate to their condition and level of understanding—namely physical punishments that could be promptly administered. Measures of lesser severity, directness and immediacy—including imprisonment—were considered inappropriate, described as unintelligible to the 'native' mentality and liable to be interpreted as weakness (Finnane 1997; Finnane and McGuire 2001; Hogg 2001).

From a relatively early point in the process of colonisation, other regulatory practices were used alongside corporal punishments, particularly in places that were subject to effective civil authority (Hogg 2001). The form of these practices varied, but commonly they involved segregation through the use of missions, government reserves or children's homes, which sought to establish an ongoing supervisory relationship between white authority (be it church or bureaucracy) and Aboriginal people. This reflected the moral and civilising mission of British imperialism that sought to bring the benefits of Christian, European (British) 'progress' to the non-European races of the world. The dominant belief at that time, informed by social Darwinism, was that Aborigines were condemned by their inferiority to die out. This view combined with pragmatic measures to erase Aboriginal culture by selectively training Aboriginal people in European values and habits. Enormous power was conferred on white officials who controlled the lives of Aboriginal people and communities. From the nineteenth century, policies and institutions established under legislative regimes, which permitted segregation on racial grounds, worked to separate Aboriginal people from white communities on reserves, missions and stations where they were subject to special regimes of control, tutelage and conversion to Christianity.

Beyond the reserves, missions or camps, institutional surveillance and control was expressed in other ways. Those not placed on reserves or stations generally lived under the threat of being moved there. From about the 1940s, state governments introduced systems that provided limited rights to some Aboriginal people under certain conditions. They had to promise to give up their traditional practices and avoid other Aboriginal people, live a European lifestyle and stay out of 'trouble'. In return, they were issued exemption certificates that removed them from the restrictions of state protection laws. Legally, these certificates meant that the people who had them were no longer 'Aboriginal'; for example, the *Aborigines Act Amendment Act 1939* (SA) allowed certain Aborigines to become 'non-Aborigines' if they behaved according to government standards. Exemption certificates, which had to be carried at all times, entitled them to exercise certain rights—like being able to vote, opening a bank account, receiving certain social security benefits, owning land, purchasing alcohol and permitting their children to attend school—denied to non-exempt Aborigines under the protection Acts. In Western Australia these were called Citizenship Certificates; in New South Wales and Queensland, they were called Exemption Certificates. Certificates could be suspended or cancelled by a magistrate and there was no right of appeal. Many Aboriginal people resented these certificates and called them 'dog licences' or 'dog tags' (up until the 1960s when records of the number of Aboriginal people in Australia were kept, they were often listed on stock registers rather than in the population census). Of the 14 000 Aboriginal people eligible in New South Wales, only 1500 chose to apply for a certificate; nevertheless, admission to conditional civic citizenship left people vulnerable to heightened surveillance and intervention by police and other government authorities (Hogg 2001; Kidd 1997; Rowse 1998).

NEW SOUTH WALES GOVERNMENT
ABORIGINES PROTECTION ACT, 1909–1943, SECTION 18c.
[REGULATION 56]

CERTIFICATE OF EXEMPTION

From provisions of the Act and Regulations

THIS IS TO CERTIFY that _____

_____ Aborigine, aged _____ years, residing at
(Caste)

_____

is a person who, in the opinion of the Aborigines Welfare Board, ought no longer be subject to the provisions/following provisions of the *Aborigines Protection Act and Regulations*, or any such provisions, and he/she is accordingly exempted from such provisions:

_____

Issued in compliance with the

Resolution of the Aborigines

Welfare Board and dated

the_____ day of _____

_____ Chairman

_____ Member of the Aborigines Welfare Board.

	Photograph of

Countersigned by
The Secretary,

Signature of
The Holder

_____   _____

Source: State of New South Wales through the Department of Education and Training (2008).

MORE CONTEMPORARY ALTERNATIVES TO PRISON

According to Finnane (1997), penal reform at the beginning of the twentieth century, which diverted certain groups away from prison and introduced conditional release and the supervision of offenders in the community, was the first of three stages in the development of alternatives to imprisonment. The second phase of decarceration involving the development of 'community-based sanctions' began in the 1950s, and was characterised by the formal bureaucratisation and codification of the non-custodial management of offenders. While the concept of aftercare for prisoners had existed in practice through the work of church and welfare agencies since the first organised prison systems were developed in the nineteenth century (Daley 2004), it was not until the mid-twentieth century that formalised systems of probation and parole were created in Australia. Tasmania established the first probation service in 1946. New South Wales set up its adult probation service five years later in July 1951 (O'Toole 2006). While South Australia had legislation providing for probation as early as 1913 (Telfer 2003), a state-run service did not exist until 1954. Victoria's parole board commenced operations in 1957. Queensland created a probation service in 1959. *The Offenders Probation and Parole Act 1959* was based on then recently enacted Victorian legislation; it aimed to replace a rudimentary parole system described in the *Prisoners' Parole Act 1937* and *1943* (Bradshaw 1985). Western Australia eventually joined the other states by providing for state-supervised probation and parole in 1963. As the twentieth century progressed, a range of other community-based offender management programs were also introduced. Chan and Zdenkowski (1986) mapped the formal introduction of alternatives to prison through codification across the Commonwealth, as shown in the Table 1.1.

TABLE 1.1 Community-based options by state/territory
Approximate date of introduction

Option	Probation[1]	Parole/ licence	Work release	Periodic detention	Attendance centre	Community service
Federal	1960	1967/1960	–	1982	1982[2]	1982[2]
NSW	[1961][3]	1966/1900 or earlier	1969	1970	–	1979
Vic.	1958	1958	1975	1973[4]	1975	[1982]
Qld	1959	[1937/1943][5]	1969	1970[6]	–	[1981]
SA	1913	1969	–	–	–	1981
WA	[1965]	1963	1970	–	–	1976
Tas.	1973	1975	–	–	–	1971
NT	[1972]	1971	–	–	1979	1979
ACT	1929[3]	1976	–	–	–	1985

General note: the dates refer to the year the relevant legislation was passed or dates of commencement, which are noted in square brackets.

Notes:
1   In the sense of supervised release. Distinguish legislation providing for 'good behaviour' bonds which has a much longer history.
2   Not proclaimed except in the ACT where periodic detention/attendance centres are not currently available.
3   Probation orders based on bond legislation.
4   Never implemented, restyled as attendance centre orders.
5   Chan and Zdenkowski (1986) cite 1959 as the date for the introduction of *The Offenders Probation and Parole Act*, earlier rudimentary provisions were introduced with the *Prisons Parole Act 1937* and *1943* (Bradshaw 1985).
6   Repealed 15 May 1984.

Source: Chan and Zdenkowski (1986), p. 76.

Three dominant justifications are regularly linked with the introduction of alternatives to incarceration: the cost of imprisonment, the ineffectiveness of prisons as a sanction and the inhumanity of prison conditions. In the reform literature there is rarely any discussion about the relative priority or ordering of these criteria (Chan and Zdenkowski 1986). By the 1980s the search for alternatives to prison had resulted in a proliferation of sentencing options and a new spectrum of penalties with varying degrees of state supervision. Chan and Zdenkowski (1986) list the non-custodial sentencing options available in Australia during the twentieth century as including: capital and corporal punishment; monetary penalties—the fine is the most frequently used non-custodial sentencing option; compensatory penalties; forfeiture/disqualification; unsupervised release; supervised release; parole; release on licence; remissions; work release; temporary leave; pre-release and pardon/royal prerogative of mercy. They explain that non-custodial sanctions are generally distinguished from custodial ones by the absence of the prison wall. In practice, however, the distinction is somewhat less well defined because offenders can move between different types of sanction. Chan and Zdenkowski suggest that it is more useful to think of a correctional continuum in terms of degree of deprivation of liberty from high to minimal and the status of the offenders under law—that is, as unsentenced, sentenced non-prisoners or sentenced prisoners.

By the beginning of the twenty-first century, the underlying principle of community corrections was that a proportion of offenders would be best managed in the community rather than spending a lot of time in prison (White and Perrone 2005). It is also arguable that the intermediate penalties that emerged as a result potentially decrease the demand for prison beds and the costs associated with building, staffing and maintaining prisons, reduce recidivism and provide safety for the public while providing credible and proportionately scaled punishments that reflect both the nature of the crime and society's denunciation of it. Moreover, these principles are compatible with the neoliberal and economically based rationales that provided for introduction of private prisons in this country. Contemporary examples of community-based intervention include:

- pre-trial interventions, like family group conferencing and community panels
- problem-solving courts
- drug diversion
- Indigenous justice options
- types of release, such as weekend, work, study, supervised and unsupervised
- electronic monitoring
- community residential centres and supported accommodation projects
- homes (foster or group)
- houses (halfway and quarter-way)
- forestry camps, and wilderness and outward bound projects
- centres (attendance, day, training, drop-in and shop front)

- ○ hostels, shelters and boarding schools
- ○ weekend detention and other forms of partial detention
- ○ community service orders and reparation schemes
- ○ citizen alert programs, hotlines, listening posts and radio watches
- ○ the use of pre-emptive test scales and diagnostic devices (White and Perrone 2005).

Some of these very recent programs represent the third stage in the development of non-carceral modes of penalty in Australia (Finnane 1997). They are not distinctive simply because they divert offenders from the formal institutions of the criminal justice system—diversion has been the aim of reform at least since the introduction of the first offenders' probation in the 1880s (Garton 1986)—nor is community involvement the key; that rhetoric has been associated with sanctions innovation since the 1960s (Chan and Zdenkowski 1986). As we will see in Chapter 9, the introduction of community justice mechanisms, like restorative justice and family or community conferencing, does bring the community back into the system of responding to offending, but the most significant change is the appearance of the victim, or potential victims, in the debate over responding to crime (Finnane 1997). Family conferencing and citizen alert programs, for example, not only focus on changing the behaviour of offenders, but they also address matters of community safety and the well-being of victims. Finnane (1997, p. 164) suggests that the emergence of the victim—as an independent actor for whom the state is no longer presumed to speak conclusively—is possibly the most significant change to occur in the criminal justice debate and policy since the emergence of the prison as the centrepiece of the state's response to crime during the nineteenth century. Some critics might argue that consideration of the victim does not belong in a book about sentencing and punishment, but it is hard to ignore the profound ways that victims influence or shape outcomes in some of these newer modes of intervention (Garland 2001).

CONCLUSION: WHERE TO FROM HERE?

This chapter surveyed the history of punishment in Australia. At the end of the eighteenth century, transportation to Australia provided an alternative to warehousing a growing population of prisoners in hulks on the Thames in England. It satisfied both punitive and imperial needs. Australia was colonised largely as a prison without walls. There are two basic stories of the convict experience (Braithwaite 1999a). Assignment to work that involved the freedom to roam the countryside was the fate of the majority, and their good behaviour was rewarded with greater freedom offered by ticket-of-leave and emancipation (including land grants). Some convicts did, nevertheless, die in chains and in conditions of relentless, savage confinement at the scaffold or on the voyage. As the colonies became better established and ex-convicts prospered, transportation was redefined as 'not punishment enough'. Transportation to Australia ended in the second half of the nineteenth century as a result of its perceived inability to fulfil penal objectives, the growth of free immigration that reduced the need for convict labour and a program of prison building in Great Britain, a program which itself was transported to the colonies. In the nineteenth century, the foundations of the physical infrastructure of Australia's prison system were laid. A significant commitment was made to prison building in this country between the 1850 and 1890s. By the end of the century, debates about the purpose of punishment introduced reform, and alternatives to prison were developed for specific populations, like first offenders, delinquent youth, drunkards and the mentally defective. The reform process continued into the twentieth century, by the end of which the terrain of imprisonment expanded from an exclusively government-run domain to include institutions built and managed by the private sector. Community corrections also expanded beyond diversion to medical institutions and supervision in the community to include an array of sentencing options for the management and treatment of offenders.

It is clear from this story that punishment in Australia from the outset has been a diverse and dynamic social institution. It has never been just about the prison. Symbolically the prison may lie at the heart of how we think about punishment, but it has never been the main form of the institution in Australian corrections (Finnane 1997; Braithwaite 1999a). Why is it then that when we think of punishment—in the past or present—we are so captivated by the prison? Braithwaite (1999a) claims that it is because the sociology of punishment has been obsessed by the emphasis in Foucault's *Discipline and Punish* (and in mainstream penology) on the birth of the prison in the nineteenth century as the crucial development. But Foucault's book was not the first on this topic and surely will not be the last. Many compelling histories of punishment that focus mainly on the prison have been written: Rusche and Kirchheimer (1939/1968), Ignateiff (1978) and Garland (1985). After all, why prison emerged as a mode of punishment in the nineteenth century and why it persists despite its failings are interesting questions. Describing the sociology of punishment as obsessed by Foucault's account of the prison, Braithwaite (along with some other critics) assumes a more literal reading than was ever intended. He overlooks the many books that have used the general ideas outlined in *Discipline and Punish* to analyse how the institutional practices described in relation to the first penitentiaries have worked more generally to regulate behaviour and the social world beyond the prison.[2] Nevertheless, he argues that this type of regulation is a more fruitful topic of study and, in this respect, that the more developed ideas of later Foucault (1991) 'On governmentality' have greater appeal than the Foucault (1977) of *Discipline and Punish*.

Consistent with this assessment, Garland (1997; 2001) proposes that three key modes of regulation currently play an important role in contemporary programs

---

2   There is a rich literature exploring the expression of these strategies in the present and the past (Finch 1993; Carrington 1991; McCallum 2001; Rose 2000; Fischer 2003; Bull 2008).

of crime control. These can be described in terms of containment through the expression of sovereign power, disciplinary strategies that aim to correct and rehabilitate offenders and last, but not least, strategies that seek to govern crime though the manipulation of interests and the promotion of mechanisms of self-regulation (Foucault 1991). These rationales are no less evident in penological pursuits, where they are linked to three concepts that currently shape the practices of sentencing and punishment. Risk, rehabilitation and restitution arguably constitute the three Rs of contemporary programs of punishment. A fourth R might be recidivism: while recidivism is arguably an important concern when thinking about punishment, its relevance is mediated through the other three. For example, serious offenders are subject to indefinite sentencing. They are too dangerous to be released into the community because the *risk* of re-offending (recidivism) is high. Programs concerned with *rehabilitation* are designed to develop capacities in participants that enhance their ability to live law-abiding (non-offending) lives, while strategies focused on *restitution* see the offender as a rational actor, who when made aware of the costs of offending behaviour will elect to self-regulate and abstain from further unlawful acts. Those falling into the latter categories are suitable for management in the community when the risk, or effects, of recidivism are acceptable.

This book will use the concepts of risk, rehabilitation and restitution to explore contemporary punishment practices. They provide a useful framework for the text because they facilitate:

- the exploration of the relationship between sentencing principles and forms of punishment
- an analysis that is not only focused on the prison, but also ranges across fines, community corrections and confinement
- consideration of recent innovations that have blurred distinctions between practices traditionally associated with policing, sentencing and punishment in innovative ways—for example, problem-solving courts
- an evaluation of theoretical perspectives. As Garland (1997) explains, a range of theories have something to offer the analysis of punishment—where some fall short, it is often not because they are incorrect, but rather they are not the whole story, or not able to explain everything.

Following these guidelines, this book is divided into four parts. This initial section is focused on providing a foundation for the later exploration of the themes of risk, rehabilitation and restitution through case studies of punishment in contemporary Australia. Along with this introduction, Chapters 2 and 3 make up this first part. This chapter has established that punishment in Australia has always been a complex and dynamic domain made up of diverse practices and institutions. To understand punishment, we need to look beyond the prison while locating it as a key institution in a broader terrain. Chapter 2 introduces the range of principles that are most commonly employed in determining punishment. Rather than simply providing a dry descriptive account, it examines how these principles have influenced punishment and sentencing practices since colonisation. This historical case study is analytical rather than archival. This means that, rather than reproducing a complete chronological account, relevant aspects are highlighted for their illustrative value. Reviewing the changing nature of sentencing demonstrates how the way we think about crime and punishment influences practice. This provides a foundation for Chapter 3, which is an overview of key social theories of punishment. It begins by reviewing the influential ideas of consensus and critical perspectives that shape understandings of modern penal systems and concludes with a survey of more recent theoretical developments that tackle the changing terrain of penality in more recent years. Chapters 2 and 3 respectively highlight links between principles of punishment and social theories, and the themes of risk, rehabilitation and restitution that structure the remainder of the book.

The second section of this book is focused on the concept of risk. It consists of two chapters that feature case studies of predatory sex crimes and terrorism. Specific regulatory responses are explored—for example, notification statutes, indeterminate sentencing and containment or incapacitation. This provides scope to address recent work on punishment focused around the ideas of dangerousness and risk (Pratt 1997; Pratt and Brown 2000) and the 'new punitiveness' (Pratt et al. 2005). It also provides a context for discussion of the theoretical ideas of Durkheim, Douglas and Elias, Foucault, Feeley and Simon.

Taking the theme of rehabilitation, the third part of the book explores the recent introduction and seeming proliferation of problem-solving courts. These courts blur boundaries between sentencing and punishment. Chapter 6, for example, investigates how drug courts work to divert offenders from prison by providing regular intensive and direct supervision by a judicial officer, which can last for several years. Politicians are at pains to make the community aware they are no easy option; indeed many participants complain that it would have been easier just to 'do their time'. Such courts involve preventive partnerships (Garland 2001) with treatment service providers in the community; they are not so much concerned with victims or vulnerable situations, but are intensely focused on the offender. Here we engage, for example, the work of Goffman (1961/1990), Foucault (1977; 1991) and Rose (1996), and the range of sociol control perspectives (Cohen 1979; 1985; Schull 1977; Young 1999). Chapters 7 and 8 respectively address the over-representation of Indigenous people in traditional institutions of punishment and the difficulty of developing judicial responses to domestic and family violence. These chapters describe how different types of problem-solving courts engage with the needs of particular—generally less powerful—groups. These case studies provide an opportunity to see the relevance of critical criminological approaches concerned not simply with the class divisions central in Marxist perspectives, but with more complex understandings of inequality shaped by multiple factors and linked to social categories, like race and gender.

The last part of the book, which is focused on restitution, positions the offender as opportunistic. This figure is not the poorly socialised misfit in need of assistance, but an illicit, opportunistic consumer who lacks a strong moral compass or any effective internal controls, aside from a capacity for rational calculation and a will to pleasure (Garland 2001; Lynch 2005). The remaining chapters provide examples of how interventions in this domain rely on the capacity of the offender to make 'the right' choices once informed of the consequences of their behaviour. Youth conferencing and fines and anti-hooning legislation (Chapters 9 and 10 respectively) can be understood as exemplars of neoliberal governmental approaches to crime (Bottoms 1995; Braithwaite 2000).

This format is not intended to imply that the three *Rs* are mutually exclusive—that a punishment shaped by risk assessment is never concerned with rehabilitation or restitution, or vice versa. Rather, exploring the relationships between these concepts and particular forms of punishment provides insight in regard to current sentencing trends. Adopting an issues-based approach, the case studies illustrate how these principles shape sentencing outcomes and punishment practices. Each chapter considers a particular crime problem and critically reviews how sentencing options and outcomes are shaped by these principles, at the same time exploring the moral and ethical justifications of sentencing and how these translate into the practices of punishment. This takes into account the actual techniques of punishment, as well as the way we think about punishment. Empirical research relating to each case study is reviewed in an examination of how the various strategies have an effect, highlighting both intended and unintended consequences. This process works to link abstract theoretical ideas and concepts to the applied domain through each of the case studies described.

Principles and practices of punishment and sentencing

INTRODUCTION

The previous chapter described Australia's colonial beginnings as a penal settlement, whose population grew initially as a result of the punishment of offenders through transportation from England and Ireland. While Australia's early penal settlements are often portrayed as brutal places for most convicts, for many, transportation was less onerous than the life of a pauper in the British Isles. By the early nineteenth century, the potential deterrent effect of an uncertain voyage and an indeterminate fate had been tempered by the system of assignment, tickets-of-leave and emancipation. For authorities in England this system gave too much liberty to those who were supposed to be undergoing severe punishment. By the 1840s the penitentiary emerged in England as a new and dominant mode of punishment, and the proportion of convicted felons sentenced to transportation declined. This was the result of opposition to transportation as an uncertain punishment and growing colonial resistance.

Jeremy Bentham (1748–1832) was a significant figure in this development. He was an English jurist, philosopher and legal and social reformer. He is best known as an early advocate of utilitarianism, which is the ethical doctrine that the moral worth of an action is determined solely by its contribution to overall utility. This is a form of consequentialism, meaning that the value of an action is determined by its outcome. Utilitarianism is the basis of theories of punishment concerned with preventing future crime. An alternative approach is provided by past-oriented theories whose aim is to exact retribution from offenders for their crimes. Central to retributive perspectives is the idea that the purpose of judicial punishment is to place moral blame on the offender for the offence committed, and that the future conduct of the offender or other members of society is not a proper concern of punishment (Hudson 2003a, p. 3).

The aim of this chapter is to introduce a range of philosophies that have influenced the form of punishment in Australian society. It begins by exploring utilitarian principles and Bentham's ideas in more detail, describing how they helped to put an end to transportation in the nineteenth century. It maps the impact of reformist ideals that displaced deterrence and came to have an enduring effect on sentencing and punishment throughout the twentieth century. By the end of that century these forward-looking or consequentialist approaches were challenged by calls for 'just deserts'. The chapter describes this retributive trend and the socio-political context that provided for a renaissance of expressive approaches. It concludes by positioning these familiar principles in relation to factors like managerialism and communitarianism, which have become important in the opening years of the twenty-first century.

BENTHAM'S UTILITARIANISM AND THE END OF TRANSPORTATION

Although Jeremy Bentham never practised law, he spent most of his life critiquing the existing law and strongly advocating legal reform. Bentham is primarily known today for his moral philosophy: his principle of utilitarianism evaluates actions based on their consequences—in particular, the overall happiness created for everyone affected by such action. Bentham's penal theory drew on his utilitarian philosophy. Punishment, he wrote, 'in itself is evil' and 'ought only be admitted in as far as it promises to exclude some greater evil', namely the suffering resulting from the commission of further offences (Bentham 1843/1995, p. 379). The main benefit was expected to flow from the effect of punishment on the actions of people besides those undergoing it. Punishment would achieve this by altering the balance between pain and pleasure as seen by potential offenders. Bentham regarded the prevention of future offences by example as fundamental. He argued that reform and incapacitation were important but secondary, affecting only 'the comparatively small number of individuals, who having actually offended, have moreover actually suffered for the offence'. Example, on the other hand, affected 'as many individuals as are exposed to the temptation of offending; that is … all mankind' (Bentham 1843/1995, p. 174). This emphasis on example indicated a willingness to punish an individual according to the social consequences that would follow. It could justify excessive punishment, or the punishment of an innocent person, if this would prevent future offending. These features were later to limit the appeal of Bentham's penal theory, but at that time the emphasis he put on example was uncontroversial.

Bentham was opposed to transportation. He developed his arguments against it in his general works on law and punishment that were written before the colonisation of New South Wales. In the 1770s he argued that the transportation of offenders to the American colonies had been 'unexemplary'. It was a poor punishment because it was uncertain. No one knew how much or how little pain was actually going to be inflicted when an offender was shipped across the seas to work in the colonies. Transportation was therefore regarded as a lesser punishment than death, but death might actually be inflicted if the ship carrying the offender to the colonies was wrecked. People were sentenced to different periods of transportation, but the experience might be very burdensome or involve no pain at all. Bentham was critical of such variations because, in practice, they could not be scaled to match the offence. In his view, deterrence was more effective when the punishment for an offence was known precisely and was sure to be inflicted. Men [sic] were not likely to be deterred from crime if they are threatened with one punishment—death—commuted to another—transportation—which itself was a great unknown. In short, because transportation was an uncertain fate, it was a very poor deterrent. Even if it could be arranged to exact the same amount of pain on all those sentenced to it, transportation would still be a poor punishment because it was delivered at a distance—remote from those who were to be deterred. The second purpose of punishment, according to Bentham, was to reform the offender. Here, too, transportation rated poorly. A man sent to compulsory labour in the colonies might become a reformed character, but this was more the result of accident than design. The chief interest of those for whom he laboured was to get work out of him, not to amend his morals (Hirst 1983).

The NSW settlement was established in the wake of the American revolutionary war, which had put an end to the practice of transporting British convicts to the thirteen American colonies. The decision to send convicts to New South Wales disappointed Bentham, who had seen the interruption to transportation in 1776 as an opportunity for penal reform. Intellectual opinion was turning against transportation and moving in favour of imprisonment, with hard labour as punishment for serious offences. When the first reports of the colony reached London, Bentham thought he had an irrefutable case against it (Hirst 1983). Between 1791 and 1802 he waged at least three campaigns to have the penal colony in New South Wales abandoned. He set forth his complete case against the colony in *Panopticon v New South Wales* published in 1802, arguing that the transportation of convicts to New South Wales served none of the proper ends of penal policy. Punishment ought to make an example of offenders with a view to the 'prevention of similar offences on the part of individuals at large' ... '[b]y the repulsive influence exercised on the minds of bystanders by the apprehension of similar suffering in case of similar delinquency' (Bentham 1843/1995, p. 174). In his view, deterrence of would-be offenders was more likely to be achieved by making an example of convicts in a strictly run penitentiary than by shipping them off to the other side of the world: 'The moon was then, as it continues to be, inaccessible: on earth there was no accessible spot more distant than NSW' (1843/1995, p. 186).

He contrasted New South Wales with the panopticon—a type of penitentiary in which punishment could be varied in length of time but also in intensity. It would be visible to all—the public would be given free access to make it more effective as a deterrent. The inmates would be kept at labour by the effortless operation of the inspection principle—the unseen and unknown eye in the observation towers. This discipline, coupled with the work of a chaplain, would guarantee reformation. Bentham's efforts to have the panopticon built failed; nevertheless, his ideas did finally play a great part in ending transportation to New South Wales. This was achieved not through the panopticon, but through the principles he gave to the law reformers who followed him. From the 1810s Romilly, Mackintosh and Brougham argued in the English House of Commons for reform of the criminal law and, in particular, for a reduction in the use of the death penalty. They attacked transportation and the convict colony with

Bentham's arguments. For twenty years they made little progress, but when the Whigs replaced the Tories in the 1830s, there was more support for their views among the new ministers (Hirst 1983, pp. 10–15).

Deterrence

Deterrence is one of several utilitarian rationales of punishment described as 'consequentialist' because it looks to preventive consequences of sentences. It relies on the offender calculating the cost of their actions: if the risk of detection is great and the penalty outweighs the value of the act, crime will be deterred.

There is a distinction between individual (or special) deterrence and general deterrence. Individual deterrence is concerned with preventing a specific person from reoffending, whereas general deterrence is concerned with deterring all people from committing a particular type of offence. The distinction between the two, however, is not straightforward as a penalty framed to deter potential offenders will be undergone by actual offenders. True individual deterrence would require a sentence of indeterminate length, with the content tailored to the individual offender, and the degree of disparity involved would generally be unacceptable (Hudson 2003a).

The problems with deterrence-based sentencing include:

- the difficulty of defining deterrence
- the lack of empirical evidence that it is effective; for example, attempts to evaluate the deterrent effects of harsh penalties, like the death penalty, provide ambiguous results
- deterrence relies on the potential offenders' knowledge of the risk of detection and the magnitude of the penalty
- not all offenders are rational calculators: some are impulsive or opportunistic, while others are overly optimistic
- the principle of deterrence could justify exemplary sentences, resulting in a disproportionately harsh sentence, or even the punishment of an innocent person, to deter others from committing a similar offence (Ashworth 2005).

PUNISHMENT AND REFORM: OFFENDERS AS BROKEN MACHINES

In the eighteenth century, imprisonment changed from being a means for holding people awaiting trial or deportation to being primarily a mode of punishment. It was introduced as an alternative to the death penalty or transportation at a time when there was growing recognition of the value of population as a resource. Death or transportation removed offenders permanently from the workforce, while older punishments, such as the stocks, did nothing to enhance their ability or willingness to behave as productive law-abiding citizens. Reform became a prime concern of the penal system in the late eighteenth and early nineteenth centuries, and the associated penalties were intended to instil in offenders both a desire for work and self-discipline suited to the then new routines of factory labour (Foucault 1977; Ignatieff 1978; 1983; Melossi and Pavarini 1981). In the 1840s new prisons were built in England and the penitentiary became the dominant mode of punishment. In Australia the foundations of the physical infrastructure of the prison system were also laid in the nineteenth century.

At that time Australia was changing: in the mid-1800s, it was a frontier society, with a population dominated by convicts and a crime rate that was high; by the end of the century, crime rates had decreased and convicts were increasingly integrated into a largely law-abiding, industrious society (Braithwaite 1999a). Punishment shifted from a system in which the prisoner was 'the enemy of the state' and disposed of by execution or severe physical punishment to one that involved a harsh disciplinary regime, and imprisonment became the most common criminal sanction for minor offenders.

Initially, Australia's prison systems were characterised by a severe brutality that was designed to break the spirit (O'Toole 2006); by the end of the nineteenth century, however, a movement for reform had gathered momentum. An increase in admissions to prison in the early 1890s prompted a reassessment of the function and aims of criminal incarceration (Garton 1982). A constant theme of debate was whether prisons were primarily reformative or deterrent institutions. The difference between deterrence and reform (or rehabilitation) is that the former is only concerned with whether or not offenders commit further crime, whereas the latter aims to help them become better, more productive people. By the late 1890s the rationale of imprisonment shifted the role of the prison from harsh punishment to a mechanism of reform and rehabilitation. Prisoners were seen as a 'broken or damaged machine' in need of moral repair and, according to progressive penal reformers (like Thomas Walker in a Perth lecture in 1898), prisons were to be moral hospitals, providing a 'cure from crime' (Finnane 1997, p. 71).

The interest in penal reform extended from the process of sentencing, enacted through new options described in legislation, to institutional design and internal management. It was driven by a range of groups, including those concerned with the welfare of women and children. Reformatories and prison farms were established to allow a finer grading of the prisoner population according to its social characteristics. Women's prisons were founded in some states from the 1890s. While they were the result of progressive social reform responding to a demand for the recognition of the distinctive needs of women, they involved regimes that diminished the adult status of the inmate. Early critics highlighted the limited range of work opportunities and a daily schedule that treated the women inmates as children (Finnane 1997, pp. 84–92).

Reform in the nineteenth century was unsophisticated, acknowledging only basic differences between prisoners. Generally, inmates were subject to the same regime. The human sciences—psychology, physiology and sociology—that emerged as the century progressed drove the movement for change, and the modern field of criminology had its genesis in its service of the state's corrective efforts (Foucault 1977). The project of reforming offenders occurred through the application of science, in which offenders were classified into various types, and diagnosis and treatment supplemented, and in some jurisdictions replaced, work and penance (Garland 1985; 1997). In Australia it was not until the beginning of the twentieth century that this influence became apparent. Various penal institutions were designed to address the expectation that a prisoner would one day return to the social world a better citizen. In the larger jurisdictions, there was a multiplication of types of 'corrective' institutions. By the 1950s at least fourteen separate penal establishments were in New South Wales, ranging from penitentiary to prison farm and afforestation camp (Finnane 1997; O'Toole 2006). As we saw in the previous chapter, the apparent failure of the prison to reform or rehabilitate the offender was one of the factors that encouraged moves to decarceration and the proliferation of community-based programs in the second part of the twentieth century.

In the 1960s rehabilitation (and its corresponding features: individual-isation, treatment, conditional release, remissions) formed an important part of the sentencing landscape. But by the early 1970s, disillusionment with rehabilitation as a punishment objective and the corresponding rise of just deserts (discussed below) led to a decline in support. Concerns about rehabilitation included the threat to political freedom from state intrusion, its vulnerability to manipulation, its conceptual vagueness, the conflation of coercive and voluntary techniques, and the lack of rigorous proof of its efficacy (Allen 1981). The conclusions regarding its lack of efficacy remain controversial: programs were never properly funded, evaluated or targeted (Cullen and Gilbert 1982). Rehabilitation never completely disappeared as a justification for punishment, and since the 1990s there has been a revival of the rehabilitative goal (Brown 1998; Zdenkowski 2000; see Chapters 6 to 8).

Rehabilitation

Rehabilitation is based on utilitarian philosophy that is forward-looking and concerned with the consequences or outcome of punishment. In contrast to deterrence theory, which sees offenders as rational and calculating, this perspective sees them as needing help and support. The aim is to achieve the prevention of crime by changing the offender. This usually requires a range of sentences and facilities designed to offer various programs of treatment. The focus may be on the modification of attitudes and behavioural problems, or the objective may be to provide education or skills that might enable offenders to find work rather than resort to crime. The key consideration is therefore the perceived needs of the offender rather than the gravity of the offence committed. These needs are determined by expert assessment—for example, a pre-sentence report prepared by a probation officer, or a psychiatric report. The sentencer then decides on the form of treatment that matches the perceived needs of the offender (Ashworth 2005).

The operation of rehabilitative model has led to sentences that are indeterminate, on the basis that a person should only be released from obligations when, in the opinion of the experts, a 'cure' had been achieved. The problems associated with rehabilitative approaches include:

○ limited empirical evidence of their success (Martinson 1974), although recent meta-analysis of large numbers of small rehabilitative schemes has suggested that positive results can be obtained in favourable circumstances and selected offenders (Hudson 2003a, p. 30)

○ a lack of due process: indeterminate or semi-determinate sentences place the release of offenders in the hands of prison or probation authorities, often without firm criteria for decision-making, clear accountability or avenues for appeal

○ a disregard for the rights of individuals, that they are not to be subjected to compulsory state intervention that is disproportionate to the seriousness of the crime committed

○ the potential for net widening: even if the crime is relatively minor, an offender who is assessed as needing help might be drawn into the criminal justice system and subject to state control for a considerable period.

INCAPACITATION

Incapacitation is a theme that is in the background of the stories of deterrence and rehabilitation. It is the third corner of the utilitarian theory of punishment, which is focused on preventing future crime. According to Bentham, punishment reduced crime through example and reformation operated on the will of offenders and others. Where example and reformation failed, it became necessary to rely on reducing a convict's physical power to offend again. In the case of transportation to New South Wales, the British government's desire to make it physically impossible for convicts to commit further offences in England was key: because the colony was so far away, few convicts would return once their sentences had been served. For the government, the behaviour of convicts after their release—as long as they did not return—was not a consideration.

The reforms of the late nineteenth century were designed to prevent some people from reaching prison and to ensure that others were detained for longer periods. The shift in the focus of punishment in Australia away from deterrence was not only about the diversion of minor offenders from prison. Rehabilitation was linked to reforms that narrowed the definition of who should be in prison: '[F]irst offenders, old feeble vagrants, diseased and friendless incapables, inebriates, lunatics and juveniles' were to be kept out of prison (Garton 1982, p. 99); those who were considered 'criminals' would be subjected to more extensive periods of imprisonment. Prisons were moral hospitals; however, unlike mental hospitals that detained patients until they were sane, the prison moral hospital had to discharge the inmate after a pre-determined amount of time (Neitenstein 1897, p. 44, in Finnane and Woodyatt 2002, p. 93).

One answer was the indeterminate sentence. *The Habitual Criminal Act 1905* introduced a system of indeterminate sentencing in New South Wales to resolve the problem of habitual offenders serving endless short sentences and being returned to the community only to recommit the same offences. Society would be both protected from repeat offenders and receive rehabilitated citizens back into itself at a future stage. Similar legislation was introduced in Victoria in 1907; and in Western Australia, a decade later. In Victoria, the *Indeterminate Sentences Act* was intended to address the repeat offending of three-times convicted offenders; it was also applied to first offenders on multiple charges (Finnane 1997, pp. 79–80). The adoption of systems of classification of prisoners associated with the reform movement had a rehabilitative rationale, but it was also a means of management for rebellious prisoners. In the postwar period, the goal of the criminological and penological enthusiasm for rehabilitation was expressed in the development of prisoner programs and the probation and parole systems. The objective was the production of useful citizens; however, as Finnane and Woodyatt point out, 'containment remained fundamental' (2002, p. 94).

Sentencing and punishment involving incapacitation consists of dealing with offenders in such a way as to make them incapable of offending for substantial periods of time. Selective incapacitation has attracted considerable interest in recent years. It has drawn support from research that suggests that a significant proportion of crime is committed by an identifiable core of persistent offenders. Based on this, proponents argue that, in order to reduce crime, authorities should develop ways to accurately identify this group of serious recidivists and develop rules for their long-term incarceration. Such measures might involve: mandatory three strikes laws (Hogg 1999, p. 262), indefinite imprisonment or preventive detention. While selective incapacitation has enjoyed support in the United States, the use of such techniques has been more modest in Australia: while habitual offender legislation has been either abolished or fallen into disuse, indefinite sentences (by way of imprisonment) are authorised in various forms. For example, there has been a rapid growth in new legislation authorising a court that has imposed a prison term for a designated serious offence to extend that term indefinitely subject to judicial review (see Queensland's *Dangerous Prisoners (Sexual Offenders) Act 2003*). Such sentences may be imposed if the offender is judged to be a serious danger to the community (Zdenkowski 2000, p. 182).

In recent decades the use of protective orders imposed by way of preventive detention has attracted criticism. Such orders are not a response to a criminal offence; rather, they provide the authority to detain someone because of apprehended future danger. They were introduced in New South Wales and

Victoria during the 1990s. In each case, the legislation was *ad hominem* (directed at a specified individual), did not require a crime or conviction as a precondition and entitled the Supreme Court, on the application of the Director of Public Prosecutions, to order the detention of the named individual if the court was satisfied on the balance of probabilities that he was more likely than not to commit a serious act of violence. The rationale for the law was the alleged gap in the protection offered to the community by the criminal and mental health laws against potential violence. Critics drew attention to the legislation's lack of constitutionality, its violation of human rights; the lack of due process safeguards; its discriminatory (*ad hominem*) nature; the flawed assumption that the existing law was inadequate to deal with potential violence; and the serious problems involved in predicting violence. In both states the law has since ceased to have effect.

Selective incapacitation can also be understood more broadly, and in a way that does not always involve imprisonment. At one extreme, capital punishment and the severing of limbs are forms of incapacitative punishments; however, today there are formidable humanitarian arguments against such irreversible measures. Less controversial examples might include disqualification from driving and measures such as curfews and additional requirements in probation orders—like restrictions on movement or chemical management of sex offenders. In the case of indefinite incarceration, research suggests that the costs outweigh the benefits. Nevertheless, there are continuing attempts to improve techniques that claim to identify offender target groups more effectively, rather than develop alternative approaches that are not reliant on selective incapacitation (which is discussed in greater detail in Chapters 4 and 5).

Incapacitation

Incapacitation has its foundation in consequentialist utilitarian philosophy. The concept refers to obstructing or reducing the offender's capacity to commit new crimes through some sort of confinement. The offender is incapacitated by being taken out of social circulation. There are two types of incapacitation: collective and selective. Collective incapacitation refers to the containment of particular categories of offenders, while selective incapacitation refers to the containment of individuals.

Selective incapacitation is appealing because it is based on the principle that likely reoffenders can be identified and the public protected against future crime by incarcerating a small group of serious repeat offenders. It promises (but doesn't necessarily deliver) the following benefits: the amount of crime will be reduced by removing from circulation those who would otherwise commit many offences; the amount of crime will be further reduced by not excessively punishing those whose reoffending probabilities would be increased rather than decreased by severe punishment; and state expenditure can be kept down by not punishing the majority of offenders more than is useful in crime reduction terms.

Community protection is cited as the main justification for selective incapacitation. Proportionality principles give way to the greater good of public safety. Due process concerns are said to be addressed by insisting on suitable criteria, expert assessment and strict forms of proof.

The problems associated with the use of selective incapacitation include:

- Overprediction of serious repeat offenders, with a false positive rate that has often reached two out of every three (Ashworth 2005)—punishment may not only be undeserved but also unnecessary to prevent further serious offending.
- It is morally indefensible because it amounts to sacrificing one offender's liberty in the hope of increasing future safety of others.
- It is a violation of human rights through arbitrary punishment.
- It violates principles of proportionality in sentencing.
- There is lack of relevant expertise to make the assessments required.
- Appropriate procedural safeguards do not exist.
- Selective incapacitation discriminates against the disadvantaged (consider, for example, the demographic profile of death row in the United States).

JUST DESERTS AND RETRIBUTION

Just desert theory is a modern form of retributive philosophy. Retributive penal systems have existed throughout history; an early example is the *lex talionis* of biblical times—an eye for an eye, a tooth for a tooth, a life for a life. This system calls for equivalence between the punishment and the crime, such that the offenders should forfeit that which the victim has lost. Up until the 1970s, criminologists generally thought of retribution simply in terms of vengeance, which has limited appeal as a basis for punishment. But dissatisfaction with rehabilitative penalties, mainly as a result of wide disparities in sentencing, stimulated the 'back to justice' movement in most modern Western liberal democracies.

In Australia the rise of 'just deserts' sentencing principles in the 1980s and 1990s was in reaction to the upheaval and reform in the 1960s and the 1970s (Brown 1998). In the 1960s and 1970s, the prison became more and more visible as a site of political struggle as a result of significant riots in a number of prisons, like those at Bathurst, in New South Wales, in 1970 and 1974. Vocal prison action groups emerged promoting anarchist, neo-Marxist and abolitionist programs. These attacks on the state created the focus for government inquiries into the penal system, which mostly supported the claims of critics (see the NSW Nagel Royal Commission in 1978): prisons were brutal, counterproductive, stigmatising and recidivist-producing in their effects. As an institution the prison was perceived as a failure: it did not fulfil its utilitarian functions, it did not protect the community from crime, and it neither rehabilitated nor deterred offenders. Community service orders were introduced as alternatives; however, these too came under attack. Stanley Cohen's 1979 assessment of community corrections as a means of extending the net of social control into the community was widely accepted (Brown 1998).

A counter-response to the movement for reform emerged in the 1980s from populist politicians and those sections of the public who believed that any problems in the prison system were the result of a loss of discipline stemming from the reform processes that followed the royal commissions. Declining support for rehabilitation provided a platform for arguing that the signs of failure—riots, high recidivism and so on—were products of ill-conceived objectives. Prisons were intended to punish, and this fundamental objective had been obscured in the notion of prisoners' rights and the meddling social work practices of parole, prisoners' programs and community alternatives. In New South Wales, a concerted attack on prison conditions aimed explicitly to intensify the punitive experience through measures like the abolition of remissions, reduced availability of parole, the removal of welfare and rehabilitation programs, the confiscation of prisoners' property and the removal of mechanisms of scrutiny and accountability (Brown 1998). Ironically, this backlash built on the earlier arguments of the radical and abolitionist critiques of imprisonment. Paul Hirst (1986) explains that constant talk of the failure of the prison to fulfil the utilitarian aims of deterrence and rehabilitation created an opportunity for those who argued that these aims were misconceived: the only function of the prison was to punish. The climate conducive to the rise of the new retributivism was also fuelled by liberal reformers who claimed that there was a fundamental problem in the mix of sentencing objectives. In their view, the confusion of, and contradiction between, the various sentencing objectives, like deterrence and rehabilitation, highlighted the need to adopt a single 'coherent' rationale for imprisonment and sentencing and they looked to just deserts (Brown 1998).

In North America the rise of just deserts was marked in many jurisdictions by the introduction of clear sentencing guidelines (for example, the Minnesota grid) aimed at preventing the disparities associated with the rehabilitative ideal (Zdenkowski 2000, pp. 163–4). Australian jurisdictions resisted change that might challenge judicial discretion, and the legislative adoption of 'just deserts' has been varied (Brown 1998, p. 384). The *Sentencing Act 1989* (NSW) adopted just deserts rhetoric in a general way as part of the argument for 'truth in sentencing', which was expressed through the abolition of executive remissions on sentences and the fixing of a relation of three-quarters between imprisonment and parole. Besides this, no direction or guidance was given to sentencers. The effect of the Act was to increase the length of prison sentences and contribute to a significant 50 per cent increase in the NSW prison population of between 1989 and 1995 (Brown 1998). In Victoria a lengthy period of sentencing review led to a more structured system, with legislative guidance on sentencing and the gradation of penalties into fourteen sentencing bands (Freiberg 1995).

In the late 1980s the Australian Law Reform Commission described the adoption of just deserts in Australia as having a primary emphasis 'on just deserts for the offender and reparation for the victim'; however, '[d]eterrence, rehabilitation and incapacitation should still be relevant but given a lesser priority' (ALRC 1987, p. 17, in Brown 1998, p. 383). This approach aimed to accommodate rehabilitation within a sentencing framework that emphasises proportionate sentences. It challenged the assumption that there is a fundamental incompatibility between retributive (backward-looking) justice goals and consequentialist (forward-looking) rehabilitationist goals. This is possible according to Bottoms (1995), through a reconceptualisation of rehabilitation as no longer involving training or expert treatment of obedient subjects; instead, offenders are seen as rational agents who can be persuaded to cooperate in their own longer term interest.

Over the last decade, justice deserts ideas have continued to influence sentencing policy and practice. This is because of persistent pessimism about the value of treatment, and claims about offenders' rights, or the obligation of state authorities to treat them with fairness (Bottoms 1995). In the policy domain, while the broad concept of just deserts is clearly prominent, what counts as just deserts can vary from one jurisdiction to another. This is because:

1   There are no positive absolute scales, and judgments about the seriousness of given offences may vary culturally from one country to another.

2   There is a continuing and unresolved debate as to what role previous convictions should play in just desert theory.

3   No modern just desert theory completely excludes instrumental (that is, utilitarian) considerations of sentencing.

Just deserts

Just deserts-based punishment aims to communicate official censure or blame chiefly to the offender, but also to the victim and society at large (von Hirsch and Ashworth 1998). General deterrence is a subsidiary element, but it operates only within the censuring framework (Ashworth 2005). The primary principle of just deserts is that punishment should be commensurate with the seriousness of the offence. Instead of the equivalence of *lex talionis*, the modern version interprets commensurate as proportionate. The most serious punishments should be reserved for the most serious offences, and penalties should be graduated according to the gravity of the offence. Possible future offending is not a consideration; however, previous convictions are taken into account. Reductions in sentence are allowed for first offenders because just desert is derived from the seriousness of the offence and from the culpability of the offender. An accidental or coerced act should not carry the penalty of a freely chosen fully willed action, even for serious crime. The intentionality, or *mens rea*, which is important in Western legal systems, is part of the idea of punishment being imposed to the extent that it is deserved. First offenders might not realise either the consequences of their actions or their impact on victims; this mitigation is less plausible for repeat offences.

Key problems associated with just deserts sentencing include:

○ the difficulty of ranking offences in terms of seriousness—whose views of seriousness should be taken into account?
○ the difficulty of ranking punishment in order of severity—in other words, the concept of proportionality is also in contention
○ an over-reliance on the court to remedy injustices
○ a lack of attention to the biases inherent in the criminal justice system
○ a disregard for the effects of social deprivation and disadvantage that are consistently correlated with the commission of crime (Cunneen and White 2002).

MANAGERIALISM

The rise of managerialism in the public sector and within criminal justice has been well documented. Recent years have seen the influence of economy, efficiency and effectiveness on the shape of penal systems. As governments have scrutinised their expenditure programs, the large sums spent on penal systems in general and prisons in particular have been questioned. Assessing whether the state gets value for money from this expenditure is another way of asking whether offenders could be dealt with equally effectively in some cheaper way. This has undoubtedly been one reason behind the development of new forms of non-custodial measures, and it continues in the shape of government enthusiasm for the 'what works' approach—testing specific and targeted methods of dealing with offenders, especially in the community, to reduce reoffending. There is much interest in 'evidence-led initiatives' and, more specifically, the cost of different sentences and their relative effectiveness in preventing reoffending (Ashworth 2000, p. 82).

George Zdenkowski (2000, p. 187) describes the effect of managerialism on the Australian criminal justice system at the beginning of the twenty-first century in terms of 'pragmatism in the punishment process'. He cites policies and practices that subordinate justifications for punishment to the imperative of administrative convenience, explaining that this is demonstrated in sentencing discounts for guilty pleas and for the provision of information to authorities and the rapid expansion of summary jurisdiction of magistrates' courts in the area of indictable offences. Ironically, perhaps in light of public concern about severity levels, this has led to a decrease in the potential and actual penalties being imposed for relatively serious offences.

Managerialist effects are evident in other parts of Australia's justice system. Administrative sanctions have been used increasingly for significant cases of corporate fraud, and administrative regulation is now commonplace in both the private corporate world and the public sector (Tomaino 1999). These types of remedies are frequently used for breaches of the law in areas such as occupational health and safety; food and health; tax; social security; equal opportunity; fishing;

and environmental standards. This approach is not without drawbacks, namely the scope for inconsistent use of such remedies and potential for anomalies and capricious justice, the erosion of due process and reduced accountability because of invisibility, and the lack of deterrence. Recently, there has also been greater use of infringement notices (that is, on-the-spot fines) that allow offenders to discharge their liability by paying a fixed sum (discussed in Chapter 10). This system can benefit individuals who wish to avoid the trauma of court proceedings; economic and administrative advantages may also arise from the diversion of minor offenders from the court system, provided that the offences to which the system is applied are carefully monitored. But there is a potential for negative outcomes in terms of punishment and justice (Zdenkowski 2000). The use of on-the-spot fines can result in the lessening of the moral content of particular offences; a departure from traditional principles of criminal law; the failure to consider individual cases; pressure on an individual to pay even if innocent; net widening; and potential victimisation.

Bottoms (1995) describes this new managerialism in terms of its systemic, actuarial and consumerist dimensions. The managerialist approach glosses over dissonance to emphasise the criminal justice system, conceived as a system rather than a collection of different and sometimes conflicting parts. Such conceptualisations have become commonplace in official crime policy in most Western countries over the last thirty years. In most jurisdictions, the recent emphasis on the systemic character of criminal justice tends to emphasise inter-agency cooperation—the creation of an overall strategic plan with each criminal justice agency linking its mission to the overall goals of the system. Agencies create and actively monitor information about the system and its function, paying attention to key performance indicators that measure efficiency and effectiveness in terms of managerial standards. Feeley and Simon note that one result of this 'systemic' aspect of managerialism is that 'increasing primacy [is] given to the efficient control of internal system processes' (1992, p. 450). Concentration on such matters can even, in some cases, result in the displacement of more traditional 'external' objectives, such as reducing recidivism.

Peters (1986, cited in Bottoms 1995, p. 28) argues that this amounts to a shift in focus in the criminal law, which is no longer driven by distinctions between right and wrong according to the retributionist principles, or the treatment of offenders pushed by the ideal of rehabilitation. These rationalities have been replaced by the rationality of the organisation. This change has significant consequences for individuals who come to the attention of the criminal justice system. The systemic approach tends to 'target offenders as an aggregate' (Feeley and Simon 1992; 1994). From this perspective, the individual is understood not through moral or therapeutic assessments, but simply as a unit within a framework of policy. Data of parole boards or arrest rates for police become performance indicators. Official statistics that might have raised concerns by highlighting high rates of recidivism or crime now measure productivity and the successful detection of parole breaches or police activity; they are positive results that demonstrate the agencies are effectively doing their job.

The actuarial dimension is highlighted by Feeley and Simon who claim that:

> [a] central feature of the new discourse is the replacement of a moral or clinical description of the individual with an actuarial language of probabilistic calculations and statistical distributions applied to populations ... (hence) the new penology is neither about punishing nor rehabilitating individuals, [rather] it is about identifying and managing unruly groups. (1992, p. 455)

While punishment and rehabilitation are still important considerations of the criminal justice system, the aggregative tendencies of managerialism can to lead to an interest in the 'actuarial language of probabilistic calculations'. For sentencing this translates into an interest in the possibilities of selective incapacitation and 'dangerousness'; or in complex cost–benefit calculations about the value of particular sentencing innovations, such as electronic monitoring. In such an environment, traditional concerns of justice are challenged by the instrumental assumptions of the actuarial approach.

The consumerist dimension is based on some of the managerialist systemic characteristics. The pressure for the effective delivery of individuals' entitlements — together with an increasing pressure from legislative and executive branches of government for efficient service delivery, greater productivity and so on — encourages service providers to adopt a managerialist approach because it seems to be the most successful method of meeting these kinds of demands. As a result, agency managers are increasingly interested in the views of those to whom services are delivered, to test whether, in their view, the services are being delivered satisfactorily (evidenced in the recent proliferation of process evaluations, Health Outcomes International 2003). The consumerist dimension sees those subject to the system in a different way to systemic managerialism. While the latter tends to see the individual as simply a statistical unit within an aggregated policy system, consumerist managerialism sees the individual as someone well able to judge (like a consumer in the private market) whether or not services are being well delivered. This consumerist dimension indicates that managerialism is not simply a top-down approach: information about the views of 'consumers' can and does affect aspects of the higher organisation of the system (see Chapters 8, 9 and 10).

RESTORATIVE JUSTICE AND COMMUNITARIANISM

A major development in criminal justice in the final quarter of the twentieth century was the increasing recognition of the rights and the needs of victims of crime. Finnane (1997, p. 164) argues that this emergence of the victim — as an independent actor for whom the state is no longer presumed to speak conclusively — is possibly the most substantial change to occur in the criminal justice debate and policy since the nineteenth century. The changed profile of victims in the domain of sentencing and punishment is evident in two ways. The first is the increased attention given to victims' rights generally in the criminal justice system. This has included granting victims the right both to make a factual statement to the court about the offence and, in some jurisdictions, to make a submission before sentencing. The second is the growing number of restorative theories of criminal justice (Ashworth 2000).

The victims' movement developed in the United States and United Kingdom in the 1970s, and emerged in Australia during the 1980s. It gained momentum from increasing concern for domestic violence and sexual assault victims. At an international level these concerns were reflected in the *UN Declaration on the Basic Principles of Justice for Victims of Crime and Abuse of Power*. This declaration sets out benchmarks for the treatment of victims in relation to access to justice and fair treatment, restitution, compensation and assistance. In Australia, the two predominant responses addressed welfare services and procedural rights (Zdenkowski 2000). Welfare services have consisted of witness assistance, information, prosecution liaison, counselling referral services and compensation (Israel 1999, pp. 223–64, see Chapter 8). Procedural rights potentially include: 'the right to be consulted on (or to veto) the decision to prosecute; the right to be consulted on the acceptance of a plea; the right to make submissions to sentencing or parole authorities' (NSW LRC 1996a, p. 417 in Zdenkowski 2000, p. 169). Victim impact statements have been widely embraced. Such statements containing the particulars of the injury suffered by the victims as a result of the offence are tendered on behalf of the victim at the sentencing hearing. They are intended to enhance the court's understanding of the seriousness of the offence. There is much debate regarding their value, and whether or not they augment pre-existing processes or simply address a perceived need to express the victim's concerns. Beyond matters relating to the procedural rights of victims, another important development has been the emergence of restorative justice theories and schemes involving victims based on such theories.

At the start of the 1990s, restorative justice was confined to the margins of criminal justice policing and practice; and although enthusiastically promoted by its advocates, it was more of a movement than a theorised approach to punishment. Over recent years, however, it has developed into a model of justice that is more clearly defined in scholarly penological literature through evaluations of programs, critiques and debates that are linked to a growing theoretical base. Barbara Hudson (2003a) explains that restorative justice is advocated by those concerned with making criminal justice more responsive to the needs and the suffering of victims. Their starting point was the argument that formal criminal justice disempowered and often excluded victims by not allowing them to describe their suffering in their own words; victims only had a part in the process if and insofar as they were asked to give evidence that the court decided was relevant. Restorative justice was promoted as a way of making victims central to criminal justice without further undermining offenders. Although victims are at the heart of the process, restorative justice is not simply a part of the victim movement: it is proposed as a way of avoiding the zero-sum thinking that what helps victims must hurt offenders. It has also been promoted by many 'First Nation' groups who wish to retain the values and traditions of their justice processes. These groups have used this approach to challenge the prosecution and sentencing processes of white justice that have continually resulted in overrepresentation of minority groups in prosecution and imprisonment rates. The Māori tradition in New Zealand and First Nation traditions in Canada have been particularly influential, as have some religious groups, such the Canadian Mennonites (Hudson 2003a). Australian criminologist John Braithwaite has been an important protagonist of restorative justice. In *Crime, Shame and Reintegration* (1989) he argued that responses to crime should use reintegrative shaming (inclusive shame focused on the offence, not the offender), rather than stigmatic shaming of offenders (shame that censures and excludes). Braithwaite and Mugford (1994) developed this idea using Garfinkel's (1956) analysis of the court process as a status degradation ceremony to highlight what was wrong with the criminal justice system. They argued that while the criminal acts should be denounced, individuals ought not to be denounced or stigmatised. Reintegrative shaming aims to separate bad acts from potentially good individuals.

The wide range of proponents and programs linked to restorative justice are so diverse that it is difficult to come up with an agreed definition. Essentially the term refers to a process in which offenders, victims, their representatives and representatives of the community come together to agree on a response to crime (Braithwaite 1999b, p. 5). Van Ness explains the purpose of restorative justice as '[t]he restoration into safe communities of victims and offenders who have resolved their conflicts' (1993, p. 258). The key is an emphasis on process as much as outcome; on victims, offenders and communities; on relationships; and the forward-looking consequentialism of the approach. Zehr, for example, proposes that restorative justice emphasises 'right relationships' rather than 'right rules' (1990 in Hudson 2003a, p. 81). The important task of justice is to restore the balance to relationships that have been damaged by crime (victim–offender; victim–offender–community; offender–community; offender–family), rather than making sure that the correct legal rule is followed and that it is interpreted and applied correctly.

Several limits of restorative justice have been identified:

- Victims, offenders and their supporters may not be prepared for restorative ways of thinking and acting.
- There are legal constraints on the process.
- Because restorative justice does not have a fact-finding or investigating mechanism, it cannot replace established criminal justice.
- As a diversion from court, restorative justice is principally used for youth as opposed to adult cases; and most jurisdictions restrict the kinds of cases that can be diverted.

○ As pre-sentence advice to magistrates, restorative justice can be used in some jurisdictions for youth cases but not in others (that is, it not available for all); for example, restorative justice for adults is not widely available.

○ Restorative justice may be better at addressing victims' rights but may compromise the justice experience of offenders (Daly et al. 2006, p. 445, see Chapter 10 for more detail).

OTHER INNOVATIONS IN JUSTICE

Indigenous justice is an innovation currently emerging in criminal justice systems in different parts of the world. It refers to a range of contemporary justice practices in which Indigenous people have a central role in responding to crime. They include urban sentencing courts, the participation of community justice groups, both community and elder panels in sentencing, and a variety of forms of sentencing circles (Daly et al. 2006).

Indigenous justice has developed as a response to the destruction of Indigenous cultures and social organisations brought about by colonialism and state violence. These innovations aim to address the over-representation of Indigenous people in the criminal justice system. Such over-representation is one of the distinguishing features of Australian imprisonment. Indeed, criminologists have described these people as the most imprisoned race in the world (Brown 1998): Australian Indigenous adults are thirteen times more likely to be imprisoned than non-Indigenous Australians (ABS 2008b). Indigenous justice initiatives also respond to the recommendations by the 1989 Royal Commission into Aboriginal Deaths in Custody (RCIADIC). Initially, in the 1990s, diversionary programs such as police cautioning and family conferences were introduced 'front end' of the criminal justice system to provide options for young offenders (Blagg 2008). By the late 1990s, court-focused programs began to be implemented at the 'back end' of the system. They aimed to reduce Indigenous incarceration, increase the participation of Indigenous people in the justice system as court staff or advisers, and identify mechanisms for Indigenous communities to resolve disputes and deal with offenders in culturally appropriate ways.

Similar to restorative justice, Indigenous justice practices are diverse; the degree to which Indigenous people have control over the process varies widely (Daly et al. 2006). Rudin argues that unless Indigenous people 'are given some options and opportunities to develop processes that respond to the needs of [their] community' (2005, p. 99), such practices should not be termed Indigenous justice. This is fundamental and one key way of distinguishing between Indigenous justice and restorative justice. Indigenous justice practices in Australia usually include some form of input from Indigenous groups or communities into sentencing decisions. This input may take the form of advice arising from consultation with Indigenous groups who have a degree of control of the process and the outcomes.

Alternatively, these practices can be almost completed imposed by 'white justice' (Daly et al. 2006).

Indigenous groups are positive about Indigenous justice programs, indicating that they have more trust in, and better understanding of, the court's decisions because they are involved and have a say in the process. Marchetti and Daly (2004) argue that the courts' strengths lie in improved communication, reliance on Indigenous knowledge and mechanisms of social control, and the development of more appropriate penalties. Attention is paid to the reasons for and contexts of offending behaviour; this is linked with 'Indigenous friendly' procedures and Aboriginal justice workers. Anecdotal reports from magistrates indicate higher rates of court attendance and reductions in reoffending (Daly et al. 2006). On the other hand, Tauri (1999) argues that such practices are tokenistic and paternalistic, while Rudin suggests that they can be a form of 'bureaucratic colonialism' (2005, p. 108). Other limits are highlighted by Daly et al. (2006, p. 451). For example, urban courts may appear to deliver a separate 'apartheid justice': one for Indigenous people and another for non-Indigenous people. This is further complicated because courts are available in some cities and regional areas but not in others; and some Indigenous offenders may be deemed more suitable than others. And some officers of the court can find it difficult to work outside of Western legal paradigms (see Chapter 7).

Therapeutic jurisprudence is a recently introduced legal concept that was originally described by Wexler and Winick (1991). It refers to the extent to which substantive rules, legal procedures and the roles of lawyers and judges produce therapeutic or anti-therapeutic consequences for individuals involved in the legal process. More recent literature has expanded this definition, suggesting simply that therapeutic jurisprudence practices are based on knowledge derived from social sciences (Goldberg 2005). The term was introduced in the United States in the late 1980s for mental-health cases, but it has since been expanded to include family, criminal and civil cases. It is linked to the recent proliferation of 'problem-solving courts' (Michandani 2005; Van de Veen 2004). Problem-solving courts were established in the United States in 1989, with the founding of the first drug court in Miami.

Therapeutic jurisprudence is an evolving concept. It is most clearly defined as a way of judging that is associated with a set of practices, including the integration of treatment services with judicial case management, ongoing judicial intervention and close monitoring, multidisciplinary involvement and collaboration with community-based and government organisations. The cultural shift involved in the application of therapeutic jurisprudence cannot be underestimated (Murphy 2000; Nolan 2001; Tapin 2002). The traditional roles of the adversarial players in the criminal justice system and the divergent focuses of law enforcement and treatment systems are at stake. Melding the roles of all the players into a coherent team with a shared objective of managing an offender through a sentence, participation in treatment and recovery is a major challenge. It strikes at issues of confidentiality, privilege and legal counsel acting on instruction (Belenko 2000; Tapin 2002). It necessitates clarity of purpose and openness of communication that does not normally characterise the interactions of those participating in court processes. As Nolan (2001) points out, this is often met with opposition. Conflict arises in the interpretation of therapeutic jurisprudence: sentencers have varying views and expectations regarding appropriate forms of intervention and the behaviour of offenders (Nolan 2001); at times they fail to take account advice from treatment providers represented on the court team, preferring to rely on their own assessment of the path that therapeutic intervention should take (Nolan 2001; Tapin 2002).

Therapeutic jurisprudence allows officers of the court to take a hands-on approach to their cases, to know more about offenders and the contexts of their offending, and to be attentive and sympathetic listeners (Wexler 2004). The processes involved are offender focused, designed to develop capabilities in the offender for law-abiding self-governance. Participants and drug court teams are positive about the process. Drug courts have been much evaluated and the quality of these studies varies (Bull 2003); the general finding is that that graduates fare better than others in reduced reoffending; however, there is a great deal of attrition from entry to the program to graduation. Problem-solving courts are labour intensive, time-consuming, and require a particular level of resourcing to be effective; it is not possible to have them in all jurisdictions. Program participation can be experienced as intrusive and controlling of offenders' movements and social interactions; as a result, drug court programs are often perceived as more onerous than the usual sentence.

In Australia, therapeutic jurisprudence is deployed not only in the context of problem-solving courts but also in corrections (in New South Wales the Compulsory Drug Treatment Correctional Centre [CDTCC] based near Parklea Correctional Complex), administrative tribunals and appellate procedures (Freiberg 2002, p. 9). Drug court programs have been established in New South Wales, Queensland, South Australia, Western Australia, Victoria, Tasmania and the Northern Territory. Therapeutic jurisprudence in drug treatment courts provides a distinct forum for the application of this principle (Hora et al. 1999; Senjo and Leip 2001), which we will investigate in more detail in Chapter 6. A problem-oriented mental health court was set up in South Australia in 1999, and subsequently in Victoria, New South Wales, Queensland and Tasmania. In Victoria the Collingwood Neighbourhood Justice Centre is a one-stop problem-solving court that involves the integration and on-site availability of a range of services for both victims and offenders (see text box). Family violence courts, which according to Stewart (2005) claim therapeutic jurisprudence as their foundation, were first established in South Australia in 1997, then in Western Australia, Victoria, Queensland and New South Wales (see Chapter 9 for a critical assessment of this claim).

Collingwood Neighbourhood Justice Centre

The Neighbourhood Justice Centre (NJC) is an example of recent innovation in the delivery of justice. It was established as a three-year pilot project of the Victorian Department of Justice and the first of its kind in Australia. Located within the diverse inner urban Yarra municipality, the NJC aims to enhance community involvement in the justice system.

The NJC provides:

○ a court
○ on-site support services for victims, witnesses, defendants and local residents
○ mediation and crime prevention programs for the City of Yarra
○ community meeting facilities.

The NJC works closely with the City of Yarra community to:

○ address the underlying causes of offending
○ provide opportunities, education and support for victims, witnesses, defendants and local residents
○ assist in preventing crime
○ stop the 'revolving door' of crime and punishment
○ increase the community's involvement in the administration of justice
○ increase access to justice.

Source: <www.justice.vic.gov.au/wps/wcm/connect/DOJ+Internet/Home/ The+Justice+System/Neighbourhood+Justice>.

CONCLUSION

Since colonisation, a range of principles have shaped the delivery of sentencing and punishment practices in Australia. The uncertain fate of those transported to Australia in the eighteenth and early nineteenth centuries was intended to deter offenders; however, the early governors' concern with the viability of the settlement had the effect of tempering the perceived harshness of the sentence. Jeremy Bentham, a man whose name is frequently associated with ideas about punishment, had a particular interest the development of the colony at Botany Bay. His utilitarian philosophy underpins the punitive principles of deterrence, rehabilitation and incapacitation. His model prison—the panopticon—was the prototype for the penitentiary that revolutionised punishment—not to mention other social institutions—in the nineteenth century; it was linked to the rise of the prison as the preferred form of punishment. In Australia, Bentham's ideas played a part in ending transportation, and they continue to shape the delivery of punishment today. The purpose of this chapter was to introduce the range of principles that have shaped punishment. Undeniably, utilitarianism was important from the outset. In the later twentieth century, other factors came into play—a return to retribution with just deserts, managerialism and communitarianism, along with other innovations. Due to space limitations, the overview of each concept here has been necessarily brief; it is therefore intended as an introduction. How these principles work, or the difficulty of getting them to work, in the applied delivery of punishment is explored in more detail in Parts 2 to 4 of this book. For example, in Chapters 4 and 5, containment through incapacitation and preventive detention is explored as a means of responding to child sex offenders and those suspected of, or linked to, terrorist activity. Recent reconfigurations of rehabilitation are examined in Chapters 7, 8 and 9, which provide examples of how therapeutic jurisprudence shaped by managerialist pursuits is put to work in both drug and domestic violence courts and describe emerging trends in Indigenous justice. The final part of the book focuses on responses that understand offenders as rational actors, who are able to choose to modify their own behaviour in the face of deterrence or responses driven by the regulatory state.

3

Some social perspectives on punishment

INTRODUCTION

The previous chapter introduced a range of philosophies that have influenced the form of punishment in Australian society since colonisation. These were divided between forward-looking approaches inspired by Bentham's utilitarian ideal—of deterrence, rehabilitation and incapacitation—and expressive past-oriented principles that aim to exact retribution from offenders. Garland (1991) describes these ideas in terms of penology and philosophy. While penologists see punishment as a means of reducing or preventing future crime, philosophers understand it as a moral problem and thus are more concerned with how penal sanctions can be justified, their proper objective and the circumstances of imposition. Garland argues that these perspectives are too limited: they are either too focused on organisational or instrumental objectives or caught up in abstract debates about the regulation of freedom. They tell us little about punishment as a social institution; saying nothing of how specific penal measures come into existence, the social functions of punishment, the relationships that exist between penal institutions and other social institutions, punishments contribution to social order, state power, class domination or the cultural reproduction of society, its unintended social effects, functional failures or wider social costs (1991, p. 119).

Although punishment is clearly concerned with crime control, it is shaped by a range of social forces and has a significance that reaches well beyond the population of criminals. Through the sociology of punishment, we can explore the social foundations of punishment, trace out the social implications of specific penal modes, and 'uncover the structures of social action and webs of cultural meaning that give modern punishment its characteristic function, forms and effect' (Garland 1991, p. 119). The value of the sociological literature on punishment is that it consists of a range of theoretical approaches rather than a single comprehensive account. These competing models of sociological explanation highlight different characteristics of punishment and its social role, explaining punishment in various ways. This chapter surveys a range of key sociological interpretations of punishment. Along with the previous chapter, its aim is to provide a foundation for the remainder of this book, which will bring different theoretical perspectives into critical conversation with one another in each of the cases studies.

With this in mind, this chapter begins by describing theoretical interpretations concerned with the development of the systems of punishment that emerged with industrial capitalism. It outlines key sociological ideas about punishment influenced by the work of Durkheim, Marx and Foucault. These theorists highlight different aspects of modern penal systems and how they are shaped by constitutional, economic or disciplinary factors. The second part of the chapter covers more recent theoretical developments that seek to grapple with an apparently bewildering array of changes in penal policy and practice at the end of the twentieth century, many of which are mutually incoherent or 'volatile and contradictory' (O'Malley 1999). Most sociological accounts locate the roots of this transformation in the culture of late modernity, and identify neoliberalism and the containment of risk as important concepts. Here, the theoretical ideas of Beck, later work by Foucault, Mary Douglas and Elias are central.

DURKHEIM

Emile Durkheim (1858–1917) was a sociologist who worked in nineteenth-century France. His approach is referred to as functionalist because he argued that any aspect of social life that is studied must be approached from the perspective of discovering what role it performs in preserving social stability and promoting moral consensus. He analysed the processes of social change involved in industrialisation. In *The Division of Labor in Society* (1893/1983), Durkheim described these processes as part of the evolution of society from a more simple 'mechanical' form to a more advanced 'organic' form. In mechanical society, each social group is relatively isolated from all other social groups and is largely self-sufficient. People behave and think similarly, perform most of the same work tasks and have group-oriented goals. Social solidarity is based on the uniformity of its members. As society becomes more complex, work and social relationships become more intricate and specialised. Organic societies are characterised by highly interactive sets of relationships, specialised labour and individual goals. Highly structured relationships are required to distribute the products of each person's skills. Solidarity is not based on the uniformity of the individuals, but on the diversity of the functions and interdependency of the parts of society. Durkheim saw all societies as being in some stage of progression between mechanical and organic structures, with no society being totally one or the other.

Durkheim uses law and punishment as indicators of societies approximating his models of mechanical and organic solidarity (Durkheim 1893/1983). By providing a measure of less-easily observed social phenomena, such as morals and trends in public opinion, they gauge the nature and condition of various levels of social organisation and culture in society (Thompson 1988). According to Durkheim, the social organisation and cultural expressions of simpler societies were dominated by collective beliefs of a religious nature; as a result, the law was largely religious law. Infractions were punished immediately, passionately and severely because they threatened the solidarity of the society that was based on the sameness of the mentalities of its members. Law functioned to repress deviance, and the most severe sanctions were reserved for offences against religious proscriptions because these hit at the core of the *conscience collective*. The function of repressive sanctions was to reaffirm solidarity in society by taking vengeance on the offender. Durkheim asserted that this is still the case in modern societies as far as repressive sanctions, or the criminal law, is concerned. This is because it is only the forms, not the function, of punishment that have undergone historical change (Durkheim 1893/1983). Modern sanctions are considered less severe than ancient ones because our modern *conscience collective* is more attentive to the rights of individuals—even criminal individuals—and less dominated by religious or absolutist values (Durkheim 1901/1983). We have not ceased to react punitively when collective values are breached—these values themselves dictate that punishment should be less destructive of human life. The difference is that 'punishment now produces its effects with a greater awareness of what it is about'. Despite this greater consciousness of cause and effect in the modern penal system, 'the internal structure of phenomena remains unchanged, conscious [of it] or not'. Durkheim concludes that 'the essential elements of punishment are the same as before. And indeed, punishment has remained an act of vengeance, at least in part' (Durkheim 1893/1983, p. 61).

Durkheim explains the difference between law and punishment in both primitive and more complex societies in terms of changes in the *conscience collective*. Mechanical solidarity based on sameness had decreased as the division of labour increased. Some criminal law—repressive in its sanction—still functioned to reaffirm the *conscience collective* when it was offended directly or indirectly by actions against its representative organs, the state institutions, such as government agencies and regulations, or the police. Beyond this, however, law and punishment worked to restore relations between individuals, or contractual parties, to their previous state. In societies with an advanced division of labour, there were more differences based on specialisation of function and less sameness of the type in 'mechanical' simpler societies. In complex societies, social solidarity depended on the successful regulation of social relationships to ensure cooperation between specialised functions and their agents; restitutive sanctions and civil law reflected these structural realities. The extension of restitutive law and the reduction of repressive law were an index of an increase in the division of labour and the changed base of social solidarity (Thompson 1988). The interdependence between specialised functions created what Durkheim called 'organic solidarity'. In complex societies the modern state had a privileged position with regard to the law because of its centrality and representative nature. It claimed to represent the *conscience collective*, and so any offence against the state constituted a threat to social solidarity. Crimes that challenged the authority of the state and its agencies, like the police, were severely punished even though they did not seem to directly offend public opinion.

In sum, for Durkheim the criminal law reflects the basic moral values of society. Crimes that violate this *conscience collective* tend to provoke collective moral outrage and a passionate desire for vengeance. Punishing offenders is a way of expressing the 'passionate reactions' of collective moral sentiment in routinised and institutionalised ways. Garland (1991) explains that Durkheim makes two important points. First, even though the state monopolises the delivery and administration of punishment, a much wider population feels that it is involved in the act of punishment. This provides the institution of the state with social support and legitimacy. Second, despite all attempts in the nineteenth century to make punishment a rational, impartial and utilitarian process, it continues to be influenced by the punitive sentiments and emotive reactions at the base of society's response to crime. Taking this into account, punishment is therefore symbolic: it is more about the ritualised expression of social values and the controlled release of psychic energy than the instrumental deterrence and regulation of offenders. It is useful as a reaction against violators of the *conscience collective*. The penal institutions that put it into effect demonstrate the material force of social values and restore collective confidence in the integrity and power of the moral order. The rituals of punishment are directed less at the individual offender than at impassioned onlookers whose values and security have been challenged by the offender's actions. Punishment's significance is social and moral rather than simply penological. Moreover, punishment from Durkheim's perspective 'transforms a threat to social order into the triumph of social solidarity. Instead of damaging the cohesiveness of society, crime sets in motion a complex moral circuitry that channels the energy of outraged sentiments into a socially binding ritual of moral affirmation' (Garland 1991, p. 123).

Durkheim's theory is based on an assumption of order and consensus: social order is the consensus of the people in that society. He adopts a functionalist view, where each aspect of society works to support and maintain the operation of the social system as a whole. The main problem with this is the way in which it highlights how societies are integrated, how there are shared values and how there is consensus. This may be true of relatively simple societies; however, as societies become more industrialised and more fragmented, any claim that there is shared agreement on morality is difficult to sustain. In short, the concept of a general social consensus denies the plurality of values in contemporary society. By definition, since there is consensus, a conflict of values must mean that one group's values are wrong; by accepting the status quo in terms of 'core values', this approach fails to account for structural inequalities that mean that some values are privileged over others.

CRITICAL THEORY: MARXISM, FEMINISM AND POST-COLONIALISM

Critical theory is a broad term that provides an umbrella for perspectives that are concerned with the distribution of power in society and the effect of this on social processes, like punishment and sentencing. The focus is to highlight how the institutionalisation of particular relations of power, and the structures that support them, reflect social interests that oppress specific categories of people, such as women, young people, Indigenous people, the poor or the homeless.

Its general aim is to expose the power relations that shape how different groups are treated unfairly in and by the criminal justice system and to inform social change.

Critical criminologists were initially influenced by Marxist ideas and focused primarily on class; attention to race or gender-based oppression began to emerge in the 1970s. Since then, other forms of social relations (for example, heterosexist and religious oppression), questions related to imperialism and colonisation and more complex consideration intersections between social categories have become more central in critical scholarship (Anthony and Cunneen 2008).

The early focus on class was not, however, a product of the work of German philosopher and political economist Karl Marx (1818–1883), whose legacy for sociology was to insist that societies must be understood in terms of how economic structures influence social practices. Besides a few passing comments, Marx and his colleague and patron Friedrich Engels had little to say about crime and less about punishment. Theories of punishment from this perspective are the product of more recent neo-Marxism: punishment is considered in relation to the economic structures and the class interests served by penal practices. Marxist theorists do not see it as functional in the way that Durkheim did; rather, they ask questions about the economic and political drivers of penal policy, the role of penal institutions in strategies of class rule, and the ways in which punishment serves class power—symbolically or materially. The relations either between punishment and popular morality or between the state and the people are reframed to suggest ideological domination or repression instead of the implicit agreement described by Durkheim (Garland 1991). Marxist accounts of punishment can be divided between those who stress interconnections between penal institutions and economic requirements of modes of production (Melossi and Pavarini 1981; Rusche and Kirchheimer 1939/1968), and others who profile the role of punishment in political and ideological class struggles and the maintenance of state power or ruling class hegemony (Pashukanis 1924/1978). Ideology is a set of ideas that govern people's perceptions of the world. Marxist theories argue that, in capitalist society, ideas that support or facilitate the relations of production come to be seen as ideas that are essential to the continuation of society itself, rather than merely society in its capitalist mode. The ideas of the capitalist class are taken as being the ideas of the society as a whole. Hegemony is an important aspect of Marxist theories of ideology: it refers to the way that the ideas of the ruling class—the capitalists—are accepted by the rest of society as their own (Hudson 2003a).

In the 1970s Marxist criminology put questions of power on the agenda. Developing at about the same time, feminist criminology began to examine who holds and wields power in society and questioned how this affects women. Feminist perspectives are based on the premise that women are structurally disadvantaged in society. The introduction of feminist perspectives challenged the male biases and neglects of mainstream criminological theorising. In the 1970s feminist criminology made its first contribution by criticising the male bias inherent in the theories and writings of criminologists. Not only were nearly all leading theorists men, but they also wrote almost exclusively about men. When they did look at female offenders, it was usually with a set of stereotypical, sexist assumptions. The feminist criminologists argued that women should not be left out of criminological research just because they comprised a small proportion of the criminal population—women make up 7 per cent of the Australian prison population (ABS 2008b). To correct this gender blindness, they argued for the inclusion of women in studies of crime and punishment. In the late 1980s and early 1990s, feminist scholarship encouraged the outright rejection of criminology's core disciplinary assumptions and boundaries. Following broader developments in feminist theory, it promoted a radical scepticism about male-centred modes of inquiry dominant in disciplines such as history, science, sociology and criminology, and challenged their key concepts, methods of enquiry and claims to neutrality.

This theoretically informed body of feminist scholarship rejected positivist research methods that had dominated mainstream criminology (Carrington 2008); however, it tended to fall into the trap of universalising women as the 'Other'. By solely focusing on gender as the primary category of analysis and source of female oppression, feminist scholars often failed to take into account the historical, cultural and material diversity of women's offending and victimisation. Such diversity could not be adequately represented by adopting a singular feminist standpoint. Deconstructionist approaches that developed later rejected universal knowledge claims and the idea of a single feminist standpoint. This kind of feminism no longer insisted on any singular relation between gender, deviance, law and crime; instead, it sought to locate its analysis more broadly in the field of power relations. The aim was not to construct a more correct feminist version of the truth, but to deconstruct and analyse power relations underpinning truth claims that shaped gendered experiences of the criminal justice system, including sentencing and punishment.

Contemporary feminist perspectives typically include the following assumptions: gender is a social construction, not a biological fact; it 'orders social life and social institutions in fundamental ways'; established gender orders assume male superiority and reflect and embody male dominance over women; and existing knowledge claims and systems reflect 'men's views of the natural and social world' (Daly and Chesney-Lind 1988, p. 108). Feminist criminology, like feminism more generally, has always had practical and theoretical components, aiming to change the social, political and economic structures responsible for the oppression of women. Feminist theorists opened up a whole field of new questions and issues. They highlighted the importance of the fear of crime in women's lives, the gendered nature of sexual violence, the problems of domestic violence, rape and incest, and the gendering of social control. Noting that certain types of crime were more associated with women, feminist criminologists established that patterns of offending are different for women and men, and that women are treated differently by police, the courts and prisons. They have also drawn attention to the link between particular types of masculinity and crime (Heidensohn 1997).

Post-colonial perspectives focus on cultural, social and political conflicts and debates that occur within societies sharing the experience of colonisation. In 1970s and 1980s the concept of colonisation tended to be studied through the lens of 'development' and underdevelopment, progressive Marxist movements, revolution and modernisation (Worsley 1991). Recently, key thinkers associated with post-colonial discourse have offered an alternative view of the relationship between the colonists and colonised, focusing on the extent to which colonisation operated at a cultural and an economic level. The process of colonisation involved a blend of not only physical marginalisation and theft of land but also a profoundly cultural form of violence. Blagg (2008) argues, for example, that the criminal justice system played and still plays a role in this process of cultural deracination in Australia.

Colonialism relied on particular narratives—ways of thinking and speaking—that had the effect of unifying the colonists on the basis of shared whiteness; they also worked to minimise pre-existing Anglo-Celtic class and regional differences. A shared sense of colonial privilege tended to unify groups who might on other levels appear to have radically different or competing interests. In Australian history, differences and conflicts between government agencies, economic interests and church groups did exist; however, when it came to dealing with the Aborigines there was considerable underlying unity of purpose. This was supported by a belief in the fundamental superiority of white men, white civilisation, white law and white religion. Until the 1960s, social, cultural, economic and administrative policies were premised on the 'doomed race' thesis (McGregor 1997). Extinction 'was regarded as the Aboriginals' inescapable destiny, decreed by God or by nature' (1997, p. ix). Police officers, missionaries, anthropologists, stockmen, doggers and pastoralists might have had conflicting ideas about the ways to treat the Aborigines, but each generally maintained the belief that they were a lesser species, destined to disappear in the face of the superior white civilisation (Blagg 2008). In this context, colonial relationships were not only imposed through violent conflict, they were also reinforced and maintained in the philanthropic distribution of rations and material goods that locked Aboriginal people into subordinate relationships with white people who were the owners and controllers of these goods. Acquiring them often meant accepting enclosure in institutions, particularly missions. At the same time, Aboriginal people were systematically dispossessed of their land; in many respects, it seemed as if they were expected to give up their cultural identity—their Aboriginality and their claims to land—in exchange for the 'bounties' of white civilisation.

From a post-colonial perspective, colonised peoples depend on the development of an oppositional identity as the basis for struggle with the colonising power: this identity offers self-worth, dignity, and the renewal of pre-contact cultures. Blagg describes Indigenous people's challenge to the current dominant hegemonic culture in terms of the deployment of a 'strategic essentialism' based on race (2008, p. 37). He argues that the strength of this post-colonial critique is that it seeks to 'deprivilege hegemonic narratives and hear voices marginalised in the colonial encounter, taking heed of the subjugated knowledges they bear' (Marshall-Beier 2004, p. 87; Blagg 2008, p. 37). As we will see in Chapter 7, rather than taking over the state or reproducing its structures and institutions, the aim for Indigenous people from the post-colonial perspective is to actively create distance from state structures and re-imagine and reframe traditional forms of order.

FOUCAULT

Over the last thirty years, the work of French philosopher Michel Foucault (1927–1986) has greatly influenced discussions about punishment. His work is broadly focused on key social institutions and their allied knowledges and disciplines. It covers the history of the birth of the clinic as a distinctly modern way of managing health, the development of psychiatry and modern approaches to mental health, modern understandings of sexuality, the relationship between criminology and the rise of the prison, the mentalities of government and the emergence of modern nation states. Foucault examined the roots and patterns of ideas found in social life and asked how they help make up what is going on in social worlds. The significance of his ideas in relation to punishment can be divided between two phases in his work. The first is linked to what is perhaps his best known book, *Discipline and Punish: The Birth of the Prison* (1977); the second relies on the influence of his later work 'On governmentality' (1991). This part of the chapter explores the key ideas and influence of his earlier work on the prison; governmentality will be discussed later in the context of social theories about risk.

A central theme for Foucault is how power is exercised and individuals are governed in the modern world. *Discipline and Punish* is an analysis of the apparatus of power that the prison deploys and the forms of knowledge, technologies and social relationships that it depends on. His book traces the development of the prison in the nineteenth century, asking how this institution replaced the public spectacle of bodily violence to become the preferred form of punishment. Foucault argues that this process involves a qualitative shift, rather than simply a decrease in the quantity and intensity of punishment (Foucault 1977). The target of punishment changed: although the body remained the focus of some penal measures, it became an instrument for transforming the soul rather than simply a surface for the infliction of pain. The character of justice changed as well: concern shifted from avenging the crime to transforming the criminal. The focus of judgment moved away from the offence itself towards an assessment of the individual, and the new objective was to know the criminal, understand the sources of his criminality, and intervene to correct him or her wherever possible (Foucault 1977; Garland 1991). Various experts were employed to provide this knowledge, identify abnormalities and help bring about reformation. These changes introduced a system of dealing with offenders that was corrective rather than simply punitive.

The transformation described by Foucault has broader implications than its effects on the form of penalty: it exemplifies how power tends to operate in modern society. Open physical force, the apparatus of violence and the ceremonies of might are increasingly replaced by a mode of power based on detailed knowledge, routine intervention and correction. These disciplinary arrangements rely on normalisation, which involves a means of assessing an individual's performance in relation to a desired standard of conduct. Surveillance arrangements, case records and examination procedures provide this knowledge, allowing non-conformity to be identified and dealt with. The object is more to correct than to punish; sanctions tend to involve repetitive exercises and training. Such measures seek to bring conduct into line and make individuals more self-controlled. The human sciences are a key part of this process because they are only made possible through the production of detailed, systematic knowledge about individuals and, in turn, contribute to the normalising power and control that is exercised over individuals (Foucault 1977, pp. 107–95).

Bentham's panopticon (see pp. 24–5) is the archetype of these power–knowledge principles. Foucault sees it not just as the prototype for prisons but for all institutions that implement regimes of surveillance and discipline (1977, pp. 200–6). The boundaries between judicial punishment and other social institutions—school, family, workshop, social welfare—are blurred by the development of similar disciplinary techniques in each. Foucault refers to this as the carceral archipelago, where the whole social body is linked by a concern to identify deviance, anomalies and departures from the relevant norm. From this perspective, the process of punishment has much in common with educating or curing and tends to be represented as an extension of these less coercive practices. One consequence is that the legal restrictions that bound the power to punishment—tying it to specific crimes, determining its duration, guaranteeing the rights of those accused and so on—tend to disappear. Penal law becomes a hybrid system of control, combining the principles of legality with those of normalisation. It is this transformation that extends the scope of its effective power, allowing it to sanction not just violations of the law but also deviations from the norm (1977, pp. 293–300; Garland 1991).

Discipline and Punish concludes that the underlying principle of modern penalty is exclusion, combined with differentiation and classification; however, nineteenth-century imprisonment did not exclude criminals to make them invisible (Hudson 2003a). The newly developing social sciences were enlisted to transform the criminal into an object of knowledge—a delinquent. Criminology (Pasquino 1991) emerged as the body of knowledge concerned with diagnosis, classification and correction of the types of criminals and the causes of their criminality. The value of the prison did not lie in its success—Foucault argued modern prisons cause recidivism. Instead, he proposed that it lay in the constitution of delinquents as a social category and the of transformation of crime from 'popular illegalities' (acts like poaching were not disapproved by the general population because they were seen as ordinary acts necessary for material survival) into delinquencies that were no longer seen as part of mainstream life, but as threatening its social order and values. The effect of imprisonment was to create a criminal subculture that the 'respectable' working class could disapprove of, and whose punishment was regarded as legitimate.

Rather than reducing crime, or even exacting retribution, penal sanctions function to manage crime in a way that reinforces the legitimacy of power. This is consistent with the Durkheimian function of giving expression to social values and the rules derived from them. At the same time it also highlights the way that the use of imprisonment and other punitive sanctions serves to differentiate crimes from each other; more specifically, the way in which it marks out the crimes of the poor as the most threatening and concentrates public concern on them, thereby shifting attention from the sorts of crime it fails to address—that is, crimes of the powerful (Foucault 1977, p. 272; Hudson 2003a).

Foucault's observations about the relationship between power and knowledge have been noted by others. Goffman wrote about power relationships between psychiatrists and their patients (see Hacking 2004 on the similarities and differences between Foucault and Goffman). Interactionists or 'labelling' theorists directed attention to the way in which deviant identities are constructed not just from deviant behaviour but also through the pronouncements of judges, social workers and others who categorise and stigmatise (Becker 1963; Goffman 1959, 1963). Foucault's contribution was to locate these insights into a wider political economy of power, and to see them as part of the modernist project of 'normalisation' (Hudson 2003a).

Chapter 1 described how, in the 1970s, Australia (along with many Western societies) seemed to be radically reversing the institutional response to deviance through processes of decarceration and the use of alternative sanctions in the community. Community corrections came to be regarded as a more humane and less stigmatising means of responding to offenders. In criminology Stanley Cohen (1979; 1985) argued that the development of community corrections marks both a continuation and an intensification of the social control patterns identified by Foucault in *Discipline and Punish* (1977). His 'dispersal of discipline' thesis insists that there is now a blurring of where prison ends and the community begins, with an accompanying increase in the total number of offenders brought into the system. Cohen's *Visions of Social Control* (1985) provided an account of the various transformations the web of social control had undergone up to the time of his writing. He described how it had strengthened and deepened, that there were broader nets with ever finer mesh. Cohen introduced expressions— such as 'net widening', 'blurring the boundaries' between freedom and control, the community and prisons—that are so often used to critique juvenile justice programs, therapeutic regimes in prisons and innovations such as electronic monitoring (Aungles 1994; Roberts and Indermaur 2006). He argued that because of the inescapable forces of normalisation the intentions of penal reformers, legislators and practitioners always result in more control, less freedom and more persons under surveillance for greater portions of their lives.

RISK

German sociologist Ulrich Beck (1992) argues that at the close of the twentieth-century, class-based industrial society characterised in Marxist analyses was replaced by 'risk society'. He (along with Giddens 1991) proposes that 'risk' has become a dominant theme in contemporary life. According to Beck, the processes of capitalist modernisation have produced a series of unpredictable manufactured risks, signalling a movement from a closely regulated class-based industrial society to an unplanned risk society. Moreover, the localised risks identifiable in industrial society have given way to the de-territorialised dangers of the risk society. These are associated with many new technologies that generate new dangers to lives and the planet itself. They are humanly produced, may have massive unforeseen consequences and may take many thousands of years to reverse. These 'manufactured risks' have consequences that may be far-reaching and are at present unpredictable. The risk society is a society of 'fate' as class divisions have been overridden by the similarity of shared destinies. Matters of social justice and equality have been eclipsed by the need to prevent the worst; therefore, a 'risk society is one obsessed with security' (L. Johnston 2000, p. 24).

The significance of Beck's argument is highlighted by Giddens's explanation that it 'is not that day-to-day life is inherently more risky than was the case in prior eras. It is rather that in conditions of modernity … thinking in terms of risk and risk assessment is a more or less ever present exercise …' (1991, pp. 123–4). A concern with risk is giving rise to a new mode of living. Instead of going ahead and doing things and then coping with any problems that may result, we now seek to anticipate problems and avoid them. As a consequence, our lives are increasingly organised around risk and the development of risk-reduction strategics. This is a qualitative shift, rather than a simply quantitative one. Risk technologies have acquired a new priority in society. Associated with this is a new risk mentality, of coping with the present in ways that will ensure that a future can be enjoyed (Shearing 2001).

While taking a different approach from Giddens and Beck, Foucault's later work draws attention to a similar trend. He identifies a shift to a style of governance that he calls 'governmentality'. This term refers both to the idea of mentalities of governance generally and to a particular way of thinking of governing that seeks 'the right disposition of things arranged so as to lead to a convenient end' (1991, p. 93). He expands on this idea of governing things as follows:

> The things in this sense government is to be concerned (with) are in fact men, but men in their relations, their links, their imbrication with those other things which are wealth, resources, means of subsistence, the territory with its specific qualities, climate, irrigation, fertility etc.; men in their relation to that other kind of things, customs, habits, ways of acting and thinking, etc., lastly men in their relation to that other kind of things, accidents and misfortunes such as famine, epidemics, death etc. (1991, p. 93)

Law within this governmentality promotes a disposition of things. 'It is a question not of imposing law on men, but of disposing things: that is to say of employing tactics rather than laws, and even laws themselves as tactics—to arrange things in such a way that, through a certain number of means such and such ends may be achieved' (Foucault 1991, p. 95). Within this mentality, law becomes a strategy or tactic for promoting security. One way that we respond to risk, as Beck has outlined, is by employing governmentality that seeks to provide for a distribution of things that will minimise hazards and insecurities (Shearing 2001).

Governmentality theorists are interested in the ways in which government power is deployed in late modern societies (Burchell et al. 1991; Rose and Miller 1992; Rose 1996). Foucault's later works, his lectures and essays on governmentality, have provided the starting point for these analyses (Foucault 1991; Gordon 1991). In this work, Foucault looks at the project of modern government, which above all else provides security for governed populations; the most fundamental aspect of this involves the identification and control of risks. He makes a distinction between discipline and security. While discipline is targeted at an individual, who is to be socialised or reformed into acting normally, security addresses itself to the population (Gordon 1991, p. 20). Security works through the identification of common risks and the provision of shared solutions; its interest in individuals is to place them into categories of risk-posing or risk vulnerability. Hudson (2003a) explains that contemporary measures of crime prevention are aimed at collectivities in this way, and it has been argued that contemporary penality is a new penology that is more consistent with this idea of security rather than the disciplinary power that was the focus of Foucault's earlier work on the prison (Feeley and Simon 1992; 1994; Simon 1988). In this context, punishment has become impersonal, similar to crime prevention and other strategies of social protection. The technique for dealing with risks that people pose and face in common is insurance, which works on actuarial principles for calculating risk. Actuarial techniques place people into categories and estimate the riskiness of these groups rather than looking at individuals as unique cases and trying to reform them. Simon (1988) describes the shift from discipline to actuarial practices:

> Over the past half century we have been moving away from the disciplines and toward actuarial practices ... Disciplinary practices focus on the distribution of behaviour within a limited population ... This distribution is around a norm, and power operates with the goal of closing the gap, narrowing the deviation, and moving subjects towards uniformity ... Actuarial practices seek instead to maximise the efficiency of the population as it stands. Rather than seeking to change people (normalise them in Foucault's apt phrase) an actuarial regime seeks to manage them in place. (Simon 1988, p. 773)

Over the last two decades, the logic of risk has begun to influence the institutions of the state in ways that are reshaping criminal justice. There is a renewed emphasis on risk, which has always been a feature of state policy especially with respect to what used to be thought of as the 'dangerous classes' in the eighteenth and nineteenth centuries (Pratt 1997). This rethinking of risk has not led to a replacement of other ways of regulating security; rather than disappearing altogether, these modes of thought and practice have been adapted to fit a risk-focused mentality (Garland 2001). Ways of thinking and acting that were developed within the logic of retribution and deterrence take on new meanings and functions under the influence of risk. For example, familiar institutions like prisons do not disappear but are employed in different ways. Feeley and Simon note:

> Possibly the clearest indication of actuarial justice is found in the new theory of incapacitation which has become the predominant model of punishment. Incapacitation promises to reduce the effects of crime in society not by altering either offender or social context, but by rearranging the distribution of offenders in society. If the prison can do nothing else, incapacitation theory holds, it can detain offenders for a time and thus delay their resumption of criminal activity. (1994, p. 174)

An appreciation of the importance of risk in penality is a significant ingredient in explanations of contemporary penal trends. Penality is fundamentally bound up with risk: the whole point of criminal law and penal sanctions is to reduce the risk of crime. What is new in contemporary penality is the approach taken to risk. Risk-reduction techniques are now concentrated on aggregates rather than individuals, and risk management has given way to risk control. Risk management accepts risks but tries to make some improvement by reducing the likelihood of feared incidents through the education and treatment of offenders, parole assessments and post-release supervision, realising that some incidents are bound to take place whatever is done. Risk control seeks to avoid incidents altogether by excluding or eliminating the risk poser (Clear and Cadora 2001; Rose 2000).

Another influential theorist concerned with risk is British anthropologist Mary Douglas (1921–2007), whose work *Risk and Blame* (1992), like that of some criminologists (Garland 1996; 2001), is interested in understanding how the organisation of communities relates to their attributions of threat and blame. Douglas describes her argument about blame as an extension of Durkheim's explanation of the relations between crime and the *conscience collective* (1992, pp. 6–7). Her approach to risk centres on the political implications of judgments (including ostensibly technical and dispassionate ones) (1992, p. 8), on the relationship between notions of risk and the structure of institutional authority (1992, p. 14), and on risk as the contemporary cloak for societal conversations about morality and identity (1992, pp. 15–16). Douglas argues that it is the language of risk in contemporary culture that provides 'a common forensic vocabulary with which to hold persons accountable' (1992, p. 22). In this process, risk is removed from its original and particular application to probability calculations, and becomes a cultural key word with much wider implications in 'a debate about accountability':

> [t]his dialogue, the cultural process itself, is a contest to muster support for one kind of action rather than another … The cultural dialogue is therefore best studied in its forensic moments. The concept of risk emerges as a key resource in modern times because of its uses as a forensic resource. (Douglas 1992, p. 24)

Douglas's cultural theory draws attention to the mixing of discourses involved in the punishment of offenders (Sparks 2000). Even though the field of punishment has acquired new technical vocabularies, and these work to restructure some of its practices, it remains political. For Douglas, political cultures act as filters for risk—they select problems for attention, suggest images of threatening people and situations, propose diagnoses and so on. This makes risk inherently a plural and contested idea.

ELIAS

The work of German sociologist Norbert Elias (1897–1990) is valuable because it provides a detailed account of certain cultural and psychic structures, termed 'civilised sensibilities', that are characteristic of modern Western societies and that can be shown to have major implications for the ways people are punished. Elias's *The Civilising Process* (1939/1979; 1939/1982) describes how Western sensibilities have altered since the late medieval period. It identifies a number of broad developmental patterns that seem to underlie the very gradual changes of attitude and conduct that historical sources describe. His book maps this pattern of change and the typical directions that it has taken, and then sets out an explanatory account that links changes in sensibility and individual psychology with broader trends of social reorganisation and changing modes of interaction. For Elias (1939/1982), what was understood as 'civilised' represented the current and contingent configuration of three characteristics, operating on different levels from the thirteenth century onwards. First, in relation to state processes, there was the growth of the central state's monopolistic control of the use of legitimate violence and the raising of taxes. Second, in relation to sociogenesis, there was an increase in the scale and scope of what Elias refers to as 'interdependencies' between citizens as a result of the complex division of labour now characteristic of Western social arrangements. Third, in relation to psychogenesis, there was the internalisation of restraint among individual citizens. This relates to keeping displays of emotion in check and suppressed to the point where such controlled behaviour becomes second nature (Pratt 2000; 2005).

Elias has little to say about the way in which the history of punishment fits into the broad developments that he describes; however, Garland (1991) argues that it is clear that Elias's analysis of the development and characteristics of modern sensibilities has a profound importance for the understanding of penality.

Forms of punishment are shaped by political forces, economic interests, penological considerations and by conceptions of what is or is not culturally and emotionally acceptable. Penal policy decisions are made against a backdrop of mores and sensibilities that, under normal circumstances, set limits to what will be tolerated by the public or implemented by the penal system's personnel. Such sensibilities force issues of 'propriety' on even the most immoral governments, dictating what is and is not too shameful or offensive for serious consideration.

Garland (1991) suggests Elias's claim that the civilising process brings with it a move towards the 'privatisation' of disturbing events is directly relevant to our understanding of penal methods. In the process of privatisation, certain aspects of life disappear from the public arena to become hidden behind the scenes of social life. Sex, violence, bodily functions, illness, suffering and death gradually become a source of embarrassment and distaste and are increasingly removed to various private domains, such as the domesticated nuclear family, private lavatories, bedrooms, prison cells and hospital wards. There is a tendency to suppress the more animalistic aspects of human conduct because of the belief that they are crude and uncultivated. Individuals are taught to avoid shocking their superiors by not displaying such distasteful and unmannerly behaviour. Eventually, this cultural suppression becomes more general and more profound. New and more private enclaves are developed 'behind the scenes' where such activities can be undertaken more discreetly, withdrawn from the sight of others and often surrounded by an aura of shame and embarrassment.

The concept of privatisation is important because it helps us to understand the heavy reliance in modern society on institutional enclosures for dealing with troublesome individuals. It also makes it clear that civilisation involves a displacement and relocation of 'uncivilised' behaviours, rather than their suppression or disappearance altogether (Garland 1991). Violence is disturbing to modern sensibilities and is minimised whenever possible. In areas where violence persists, it is usually removed from the public arena and sanitised or disguised in various ways, often becoming the monopoly of specialist groups such as the army, police or prison staff, who conduct themselves in an impersonal, professional manner, avoiding the emotional intensity that such behaviour threatens to arouse.

According to Pratt (2005) there are, however, two sides to the Eliasian coin: both civilising and decivilising processes can shape the cultural sensibilities of modern life. Citing Fletcher (1997), he describes three main characteristics of the decivilising process: a shift away from self-restraint towards restraint imposed by external authorities; the development of behaviour and sensibilities that generate the emergence of less even, stable and differentiated patterns of restraint; and a contraction in the scope of mutual identification between constituent groups and individuals. When these occur, they are likely to be accompanied by a decrease in the state monopoly on violence, a shortening of interdependences and a concomitant rise of fear, danger and incalculability (Pratt 2005, p. 259).

In contemporary Western societies, however, bureaucratisation, which is one of the consequences of the civilising process itself, works against decivilising trends to maintain governmental authority and certainty. This tends to limit the full disintegration of the social order brought about by these tendencies. Equally human capacities for learning also present a buffer. Fletcher notes that social processes under decivilising conditions 'do not simply reverse and go backwards, as it were, down the path along which they have already travelled. It is extremely unlikely that the composite relations of the networks of interdependencies go into "reverse" to the same degree, resulting in a different composition of the new configuration' (1997, p. 83). This suggests that any decivilising trends are likely to have only partial effects. What is likely to happen is that 'civilising and decivilising processes [will] occur simultaneously in particular societies, and not simply in the same or different societies at different points in time' (Dunning and Mennell 1996, p. xv in Pratt 2005, p. 260). Extending this argument, Pratt suggests we are likely to see the emergence of new practices, behaviours and cultural values that represent a fusion of these influences rather than the exclusive ascendancy of one or the other (2005, p. 260).

Penal trends over much of the nineteenth and twentieth centuries correspond to the characteristics of the civilising process. In regard to state processes, in the late nineteenth century there was an assumption of the monopolistic control of punishment by central state authorities. Punishment was increasingly standardised within jurisdictions instead of being fragmented and differentiated as before. The general public was increasingly excluded from any formal involvement or influence on penal processes. A firm dividing line was therefore placed between the bureaucratic administration of penal affairs and the general public. Since the 1970s, profound cultural and economic changes that have been linked to late modernity (Garland and Sparks 2000) have impacted on punishment. There has been the emergence of two competing sets of developments consistent with civilising and decivilising trends. On the one hand, the characteristics of the civilising process have been enhanced: trends toward globalisation, technological development and mass communications are likely to strengthen interdependencies (such as transnational trade and international alliances) and increase identification with, and tolerance of, citizens from other countries as societies become more heterogeneous. The increasing cosmopolitan and pluralistic nature of societies since the 1970s is likely to lead to an increased tolerance of minority groups and differing personal arrangements regarding marriage, sexual preferences and so on. On the other hand, some aspects of this civilising process have the potential to bring about uncivilised consequences. Globalisation not only fosters international alliances and leads to interdependencies between states, but it also leads to a weakening of the sovereignty of nation states. Transcending national boundaries as a result of trade agreements has led to massive population movements (particularly from the Eastern bloc and developing countries), which can undermine social stability in some societies. Heterogeneity may be embraced by some, but for others it seems threatening and unfamiliar, leading to contracting and more shallow interdependencies with these 'strangers'. The technological advances associated with the civilising process enables mass communication industries to become our main source of knowledge of risks, making them seem broader and more incalculable (Pratt 2005).

Pratt (2005) argues that these developments coincide with decivilising trends that have resulted from recent political, economic and social changes. The pre-eminence of neoliberal polities has seen the reconfiguration and fragmentation of the authority of the central state, which has come to assume a more residual role in government than was previously the case. Providing protection from risks and dangers may now be undertaken by private or voluntary sectors as citizens increasingly have to accept responsibility for themselves (Garland 1996). Government bureaucracies have been increasingly criticised for their remoteness, expense, inefficiency and their inability to solve the social problems. Alternative modes of government have developed that no longer privilege the idea of a strong central state working as one with its own bureaucratic organisations, with its citizens excluded. Emphasis has been on empowerment and ensuring government departments are transparent and accountable. Interdependencies have been dramatically restructured. There has been an erosion of many of the long-standing institutions and cultural expectations that had become deeply embedded in these societies: durable class cultures, or the traditional relations and arrangements of the family. The reversal of the trend towards a centralised state authority, which had assumed overall management for the risks threatening its population and the breaking up of previously secure and wide-ranging interdependencies, has led to a preoccupation with new areas of danger, vulnerability and uncertainty (Pratt 2005, p. 265) described in the context of the 'risk society' thesis.

CONCLUSION

This chapter surveyed a range of social theories that have been influential in making sense of the field of punishment and sentencing. The coverage of each perspective has perhaps not been as complete or as critical as it could have been. That is, while the work of these social theorists attends more broadly to relationships shaping society and human behaviour, this chapter limited its consideration to how particular ideas relate to punishment and sentencing. Punishment can be understood as a cultural and historical artefact that is shaped by various social and political forces. Moreover, it has a significance and range of effects that reach beyond the problem of crime control and the population of offenders. As a result, it should not be studied solely in terms of its declared objective—reducing crime. The practices that make up systems of crime control—including sentencing and punishment—are heavily mediated by independent considerations such as historical circumstances, cultural conventions, economic resources, institutional dynamics and political arguments. It is important to explore the relationships between these elements. Adopting a multidisciplinary approach is one way of bringing this interaction into focus. This means engaging a range of theoretical perspectives, analytical frameworks and concrete interpretations. Such an approach aims to accommodate competing interpretations by drawing on diverse models of explanation, each approaching the problem in a different way and highlighting a different characteristic of punishment and its social role. It recognises that punishment is neither a unitary process nor a continuous field of practice — its history has not been an unfolding logic of progress through reform — rather the terrain of punishment is fragmentary and at times contradictory, and is often characterised by discontinuity and tension.

Using a case-study approach, the remaining chapters of this book survey the major analytical interpretations of punishment and give some sense of the insight that social theory can provide for understanding the changing practices. It engages a range of perspectives, dealing with not only more established traditions associated with the work of Durkheim and Marx, for example, but also contemporary perspectives that build on Elias (Pratt 2000) or Foucault's (1991) concept of governmentality (Feeley and Simon 1992; 1994). The case studies will be used to provide applied examples of the distinctive questions that theoretical perspectives pose, to summarise the major interpretive themes, and to identify the kinds of insights that each theory has to offer for the understanding of particular examples of modern penality.

I am not proposing some type of overarching synthesis or simple blending of ideas. The benefit of drawing on more than one perspective is that the construction of such a multidimensional account provides an arena in which different interpretations might be played off against one another and the empirical research evidence that they are used to interpret. In an issues-based format, proceeding from one explanatory perspective to another will make it clear that each way of thinking about punishment asks slightly different questions, pursues a different aspect, reveals different determinants and outlines different connections. This guards against the appeal of reductive explanations that rely on single causal principles of functional purpose—whether moral, economic or matters of state control or crime control. It acknowledges that in the penal realm—as with all social experience—specific events or developments usually have a plurality of causes, effects and social meanings (though some will be more powerful than others). The aim of analysis should therefore always be to capture that variety of causes, effects and meanings and trace their interaction and points of tension, rather than to reduce them all to a single currency (Garland 1991).

Risk

4

Child sexual offences and community notification

INTRODUCTION

The previous three chapters set up the analytical foundation for this book. The remaining chapters have a distinctly different orientation: they adopt an issues-based case-study approach in a survey of contemporary penological practices. These case studies are arranged around the themes of risk, rehabilitation and restitution in a way that allows us to see these abstract concepts in action.

Introducing the section on risk, this chapter offers a case study of 'predatory' sex crimes involving children. Public awareness about sexual violence has increased in Australia in recent years. This is particularly so in relation to child sexual abuse. In Queensland, for example, official statistics indicate that the rate of sexual offences reported to police doubled from about 92 per 100 000 to more than 190 per 100 000 of the population between 1994 and 1998. The majority of these offences were committed against children younger than 16 years (Cook et al. 2001; Criminal Justice Commission 1999). This does not necessarily indicate that the incidence of child sexual abuse is increasing; rather, increased reporting rates appear partly to reflect a greater willingness by victims and others to register formal complaints with various authorities regarding allegations of child sexual abuse. Indeed, many alleged child sexual offences are not reported until long after they have occurred. Nevertheless there is widespread agreement that sexual abuse is a major social problem (Smallbone and Wortley 2000).

Reflecting this changing state of awareness during the 1990s, most Australian states reformed or introduced stricter laws addressing the problem of sexual offending. Sexual violence and particularly the sexual abuse of children continue to be matters of significant public concern. Popular alarm is fuelled by fears that the internet potentially allows offenders to access and groom those children who are thought to be safe in their own home. Public spokespeople and lobby groups, like the Movement Against Kindred Offenders (MAKO), argue that new provisions for harsher penalties, potentially indefinite sentencing and registration do not go far enough and that, like the United States, Australia should introduce legislation that allows for the public notification of the names and addresses of convicted sexual offenders—particularly those that offend against children. While a national offender registration system does exist, Australian parliaments have been reluctant to introduce systems of public notification. This chapter critically reviews a range of criminal justice responses to sex offending against children; exploring the reasons why some interventions and not others might be considered appropriate in the contemporary social context. It begins by describing what we know about the problem of child sexual assault, and outlines a range of responses that are currently available. It then discusses the possibility of each of these while taking into account the principles and practices of punishment and social theories surveyed in earlier chapters.

THE PROBLEM: CHILD SEX OFFENDING

Although research efforts have expanded in recent years, sexual offending against children remains difficult to study. The main problems are the secrecy that typically surrounds the commission of these offences and the reluctance or difficulty of getting victims to report. What we know about child sexual offending primarily comes from clinical studies of convicted (usually incarcerated) offenders undergoing treatment. While these studies are able to provide rich empirical information, it is unclear if their results can be generalised. As Smallbone and Wortley (2000) point out, the reliability and validity of these data are typically compromised by the absence of confidentiality, since offenders would normally be aware that information provided by them may affect decisions relating to their progress in treatment and their release from prison. Many studies do not provide sufficient descriptive data to allow for the comparison of findings from different samples and jurisdictions. And comparisons between different subtypes of sexual offenders are often made difficult by the use of small samples and/or by differences in the typological frameworks employed by researchers.

Nevertheless, there is broad consensus among researchers that considerable variation exists in both the ways sexual offences against children are perpetrated (that is, in the tactics of selecting and accessing children, sexual and other behaviours involved in the commission of offences, and methods of avoiding detection) and the characteristics of the perpetrators themselves (age, ethnicity, education, psychological and psychosexual background, level of sexual interest in children, relationship with victims and general criminality). Sex offenders comprise a wide range of offence patterns and reoffence risk. Causal explanations are also varied. Therefore most researchers agree that sexual offending against children is a multidimensional and multidetermined phenomenon.

What is known from research is that recidivism rates for sexual offences are much lower than commonly believed (Levenson and D'Amora 2007). In the United States, for example, the Bureau of Justice Statistics found that of 9691 sex offenders released from prison in 1994, just over 5 per cent were rearrested for a new sex crime within the three-year follow-up period. However, a Canadian government study of nearly 30 000 sex offenders found that 14 per cent of all sex offenders and 13 per cent of child sexual offenders were rearrested for a new sex crime within four to six years (Hanson and Bussiere 1998;

Hanson and Morton-Bourgon 2004; 2005). Harris and Hanson, who reported the highest recidivism rates over a fifteen-year follow-up, concluded that:

> Most sexual offenders do not re-offend sexually over time. This may be the most important finding of this study as this finding is contrary to some strongly held beliefs. After 15 years 73% of sexual offenders had not been charged with, or convicted of, another sexual offence. The sample was sufficiently large that very strong contradictory evidence is necessary to substantially change these recidivism estimates. (2004, p. 17)

Some types of sex offenders do reoffend at higher rates than those reported above. Levenson and D'Amora (2007, p. 177) summarise an extensive literature that suggested that:

○ higher rates of recidivism are found among those who assault boys and adult women
○ sex offenders with past arrests are more likely to reoffend than first-time offenders
○ those who comply with probation and treatment have lower reoffence rates than those who violate the conditions of their release
○ some sex offenders have victimised many more individuals than those for whom they have been arrested
○ most child sexual offenders are not 'predatory paedophiles' with an exclusive attraction to children, and intrafamilial offenders have consistently lower rates of recidivism
○ sex offence recidivism appears to decline with age
○ the longer that offenders remain offence-free in the community, the less likely they are to reoffend sexually.

In popular culture the stereotypical image of a sex offender is that of a predatory stranger; however, most sex offenders are well known to their victims. In the United States, police reports reveal that child sexual abuse victims identified their abusers as family members in over one-third of cases and as acquaintances in almost 60 per cent of cases (Bureau of Justice Statistics 2000); only 7 per cent were strangers (Bureau of Justice Statistics 2002). Simon and Zgoba (2006) reported similar trends in their analysis of arrest data. An earlier Bureau of Justice Statistics study also found that about 40 per cent of sexual assaults take place in the victim's own home and 20 per cent occur in the home of a friend, neighbour or relative (Bureau of Justice Statistics 1997). Recent Australian research challenges the view that most sexual offenders are dedicated, serial offenders driven by irresistible sexual urges. Smallbone and Wortley (2000; 2001) examined official records of 323 convicted child sex offenders. They concluded that there was an absence of strong deviant motivations in many cases and that environmental factors may instead have been important. For example, the largest proportion of their sample—nearly 40 per cent—was aged between thirty-one and forty. This relatively late onset of behaviour suggests that many offenders were able to resist sexually abusing children and that there is an absence of strong sexually deviant motivations. Moreover, the early thirties is an age when many men are assuming child-care and other supervisory roles with children; as a result their opportunities to offend are significantly expanded (see Hanson 2002).

Less than one-quarter of Smallbone and Wortley's sample had previous convictions for sexual offences, and almost half reported having restricted their offending to one victim. Their findings suggested the absence in many offenders of strong deviant motivations. In contrast to the low incidence of previous sexual offending, around 60 per cent of the sample had prior convictions for non-sexual offences. Of those offenders with previous convictions, their first conviction was four times more likely to be non-sexual. Smallbone and Wortley argue that, for many, sexual offending might be seen as part of a more general involvement in criminal activity. Therefore, the problem seems to be less some special motivation to sexually abuse children than a more general problem involving the failure to inhibit urges and impulses, especially within the interpersonal domain—that is, many offenders in the sample may be better portrayed as 'opportunity takers' than sexual deviants. The vast majority of offenders (over 90 per cent) abused their own child or a child who they already knew. Locating and grooming a previously unknown child for the purpose of sexual contact requires a high level of planning, commitment and effort. In contrast, most offenders had sexual contact with children with whom they had an immediate or convenient access. Only a small percentage of offenders said that they had talked to other offenders prior to their arrest, and fewer said that they were involved in an organised paedophile group. There was little evidence that offenders sought out a paedophile subculture, and there was a low incidence of paraphiliac (sexually deviant) interests.

Wortley and Smallbone (2006) propose that a control model might be more appropriate for explaining the behaviour of many sexual offenders than a sexual deviance model. According to control theory (Gottfredson and Hirschi 1990), the propensity to commit crime is widely distributed in the community, and the basic cause of criminal behaviour is universal—an absence of restraint. Criminal behaviour is intrinsically rewarding and requires neither special motivation nor specialised skills or experience. Offenders do not learn to commit crimes; rather they fail to learn not to commit them. The causes of sexual offending against children may therefore be the same as those of crime more generally. Wortley and Smallbone suggest that opportunity structures and environmental cues may play an important role in weakening controls and facilitating offending behaviour (Hirschi 1988 in Wortley and Smallbone 2006). This raises important questions about how we respond to sexual offending and sexual offences against children in particular. In contrast to the research described above, criminal justice responses to sex offenders are typically based on the perception that the vast majority of sex offenders will repeat their crimes, and that they are repeatedly arrested in alarmingly high numbers. Current criminal justice trends that are clearly shaped by these perceptions are described in more detail below.

RESPONDING TO SEXUAL VIOLENCE OFFENCES AGAINST CHILDREN

Prior to the twentieth century, 'sex offences' were not classified separately and 'sex offenders' were not differentiated from those convicted of other crimes. In the United States, the passage in many jurisdictions of sexual psychopath laws during the 1930s and 1940s signalled a significant shift in the treatment of sex offenders and their crimes (Hinds and Daly 2001). Based on the assumption that the problem could be solved by the intervention of medical expertise and psychiatric therapy, they offered an optimistic approach. Their purpose was to create an alternative to punishment for a certain subclass of sex offender: those 'too sick to deserve punishment'. Sex offenders were involuntarily detained under civil commitment statues for purposes of treatment and rehabilitation, not as punishment for past criminal behaviour (Washington Institute for Public Policy 1996). The laws were understood as creating new legal categories to reflect a new 'scientific' understanding of the links between sexual deviance and mental disorder. In 1955 Hacker and Frym explained that the California *Sexual Psychopath Act* 'recognised and adopted [the principle]' that 'our *collective conscience* does not allow punishment where it cannot impose *blame*', and that 'the commission of a sex crime was usually, if not always evidence of a mental disorder which should be treated rather than punished' (1955, p. 767). Twenty-seven states and the District of Columbia enacted mentally disordered sex offender commitment laws (Janus 2000). The frequency and nature of the use of these early laws were quite varied. Erickson reported that in the 1940s and 1950s these laws were characterised by the 'commitment of relatively harmless individuals for relatively trivial crimes' (Erickson undated p. 10 in Janus 2000, p. 8).

By the 1970s concerns addressing the civil rights of offenders, the effectiveness of treatment programs, and the lack of a consistent scientific basis for identifying and classifying people as sexual psychopaths began to be widely expressed. The loss of faith in the ability of experts to cure sex offenders, the failure to accurately predict future violent behaviour and the generalised movement away from the rehabilitative ideal during the 1970s all had a profound effect on approaches to the punishment of sex offenders (La Fond 1998; Pratt 1995). The use of civil commitment declined and its focus shifted from non-violent to violent offenders. In 1977 the Group for the Advancement of Psychiatry (GAP) published an influential report entitled 'Psychiatry and Sex Psychopath Legislation: The 30s to the 80s' that, along with the President's Commission on Mental Health and the American Bar Associations Committee on Criminal Justice Mental Health Standards, recommended the repeal of sex offender commitment legislation (Janus 2000). The GAP report characterised sex offender commitment statutes as an 'experiment [that] has failed', neither providing effective treatment nor incarcerating truly dangerous individuals (GAP 1977, pp. 942, 935 in Janus 2000, p. 74). By the 1980s, most of the states with sex offender commitment laws had either repealed them or ceased actively using them. Beginning in the late 1980s a second generation of sex offender commitment laws developed: while the first-generation laws were designed as an alternative to prison for offenders deemed too sick for punishment, the second aimed to extend the incarceration of convicted sex offenders deemed too dangerous for release from custody.

Today, sex offender laws generally take four forms: sentencing enhancement for certain classes of violent or sex offenders, sexual predator laws, registration of sex offenders, and community notification of sex offenders (Hinds and Daly 2001; McAlinden 2006) (see also Simon and Zgoba 2006). While sentencing enhancements and sexual predator laws are methods of confining sex offenders for longer periods of time in the interests of community safety, registration laws are used by law enforcement agencies to track or keep an eye on those sex offenders who have served their prison or probation time but are now living in the community. Community notification takes registration a step further by permitting law enforcement agencies to release the names of sex offenders, along with other identifying information, to the general public. With the exception of notification provisions, similar types of laws have been introduced in Australia.

AUSTRALIAN RESPONSES TO CHILD SEX OFFENDING

Enhanced sentencing

Some sentencing statutes provide for enhanced or longer terms of imprisonment for certain classes of dangerous offenders, including those commonly referred to as 'predatory' sexual offenders (that is, those who target strangers) and those with previous convictions for sex offences.

During the 1990s a number of states in Australia—including Victoria, Queensland and Western Australia—significantly increased maximum penalties for sexual offences. Freiberg describes how new laws in Victoria that permitted indefinite sentences and consecutive sentences for 'serious sex offenders', 'provisions … contrary to the prevailing sentencing culture' were 'rushed through Parliament' in response to citizen concerns that sexual and violent offenders were not incarcerated long enough' (1997, p. 151).

In Queensland the *Criminal Law Amendment Act 1945* s18(3)–(6) provides for the indefinite preventive detention of convicted sexual offenders against children under sixteen who are found on the basis of medical evidence to be incapable of exercising proper control over their sexual instincts, or whose mental condition is subnormal. The newer *Penalties and Sentences Act 1992* (Qld), ss162, 163, makes the same provision for people convicted of violent or sexual offences, attracting possible life sentences when the court is satisfied that the person does not merit reference to the Mental Health court for examination and is a serious danger to the community because of their antecedents, character, age, health or mental condition, the severity of the offence and any special circumstances (Smallbone and Ransley 2005).

In New South Wales, standard minimum sentences were introduced by the *Crimes (Sentencing Procedure) Amendment (Standard Minimum Sentencing) Act 2002*. It applies to certain serious offences, including six sexual offences—two of these specifically focus on child victims: sexual intercourse with a child under ten years, and aggravated indecent assault of a child under ten years. Some of the other sexual offences are committed in circumstances of aggravation if the victim is under the age of sixteen or under the authority of the offender. The *Crimes (Sentencing Procedure) Act 1999* was amended to provide that a person who is convicted of a sexual offence against a child under sixteen years (or convicted of a prescribed sexual offence against any person) cannot be sentenced to periodic detention. The government considered periodic detention to be an unsuitable for the punishment of serious sexual offences:

> Periodic detention has been held by the courts to be a salutary punishment involving the continuous obligation of complying with an order week in and week out over a lengthy period of time. By its very nature however, periodic detention *has a strong element of leniency already built into it and it is outwardly less severe in its denunciation of the crime* than full-time imprisonment. Periodic detention is an inappropriate punishment for these categories of offences, especially where child victims are involved. (Hon. John Hatzistergos MLC, Minister for Justice, Crimes Legislation Amendment Bill, Second Reading Speech, NSWPD, 3 September 2005, p. 3115 in Johns 2003, p. 26)

See also *Sentencing Act 1991* (Vic.), Pt 3 Div. 2(1A); *Criminal Law (Sentencing) Act 1988* (SA), Pt Div. 3; Criminal Code (WA) s662(a); *Sentencing Act 1995* (WA) s98; as well as the *Powers of Criminal Courts (Sentencing) Act 2000* (UK) s80(2)(6).

Sexual predator laws

Sexual predator laws authorise the continued detention of sex offenders beyond the time served for criminal sentence. Because they are only invoked after the offender has served a criminal sentence, they operate as a last resort to confine offenders who cannot otherwise be detained under criminal or mental health laws (Hinds and Daly 2001). Unlike the earlier sexual psychopath laws, which were justified as an alternative to incarceration and punishment, sexual predator laws are used to confine sex offenders understood to be 'the worst of the worst' (Lieb et al. 1998, p. 46) for an indefinite period of time. Moreover, while the sexual psychopath laws targeted particular behaviours or personality types for treatment, sexual predator laws attempt to target those who are *likely* to pose a future threat to community safety. The nature of that threat to community safety is highly specific. The term *sexual predator* excludes those whose victims are their own children or intimates; thus, a predator is presumed to target strangers and have multiple victims (Lieb et al. 1998, p. 43).

In Australia, laws analogous to sexual predator laws have been passed, although without targeting sexual offenders per se. The *Community Protection*

Act 1990 (Vic.) was directed at one individual, Garry David, to secure his continued detention beyond the imposed criminal sentence. The *Community Protection Act 1994* (NSW) was also aimed at the continued detention of one individual, Gregory Kable. Both David and Kable had histories of violence, actual and threatened, although neither had a known history of sexual violence. More recently, the Queensland government passed the *Dangerous Prisoners (Sexual Offenders) Act 2003* that provides for the indefinite preventive detention of prisoners in custody for serious sexual offences who would be a serious danger to the community if released. This is based on two psychiatrists' assessments of the level of risk of the person committing another serious sexual offence if released (Smallbone and Ransley 2005).

Registration of sexual offenders

Registration provisions require convicted sex offenders to register with the police after release from prison, parole or probation, and to provide a range of identifying information, including their name, address, date of birth, criminal history, photo, fingerprints and DNA material.

Precisely who a sex offender is for purposes of registration differs between jurisdictions. In the United States, there is large variation in the different offences requiring registration, the date that triggers registration and the duration of registration. In Britain, only those offenders under supervision or who are cautioned, convicted or released from prison on or after 1 September 1997 are required to register. In Canada, registration has existed since 1994; however, at the federal level, correctional officials gather the information (that is, offenders are not obliged to supply it) and decide how it should be disseminated to law enforcement authorities. In Australia, there have been initiatives to register sex offenders at the federal and state levels: federally, sex offender registers were developed between 1995 and 1997 by the Australian Bureau of Criminal Intelligence (ABCI) and Australian Federal Police (AFP); at the state level, the Victorian Parliament Crime Prevention Committee and the Wood Royal Commission into the NSW Police Service both recommended in 1995 and 1997, respectively, that sex offender registers should be established. In Queensland the *Criminal Law (Sex Offenders Reporting) Bill* was tabled in Parliament in 1997 to establish a sex offender register. The Queensland Crime Commission was set up also in 1997 to investigate the incidence of criminal paedophilia and to maintain an intelligence database on paedophile activities.

Statutory provisions for child sex offenders to register with the police were introduced in Queensland in 1989. The provisions are found at s19 of the *Criminal Law Amendment Act 1945*, which allows a court (on application from the prosecution) to order a person convicted of a sexual offence against a child under sixteen years to report to the police within forty-eight hours of being released from custody. The offender has to report their name and address and any change of those details for as long as is specified in the order. Furthermore, under the *Sexual offenders (Protection of Children) Amendment Act 2003* and *Child Protection (Offender Reporting) Act 2004*, offenders can be ordered to report to the police within forty-eight hours of being released from custody if the court is satisfied that a 'risk' exists that the offender would commit another offence of a sexual nature on a child less than sixteen years. Offenders may also be required to report to police at nominated intervals.

The NSW Child Protection Register—which is described as the model state and territory register (Johns 2003)—was established under *Child Protection (Offenders Registration) Act 2000* (CPOR). It requires particular offenders against children to keep the state police informed of their name, date of birth, residential address, employment, motor vehicle registration, the offences and travel arrangements for a specified period of time. Offences under the Act include anything done outside New South Wales that would constitute an offence in the state. Registrable persons must attend a police station near their residence within twenty-eight days of sentencing, release from custody or entry to New South Wales (whichever is later). Any change must be notified within fourteen days. Before travelling interstate or overseas, a registrable person must contact the police of each nation to be visited, providing details of the duration of stay and approximate return date. The compliance period reflects the number and type of offences, including prior convictions. It ranges through life, fourteen years, twelve years, ten years and eight years (Johns 2003).

The South Australian *Child Sex Offender Registration Act 2006* is the most recent addition of this style of response. The Act establishes a child sex offender register of convicted child sex offenders, other serious criminal offenders who have committed that offence in connection with sex offences against children or who otherwise pose a risk of offending against children, and people subject to paedophile restraining orders (s99A of the *Summary Procedures Act 1921*). It also imposes registration and reporting obligations on those people who are on the register and prohibits them from undertaking child-related work. The Act was introduced as a part of a national scheme and follows the model adopted by other states and territories. It has been drafted in a way that allows South Australia to contribute to the national monitoring of child sex offenders.

The enhancement of information-sharing arrangements and legislation over 2004–2005 saw registers established across Australia. State and territory legislation providing for registration includes:

- *Serious Sex Offenders Monitoring Act 2005* (Vic.)
- *Sex Offenders Registration Act 2004* (Vic.)
- *Sex Offenders Registration (Amendment) Act 2005* (Vic.)
- *Child Protection (Offenders Registration) Act 2000* (NSW)
- *Child Protection (Offender Reporting and Registration) Act 2004* (NT)
- *Child Protection (Offender Reporting) Act 2004* (Qld)
- *Community Protection (Offender Reporting) Act 2004* (WA)

○ *The Crimes (Child Sex Offenders) Act 2005* (ACT)
○ *Child Sex Offender Registration Act 2006* (SA)
○ *Sex Offenders Registration Act 2004* (Tas.)

Australian constitutional arrangements mean that the different states and territories and federal government each maintain offender registers. The Australian regimes, reflecting wariness about the effectiveness of community notification, involve non-public registers that have been developed from existing criminal conviction or other databases and that contain a range of information: offender name, residential address, employment address, car registration, fingerprints and nature of offence. A national sex offender system is managed by the CrimTrac agency. It shares information across state and territory borders using the Australian National Child Offender Register (ANCOR), which is an electronic database accessible to a range of federal and state and territory government agencies, police forces and some voluntary bodies, like churches. Personal details of offenders are not made available to the public and cannot be accessed through Freedom of Information applications. This system enables police to register, case-manage and share information with other jurisdictions for persons subject to child protection registration. The Commonwealth government did not support the release of offenders' details to the community because public disclosure in other countries has led to attacks against either offenders or innocent people being mistaken for offenders.

Community notification

Community notification laws authorise the public disclosure of a convicted sex offender's personal information—for example, name, address and offence history—to people and organisations in the sex offender's local community. These laws are often justified as a means of increasing public safety (by informing citizens about sex offenders who live in their area) and assisting law enforcement in the investigation of sex offences (United States Department of Justice 1997). Notification takes distinctive forms, for example:

○ general disclosure to the public of sex offender information
○ selective disclosure of information to particular 'at risk' individuals and organisations
○ limited disclosure of information on a 'need to know' basis.

While there have been calls for the introduction of such schemes in Australia, such as from the Movement Against Kindred Offenders (MAKO), currently no statutory system exists. They are federally supported in the United States, however. In 1990 the prototype community notification scheme passed into law as a response to high-profile violent sexual acts. Washington State's *Community Protection Act* authorised notification when 'dangerous sex offenders' were released from custody. It was followed in other states by statutes such as Wisconsin's *Sexually Violent Persons Commitment Act 1993* and the *Jacob Wetterling Crimes Against*

Children and Sexually Violent Offender Registration Act 1994, which encouraged US states to implement a sex-offender register by linking federal funding to the creation of a state register.

In 1996 the enactment of the federal 'Megan's Law', provided for nationwide community notification. It followed the 1995 sexual assault and murder of New Jersey child Megan Kanka by a neighbour who had a history of sexual offending against children. The Megan's Law amendment to the federal Wetterling legislation effectively mandated community notification across all states, although it prescribed limited disclosure at a minimum. The US federal *Pam Lychner Sexual Offender Tracking and Identification Act 1996* extended the Megan's Law regime, mandating lifetime registration for repeat and aggravated offenders. The legislation was further extended in 1998 through the federal *Commerce, Justice, and State, the Judiciary and Related Agencies Appropriations Act* (CJSA), which strengthened the 'violent predator' provisions and added registration of federal and military sex offenders. It covers offenders who are non-resident students or workers. It established a national sex offender registry (NSOR) under the National Crime Information Center (NCIC). By 2002 some forty-two US states published information about sex offenders on the internet.

Community notification comes in numerous forms, such as news releases and postings on the internet, calling community meetings and targeting specific organisations, groups or local areas to give advice about released sex offenders. There is great variability in the way these laws are applied across jurisdictions. For instance, the length of the notification process can range from five years to life. Variation also exists in the way that states categorise offenders: some utilise a three-tiered system in which sex offenders are rated as low, medium or high risk and the notification requirements vary according to that rating, as does the length of time that an offender must stay on the records. Furthermore, there is variation not only in the delivery method—for example, in Louisiana, released offenders are required to personally alert neighbours within a one-mile radius in rural areas, and a three-block radius in urban settings (Levi 2000)—but also in the level of access to the information and the way it is distributed, who has access or who is notified, whether the access is proactive or only upon request, whether notification is discretionary or mandatory, what kinds of appeal process are available to offenders and what kinds of information is released. In some jurisdictions, name and address are supplied; in others, just general locations at the suburb or local block level; still others give a full description of the person, including a photograph.

In Australia, unofficial forms of community notification operate through publications like the *Australian Paedophile and Sex Offender Index* (Coddington 1997), which is said to be based on media reports with some checking against court records. This register has been criticised as 'incomplete and misleading' through, for example, a failure to identify some convictions that were successfully appealed in a court at a later date, or emphasising 'stranger' rather than the family members/associates responsible for most child offences (Hinds and Daly 2001). MAKO has placed similar lists on the internet, claiming that they rely on Coddington's index for their notification activities, compiling lists from newspaper reports and checking them against court records. Each index lists the names, locations, offences and sentences of convicted sex offenders. They are incomplete because they do not list offenders whose names were suppressed by the courts. A number of persons are included by identifying information, such as age, occupation, offence and location, but are unnamed due to the unavailability of appeal details. Since 1998 MAKO members have been active throughout the country, 'notifying over sixty Australian communities of convicted paedophiles and sex offenders living secretly among them' (MAKO <www.mako.org.au/makoniti.html>, 26/2/09). In Queensland they did a letterbox drop in one suburb; however, it was later revealed that the offender was still in goal. They had previously targeted a convicted child sex offender in Victoria by distributing pamphlets containing details of past convictions, as well as the name and current address. In Australia both print and online private community registers have attracted criticism from civil liberties groups, government officials and privacy bodies.

AICrime reduction matters: Is notification of sex offenders in local communities effective?

From time to time, public pressure arises for a public sex offender register similar to those in parts of the United States. The ANCOR allows police to share information between jurisdictions on convicted offenders, but currently there are no publicly accessible registries. The best known US measure, Megan's Law, aims to promote public and community safety through heightened public awareness of the location of sex offenders (Fitch 2006). Each state is required to provide mandatory community notification when a sex offender moves into an area (Pawson 2006).

Megan's Law has been systematically reviewed by Pawson (2006) and the UK's National Society for the Prevention of Cruelty to Children (Fitch 2006). It was found that the evidence base for the law was weak and that it was developed largely as a response to community agitation (Pawson 2006). There were also variations in implementation from policy-makers through to the community, leading to a lack of uniformity in decision-making between similar cases (Pawson 2006). There was little evidence of impact on sex offending—in particular, of offender recidivism rates being affected by community notification—or of reduced assaults by strangers on children (Fitch 2006). However, both studies stressed that program inconsistency made proving the overall efficacy of the measure problematic. The following issues with the law were identified:

○ Vigilantism is not monitored, with acts being under-reported and under-recorded.
○ Offender compliance varies, and offenders can still 'go underground'.
○ The focus on a small number of known offenders may distract attention from the more common intrafamilial abuse, and lead victims of intrafamilial violence not to report abuse due to ramifications for the victim and the offender.
○ There is conflicting evidence on whether community members, informed of an offender's presence, increase measures to protect their families.

○ It can create a false sense of fear and security among parents, and exaggerates true levels of offender recidivism.

○ Practitioners often point to increased use of risk assessment, better information sharing, and additional funding for treatment and surveillance as evidence of success, but these can be achieved separately through the community notification function.

○ The financial cost of implementation is high (Fitch 2006).

The following improvements were suggested:

○ standardising decision-making on risk assessment at every level (Pawson 2006)
○ increasing public awareness of existing systems of sex offender registration
○ public education that focuses less on the narrow group of high-risk offenders
○ treatment for those outside the criminal justice system
○ treatment for children who display sexually harmful behaviour (Fitch 2006).

Source: Australian Institute of Criminology (2007).

PENOLOGICAL PRINCIPLES: THE UTILITY OF INCAPACITATION?

It is easy to see the expression of the utilitarian idea that the value of an action is determined by its outcome in the punishment and sentencing of sex offences against children. Utilitarianism is the basis of theories of punishment concerned with preventing future crime. Such an approach is sometimes referred to as reductivist (von Hirsch and Ashworth 1998) because the aim is the future reduction of crime. The US sexual psychopath laws of the 1930s and 1940s were based on the assumption that the problem could be solved by interventions driven by medical expertise and shaped by psychiatric therapy. Through civil commitment, offenders were detained for the purpose of treatment and rehabilitation—the idea was that forced treatment would ultimately end with cure. So it was not so much Bentham's early utilitarian ideas of deterrence, but the rehabilitative ideals driven by the social sciences that took hold in the twentieth century that were initially important in the differentiation of sexual offenders. This was a forward-looking approach clearly concerned with the outcome of punishment, which would be the prevention of crime through the rehabilitation of the offender. Sentences and facilities were designed to offer various programs of treatment to offenders with the purpose of modifying inappropriate sexual behaviours. The crucial question for the sentencer involved the perceived needs of the offender, not the gravity of the offence committed. These early sexual psychopath laws identified a certain subclass of sex offender who was 'too sick to deserve punishment'. Positivist criminologies that locate the causes of criminality in individual pathology supported sentencing that relied on psychiatric experts who diagnosed the needs of the offender. These assessments were translated into indeterminate sentences that exemplified the rehabilitative ideal that an offender could only be released when, in the opinion of the experts, a cure had been achieved.

By the early 1970s, disillusionment with the objective of rehabilitation as a punishment and the corresponding rise of just deserts led to a decline in support for sexual psychopath laws; by the 1980s, they were repealed or fell into disuse. This shift reflected growing concerns for the civil rights of offenders, doubts about the effectiveness of treatment programs, and the lack of a consistent scientific basis for identifying and classifying people as sexual psychopaths. As we have seen in Chapter 2, it was exactly these types of issues that led to the collapse of welfare-oriented rehabilitative sentencing practices and programs more generally. In the case of sexual offending, there was no straightforward transition to rights-based or proportionate sentencing associated with just deserts, which were past oriented and concerned with the attribution of blame (and responsibility). Blame certainly became a key concern; however, the possibility of future offending continued to be a driving influence. While the critique of the early sexual psychopath laws rejected the rehabilitative ideas that justified indefinite sentencing, the new approach that emerged in the 1980s and 1990s nevertheless reaffirmed its value as a criminal justice response. There was a new justification for continued incarceration: convicted sex offenders were to be kept in custody not because it promised the possibility of cure, but because they were deemed too dangerous for release. It was a form of incapacitation done in the interests of community safety. This somewhat extreme (not to mention expensive) option is applied selectively. Those who are identified as less risky—that is, less likely to reoffend—are subject to systems of registration that allow law enforcement agencies to track or keep an eye on those sex offenders who have served their prison or probation time, and who are now living in the community.

Community notification laws, like those operating in the United States and the United Kingdom, take registration a step further: acknowledging the limits of law enforcement and releasing the names of offenders to the community with the intention that citizens will (be able to) take responsibility for their own safety. Community notification does not attempt to deal with sex offenders through attempts to reintegrate the offender into society after being treated by experts; rather, it works by identifying and classifying offenders' risk profiles—again, not to treat or condemn them, but as a regulatory strategy designed to manage them and make crime a tolerable fact of everyday life (Garland 2001). Addressing individual dangerousness has been replaced by the prediction and management of risk factors, relying on a hybrid of expert, commonsense and administrative knowledges to manage rather than act on underlying causes of dangerousness. According to Levi (2000), this focus on regulatory measures and risk management is an example of 'the preventive state': instead of purporting to deal with an offender's past wrongdoing through a penal state sanction, the power of the state (and civil society) is said to be deployed preventively to anticipate future conduct rather than exact sanctions for past events.

This move away from the traditional language of punishment to a vocabulary that draws heavily on ideas of risk, management, positivist knowledge and commonsense—in a way that mixes expert and non-expert rationalities—has developed into a strategy for advanced liberal governance in the area of criminal law. This is an example of what Feeley and Simon (1992) describe as the 'new penology'. It shifts attention away from the traditional concerns of the criminal law and criminology, which have focused on the individual, and redirects it to actuarial consideration of aggregates. This reorientation has a number of important implications: it facilitates the development of criminal justice processes that embrace an increased reliance on imprisonment and merges concerns for surveillance and custody; and it redirects the focus of concern from the punishment of individuals to the management of aggregates of dangerous groups. These authors identify incapacitation as the clearest example the new penological method, promising to reduce the effects of crime in society not by altering either offender or social context, but by rearranging the distribution of offenders in society. According to incapacitation theory, prison can detain offenders for a time and thus delay their resumption of criminal activity. If such delays are sustained for enough time and for enough offenders, significant aggregate effects in crime can take place, although individual destinies are only marginally altered. Selective incapacitation involves the identification of high-risk offenders and maintains long-term control over them while investing in shorter terms and less intrusive control over lower-risk offenders. It is in this context that risk assessment tools are used to identify likely recidivist offenders so that punishment can be preventive. Selective incapacitation of sex offenders is appealing because it is based on the principle that likely reoffenders can be identified and the public protected against them.

The responses described above are prefaced on a number of assumptions about sex offenders and child sex offenders that research indicates are problematic. First, they assume that these offenders are predatory strangers; however, most (around 90 per cent) child sex offenders are well known to their victims (Berliner et al. 1995; Bureau of Justice Statistics 2002; Smallbone and Wortley 2001). Second, criminal justice responses are based on the assumption that there are high rates of recidivism among this group of offenders. As Hanson and Bussiere (1998) and many others (cited in Levenson and D'Amora 2007) have noted, they are much lower than commonly believed and, in many cases, less likely than non-sexual offenders to be rearrested for ongoing criminal behaviour. Third, a common belief is that such offenders have strong, sexually deviant motivations that are untreatable; hence, indefinite sentencing is the only way to truly protect the public. Large-scale correctional studies suggest otherwise: sexual offenders, including sexual offenders against children, are more versatile in their criminal career than is generally accepted. Wortley and Smallbone (2006) take this a step further, proposing that sexual offending could be better understood as part of a more general involvement in criminal activity, and that the problem for these offenders seems to be less some special motivation to sexually abuse children than a more general problem involving their failure to inhibit urges and impulses, especially within their interpersonal domain. This suggests that such offenders could benefit from more generalised criminal justice interventions aimed at reducing crime. Indeed, there is a significant amount of research that argues that early intervention and treatment, such as cognitive behaviour therapy, works for many sexual offenders. The fourth assumption is that dangerousness can be easily identified and predicted. Among many others, Smallbone and Ransley (2005) explain how recent sexual offender risk prediction research shows that current risk prediction methods provide a very tenuous basis for selective incapacitation. The final assumption is that these approaches reluctantly acknowledge that the state alone is not able to protect its citizens—this opens the way for a form of pragmatic managerialism (Garland 2001; Levi 2000). It also assumes the citizens who are notified of the presence of sex offenders in their community will behave in responsible and orderly ways. However, research suggests that vigilantism is often associated with community notification (Pawson 2006). Despite the refusal of Australian jurisdictions to adopt this strategy because of the risk of vigilantism, public notification by other means has resulted in rough justice for convicted and alleged offenders. For example, a former mayor and a local shopkeeper in Wollongong were bashed and murdered allegedly by vigilantes following publicity about their supposed paedophile interest, and an inmate in Junee Correctional Centre in New South Wales was stomped to death in 1998 allegedly because this former school headmaster was convicted of child sex offences (Wyre 1998 in Ronken and Lincoln 2001, p. 235).

THINKING THEORETICALLY: CIVILISING VENGEANCE

Even in an era of proclaimed evidence-based policy making, there does not appear to be a sound empirical base for current criminal justice responses to sexual offending. How else might we understand the styles of response described above?

Foucault's work on governmentality makes a distinction between discipline and security: while discipline, which lies at the heart of the idea of rehabilitation, is targeted at an individual who is to be socialised or reformed, security addresses itself to the population (Gordon 1991, p. 20). Security works through the identification of common risks and the provision of shared solutions; its interest in individuals is to place them into categories of risk-posing or risk vulnerability. Feeley and Simon (1992; 1994) argue that the actuarial techniques of the new penology place people into categories and estimate the riskiness of these groups, rather than looking at individuals as unique cases and trying to reform them. As Douglas points out, the acquisition of a new technical vocabulary of risk assessment and categorisation in the field of punishment does not move it beyond politics. Political cultures act as filters for risk—they select problems for attention, suggest images of threatening people and situations, propose diagnoses, etc.

The identification of risk is not value neutral. Douglas linked her argument about blame to Durkheim's explanation of the relations between crime and the conscience collective (1992, pp. 6–7).

Hacker and Frym (1955, p. 767) claim that California's early *Sexual Psychopath Act* 'recognised and adopted [the principle] that our *collective conscience* does not allow punishment where it cannot impose blame'. While critical of the law, Sutherland (1950, p. 146) explained its diffusion as a 'form of *collective activity*' which occurred in the 1930 and 1940s while treatment as a response to offending was ascendant. Both of these accounts are consistent with Durkheim's view of law and punishment as an index of social phenomena and currents of public opinion. Later repressive developments demonstrating a shift in the collective conscience can easily be understood as reaffirming solidarity by taking vengeance on the offender. The new criminal laws reflect moral values that society holds sacred so that crime that violates this 'conscience collective' will tend to provoke collective moral outrage and a passionate desire for vengeance. As we have seen in Australia, child sex offenders have been the subject of moral outrage and experienced more than the desire for vengeance. Former Democrats leader Don Chipp suggested that convicted paedophiles should be tattooed on their foreheads as a warning that 'this person is not only dangerous but will remain dangerous' (*Sunday Mail*, 18 February 1997, in Ronken and Lincoln 2001, p. 235).

A Durkheimian analysis would also argue that the lack of concern with rehabilitation and correction demonstrated by the later legislative changes acknowledges that the deterrent and regulatory impact of punishment on offenders is limited. The extended provisions and sexual predator laws, along with systems of community notification, are expressive. These rituals of punishment are directed less at the individual offender than at the audience of impassioned onlookers. From this perspective, it matters little that there is limited (if any) empirical support for the preventive effects of these types of punishment. Punishment is symbolic—an occasion for the practical realisation of moral values that make up the collective conscience. It responds to the criminal's attack on morality and solidarity by affirming the strength of that moral order, restating its terms and reasserting its authority. It draws on the support of all those of 'healthy conscience' that are outraged by crime, a reaction that the ceremonial ritual of punishing helps to elicit and express. Arie Freiberg describes how new laws in Victoria permitting indefinite sentences and consecutive sentences for 'serious sex offenders' were 'rushed through Parliament' in response to citizen concerns that sexual and violent offenders were not incarcerated long enough (1997, p. 151). In the United States, Pawson (2006) found the evidence base for notification laws was weak: they developed largely as a response to community agitation. Punishment from Durkheim's perspective transforms a threat to social order into a basis for social solidarity. Instead of damaging the cohesiveness of society, crime sets in motion a complex reaction that channels the energy of outraged sentiments into a ritual of moral affirmation. We might ask, however, exactly whose morals and values are being affirmed?

Like Durkheim, Elias's study of the civilising processes draws our attention to mores and sensibilities. From this perspective, the ways in which we punish depend not just on political forces, economic interests or even penological considerations, but also on our conceptions of what is or is not culturally and emotionally acceptable. Penal policy decisions are always taken against a background of mores and sensibilities that, under normal circumstances, will set limits to what will be tolerated by the public or implemented by the penal system's personnel. The civilising process that promotes greater interdependency and the internalisation of restraint could easily account for the '[the principle] that our *collective conscience* does not allow punishment where it cannot impose blame', and the ascendance of treatment and rehabilitative approaches in the 1930s and 1940s. But as Pratt (2005) points out, Elias argued that decivilising processes can also shape the cultural sensibilities of modern life.

The three main characteristics of the decivilising process—a shift away from self-restraint towards restraint imposed by external authorities; the development of behaviour and sensibilities that generate the emergence of less even, stable and differentiated patterns of restraint; and a contraction in the scope of mutual identification between constituent groups and individuals—are clearly evident in recent responses to sex offending against children. Examples include calls for harsher sentencing practices (Ronken and Johnston 2006), indefinite sentencing, community notification and open public expressions of vengeance, vigilantism and discrimination. Fletcher (1997) suggests that when these characteristics of the decivilising process occur, they are likely to be accompanied by a decrease in the state monopoly on violence, a shortening of interdependences and a concomitant rise of fear, danger and incalculability. Community notification statutes amount to an acknowledgement that the state is unable to ensure the protection of citizens when it comes to sexual offending against children. By providing information on the location of sex offenders, the state transfers the responsibility for security and protection (previously the exclusive domain of the state) to citizens themselves (Levi 2000). Rather than contribute to community safety, such knowledge often enhances feelings of insecurity and opportunities for violence against those who are identified (Fitch 2006). Fletcher explains that this is not a process of simple reversal. In contemporary Western societies, bureaucratisation, one of the consequences of the civilising process, works against decivilising trends to maintain governmental authority and certainty. This tends to limit the full disintegration of the social order brought about by these tendencies. A range of legislative reviews (Johns 2003; AICrime Reduction Matters 2007) describe how bureaucratisation in Australia worked to limit regulatory measures to the registration of offenders with authorities rather than extending them to allow community notification. This aspect of the civilising process provides an explanation of why statutes like Megan's Law were not introduced in this country.

CONCLUSION

The earliest statutory responses specifically addressing sexual violence were the US sexual psychopath laws of the 1930s and 1940s. They were based on the assumption that the problem could be solved by the intervention of medical expertise and psychiatric therapy. As an alternative to punishment, these laws were based on the view that 'our collective conscience does not allow punishment where it cannot impose blame', and that 'the commission of a sex crime was usually, if not always evidence of a mental disorder which should be treated rather than punished' (Hacker and Frym 1955, p. 767). Beginning in the late 1980s, a second generation of sex offender commitment laws developed. While the first-generation laws were designed as an alternative to prison for offenders deemed too sick for punishment, the second aimed to extend the incarceration of convicted sex offenders deemed too dangerous for release from custody. The new generation of laws tended to consist of: enhanced sentencing for certain classes of violent or sex offenders, sexual predator laws, the registration of sex offenders and community notification of sex offenders. With the exception of community notification, similar laws have been introduced into Australian jurisdictions. This chapter examined the principles that underpin the punishment of child sex offenders described by these laws, and considered why community notification failed to gain traction in this country.

While the early responses were clearly shaped by principles of rehabilitation, changes in the late twentieth century were more concerned with prevention through incapacitation. Offenders were assessed using actuarial techniques that categorised them according to levels of risk. Responses were no longer focused on individual cure and correction, but on the identification and management of dangerous groups. Through a Foucaultian lens, this involved a shift from the rationality of discipline, and the rehabilitation of offenders, to security that addresses itself to the population (Gordon 1991, p. 20). Security works through the identification of common risks and the provision of shared solutions. However, as Douglas (1992) points out, categorisation according to risk is not value neutral. Political cultures work as filters, selecting problems for attention and suggesting images of threatening people and situations. In this way, risk is linked to Durkheim's idea of collective conscience. Laws act as an index of social phenomena and 'popular' opinion; the later repressive developments demonstrate a shift in the collective conscience and can easily be understood as reaffirming solidarity by taking vengeance on the offender. Elias's work on civilising and decivilising processes helps us to better appreciate changing responses to this type of sexual offending. Moreover, it highlighted how bureaucratisation in Australia worked against decivilising trends through the implementation of a national system of registration, rather than one of public notification. This perspective therefore explains why Megan's Law didn't make it to Australia.

Terrorism: Risk, retaliation and preventive detention

INTRODUCTION

Since the coordinated attacks on American targets on 11 September 2001, statements by principal Western leaders on the subject of the 'war on terror' have contained few references to the previous experience of governments in tackling terrorist threats (Roberts 2005, p. 103). Despite this apparent neglect, terrorism has a much longer history. For example, Michael Ignatieff (2004) documents terrorism and counter-terrorist activity from the nineteenth to the twenty-first centuries. Even '9/11' was not the first attack on America's World Trade Center: in 1993, seven people died and 1000 were injured in a car bomb explosion. Many other examples of terrorist activity associated with organised groups like the IRA, ETA, ANC, Tamil Tigers, HAMAS, PKK, along with events including the car bombing of an Oklahoma City federal building in the United States, the release of deadly sarin gas by Aum Supreme Truth on the Tokyo subway in 1995, or the bombing of the Hilton Hotel in Sydney during the Commonwealth Heads of Government Meeting in 1978, could be cited here. Nevertheless, the events of 9/11 heralded a fresh concern that has been referred to as 'the new terrorism'. In the face of this redefined threat, we have witnessed an avalanche of legislation as countries, including Australia, try to mitigate it. While some of this new law involves refining and tightening security measures, other legislation is controversial because it contravenes civil and political rights.

Critics argue that many recently introduced counter-terrorism provisions represent an unprecedented erosion of freedom—in particular, an erosion of some of the judicial principles that have regulated the delivery of punishment in liberal democratic societies, such as equality before the law and the right to counsel, fair trial and to know charges. This chapter explores these developments by highlighting the difficulty of arriving at a clear definition of terrorism, considers briefly the causes of this type of activity and then outlines a number of recent (post 9/11) changes to how Australian governments respond to this threat. The horizon of counter-terrorist activity introduced by federal and state agencies is broad. Consideration of all such programs is beyond the scope of this book. Given the context here, discussion focuses on the punitive dimensions of the Australian responses and the principles that have shaped these interventions. The treatment of alleged terrorists is exemplified in a number cases in Australia: Jack Thomas, Mohamed Haneef and David Hicks. The chapter concludes by considering the role of risk in the expression and practices associated with this recent governmental concern. Drawing on Douglas and Beck, I argue that the perceived or socially constructed risk, rather than the actual threat of terrorist attack, has provided justification for harsh responses and the erosion of 'freedom' in the interests of security. This raises questions about the acceptability of detention without trial or the restriction of liberty without criminal conviction. More specifically, we might ask about the relationship between such deprivation of liberty (which may be justified for administrative reasons) and punishment.

THE PROBLEM OF TERRORISM

Terrorism is a hard concept to define (Hayward and Morrison 2002; O'Neill 2002a): 'one person's terrorist is another's freedom fighter'. The label *terrorist* has sometimes been applied to the activities of movements that (even if they did resort to violence) had serious claims to political legitimacy. In 1987 and 1988 the UK and the US governments labelled the African National Congress of South Africa 'terrorist'; this is a contested label in retrospect, given Nelson Mandela's later emergence as statesman. Farhang Rajaee (2002, p. 38) explains that 'on the one hand [terrorism] is a serious violation of domestic and international laws, and on the other it has direct links to social, political and historical grievances'. This means that terrorism is an act that is not easily categorised as simply criminal because it often has a political dimension. It has a link to some notion of the public good, is often carried out in support of some public cause and is an expression of public protest when the politics of inclusion fails. It may not be considered political because the legitimate use of violence has its own set of rules, but it is political because it is usually the weapon of a dispossessed group who feels it is excluded from public life and has no other means at its disposal. It is not usually an individual act—there is generally an organisation that supports that act itself, as well as a community of sympathisers behind the act who consider it to be a legitimate form of expression and a means of advancing a particular cause (Baregu 2002; Rajaee 2002).

Terrorism is a term used to refer to the systematic use of violence and threats of violence by non-state groups, which are designed to cause disruption, alarm, anxiety and submission on the part of the target population or government. States can also use terror, and sometimes secretly sponsor non-state terrorist groups (Roberts 2005). Attempts to define terrorism in recent years, especially since 2001, have reflected the fact that much contemporary terrorism is targeted against civilians. United Nations Security Council Resolution 1566 of 8 October 2004 refers to terrorism as:

> Criminal acts … committed with the intent to cause death or serious bodily injury, or taking of hostages, with the purpose to provoke a state of terror in the general public or in a group of persons or particular persons, intimidate a population or compel a government or international organisation to do or to abstain from doing any act, which constitute offences within the scope of, and as defined in, the international conventions and protocol relating to terrorism.

Terrorist acts are easier to define than terrorism. They encompasses certain violent acts that contravene national laws and, in some cases, specific international agreements. The Australian government explains that terrorism is often considered to involve acts or threats of violence or criminality that:

1 are significant in seriousness or magnitude
2 are motivated by political, social or ideological objectives; and/or
3 are intended to influence a government or intimidate or coerce the public or a section of the public (Parliament of Australia 2002, p. 5).

Goldsmith (2006) suggests that this definition provides some clues as to who is a terrorist and the motivations for terrorism. He proposes that those labelled as terrorists are 'outsiders', generally young males with a grievance against the established political system or way of life. Their methods tend to indicate that they are acting from positions of actual or perceived subordination in, and rejection or alienation from, the society in which they take action. Furthermore, they generally see little point in pursuing change through conventional political methods. Taking this into account, at its simplest, terrorism might be described as 'a highly problematic means of bringing about change' (Roberts 2005, p. 123).

Historically, much terrorist activity has occurred within, not across, the borders of nation states. The goal has been a change of regime and/or political system (as sought by revolutionary groups, such as FARC in Columbia) or the establishment of a separate state (as seen in Quebec in the 1960s or in the Basque region of Spain in the 1990s). However, activity by al Qaeda, for example, highlights the transnational origins, activities and aspirations of some more recent groups. Today's terrorists can find their justification in religious ideologies that construct the members of these groups as victims suffering humiliation and shame for their religious beliefs (Goldsmith 2006, p. 235). The source of grievance can cross national borders and is perceived as a global problem, rather than one that is locally bounded.

CAUSES AND RESPONSES

Discussion of how to respond to or prevent terrorism might logically begin with a consideration of the causes of terrorism. Academic debate frequently centres on whether terrorism is related to economic factors (O'Neill 2002a). Poverty and underdevelopment often coincide with limited or non-existent governance (Gutierrez 2002), so host states have limited or no control over what happens in large parts of their territory and local extremist groups prosper by exploiting discontent fed by corruption, poverty or authoritarian rulers. The international system of growing global institutions, trade and technological capacities can exacerbate real and perceived inequalities, creating greater inequalities between and within states. Terrorists exploit these gaps, using modern communications and jet travel to spread their ideologies, raise funds, recruit and hide. These are the characteristics of what is referred to as the 'new' terrorism.

From this perspective, critics argue that a key strategy to prevent terrorism would be to allow people to participate fully in the economic and political systems of their states or in the new globalised international system. This could be achieved through a global recognition and enforcement of human rights, development programs designed to promote a broader definition of human security, emphasising the right to development, citizen participation, and government accountability and transparency. Such proposals are based on the assumption that the greater the stake that citizens have in their societies, the less likely they will be to support terrorism (O'Neill 2002b). Other solutions included nation building or capacity building and empowerment (Gunaratna 2002; Gutierrez 2002). Empowerment, capacity building and participatory democracy are concepts associated with critical criminological perspectives; however, as Garland (2001) and O'Malley (2000) note, there has been a recent antipathy to solutions concerned with addressing inequalities. In the criminal justice state, this has amounted to a shift away from penal welfarist approaches and a rejection of strategies that address structural inequalities. Rather, emphasis has been placed more on penalty and prevention, and this characterises what Garland has come to call a 'culture of control'. A focus on penalty and prevention lies at the heart of the Australian counter-terrorism response.

RESPONDING TO TERRORISM IN AUSTRALIA

Unlike other countries, Australia has been almost entirely free of acts of political violence into the twenty-first century. Nevertheless, after 9/11 the development of a specific and coordinated policy for national security became a priority. In pursuit of this goal, and despite the adequacy of existing provisions, from 2001 to 2008 the Commonwealth government made no less than forty-four new laws that directly deal with counter-terrorism. This rush of legislative activity has also been significantly bolstered by numerous state and territory provisions.

Key counter-terrorism laws and their rationale

Of the many laws enacted by the Commonwealth government, the following are perhaps the most significant:

○ The Anti-Terrorism Act (No. 2) 2005 amends the criminal code to allow for the listing of organisations that advocate the undertaking of a terrorist act, establishes procedures for preventive detention and control orders and updates the offence of sedition.

○ The Australian Security Intelligence Organisation Legislation Amendment (Terrorism) Act 2003 empowers ASIO to obtain a warrant to detain and question a person who may have information important to the gathering of intelligence in relation to terrorist activity.

- *The Criminal Code Amendment (Offences Against Australians) Act 2002* makes it an offence to murder, commit manslaughter or intentionally or recklessly cause serious harm to an Australian outside Australia, thus making extradition easier.
- *The Criminal Code Amendment (Suppression of Terrorist Bombings) Act 2002* makes it an offence to place bombs or other lethal devices in prescribed places with the intention of causing death or serious harm or causing extensive destruction, which would cause major economic loss.
- *The Security Legislation Amendment (Terrorism) Act 2002* creates new terrorism offences, modernises treason offences and creates offences relating to membership or other specified links to terrorist organisations.
- *The Suppression of the Financing of Terrorism Act 2002* creates a new offence that targets persons who provide or collect funds and are reckless as to whether those funds will be used to facilitate a terrorist act.
- *The Telecommunications Interception Legislation Amendment Act 2002* permits law enforcement agencies to seek telecommunications interception warrants in connection with their investigation of terrorism offences.
- *The Criminal Code Amendment (Terrorism) Act 2003* (Constitutional Reference of Power) seeks to remove any uncertainty regarding the constitutional status of the counter-terrorism legislation.
- *The National Security Information (Criminal and Civil Proceedings) Act 2004* seeks to protect information from disclosure in federal criminal proceedings, where the disclosure would be likely to prejudice Australia's national security.

Source: Renwick (2007), pp. 67–77.

Responding to the events of 9/11, Australia created a series of new criminal offences that are described in the *Commonwealth Criminal Code Act*.

According to section 100.1(1), a terrorist act means an action or threat of action where:

...

(b) the action is done or the threat is made with the intention of advancing a political, religious or ideological cause; and
(c) the action is done or the threat is made with the intent of:
    (i) coercing, or influencing by intimidation, the government of the Commonwealth or a State, Territory or foreign country, or of part of a State, Territory or foreign country; or
    (ii) intimidating the public or a section of the public.

The act must cause death or serious harm to a person, serious damage to property, endanger a person's life, create serious risks to the health or safety of the public or seriously interfere with, disrupt or destroy an electronic system, such as an information, telecommunications or financial system. Ordinary acts of protest, dissent advocacy or industrial action that are not intended to cause serious harm, death or endanger the life of a person or create a serious risk to the health or safety of the public do not constitute terrorist acts. Divisions 101, 102 and 103 of Part 5.3 of the criminal code cover conduct related to committing and planning terrorist acts. Divisions 101 and 102 distinguish between offences committed by individuals acting alone and those where criminal liability depends on some connection to a terrorist organisation, whereas division 103 creates offences relating to financing terrorism. These offences criminalise a great range of acts and omissions and extend Australia's jurisdiction beyond our borders to all parts of the globe. Obvious terrorist crimes include engaging in a terrorist act (s101.1) and detonating an explosive device in a government facility or public transportation system (s72.3), both of which carry maximum penalties of life imprisonment. However, despite the fact that many offences that criminalise acts fall short of the actual commission of a terrorist act, they also carry very heavy penalties. For example, the code criminalises:

- providing or receiving training connected with a terrorist act (s101.2)—15 years imprisonment
- possessing things connected with preparation for or assistance in a terrorist act (s101.4)—15 years imprisonment
- collecting or making documents likely to facilitate terrorist acts (s101.5)—15 years imprisonment
- preparing or planning for a terrorist act (s101.6)—life imprisonment
- directing the activities of a terrorist organisation (s102.2)—25 years imprisonment
- being a member of a terrorist organisation (s102.3)—10 years imprisonment
- recruiting a person for a terrorist organisation (s102.4)—25 years imprisonment
- training or receiving training from a terrorist organisation (s102.5)—25 years imprisonment
- receiving funds from or making funds available to a terrorist organisation (s102.6)—25 years imprisonment
- providing support to a terrorist organisation (s102.7)—25 years imprisonment
- collecting funds to facilitate or engage in terrorism (s103.1)—life imprisonment.

In addition to all of these substantive offences, the code also criminalises attempts to commit these offences (s11.1), the incitement of these offences (s11.4) and the use of an innocent agent to commit the offences (s11.3). Aiders and abettors and conspirators can also be prosecuted, convicted and punished in the same manner as the principal offenders (ss11.2 and 11.5) (Boulton 2006).

In Division 101 the core offence is that of engaging in a terrorist act (s101.1); other crimes are 'ancillary offences' that do not deal with terrorist acts but actions that are connected with them. The scope of this legislation is a major source of concern (Lynch and Williams 2006). It criminalises the very formative stages of an act, making individuals liable to very serious penalties, despite the lack of a clear criminal intent. This involves a significant extension of criminal responsibility since it is far removed from the commission of an unlawful act. Admittedly, the law has long recognised offences based on an attempt to commit a crime, or even a conspiracy to do so; however, as Lynch and Williams (2006 among others) explain, the ancillary offences in Division 101 establish crimes at an even earlier point. In November 2005 former Minister for Justice and Customs, Senator Chris Ellison, offered this justification for the offences to the Australian Parliament:

> In the security environment that we are dealing with you may well have a situation where a number of people are doing things but you do not yet have the information which would lead to identify a particular act ... When you are dealing with security you have to keep an eye on prevention of the act itself as well as bringing those who are guilty of the act to justice. (Commonwealth of Australia 2005, p. 43)

This comment reveals a policy of using the law not merely to punish or deter specific conduct, but to prevent such conduct. Authorities are now empowered to act pre-emptively by arresting people before they have formed a definite plan to commit the criminal act—an approach that reflects the growing dominance in counter-terrorism law of what is known as the 'precautionary principle' (Lynch and Williams 2006, p. 19). Furthermore, the evidential burden is placed on defendants who must show that there is a reasonable possibility that they had no such intention before the prosecution will be called on to establish such an intention. While the prosecution must refute the defence's claims beyond reasonable doubt, defendants are to argue their innocence first. This is a significant departure from the accepted notion in Australian criminal law that the prosecutor should be required to prove all the central elements of an offence before a person has to mount a defence.

Detection and prevention of terrorism

One of the most controversial aspects of the Commonwealth government's response to 9/11 was its decision to grant new powers to the Australian Security Intelligence Organisation (ASIO). Under these powers, ASIO can question and detain suspected terrorists and monitor them through electronic and other means to gather intelligence that might prevent an attack. It can also monitor, question and detain Australian citizens who are not suspected of any involvement with terrorism but who might have information that is useful to the government. These new powers to detain innocent Australians generated considerable opposition and an extended and heated public debate, which was centred on whether it is appropriate to confer this power on a secret intelligence organisation and whether the detention of 'non-suspects' for information gathering purposes is ever justifiable.

The initial ASIO Legislation Amendment (Terrorism) Bill 2002 permitted ASIO to strip-search and detain without trial adults and children who were not suspects but who may have had useful information about terrorism. Such detention could be for renewable, indefinite two-day periods. George Williams described this Bill as 'one of the most remarkable pieces of legislation ever introduced into the federal parliament. It would not have been out of place in General Pinochet's Chile' (Williams 2005, p. 18). In the face of such criticism, the government vigorously defended the Bill by arguing that it was necessary for the protection of Australia against the threat of terrorist attack. The strength of opposition and criticism from two parliamentary committees, the legal community and other groups had some effect. The Bill stalled; and a revised version of the law, the ASIO Legislation Amendment (Terrorism) Bill (No. 2) was eventually passed on 26 June 2003. This legislation amended the *ASIO Act 1979*, which allowed Australians to be questioned for twenty-four hours while being detained for one week. A person can now only be held and questioned on the order of a judge, with the questioning to take place before a retired judge. While these protections tempered some of the main problems with the original Bill, the laws nevertheless gave ASIO unprecedented new powers that could be justified only as a temporary response to the exceptional threat posed by terrorism. The legislation included a sunset clause, providing that it would lapse after three years unless re-enacted. In 2005 it was reviewed and, with some modification, renewed for ten years, so it will remain in force until 2016 (Head 2003; Lynch and Williams 2006, pp. 34–5).

One of the notable effects of these new provisions is that a person who is not suspected of any crime can now be detained for longer than a suspect. Under the amended *Crimes Act 1914*, a person arrested for a terrorism offence may only be detained for the purpose of investigating the offence for four hours (or two if the person is under eighteen or Indigenous). This may be extended for up to twenty hours, giving a maximum period of twenty-four hours before charges must be laid. (In contrast, the investigation period for serious, non-terrorist federal offences may only be extended for up to eight hours to a maximum of twelve hours.) The ASIO Bill (No. 2) allowed for the detention of non-suspects for seven times longer than people suspected of a terrorism offence.

Furthermore, ASIO can now demand the surrender of a person's passport in certain circumstances, can use search warrants for ninety days (an increase from twenty-eight) and postal and delivery service warrants for six months (an increase from ninety days), and can remove and retain for a reasonable period material found during the execution of a search warrant. Since 9/11, ASIO has been given greatly enhanced powers and an enormous increase in budget and personnel (Bull and Craig 2006). Although there is no evidence that ASIO has misused its powers, there is potential for misuse (whether deliberately or by mistake, Lynch and Williams 2006).

Pre-emptive policy: Preventive detention and control orders

Preventing a terrorist attack is the core aim of the Commonwealth's national security policy, and the law has a central role to play. As former Attorney-General Philip Ruddock made clear in 2004, prevention is not just a matter of a telephone hotline, better policing and tightened transport security: 'the law should operated as both a sword and a shield—the means by which offenders are *punished* but also the mechanism by which crime is *prevented*' (cited in Lynch and Williams 2006, p. 41). The criminalisation of preparatory activities and the significant expansion of the powers of intelligence agencies are two of the ways that the aim of prevention has been taken up in legislation; however, the counter-terrorism laws, which are discussed below, offer an even more striking example of the government's attempt to use the law pre-emptively.

In late 2005, as part of a suite of agreed changes by the Council of Australian Governments (COAG) in the wake of the 7 July London bombings that year, Divisions 104 and 105 were added to Part 5.3 of the criminal code. They enable control and preventive detention orders to be imposed on a person. While both orders are designed to protect the public from a terrorist act, they differ in an important way. On the one hand preventive detention orders are fairly short term: they are aimed at either preventing an imminent terrorist attack or preserving evidence relating to a terrorist act that has recently taken place. On the other hand, control orders do not require an imminent risk of terrorist attack and may last much longer: up to a year, with the possibility of renewal. These orders highlight the problems associated with employing the law as a tool of preventive policy; they challenge the traditional understandings of legal regulation. Neither requires a finding of guilty, or even a suspicion that a crime has been committed, yet both enable significant restrictions on individual liberty. According to McDonald and Williams (2007, p. 48), this is 'more than a breach of the old "innocent until proven guilty" maxim: it ignores the notion of guilt altogether'.

The emphasis here is on prevention of a terrorist act, rather than punishment when an act has occurred. These powers are controversial. The right to personal liberty (that is, the freedom from arbitrary detention) has been described as the most fundamental and important common law right. Non-punitive detention without trial can be authorised in limited circumstances by federal laws, such as migration or quarantine detention, but there are far fewer limitations on state parliament. For example, the High Court in *Fardon v Attorney General* (Queensland—2004 210 ALR 50) upheld a law that provided for the annual but, because renewable, possibly indefinite detention in jail of serious sex offenders whose term of imprisonment had ended, because they were considered by a court to be an 'unacceptable risk to society' if released (Renwick 2007, pp. 73–4).

Control orders

Control orders impose a variety of obligations, prohibitions and restrictions on a person for the purpose of protecting the public from a terrorist act. By order of a court, they allow the Australian Federal Police (AFP) to monitor and restrict the activities of people who pose a terrorist risk to the community without having to wait to see whether this risk materialises. The potential scope of a control order ranges from minimal intrusion on an individual's freedom to an extreme deprivation of liberty. An interim control order can require that a person:

○ is restricted in relation to their movement and access to specified areas or places
○ leave Australia
○ remain at specified premises between specified times or on specified days
○ wear a tracking device
○ not communicate or associate with specified individuals
○ not have access to or use of specified forms of telecommunication or other technology, including the internet
○ not possess or use specified articles or substances
○ not carry out specified activities
○ report to specified persons at specific times and places
○ allow photographs or fingerprints to be taken (for the purpose of ensuring compliance with the order).

Unlike preventive detention orders, control orders stop short of imprisonment in a state facility. Nevertheless, it is possible to detain an individual using an order. If a person must not be at specified places or must remain at specified places at certain times, this may amount to detention. A person who contravenes the terms of a control order commits an offence with a maximum penalty of five years' jail.

PREVENTIVE DETENTION ORDERS

Preventive detention orders involve the power to detain a person for forty-eight hours under federal laws and fourteen days under corresponding state laws either to prevent a terrorist act or to preserve evidence of a terrorist act that has occurred. They allow AFP officers to take people into custody for a short period of time when they believe it is necessary to prevent an imminent terrorist act or to preserve evidence of, or relating to, a recent terrorist act. AFP officers will apply to an issuing authority, such as a magistrate, for a preventive detention order if they are satisfied that there are reasonable grounds to suspect that:

○ the person will engage in a terrorist act
○ the person possesses a thing that is connected a terrorist act
○ the person has done an act in preparation for, or planning, a terrorist act

- a terrorist act has occurred within the last twenty-eight days and it is necessary to detain the person to preserve evidence of, or relating to, the terrorist act.

The person may be detained for an initial twenty-four-hour period. This can be extended by the issuing authority for a further twenty-four-hour period. During detention, the suspect cannot be questioned, except to confirm identity or to enable safe detention. The suspect must be given a copy of the order, with a summary of the grounds on which the order was made. Their lawyer will also be able to obtain a copy of the order and a summary of the grounds for making the order. During detention, they may contact a family member and/or their employer solely for the purpose of letting them know that they are safe but that they are not to be contacted for the time being. The suspect is not permitted to disclose the details of the preventive detention order or the fact that they are being detained under the order.

PROHIBITED CONTACT ORDER

In conjunction with a preventive detention order, AFP officers may apply to an issuing authority for a prohibited contact order to prevent suspects from contacting specified persons. They may apply for this when they are satisfied that the order is reasonably necessary to:

- avoid action being taken related to a terrorist act
- prevent serious harm to a person
- preserve evidence of, or relating to, a terrorist act
- prevent interference with the gathering of information about a terrorist act or its preparation
- avoid a risk to:
  - the arrest of a person who is suspected of having committed an offence related to a control or preventive detention order
  - the taking into custody of a person in relation to whom a preventive detention order is in force or likely to be made
  - the service on a person of a control order.

Central to all of the terrorism crimes listed under the criminal code is the definition of 'terrorist act'. Although terrorism is a difficult concept to pin down, the legislative definition is sufficiently precise for the new criminal offences and it explicitly protects legitimate forms of protest and advocacy. However, the legislation is problematic because the actual offences go well beyond terrorist action. The ancillary offences outlined in Division 101 are designed to empower authorities to prevent the fulfilment of a terrorist plot. In so doing, critics argue there is a real risk that they define liability too broadly so that otherwise innocent behaviour may lead to a person being charged despite the absences of criminal intent (Boulton 2006; Lynch and Williams 2006; Renwick 2007). Moreover, the potential for control and preventive detention orders to be used to cover circumstances in which authorities do not have sufficient evidence to lay a charge is a matter for concern. The controversy over the detention and removal of Mohamed Haneef because of his alleged, but ultimately unproven, connection to a terrorist cell demonstrated the problems associated with this type of response (see the Clarke Inquiry report released on 23 December 2008).

Mohamed Haneef in brief

On 2 July 2007 Mohamed Haneef, then a Gold Coast doctor, was arrested at Brisbane Airport possessing a one-way ticket to India. He was detained without charge from 5 to 13 July under new anti-terror laws. On 14 July he was charged with providing support to a terrorist organisation, because he had given a mobile phone SIM card to his second cousin, Sabeel Ahmed, a brother of Kafeel Ahmed who died after attempting to drive a car laden with explosives into a terminal at Glasgow Airport.

On 16 July Haneef was released on bail. However, the then Minster for Immigration Kevin Andrews revoked Haneef's 457-day work visa on character grounds and he was again detained. Four days later (20 July) the AFP revealed that Haneef's SIM card was not found at the scene of the bombing. Seven days later Haneef was released into residential detention. His passport was returned but the minister refused to reinstate his work visa. On 29 July Haneef flew to India. The Federal Court quashed the decision to cancel his work visa in August.

In March 2008 the retired Supreme Court judge John Clarke QC began an inquiry into Haneef's case. In May, Sabeel Ahmed, who had been deported to India, was found not to have known about the bomb plot. In August the AFP announced that Haneef was no longer a person of interest. In documents obtained through the *Freedom of Information Act* the AFP acknowledge there was 'insufficient evidence' to charge Haneef before the charge was laid (clarke 2008).

As a result, both orders can be seen as an attempt to avoid the regular judicial procedures for testing and challenging evidence in criminal trials before a person's freedoms are removed. This is clearly the case when it comes to preventive detention orders, which may be issued by an individual officer simply on the basis of reasonable suspicion. It also an issue with regard to the lower standards of proof required by courts when issuing control orders. The introduction of these orders therefore signals a departure from the way that Australian law is generally thought to work. While community protection has undoubtedly been an important consideration for the criminal justice system in this country, these orders put that objective ahead of fundamental principles: for example, that people should not be detained without trial or their liberty restricted without a criminal conviction.

Roberts (2005) concludes from his survey of the history of counter-terror responses that respect for the law has been an important element in many operations against terrorists. One of the key figures involved in the Malayan campaign in the 1950s, Sir Robert Thompson, distilling five basic principles of counter-insurgency from this and other cases, wrote of the crucial importance of operating within a properly functioning domestic legal framework: the government must function in accordance with law.

> There is a very strong temptation in dealing both with terrorism and with guerrilla actions for government forces to act outside the law, the excuses being that the processes of law are too cumbersome, that the normal safeguards in the law for the individual are not designed for an insurgency and that a terrorist deserves to be treated as an outlaw anyway. Not only is this morally wrong, but, over a period, it will create more practical difficulties for a government than it solves. (1966 cited in Roberts 2005, p. 110)

Roberts urges that the treatment of detainees, in particular, is an issue of crucial importance in the history of terrorism and counter-terrorism. When fighting an unseen enemy who may have many secret sympathisers, all societies encounter difficulties. In such circumstances most states, even democratic ones, resort to some form of detention without trial. There are enormous risks associated with such detentions: first, a risk of arresting and convicting the wrong people; and second, the maltreatment of detainees (for example, see David Hicks's affidavit reprinted in the *Sydney Morning Herald*, 10 December 2004). Both risks tend to create martyrs and encourage support for the terrorist campaign. The treatment of detainees and prisoners—in Abu Ghraib or Guantánamo Bay, for example, not to mention the controversial practice of rendition—has been one of the major failures of the 'war on terror' since it began in late 2001. In January 2002, US Secretary of Defense Donald Rumsfeld said of the prisoners in Guantánamo: 'I do not feel even the slightest concern over their treatment. They are being treated vastly better than they treated anybody else over the last several years and vastly better than was their circumstance when they were found' (cited in Roberts 2005, p. 111). This and similar remarks were widely broadcast on radio and television stations critical of the United States. The episodes of maltreatment and torture in Iraq since April 2003 reinforced the damage. Arguments that lawful and humane treatment is relatively unimportant lose sight of the fact that ill-treatment and torture have been used to justify the resort to terrorism and discredit the anti-terrorist cause. The history of counter-terrorist operations in the twentieth century suggests that, in the long struggle against terrorism, four assets are important:

○ public confidence in official decision-making
○ public confidence in the intelligence on which that decision-making is based (for example, the controversy that surrounded claims regarding weapons of mass destruction that provided a justification in the United States and United Kingdom for the invasion of Iraq in 2003)
○ operation with respect for a framework of law
○ a willingness to address some of the problems that have contributed to the emergence of terrorism (Roberts 2005).

The first Australian convicted under Australia's anti-terrorism legislation

Jack Thomas was detained at Karachi airport by Pakistani immigration officials as he attempted to return to Australia in January 2003. He was released and returned to Australia on 6 June 2003. Over the intervening five-month period, he was held without charge in solitary confinement without consular or legal access. Hooded, handcuffed and shackled, he was taken to several locations for interrogation by representatives from Pakistani and American intelligence agencies, as well as a joint Australian team of AFP and ASIO officers. In March 2003 the AFP officers were granted permission by Pakistani officials to conduct a formal interview with Thomas on the condition that he be denied access to legal assistance. Unlike previous interrogations the purpose of this interview was not to gather intelligence but to obtain evidence for use in Australian criminal proceedings. Thomas was released without charge. He returned to Melbourne, lived and worked in the community. Eighteen months later he was arrested and spent months confined in Barwon maximum security prison, in solitary confinement, for up to twenty-three hours a day.

On 26 February 2006 Jack Thomas was the first person tried and convicted under the Commonwealth government's anti-terrorism laws. Thomas was found guilty by the Supreme Court of Victoria jury of one count of receiving funds from a terrorist organisation (Criminal Code, s102.6), namely al Qaeda, and one of possessing a falsified Australian passport (*Passports Act 1938* (Cwlth), s9A[1][e]). He was acquitted of a further two counts of intentionally providing resources to a terrorist organisation (Criminal Code, s102.7[1]). His acquittal on the charge of supporting a terrorist organisation indicates that the jury found that Thomas did not intend to use the funds to engage in a terrorist act. Nevertheless, the receipt of such funds from al Qaeda led to a conviction (McCulloch 2006). He was sentenced on 31 March 2006 to five years in prison with a non-parole period of two years.

The trial was controversial because the evidence used to prosecute Thomas consisted of an interview conducted by two AFP officers while Thomas was detained in the Pakistani military prison. In the period between his return to Australia and arrest, security forces monitored his movements, his phone calls and emails but found no new evidence. According to the prosecution the case against him rested on the interview conducted in Pakistan. On 18 August 2006 the Victorian Court of Appeal (in R v *Thomas*) quashed his conviction on the grounds that the trial judge should have ruled that the evidence given in that interview was inadmissible because the defendant was under external pressure calculated to 'overbear' his will. On 27 August 2006 the Federal Magistrates Court issued an interim control order restricting his movements and communications.

According to the control order, the obligations imposed on Joseph (Jack) Terrence Thomas pursuant to subsection 104.5(3) of the Criminal Code (Cwlth) were as follows.

He was required to:

- abide by a curfew confining him to his identified place of residence between midnight and 5.00 a.m. each day, unless the coordinator of the AFT Counter Terrorist Team (CTT) was notified in writing of another address where he will be residing between these times
- report to a member of Victoria police, every Monday, Wednesday and Saturday between 9.00 am and 9.00 pm, at Werribee, Footscray or Sunshine police station
- allow impressions of his fingerprints to be taken by Victoria Police. Furthermore, Thomas was prohibited from:
- leaving Australia, except with prior permission from the AFP CTT coordinator
- acquiring, producing, accessing or supplying documentation regarding the manufacture or detonation of explosives, weapons and/or combat skills
- manufacturing, acquiring, taking possession of or using or attempting to manufacture, acquire, possess or use any commercial, military or homemade and/or improvised explosives, explosive accessories, initiation systems or firing devices
- subject to section 104.5(5) of the criminal code, communicating (directly or indirectly, including via internet chat rooms, websites, media interviews, publications and group gatherings) with any person in relation to:
  - methodology, tactics and other knowledge connected with or likely to facilitate terrorist acts, including explosives, weapons and/or combat skills;
  - names or contact details of persons known to be associated with a listed terrorist organisation
- communicating or associating with individuals listed by the Department of Foreign Affairs and Trade, as notified in writing by the AFP CTT coordinator, or any individual he knew to be a member of a listed/specified terrorist organisation.

His access to communications services was restricted to: one mobile phone/ SIM card, one fixed landline, one email account, one internet service provider account, one Voice Over Internet Protocol (VOIP) service; each of which must be approved in writing by the AFP CTT coordinator. Sufficient details to identify each of the services to be used must be provided. Thomas was also prohibited from using any public telephone, except in the case of an emergency, or a satellite telephone.

Finally, he was prohibited from having or using any firearm or ammunitions, and was required to arrange for the surrender to police of any firearm or ammunition in his possession custody or control (Federal Magistrates Court of Australia, File No: (P)CAG47/2006).

On 20 December 2006 prosecutors used an interview Thomas gave to the ABC's *Four Corners* to successfully apply for a retrial, arguing it was new evidence (ABC Online 2006). After a failed High Court bid to stop the retrial Thomas once again faced the Supreme Court, and on 23 October 2008 was found not guilty of the terrorism charges but guilty of a passport offence, which carried a maximum penalty of two years' imprisonment. Justice Elizabeth Curtin on 29 October 2008 ordered that Thomas be imprisoned for nine months but found that he was free to go after taking into account time already served (Collins 2008).

PENOLOGICAL PRINCIPLES: PRE-EMPTIVE PREVENTION

The 11 September 2001 incident in the United States provides a clear example of how one series of terrorist attacks impacts on countries and populations around the world, contributing to a general sense of greater insecurity. As a consequence, it is certainly now easier than before to present groups that carry out these attacks as a 'common enemy'—and to consider common or at least coordinated responses. In Australia the raft of legislative changes that followed 9/11 defined and criminalised terrorism, along with behaviour that arguably falls short of the actual commission of a terrorist act, but nevertheless carry heavy penalties. Such heavy penalties might be justified as a means of general deterrence, but the presumptive nature of the provisions is unmistakably designed to be preventive, which is confirmed by the ASIO legislation that allows the detention of non-suspects. This preventive imperative was made explicit in Philip Ruddock's statement: 'the law should operate as both a sword and a shield'. Challenging the traditional purpose of legal regulation, control and prevention detention orders introduced in 2005 illustrate the tension in employing law as a tool of preventive policy. Neither order requires a person to have been found guilty or even be suspected of committing a crime; both orders can significantly restrict individual liberty. This raises the question of when the deprivation of liberty (which may be justified for administrative reasons) becomes punishment.

Critics have highlighted the importance of respect for the rule of law and the risks involved with disregarding it, particularly in relation to the treatment of detainees (linked to terrorist activity). Indeed, public criticism of the treatment of those detained in Australia suggests that the four assets that Roberts (2005) identifies as important in the struggle against terrorism are in some important respects missing. Moreover, the treatment of those who are or have been detained is perhaps as much a problem in terms of formulating an effective response in Australia as it has been elsewhere in the world. If the Australian response is governed by law, albeit fairly controversial ones, this raises the question of how these provisions (which Roberts and others argue are likely to exacerbate rather than mitigate the problem) were able to be enacted in a liberal democratic state.

Returning to the principles of sentencing and punishment described in Chapter 2, it is clear that incapacitation is a significant motivation. In the past, preventive detention was reserved for the 'dangerous offender, career criminals or other persistent offenders'. Authorities sought to develop both ways to accurately identify this group of serious recidivists and rules for their long-term incarceration through programs of mandatory sentencing, indefinite imprisonment or preventive detention. In recent Australian history, the use of each of these responses has been controversial, such as mandatory sentencing in the Northern Territory, preventive detention orders in New South Wales and Victoria, and recent provisions for indefinite sentencing in Queensland. Nevertheless, just these types of containment have been seen as justifiable in the context of terrorism and even suspected terrorism (in the case of Mohamed Haneef). Moreover, as noted, incapacitation does not always involve imprisonment: it may include curfews, additional requirements on probation orders (like restrictions of movement and association) or control orders (as in the cases of Jack Thomas and David Hicks). In the context of sentencing and punishment more generally, research has found such forms of incapacitation hard to support; in the context of terrorist activity, and suspected or predicted activity more specifically, the justification of such a response remains problematic.

While incapacitation might provide a shield, the harshness of the response — or the sword — is unquestionably punishment concerned with deterrence and retribution. The execution of these rationalities in the context of the 'war on terror' is not consistent with just deserts principles that have been characteristic of sentencing reforms in the late twentieth and early twenty-first centuries. Rather, such responses perhaps can be interpreted in terms of harsh retributive vengeance. Punishment shaped by just deserts philosophies should be consistent with a number of principles. First, they should communicate censure or blame, the communication being directed chiefly to the offender but also to the victim and society at large. Second, understanding the need for general deterrence is important, but the preventive rationale should not be overstated (Ashworth 2005). Third, punishment should be commensurate to the seriousness of the offence. Fourth, there should be a schedule of punishment in which the most serious is reserved for the most serious offence, and that penalties should be graduated throughout the scale according to the gravity of the offence.

Some of these principles, with important qualification, might be applied to terrorism. For example, punishment is to communicate censure or blame chiefly to the offender. The nature of the terrorist offences and the Acts governing terrorism in this country, as we have seen, are at times weak in establishing that an offence has been committed, so the communication of blame seems to be chiefly to the victim, which is defined as the society at large. Moreover, the preventive rationale is overstated, and critics repeatedly complain that many of the penalties are not commensurate with the seriousness of the offence. Perhaps the most telling point of tension between just deserts principles and contemporary Australian responses to terrorism is the provision that possible future offending is not a consideration. According to this rationale of sentencing, punishment should be to the extent that it is deserved by the offence already committed and estimates of the likelihood of future offending should not influence the sentence passed, or the punishment actually experienced. As we have seen above in the context of Australia's new legislation, possible future offending is an important, if not a core, consideration.

THINKING THEORETICALLY: RISK AND RETALIATION

If we accept that the new legislation represents an expression of vengeance, we might look to Durkheim to understand better how such provisions are possible in our contemporary liberal, democratic society. According to Durkheim, in the past the function of repressive sanctions was to reaffirm solidarity in society by taking vengeance on the offender. Durkheim asserted that this is still the case in modern societies as far as the criminal law is concerned. We have not ceased to react punitively when collective values are breached (1893/1983). The criminal law for Durkheim is an embodiment of the basic moral values that society holds sacred, so crimes that violate this *conscience collective* will tend to provoke collective moral outrage and a passionate desire for vengeance. The 'passionate reactions' find expression in the legal practice of punishing offenders, which however much it is routinised and institutionalised remains a mechanism for the channelling and expression of collective moral sentiment. He makes two important points. First, even though the state monopolises the delivery and administration of punishment, a much wider population feels itself to be involved in the act of punishment, thus supplying the state institution with its social support and legitimacy. Second, despite all attempts in the nineteenth century to make punishment a rational, impartial and utilitarian process, it continues to be marked by the punitive sentiments and emotive reactions that are at the route of society's response to crime.

Mary Douglas extends Durkheim's explanation of the relations between crime and the *conscience collective*. Her approach to risk centres both on the political implications of judgments about the relationship between notions of risk and the structure of institutional authority and on risk as the contemporary framework for societal conversations about morality and identity. Douglas argues that it is the language of risk in contemporary culture that provides 'a common forensic vocabulary with which to hold persons accountable' (1992, p. 22). In this process the notion of risk is distanced from its original and particular application to probability calculations, and becomes a cultural key word with much wider reference within 'a debate about accountability'. Her cultural theory draws attention to the mix of discourses involved in the punishment of offenders. Public discourse on punishment is not limited to a concern with the severity of penalties—that is, their frequency and duration; it maintains more than an interest in the morality and propriety of the form and conditions of confinement and its security. For Douglas, political cultures act as filters for risk—they select problems for attention, suggest images of threatening people and situations, propose diagnoses and so on. This makes risk inherently a plural and contested idea (Sparks 2000). From this perspective, risk is always a social product (Kemshall 2003, p. 55). We therefore need to be attentive to how risks are selected and legitimised for public attention, and how group membership and risk perception are intrinsically linked. Risk is mediated by the interaction between action and cultural systems; it is a product of 'social dynamics of particular relationships or situations'. According to Douglas, risk is a negotiated concept and product of social interaction; it is context specific and bounded by group norms and values (Kemshall 2003, p. 61). Such an interactive approach recognises that risk decisions are negotiated and subject to both constraint and opportunity.

In criminology, this approach to risk is best illustrated in work on risk and its relation to fear and victimisation, and social construction approaches to fear of crime in which the 'knowledges, discourses and experiences used by people to construct their notions of risk and fear' are the site of investigation (Lupton 2000, p. 223). Attention is paid to how fear and risk are the products of particular, and at times conflicting, discourses and cultural understanding. Lupton locates the different and at times paradoxical fears of crime presented by respondents within the broader 'normalisation of crime' and subjective responsibility for crime avoidance of late modernity (Lupton 1999; 2000). Crime was seen as frequent and therefore highly likely to happen 'someday', but also random in terms of whom, where and when it might strike. Fatalism around the likelihood of crime combines with caution and increased responsibility for self-protection against threats to the person. It is arguable that since 9/11 the risk of terrorism, like crime more broadly, has also become a routine consideration in the collective consciousness of populations of the industrialised West. Before this event—with a few exceptions—terrorist activities were seen by many in the English-speaking world to be largely confined to 'Third World' or 'poorer' non-English speaking states that were considered by core powers to be fairly peripheral in terms of global governance and economic matters (Gunaratna 2002). With 9/11, the focus on terrorist activity shifted to the United States—the most powerful nation-state in the world (O'Neill 2002a). With the Bali bombings, the bombing of the Marriott and the Australian Embassy in Jakarta, the trains and buses in Madrid and London and the ongoing struggle in Iraq, it appears that the target extended beyond the United States to her allies (Gunaratna 2002). From being a problem that most affected developing countries on the other side of the world, terrorism and national (in)security have increasingly become a daily consideration for anyone who regularly flies in a plane, travels by train or bus, works or lives in high-rise buildings, holidays at popular resorts, stays in five-star hotels, frequents popular night club or restaurant districts, or works for a transnational corporation or government department.

From this perspective, to understand the significance of risk in the criminological or penological context, we need to acknowledge the relationship between discourse and practice. As Lupton explains (1999, p. 15), 'discourses delimit and make possible what can be said and done about phenomena such as "risk"; they work as an organising frame within which some risks gain both legitimacy and saliency'. As a result, focus of analysis is not on individual risk management, but on how some risks are chosen for attention while others are not. In essence this involves directing attention to the meaning and symbolic significance of risk classification and the penal subject they 'make up', and the political rationalities and strategies that underpin them (Kemshall 2003, p. 62). Working in this vein, Mythen and Walklate (2006), for example, are concerned with how the political debate about terrorism is constructed. They argue that distinct understandings about the nature of 'new terrorism' have been created and that these impact on both public opinion and the formation of domestic and international security policy. Their analysis of public discourse in the United Kingdom demonstrates that the communication of the terrorist threat has been ambiguous, patchy and ill-conceived. Government advisories individualise the risk of attack by focusing on the functions and responsibilities of citizens rather than the security duties of the state. Through these processes of 'responsibilisation', the general climate of uncertainty is exacerbated and more repressive legal responses are made a socially acceptable possibility. Taking the United States as a case in point, Altheide (2006) paints a similar picture by arguing that public acceptance of government action taken to combat terrorism has been influenced by public discourse—entertainment media content and media logic—about crime and fear. He focuses on cultural and mass communication contexts that have promoted fear of crime on the one hand while also justifying harsh and even illegal state actions to combat crime—and now terrorism—on the other. He demonstrates how current media practices contribute to a discourse of fear and symbolic negation of the 'other' as criminal or terrorist, and to the process of valorising criminal conduct (on the part of authorities) as necessary and heroic.

This argument turns on Beck's (1992) claim that there is a cultural focus in late capitalism on avoiding 'bads' rather acquiring 'goods'. In recent years the 'bads' highlighted by Beck (1992) have captured the attention of politicians, the public and the media, raising public sensitivity to risk. In this context, risk has become an increasingly important driver of policy for the state, private business and non-government organisations. Nowhere is the significance of the idea of risk more apparent than in the current raft of policy initiatives designed to combat terrorism. Since 9/11 a string of high-profile incidents around the world—Madrid, Bali, London, Mumbai—have redefined terrorism as one of the most pressing governmental issues of the day. Mythen and Walklate (2006) propose that the idea of new terrorism is central here because it is used by commentators to distinguish between the activities of radical Islamic networks and the operations of traditional terrorist groups. They acknowledge that while there is much debate about the social significance of this apparent reconfiguration, as far as political rhetoric is concerned, since 9/11 it has nevertheless underpinned the directive to 'think security'. As Beck (2001) suggests, 'what is politically crucial is ultimately not the risk itself but the perception of risk. What men fear to be real is real in its consequences—fear creates its own reality'. It is important to acknowledge that the effect of the command to 'think security' is not only ideological and symbolic.

The prevailing discourse of insecurity has justified political decisions that have material effects, including increased spending on security (whether we are talking about the United States, United Kingdom or Australia), legislation, intelligence and policing and public campaigns. Communicating risk to the public has become more and more central to the everyday functioning of the state; through this process, fear can be effectively harnessed as political capital.

The media play an important role in influencing and shaping public perceptions of crime risks and now the risk of terrorist attack. The promotion of certain issues by the media can help set the agenda on a given issue and hence magnify or allay a sense of danger. The news media are dependent on eye-catching and sensational events, and often report on crises that appeal to both base instincts and a shared sense of morality. Mythen and Walklate (2006) argue that while different media forms will convey messages in different ways, there is a visible moral dimension at play in dominant representations of the terrorist risk. The narrative framing of the terrorist threat has acted as a means for establishing 'mass endorsement of morality'. In short, they propose that terrorist attacks are given meaning though cultural, political, economic and social processes. Public responses to terrorism are shaped not solely by the nature of the emergency, but also by pre-existing assumptions underlying cultural values and political attitudes. The capacity of the mass media to appeal to emotions and moral notions of what a decent society should look like should not be understated. The politically loaded discursive construction of a terrorist 'other' pictured and framed through the lens of Anglo-American political elites is easily identified in news media and popular culture (see Poynting 2004 for Australian examples). Following the political line, dominant media representations of radical Islam have been dehumanising and demonising, encouraging the public to accept separation between rational Western citizens and a monstrous terrorist other. This is a reductivist separation between good and evil.

The promotion of this either/or reasoning has consequences for attitudes towards human rights and civil responsibilities: the balancing of rights has gone; the only rights that matter for most people are the safety rights of selves and loved ones. 'The sense of shared risk, shared responsibility has also gone: we cope with risk by a constant scanning of all with whom we come into contact to see whether or not they pose a threat to our security, and the only way we achieve this is by adopting stereotypes of safe and risky kinds of people' (Hudson 2003b, p. 74). The amplification of difference works against rational attempts to understand the values, objectives and/or grievances of terrorists (as Roberts 2005 suggests) and instead reduces the terrorist to an inhuman object we can hate. The presentation of the terrorist as unapproachable and ultra deviant fits into a wider framework where moral judgments are decided and retributive consequences delivered. Hudson explains this type of response using Garland's (1996; 2001) idea of expressive punitivism and its relationship to 'criminologies of the other'. Expressive punitivism is exemplified in the insistence of politicians in the face of failure to curb crime or to stop to terrorism so that the state can protect its citizens that what is needed is a more forceful state-centred approach: harsher penalties, more police and more prisons. This approach relies on notions of essentialised difference that represents criminals/terrorists as dangerous members of distinct racial and social groups that bear little resemblance to 'us'. It trades in images, archetypes and anxieties. Offenders are described as evil and wicked, they are suitable enemies for whom we can have no sympathy and for whom there is no effective help. The only practical rational response is to have them 'taken out of circulation'—to remove them or to lock them up (Bull and Craig 2006).

Mythen and Walklate (2006) draw this general observation back to the functions of government, highlighting how such 'criminologies of the other' find their place within what Beck has called the surveillance state, a body politically dominated by military and security concerns. The surveillance state is one that follows strict immigration procedures, polices its borders zealously and does not discourage xenophobia. This mindset underpins the possibility of the extension of the state's coercive powers. The promise of safety for us all lies at the root of the state's ability to turn increasingly compromising liberal understandings of freedom into the neoliberal notions of surveillance that Innes (2001) has described as 'control creep'. Control creep is apparent in a number of different ways, including the extension of legislative powers.

CONCLUSION

Australia has seen the introduction of wide-ranging anti-terrorist legislation since the destruction of the twin towers of the World Trade Center in New York on 11 September 2001. Some of the most controversial aspects of this governmental response include the very broad definition of offences and the powers to act pre-emptively by arresting people before they have formed a definite plan to commit a criminal act. With the intention of using the law 'as both a sword and shield', ASIO was granted new powers, allowing for preventive detention that extends even to non-suspects; and the implementation of control orders allows the AFP to monitor and restrict the activities of people who pose a terrorist risk without having to wait to see whether the risk materialises. These new responses have been the subject of criticism, particularly as historically public confidence in decision-making, in the intelligence on which that decision-making is based, respect for the rule of law and a willingness to address some of the problems that have contributed to the emergence of terrorism have been important in preventing it.

The strength of the new responses communicates censure and blame to society—but not necessarily to the suspects and non-suspects subjected to them. At a more pragmatic level such provisions, based on the 'precautionary principle', are clearly concerned with incapacitation, which has in the past been reserved for 'dangerous offenders, career criminals or other persistent offenders'. Incapacitation is hard to support even when there is a history of offending; in the context of terrorist activity, and suspected or predicted activity more specifically, the justification of such a response remains problematic. Incapacitation might be justified as prevention, but the harshness of the response executed in the context of the 'war on terror' is not consistent with just deserts principles that have been characteristic of sentencing reforms in the late twentieth and early twenty-first centuries.

Durkheim encourages us to see punishment as an emotional reaction that works to maintain social solidarity. In the political context of terrorism the new legislation can easily be positioned as an expression of vengeance, as a response to those who stand outside the *conscience collective*. Mary Douglas' work on risk develops from Durkheim's explanation of the relations between crime and the *conscience collective*. She draws attention to the implications of political judgments that are made about the relationship between the idea of risk and the structure of institutional authority, noting the role of the idea of risk in societal conversations about morality and identity. Douglas argues that political cultures select problems for attention and identify certain images of threatening people and situations. From this perspective risk is socially constructed. Communicating risk to the public has become a central function of the state; and fear is harnessed as political capital (Beck 2001).

This chapter described how the public acceptance of government action taken to combat terrorism has been influenced by public discourses about risk and fear. Public responses to terrorism are shaped not solely by the nature of the emergency but by the assumptions underlying cultural values and political attitudes. Thus the mass media appeals to emotions and moral notions of what a decent society should be. The political construction of a dangerous terrorist 'other' as different from 'us' is easily identified in news media and popular culture. For example, dominant media representations of radical Islam have been dehumanising, promoting the acceptance of a separation between rational Western citizens and a monstrous terrorist other. This approach amounts to a reductivist separation between good and evil. It relies on notions of essentialised difference representing terrorists as dangerous members of distinct racial and social groups that bear little resemblance to 'us'. This way of thinking allows for the possibility of extending of the state's coercive powers. By promising safety for us all, and protecting 'us' from the 'other', the state is able to transform increasing compromised liberal understandings of freedom into neoliberal notions of surveillance.

Rehabilitation

PART 3

6

Drug courts: Clinic or panopticon?

INTRODUCTION

Foucault's work on governmentality makes a distinction between discipline and security. At the heart of the idea of rehabilitation, discipline targets individuals who are to be socialised or reformed, whereas security addresses itself to the population (Gordon 1991, p. 20). Security works through the identification of common risks and the provision of shared solutions. The main strategies for dealing with risks that people pose and face in common work on actuarial principles that place people into categories and estimate the riskiness of these groups, rather than looking at individuals as unique cases and trying to reform them. The chapters in the previous section on risk focused on the role of these techniques in relation to responding to particular types of offenders: sex offenders who target children and suspected terrorists (and others who may only be linked to terrorist activities). The punitive interventions described, including incapacitation through detention and curfews, were justified by a preventive rationale. In this next section, prevention remains a driving force; however, it is achieved by different means. Here we explore the influence of rehabilitation—practices that are focused on changing the individual (or getting individuals to change themselves). This usually requires a range of sentences and facilities designed to offer various programs of treatment. Sometimes the focus is on the modification of attitudes and behavioural problems; alternatively, the objective may be to provide education or skills that might enable offenders to find occupations other than crime. The crucial consideration is the perceived needs of the offender rather than the gravity of the offence committed. In the next three chapters, we will explore examples of this style of offender-focused program of punishment and sentencing in three recent justice innovations: drug courts, Indigenous courts, and domestic violence courts.

Chapter 1 described a recent trend towards punitivism marked by greatly increased rates of imprisonment throughout the industrialised world (Garland 2001). One of the characteristics of this is the proportion of people whose imprisonment is linked to their use of illicit drugs; for example, some estimates indicate that as many as 80 per cent of those currently held in Australian prisons report the use of illegal drugs (Makkai and Payne 2003). While the relationship between drug use and crime remains unclear (see Makkai 1999), it is apparent that punitive responses alone have been unsuccessful in reducing illegal drug use. Moreover, they impact in negative ways on the lives of offenders who have drug problems. With significant numbers of drug-related crimes and disillusionment with traditional criminal justice approaches to drug-using offenders, there has been renewed interest in Australia, and elsewhere in the world, in programs that divert drug-dependent offenders from the criminal justice system into education and treatment programs. This trend is based on the view that these types of intervention are more effective than punishment in achieving behavioural change (Murphy 2000; Walker 2001). The range of diversionary approaches for drug offenders includes police arrest, referral and court-based pre- and post-plea schemes. While examples of each of these are operating in Australian jurisdictions, this chapter focuses on the role that drug courts have come to play in Australia's criminal justice system and the types of punishment they deliver. It begins by describing the factors underlying the development of drug courts and then reviews how they work. The concluding parts of the chapter consider whether drug court practices are consistent with principles of punishment and how they work to achieve these ends.

ALTERNATIVE STRATEGIES IN THE UNWINNABLE 'WAR ON DRUGS'

Responding to drug-related crimes by diverting offenders into treatment is not new. In the United States, such strategies have been applied throughout the twentieth century, beginning with morphine maintenance clinics during the 1920s; the establishment of federal narcotics treatment facilities in Fort Worth, Texas, and Lexington, Kentucky, in the 1960s; broad-based civil commitment procedures in the 1960s; and the introduction of community-based treatment as an alternative to incarceration or as a condition of probation or parole in the 1970s (Anglin et al. 1999). The more recent innovation is specialised drug treatment courts built on this latter scheme, with the first court serving Miami Dade County, Florida, in 1989 (Nolan 2001). Drug courts arose within the context of the multiple efforts at all government levels—federal, state and local—to carry out a 'war on drugs' in the 1980s. In the face of the crack cocaine epidemic and growing public concern, a zero-tolerance response to drug offences was expressed through federal and state legislation that substantially reduced judicial discretion in the sentencing of offenders convicted of drug-related offences. This placed a heavy burden on both state and federal courts by subjecting more individuals to arrest and prosecution. This overloaded both existing court dockets and federal and state correctional systems by increasing prison and jail populations beyond capacity. According to the Bureau of Justice Statistics (BJS), the number of adults arrested for drug-related violations increased 273 per cent between 1980 and 1995, from 471 200 to 1 285 700 (BJS 1997b in Burdon et al. 2001).

Some jurisdictions' attempts to alleviate the saturated court systems and overcrowded prisons and jails took the form of specialised drug courts that focused primarily on improving case flow management to expedite the processing of the large volume of drug cases (Goldkamp 1994). The experience of those early efforts made it clear that, without treatment interventions, many offenders would simply recycle through the system, albeit more quickly. Some of these courts began integrating drug treatment into the criminal justice process. The first drug 'treatment' court 'established itself as an integral part of the treatment process' (Goldkamp 1994, p. 110). This was accomplished by identifying drug-dependent offenders early in the adjudication process, and offering them immediate access to treatment under the direction and close supervision of the judge as an alternative to jail or prison. Within a non-adversarial atmosphere, this alternative brought together judges, prosecutors, defence attorneys, probation officers and community-based treatment providers in a collaborative effort to reduce illicit drug use and related criminal behaviour and, secondarily, to reduce the increasing burden on the courts. The approach adopted in Miami Dade County, Florida, became the model, with local variations for similar drug-treatment courts established elsewhere in the United States and throughout the world.

The primary goals of drug courts are to:

- reduce drug use and associated criminal behaviour by engaging and retaining drug-involved offenders in treatment and related services
- concentrate expertise about drug cases into a single courtroom
- address other defendant needs through clinical assessment and effective case management
- provide free judicial, prosecutorial and public defence resources for adjudicating non-drug cases.

The key components of drug courts typically include:

- judicial supervision of structured community-based treatment
- a dedicated courtroom reserved for drug court participants
- the timely identification of defendants in need of treatment and referral to treatment as soon as possible after arrest
- regular status hearings before a judicial officer to monitor treatment progress and program compliance
- increasing defendant accountability through a series of graduated sanctions and rewards
- mandatory periodic or random drug testing
- the establishment of specific treatment-program requirements, with compliance monitored by a judicial officer
- the dismissal of the case or a reduced sentence on successful treatment completion.

The drug court offers drug offenders the option of court-monitored treatment as an alternative to the normal adjudication process and prison. Defendants participate in various treatment modalities; submit to periodic urine analysis; and regularly (every one to four weeks) report back to the judge who oversees their overall treatment program. The program is usually expected to last one year but can last much longer (Bull 2003).

In the United States, judges reward participants who succeed in the program (for example, graduating to a higher level—there may be as many as three or four stages of treatment) with praise, applause and prizes. Small incentives for good performance may include T-shirts, key chains, donuts, pens, mugs, coloured star stickers and sweets. Graduation ceremonies are celebrated with cake, speeches, graduation certificates, individual testimonies by graduates and visits from politicians and other local dignitaries.

Failure to comply with treatment can result in the imposition of sanctions that may come in the form of increased participation in twelve step groups (like Narcotics Anonymous), community service, one or two days sitting in the jury box during drug court sessions, or short stints (of several days to two weeks) in the county jail (Nolan 2001). As an incentive for participation, most drug courts offer defendants the dismissal of their criminal charge or the expungement of their drug arrest on successful completion of the program.

THE AUSTRALIAN ALLIANCE

In Australia, the diversion of drug-related offenders has also been practised both formally and informally for some years; however, it was the introduction of a new illicit drug strategy by the Council of Australian Governments (COAG) in April 1999 that first aimed to establish a nationally consistent diversion initiative (Commonwealth Department of Health and Ageing 2001). In response to their particular local priorities and conditions, the states have since implemented a range of diversionary programs that differ significantly, despite COAG's desire for consistency. An Australian Bureau of Criminal Intelligence report (cited in Swain 1999) identified five distinct types of diversion practices: informal police diversion, formal police diversion, statutory diversion, prosecutorial diversion and judicial diversion. The programs vary in the offender profile targeted, the degree of intervention or supervision offered, the treatment or form of intervention offered and the stage of the prosecution process at which offenders are recruited into the diversion process (Lawrence and Freeman 2002). Currently, diversion programs for drug offenders are being run in every state for cannabis and other drug offences. These programs operate at both the police and non-police (that is, between charging and jailing) levels and range from well-developed and documented schemes supported by legislation through to informal local arrangements between police, alcohol and drug workers and the courts. Offenders targeted by these programs include: those facing use and possession charges; those whose use has led to offences while intoxicated; and those who have committed offences to support their drug taking (Alcohol and Other Drugs Council of Australia 2000).

Court diversion programs are available in all states. In contrast to much shorter twelve-week bail-based programs, like CREDIT (Court Referral and Evaluation for Drug Intervention and Treatment) or MERIT (Magistrates Early Referral into Treatment), specialised drug courts operate as an alternative to imprisonment and are available in Queensland, New South Wales, Victoria, South Australia, Western Australia and Tasmania; however, they are not available in all parts of these jurisdictions. For example, in New South Wales there is only one drug court that works out of the Parramatta District Court; there is also a youth drug court (working out of Campbelltown Children's Court, Bidura Children's Court and Cobham Children's Court). Queensland has the most extensive provision of this type of service, with courts operating part-time (one to two days a week) in the magistrates' courts of Ipswich, Beenleigh and Southport in the south-eastern metropolitan area and in Townsville and Cairns in the north of the state. Tasmania, Victoria, South Australia and Western Australia have limited editions operating in their metropolitan areas. The Queensland and New South Wales programs are distinctive because they are explicitly defined and provided for in legislation: *Drug Court Act 1998* (NSW) and *Drug Rehabilitation (Court Diversion) Act 2000* (Qld).

The NSW drug court was the first to begin operation in Australia in 1999. It targeted drug-dependent adult offenders who were facing a custodial sentence using 'the threat of imprisonment as an incentive for treatment entry and the fear of return to prison as a reason for complying with drug treatment while on parole or probation' (NSW Hansard 27/10/1998, p. 9031 in Taplin 2002, p. 1). It is based on the models that have been operating in the United States, as described above. A 1999 review of NSW drug court procedures outlined ten components of the US drug courts that were applied by the NSW court. They included:

○ Treatment is integrated into the criminal justice system.
○ Prosecution and defence lawyers work together as part of a drug court team.
○ Eligible offenders are identified early.
○ Participants have access to a continuum of quality treatment and rehabilitation services that meet their health needs.
○ Participants are frequently monitored for illicit drug use.
○ Any non-compliance by a participant results in a swift and certain sanction by the court.
○ There is ongoing judicial supervision and regular judicial interaction with each participant.
○ An evaluation of the rehabilitation outcomes achieved through the drug court.
○ The drug court team and others associated with the court receive ongoing interdisciplinary education.
○ Networks are forged with other drug courts, law enforcement authorities, public bodies, treatment providers and the community. (NSW Drug Court 1999a, point 3.10 in Talpin 2002, p. 8)

The NSW edition differs from the US courts in a number of ways:

○ A higher proportion of NSW drug court participants are dependent on heroin than in US drug courts, where there is greater usage of amphetamines and cocaine.

○ In New South Wales the target criminal population is at the higher end of criminality than in the United States (NSW Drug Court 1999a in Taplin 2002).

○ Most drug courts in the United States are abstinence-based; however, the NSW court provides a range of treatment options, including methadone and naltrexone.

○ The NSW court limits the use of material rewards (Taplin 2002).

Offenders appearing before both the local and district courts can be referred to the NSW drug court. Eligibility criteria are clearly laid out in section 5 of the *Drug Court Act 1998* (NSW). To participate, an individual must:

○ be charged with an offence under the jurisdiction of the local and district courts, excluding charges of physical violence, sexual assault or drug trafficking

○ be dependent on illicit drugs

○ be willing to plead guilty to the offence for which they have been charged

○ be highly likely to be sentenced to full-time imprisonment

○ be willing to participate in the drug court

○ be a resident of the area in which the court operates

○ not be suffering from any mental condition that could prevent or restrict their active participation in the program (Lind et al. 2002, pp. 7–8). (Similar provisions exist in the Queensland legislation.)

However, access to the program can be limited by the availability of beds in the Detoxification Unit, where a preliminary health assessment stage is conducted before offenders are accepted, or by the availability of facilities (like treatment places) for their continuing participation.

Three types of treatment programs are available to participants: abstinence-based programs or pharmacotherapy involving methadone or naltrexone. Each of these can be undertaken in either the community or a residential treatment environment. The drug court team[3] has a clearly defined policy for matching treatment to offenders (see Taplin 2002, p. 17). There is a list of specific agencies that can be involved in the provision of services to offenders, including gender-specific services or agencies that accept both men and women. Some of these programs accept participants with their children, though most do not. Those who undertake a community-based treatment program must satisfy the drug court team that their place of residence is suitable. The court has a policy that describes what is considered unsuitable residential accommodation (see Taplin 2002, p. 18).

The drug court program has three phases: initiation and stabilisation, consolidation and early reintegration, and final reintegration. Each has its own specific goals and associated restrictions and requirements. The degree of judicial

---

3 The NSW drug court team includes the judge, judge's associate, a registrar and other officers for the administration of the Act, two solicitors for the DPP, solicitors from the Legal Aid Commission, a police inspector, two probation and parole coordinators (representing case managers), and a nurse manager from Corrections Health Service (representing treatment providers).

supervision decreases as participants progress through the phases. Program participants must maintain contact with their case manager and participate in regular home visits. They are required to attend counselling and day programs on topics covering social and lifestyle issues, such as financial planning, parenting, nutrition, oral hygiene and smoking. They must also provide a minimum of two supervised urine samples per week either at the court registry, their treatment provider or the mobile drug court urinalysis (drug testing) bus. Individuals are terminated from the program when they successfully complete the program, on their own request or if the drug court decides to terminate the program. The criteria for termination are clearly laid out in policy. Participants must be drug-free for six months prior to graduation. As with the US drug courts, clearly defined sanctions are an integral part of the program and are used to ensure that participants comply with the conditions.

The needs of certain population groups are not always well addressed (Bull 2003; Payne 2005). Taplin (2002) identified a failure in the planning phase of the NSW program to anticipate the high proportion of participants experiencing multiple health problems, most notably mental health problems. As a result, the needs and management of participants with mental health problems were poorly addressed. Aboriginal offenders have been disproportionately excluded from entry into the program because of their 'antecedents' or having committed some 'violent' offence in the past under s7(2) of the *Drug Court Act 1998* (NSW). The facilities and services available to women are of a poorer standard than those available for men. Evaluations have also noted that the level of activity required by the drug court program resulted in difficulties for participants with the primary responsibility for childcare (Payne 2005, p. 77; Taplin 2002), most of whom were women. The intensity of the program also placed limits on participation in employment.

The level of intervention and supervision described in process evaluations is very intensive. Some service providers see this degree of intensity as a positive aspect. One explained that 'the intensity of the whole package and the resources and time being put into them, the feeling that someone cares about them is a major advantage' (in Taplin 2002, p. 80), while others thought that it was 'unethical and harmful to the participants to provide so many resources and support when they are on the drug court program, then suddenly take it away', explaining that 'some fall apart when they leave and there is a sudden withdrawal of services' (Taplin 2002, p. 60). Similar views have been expressed by probation and parole case managers who explained that once supervision stops, participants often cannot maintain the changes (Taplin 2002, p. 60). These views highlight the importance of additional follow-up and aftercare for those who complete or leave the program, as the removal of intensive supervision was often associated with the likelihood of relapse to drug use and associated recidivism. Other positive aspects of the program include the ability of participants to change the type of drug treatment they were receiving, and the intersectoral approach that led to some breaking down of barriers between professions and a better way of dealing with drug-dependent offenders. On the less positive side, the criteria for graduation were considered to be too onerous, resulting in a small number of graduates from the program (Taplin 2002) or unusually long sentences as relapsing participants were repeatedly returned to stage one of the program with each offending event. The drug court program is ideally a twelve- to eighteen-month commitment; however, for some participants, it has lasted much longer—up to three years in some cases (Bull 2005; Payne 2005). Sentences have an indeterminate aspect as participants are only able to graduate when they have had a sustained period (six months) free of drugs and crime, and when they are able to demonstrate sufficient social support and resilience.

PENOLOGICAL PRINCIPLES: JUST TREATMENT OR PREVENTIVE PUNISHMENT?

The principle of rehabilitation in sentencing is based on utilitarian philosophy that is forward looking and concerned with the consequences or outcome of punishment (Ashworth 2005). The aim is to achieve the prevention of crime through the rehabilitation of the offender. This is clearly an objective of drug courts that offer a range of court-monitored programs of treatment. Through regular and graduated judicial monitoring, the court itself is directly involved in attempts to modify the attitudes and behaviour of those appearing before it. These efforts are augmented through programs providing education or skills. A crucial consideration is the perceived needs of the offender. A key element in determining those needs is a report from an expert—for example, a pre-sentence report prepared by a correctional officer or, occasionally, a mental health assessment. The drug court team then decides on the treatment that matches the perceived needs of the offender. Sentencing is clearly informed by the social sciences demonstrating a link with forms of positivist criminology that locate the causes of criminality in individual pathology or maladjustment, whether psychiatric, psychological or social. The operation of the rehabilitative model has led to sentences that are indeterminate, on the basis that a person should only be released from obligations when, in the opinion of the experts, a cure had been effected. This tendency is reflected in criticisms that drug court sentences, despite their altruistic intent, can be longer and more onerous that those traditionally applied for a similar offence (Indermaur and Roberts 2003; Roberts and Indermaur 2006).

In recent years, managerialism has become an influence on punishment and sentencing, expressed through concerns for economy, efficiency and effectiveness. The introduction of the first drug courts in the United States was driven by this preoccupation: their initial focus was simply on improving case flow management to expedite the processing of the large volume of drug cases. The outcome was greater efficiency; and offenders were recycled through the system more quickly. Some of these courts, such as the one in Miami Dade County, Florida, in 1989, began integrating drug treatment into the criminal justice process. This change reflects a managerialist concern with systems (see Bottoms in Chapter 2, p. 36) promoted by inter-agency cooperation. Partnering agencies in drug courts create and actively monitor information about the system and its function, paying particular attention to key performance indicators that measure efficiency and effectiveness in terms of managerial standards. One result of Bottoms' 'systemic' dimension of managerialism can be that, within criminal justice systems, 'increasing primacy [is] given to the efficient control of internal system processes' (Feeley and Simon 1992, p. 450). Concentration on such matters can even, in some cases, result in the displacement of more traditional 'external' objectives, such as the reduction of reoffending. In the case of drug courts (and programs diverting offenders from the criminal justice system more generally), this is evident in the early proliferation of program evaluations focused on process rather than outcomes in terms of recidivism (Bull 2003; Hales et al. 2004; Hughes and Ritter 2008).

Indeed, drug treatment courts continue to be a controversial addition to the criminal justice system because there is a lack of clear empirical evidence that they are effective in reducing crime (another demand of the managerialist trend) (Hughes and Ritter 2008; Lawrence and Freeman 2002; Spooner et al. 2001). While some positive outcomes are evident in evaluations, advocates tend to base their support for these programs on the view that 'treatment is more effective than punishment in achieving behaviour change' (Murphy 2000; Walker 2001). They explain that the court is founded on the principle of therapeutic jurisprudence. This relatively new legal concept was originally described by Wexler and Winick (1991) as the extent to which substantive rules, legal procedures, and the roles of lawyers and judges produce therapeutic or anti-therapeutic consequences for individuals involved in the legal process. Recently, this definition has been expanded to acknowledge the relationship between the practice of therapeutic jurisprudence and knowledge derived from social sciences (Goldberg 2005).

Drug treatment courts provide a distinct forum for the application of this principle (Hora et al. 1999; Senjo and Leip 2001). According to Tauber (1999), the therapeutic orientation of drug courts requires that the traditional adversarial approach of court procedures be replaced by a collaborative style of case management. For this to be effective, the judge, prosecution, defence counsel, drug treatment providers and probation representative must work as a team to monitor the treatment process of each offender to help them change their drug usage and criminal behaviour. This practice creates new roles for judges, prosecutors and defence counsel; they must work together to apply 'smart punishment' to offenders rather than punishment for the sake of retribution (Tauber 1999).

The drug court alters the traditional adjudication process. The judge engages the clients directly, asks personal questions and encourages them in the treatment process. In many ways, judges take on the role of the therapist. The role of the public defender and the prosecutor is no longer adversarial, and lawyers generally play a less prominent role. The primary objective of drug courts is to reduce drug abuse and associated criminal activity. Tauber (1994, p. 2 in Nolan 2001) explains that successful drug courts are 'based on an understanding of the physiological, psychological and behavioural realities of drug abuse and are designed and implemented with those realities in mind'. How drug courts are implemented and the exact shape they take vary among different jurisdictions (Hughes and Ritter 2008). The design of each drug court is a function of the unique set of circumstances that exists within each jurisdiction—the characteristics of the drug-involved criminal justice population being served; the available resources of the community to support the existence and operation of the drug court; and the unique characteristics of the judge (Huddleston 1998).

THINKING THEORETICALLY: THE PANOPTICON AND BEYOND

The 'human' sciences and adjudication of correction

In *Discipline and Punish*, Foucault (1977) examines the rise of the prison in the nineteenth century, arguing that this was associated with a qualitative shift in the form of punishment. The objective of punishment was less to avenge the crime than to transform the criminal. The new concern was to know the criminal, to understand the sources of criminality and to intervene to correct him, or her, wherever possible. The focus of judgment moved away from the offence itself and towards an assessment of the individual (Foucault 1990). Various experts are employed to provide this knowledge, identify abnormalities and help bring about reformation. The result of these changes is a system of dealing with offenders that is not so much punitive as corrective and is more intent on producing normal, conforming individuals than on dispensing punishment and penalties. It is easy to argue that the characteristics Foucault links to the rise of the prison in the nineteenth century have traction in the drug court today. In drug courts, offenders, their particular biography and capacity for correction, rather than the offence, is the focus of judgment. Indeed, because entry into the program relies on a guilty plea, no time at all is spent considering whether the offender (often referred to as a participant or client, suggesting a voluntary aspect) is innocent or not. The initial concern is with their capacity to 'actively participate' in the program. The drug court team advises on matters of health, social well-being and possible recidivism, explicitly illustrating expert intervention through the human sciences.

Foucault (1977) sketched out how imprisonment as a form of punishment worked through power relations based on detailed knowledge of offenders, routine intervention and correction. He explained that these disciplinary arrangements rely on normalisation, which involves a means of assessing an individual's performance in relation to a desired standard of conduct. Surveillance arrangements, case records and examination procedures provide this knowledge, allowing non-conformity to be identified and dealt with. Since the object is to correct rather than to punish, the actual sanctions tend to involve exercises and training; measures themselves that help bring conduct into line and make individuals more self-controlled. The human sciences are bound up in this process of normalisation since they are only made possible by the production of detailed, systematic knowledge about individuals and, in their turn, are made to contribute to the normalising power and control that is exercised over individuals (1977, pp. 107–95). Jeremy Bentham's panopticon (see Chapter 2, p. 24–5) is the archetype of these power–knowledge principles. Foucault (1977, pp. 205–6) sees it not just as the prototype for prisons but for all institutions that implement regimes of surveillance and discipline.

The daily operation of the drug court relies on a broad array of practices. Principal among these are panoptic techniques that have the potential to make the behaviour of participants visible, even when there are not the resources or will to track every movement and action. As Queensland Magistrate John Costanzo explained:

> The drug court program was designed recognising the target group needed a continuum of supervision … The program combines court processes with local drug, health and mental health services, specifically funded residential and outpatient rehabilitation services, housing, employment and other services … Key features which link together the elements of this continuum are frequent random drug testing and the incorporation of court monitoring and reviews in each offender's rehabilitation program. (Costanzo 2003, p. 3)

Drug court treatment orders contain provisions in relation to place of residence; these are sometimes accompanied by curfews or specific conditions in relation to social interaction. For example, the undertaking that participants in the NSW program sign as a behavioural contract while in the program stipulates that during the first month of the program they must be at their place of residence between 7 p.m. and 7 a.m. each day, unless they have approval to be absent. A key component of an order is regular judicial review, which consists of weekly court appearances in phase one, extending to two weekly appearances as a result of reward for compliance and/or graduation to phase two, and monthly in phase three.

Drug testing, which involves observed urinalysis, is considered to be key (Costanzo 2003). Policy documents and protocols explain that there is an agreed plan for drug testing that requires that unless the court otherwise orders or a case manager directs, defendants are to be tested a minimum of twice weekly during phase one, once a week during phase two and twice fortnightly during phase three. The *Drug Rehabilitation (Court Diversion) Act 2000* (Qld) also provides that participants may be required by their case manger to report for further random testing. The literature on drug testing through urinalysis indicates that it is most effective when randomly delivered and observed (Ward et al. 1992). To facilitate random testing, all participants are required to be able to be contacted between 7 a.m. and 8 a.m. every day of the week. They must be prepared to report for a urine test or receive a home visit from a mobile drug-testing van

(Costanzo 2003). Besides urinalysis, participants have regular appointments with Queensland Health counsellors and Community Corrections case managers. Phase one participants have twice-weekly case manager contact, at court where directed, or receive visits. In phases two and three, these contacts are reduced to fortnightly. Participants are to be available for home visits when required. Beyond this, they must participate in treatment, service providers report to case managers who then report to the drug court team regarding compliance, confirming course attendance. Compliance with their program involves restitution through financial payment based on their income or community service. Participants also report on their attendance at a range of other courses—life skills, personal development, educational and vocational and parenting and/or anger management where considered necessary[4].

These aspects of the drug court program can be understood as contemporary examples of practices of normalising discipline (Foucault 1977). They work together in a panoptic way: regulating individuals enrolled in the program through techniques of surveillance, examination and the normalising judgment (Bull 2008). Once enrolled in the drug court program, the participant must routinely attend court appearances and other appointments at designated times. The possibility of random urine testing and home visits (if not in residential treatment) adds to this potential visibility, by both tracking movement and making hidden drug use visible. In an assessment of the Canadian drug courts, Fischer (2003) described these processes as 'holistic disciplining' through a corresponding comprehensive and pervasive system of behaviour surveillance and correction.

> Urine tests, weekly court appearances and comprehensive 'performance updates' from treatment counsellors and probation staff, as well as regular performance reports by the offender themselves to the court function as a panopticon-like 'gaze' into the subject's everyday life, triggering the described corrective interventions where norm-breaking occurs.

He argues that:

> … while traditional or explicit forms of punishment may have disappeared as the primary form of intervention, the drug treatment court (DTC) presents an instructive illustration of a dispersed yet comprehensive and pervasive regime of behavioural 'discipline' acting upon the offender from many sides … As such, the DTC may be viewed as a microcosm of late modern governmentality, in which singular expressions of punishment have been replaced with a dispersed regime of disciplinary tools and technology. (Fischer 2003, p. 237)

---

4   In Queensland the core programs may include programs about: substance abuse education, cognitive skills development, anger management, relapse prevention and ending offending. Elective programs may include programs about: domestic violence, good parenting practices and relationships, grief loss, post-traumatic stress disorder, sexual abuse, financial or other counselling. The health programs may include detoxification, methadone maintenance, naltrexone or buprenorphine, drug counselling, live-in rehabilitation or residential treatment, attendance at AA or NA, the TripleP Positive Parenting Program, and the dual diagnosis program for mental health and substance abuse (Phase I/II). The life skills program may include: cooking healthy meals on a low-income budget, budgeting, assertiveness, self-esteem and so on (Phase III).

Net widening

Cohen (1979; 1985) argued that the development of community corrections in the 1970s (see Chapter 1) marks both a continuation and an intensification of the social control patterns identified by Foucault in *Discipline and Punish* (1977). Cohen's 'dispersal of discipline' thesis insists that there is now a blurring of where prison ends and the community begins, with an accompanying increase in the total number of offenders brought into the system. Clearly this is true for the drug court, where it is promoted as an alternative to prison, and sanction for breach of a treatment order often involves time in custody. Cohen's *Visions of Social Control* (1985) provided a compelling account of the various transformations that the web of social control had undergone up to the time of his writing. He explains how it had strengthened and deepened, that there were broader nets with ever finer mesh. He described the process of net widening in terms of society as an ocean: 'vast, troubled and full of uncharted currents, rocks and other hazards' (pp. 41–2); deviants as fish who are caught and sorted and the criminal justice system as the fishing net. Net widening involves extending the reach of the criminal justice net to capture more offending 'fish'/offenders or provide more intensive processing. He differentiates between wider nets, denser nets (stronger nets) and different nets (new nets).

Net widening has been linked with a number of criminal justice system reforms: decarceration, due process, deterrence, just deserts and diversion reform movements. Austin and Krisberg (1981) point out that, theoretically, reducing the net at the points of arrest and prosecution should result in reductions in incarceration; however, in practice, it results in enlarged prison populations. Diversion effectively extends the net, making it stronger and creating new nets through the formalisation of the informal and the creation of new practices that erode due process and increase formal interventions.

Net widening can occur at different stages in the criminal justice process, depending on the nature of the diversion program. Front-end net widening happens when there is a greater level of involvement at the point of contact with the criminal system. The recruitment of program participants for drug diversion initiatives has the potential to result in wider nets in a number of ways (Roberts and Indermaur 2006). Drug courts require and depend on offenders admitting their guilt to at least some of the charges they are facing. Some, or all, charges that may otherwise have been contested then form part of the individual's official offence history. The requirement to plead guilty to qualify for diversion can lead to a fundamental aberration of justice, whereby the offender who does not plead guilty faces not only a more onerous path but also a perception by a range of criminal justice decision-makers that they are 'recalcitrant' or 'uncooperative'. Beyond this, there is a real possibility that individuals will be drawn into the criminal justice system so that they can access sometimes scarce treatment services (Payne 2005). Programs can be offered to individuals who fall outside the target group for whom the program was designed. This may happen when an offender who is not facing a sentence of imprisonment is placed on a drug court program. Roberts and Indermaur (2006, p. 223) argue that net widening occurs with the 'temptation … to reach into the vast supply of "needy" cases to provide help rather than the use of drug court as an alternative to custody'.

Back-end net widening refers to the increased likelihood of further sanctions because of technical violations arising from the greater surveillance and closer monitoring often associated with diversion. Back-end net widening in the form of denser and different nets can occur through the conditions imposed as treatment. Best practice guidelines for diversion programs recommend that treatment participation should not be disproportionately more onerous for the individual than the criminal justice alternative (Bull 2005). Net widening may occur when the conditions of diversion are more onerous than the sentence may have been. We have seen that the program may include attendance at treatment, supervisory sessions, mandatory drug testing and curfews. In addition, the length of treatment may be longer than the likely sentence. For example, the average length of time to complete the three phases of the North Queensland Drug Court is 354 days. A male offender who failed to complete the program explained that he couldn't stop thinking about how his head sentence was only four months, and that it was easier just to go to prison. Another asked to be terminated for family reasons (children), commenting that 'I would have liked to have finished, but it was taking too long' (Payne 2005, p. 77).

Alternatively, the consequences of failure to comply with treatment conditions may be more severe than traditional sentencing; that is, sanctions imposed during the course of the 'treatment' may exceed the likely sentence. Drug courts often impose imprisonment as a sanction during the treatment period. In some cases, the accumulation of sanctions of imprisonment can exceed the length of the sentence that may initially have been imposed if diversion had not occurred (Roberts and Indermaur 2006). Closer scrutiny of participants increases the likelihood of breaches of condition and results in the increased frequency of sanctions in diversion programs. Breaches for illicit drug use, for instance, are more likely to be detected when monitoring systems such as urine analysis are in place. At the time of final sentencing (drug court often involves a suspended or deferred sentence) and in addition to the original charges, failed diversion clients may face additional charges relating to breaches of treatment orders.

In the context of the criminal justice system, net widening is generally considered a negative outcome as increasing numbers of individuals are brought into contact with corrosive elements and labels. In drug diversion programs the aim is specifically to provide treatment for drug problems; from the point of view of health professionals, widening the net can be a positive outcome because it draws people into treatment, providing early intervention for drug users with the potential for avoiding or reducing subsequent pain associated with a drug-using 'career'. These opposing views reflect the tension between principles of punishment and treatment that are evident in the daily delivery of drug court diversion programs. Chan (1992) warns, however, that we should not automatically disregard the possibilities that diversionary programs offer; rather, each must be evaluated in its own right. Not every initiative constitutes a further net widening. Not all state intervention or policy implementation is necessarily oriented to negative social control. If community-oriented programs are simply criticised in total, we are left with only much harsher and socially unredeeming measures, such as prison.

Not the total institution

With this in mind it is important to remember that drug courts are used in most cases as an alternative to imprisonment. Indeed, if we consider the work of Canadian sociologist Erving Goffman (1922–1982), it is possible to identify some important differences between these diversion programs and their carceral alternative. Goffman identified a class of institution in Western societies as total institutions. Their encompassing character 'is symbolised by the barrier to social intercourse with the outside that is often built into the physical environment: locked doors, high walls, barbed wire, cliffs and water, open terrain, and so forth' (1957/1997, p. 97). He lists prisons as a key exemplar, along with mental hospitals, army barracks, boarding schools and monasteries.

In total institutions, all aspects of each inmate's life are conducted in the same place and under a single authority. Each phase of the member's daily activity is carried out en masse, with all members treated alike and required to do the same thing at the same time. Daily activities are tightly scheduled, with one activity leading at a prearranged time into the next, the whole circle of activities being imposed from above through a system of explicit formal rulings and a body of officials. Finally, the contents of the various enforced activities are brought together as parts of a single overall rational plan purportedly designed to fulfil the official aims of the institution. Because blocks of people are caused to move in time, it is possible to use a relatively small number of supervisory personnel. The central relationship of the institution is not guidance or periodic checking, but rather surveillance: ensuring that everyone does what is required, 'under conditions where one person's infraction is likely to stand out in relief against the visible, constantly examined, compliance of the others' (1961/1990, pp. 6–7). Here there is an obvious link to Foucault's assessment of the panopticon; however, Goffman argues that cultural change occurs in total institutions, not through a process of acculturation or assimilation or, as Foucault describes, the means of correct training according to accepted norms and practices of behaviour. Instead, it involves the removal of certain behavioural opportunities and the failure to keep pace with recent social changes on the outside. It is therefore more a process of disculturation—an untraining that renders inmates incapable of managing certain features of daily life on the outside if and when they get back to it.

Another important aspect of the experience of the total institution is its effect on the identity of inmates who enter the establishment with a conception of themselves made possible by certain stable social arrangements in their home environment. Once inside, they are immediately stripped of the support provided by these arrangements and are subjected to a series of abasements and degradations. Goffman calls this process the 'mortification of the self' and suggests that it involves some radical shifts in the inmates' moral career, a career composed of the progressive changes in their beliefs about themselves and significant others. If undertaken in a fairly standard manner, the process of mortification involves a loss of social roles, possessions and control over one's actions. In this way, total institutions automatically disrupt social roles since the inmates' separation from the wider world lasts around the clock and may continue for years. On release, there may be some opportunity to re-establish these relationships, but other losses are enduring. For example, it is impossible to retrieve time not spent in educational or job advancement, or rearing one's children. One of the problems of the drug-dependent lifestyle is the disconnection from the routines of everyday life. The potential for 'recovery' is said to be enhanced by social integration: maintaining connections with non-dependent others, family relationships, employment and educational opportunities. Harsh responses to drug-related offending generally result in large numbers of people ending up in prison, the effects of which exacerbate their poor life circumstances, recidivism and drug dependence. A key objective of drug court programs is therefore to establish/re-establish/maintain the offenders' connections to civil society, often through the use of personalised vocational, educational and parenting/relationship programs.

Admission to total institutions (prisons) marks a leaving-off and taking-on process. Leaving off entails a dispossession of property. This is important because people express who they are and gain a sense of themselves through their possessions. Goffman explains that one of the most significant of these possessions is not physical at all: one's full name. Once inmates are stripped of their possessions, some replacements are made by the institution; however, these take the form of standard issue—uniform in character and uniformly distributed. These substituted possessions are clearly marked as really belonging to the institution (Goffman 1961/1990, p. 28). Their name is replaced by a number or a status of 'inmate'. Inmates no longer have control over how they present themselves to others, and the ability to shape how others engage with them is severely circumscribed. These processes work to erase the unique biography of inmates, making them no different from their fellows. In contrast, drug courts are offender-focused. Participants are encouraged to take an interest in how they present themselves to court. The decisions of the drug court team theoretically acknowledge and respond to each offender's unique biography by tailoring the drug treatment orders they issue to specific needs. Participants are even asked to identify for themselves what these might be. For example, in the Queensland drug court, at the end of each phase participants are asked to identify issues for counselling. They are provided with a checklist that includes things like grief/loss; abuse, abandonment; drug and alcohol abuse; criminal issues/dishonesty; self-esteem/confidence/self-sabotage; authority/trust; specific health issues; relationship intimacy; family; gambling or other non-drug addictive behaviours; prisons/institutionalism; depression/stress, anxiety; anger; budgeting/parenting or any other relevant factor. They are instructed that:

> It is *your responsibility* to identify issues *you know you need to deal with* in counselling during your Drug Court program … The issues should be those that led to drug use, kept you in addiction or which affect your progress in life. (Queensland Department of Justice and Attorney General undated)

They are asked to prioritise the issues they identify in order of importance. Admittedly, such needs are also the subject of a range of specialist assessments and reports.

Drug courts are different from traditional courts because the magistrate or judge speaks directly to the offender (not to them through a legal representative), using their name and inviting them to respond and explain themselves and their individual situation and needs. This is another example of difference between this type of intervention and that offered by a total institution like prison. Goffman (1957/1997; 1959) sees the denial of voice as a clear-cut expression of personal inefficacy. By responding to questions in their own words, individuals can sustain the notion that they are somebody to be considered, however slightly. Inmates in the total institution are generally denied this kind of self-action. A positive aspect of the drug court frequently identified by participants in evaluations is that they were able to speak for themselves and that the magistrate or judge listened to them. Participants described this as a self-validating experience (Payne 2005).

Finally, total institutions frequently claim to be concerned with rehabilitation, resetting the inmates' self-regulatory mechanisms so that after they leave they will maintain the standards of the establishment of their own accord. This is also the aim of drug courts. Goffman makes the point that this claim of change is seldom realised in total institutions; and when permanent alteration occurs, the changes are often not of the kind intended. Neither the stripping process nor the reorganising processes seem to have desirable lasting effects. What ex-inmates do retain of their institutional experiences is nevertheless important: Goffman highlights the impact of its stigmatising and life limiting effects. Total institutions disrupt or destroy actions that have the role in civil society of confirming to actors and those in their presence that they have some command over their world— that they possess 'adult' self-determination, autonomy and freedom of action. Diversion generally, and drug courts in particular, provide an opportunity for participants to avoid such negative effects. Whether or not participants are able to overcome what often amounts to a lifetime of stigma and limitations so often linked with a career of dependent drug use is another matter.

CONCLUSION

In this chapter we have seen how drug treatment courts initially emerged in the United States as a managerialist response to overloaded court dockets, resulting from the harsh penalties prescribed by 'the war on drugs'. While offenders cycled through the system with expedited efficiency, it quickly became clear that dedicated courts alone were no solution to the problem of drug-related offending. The alternative that emerged significantly challenged traditional norms of judicial practice. Treatment was integrated into the criminal justice system and the court itself became a therapeutic domain. Prosecution and defence lawyers swapped their role as adversaries to become part of a multidisciplinary team. Eligible offenders were provided access to a broad continuum of treatment. Illicit drug use was routinely monitored, with non-compliance resulting in swift and certain sanctions by the court. A key difference was ongoing judicial supervision and regular and personalised judicial interaction with each participant.

Drug treatment courts were a controversial addition to the criminal justice system. Supporters based their advocacy for them on the view that 'treatment is more effective than punishment in achieving behaviour change' (Murphy 2000, Walker 2001), explaining that the court is founded on the principle of therapeutic jurisprudence — or the extent to which substantive rules, legal procedures, and the roles of lawyers and judges produce therapeutic or anti-therapeutic consequences for individuals involved in the legal process. The practice of therapeutic jurisprudence in drug courts is shaped by knowledge derived from social sciences. Successful courts are said to understand 'the physiological, psychological and behavioural realities of drug abuse and are designed and implemented with those realities in mind' (Tauber 1994, p. 2 in Nolan 2001).

The influence of the social sciences is a contemporary indicator of the durability of the Lomborsian project and the continuing relevance of positivist criminology (Garland 1991). The characteristics that Foucault links to the rise of the prison in the nineteenth century are evident in the drug court, where offenders and their specific biography and capacity for correction and change, rather than the offence, are the focus of judgment. Entry into the program relies on an admission of guilt and an assessment of their capacity to 'actively participate' in the program, to be reformed or rehabilitated. The drug court team makes its decisions in relation to matters of health, social well-being and possible recidivism, explicitly illustrating expert intervention through the human sciences. More than this, as an alternative to prison, the court unambiguously functions as part of the carceral archipelago. The panoptic qualities of its services ensure a continuum of surveillance and control. While the potential for net widening, through a desire to get more people into treatment or more rigorous monitoring as part of the program, warrants critical consideration; as an alternative to prison, drug treatment courts can offer some redeeming possibilities. Remaining outside the 'total institution' allows offenders to avoid disculturation — the untraining that renders the inmate incapable of managing certain features of daily life following release from prison. It also provides an opportunity to maintain connection with civil society and non-drug-using networks, which is an important factor in overcoming and developing future alternatives to drug-dependent (offending) behaviour.

7

Indigenous justice and the decolonisation of punishment

INTRODUCTION

No book on punishment in Australia would be complete without a chapter (at least) focused on the troubled relationship that has persisted between this country's Indigenous peoples and the criminal justice system since colonisation. From the outset the experience of Aboriginal people who have come to the attention of various Australian authorities has been distinctly different from that of other people. Hogg (2001) and Finnane and McGuire (2001; see also Edney 2002), for example, outline the complexities of a historically differentiated system of punishment that emerged in the 1960s when the citizenship status of Indigenous people was formally recognised. From that time onwards, the criminalisation of Australian Aboriginal people increasingly became a problem for governments. In 1987 the Royal Commission into Aboriginal Deaths in Custody (RCIADIC) was created 'in response to a growing public concern that deaths in custody of Aboriginal people were too common and public explanations too evasive to discount the possibility that foul play was a factor in many of them' (Johnston 1991, p. 1). The deaths of ninety-nine Aboriginal and Torres Strait Islander people were closely examined. Perhaps the most important finding was that Indigenous people did not die in custody at a greater rate than non-Indigenous people, but that they came into police and correctional custody at an overwhelmingly high rate (Johnston 1991, p. 6).

In 1991 the RCIADIC released its findings and made 339 recommendations that addressed wider social issues underpinning the over-imprisonment of Indigenous people. It sought improvements in policing, police use of custody, court operations and the adult correctional system. Some improvements and a greater sensitivity to this issue have eventuated. However, in a climate of increasing punitiveness (see Chapters 1 and 2), the RCIADIC recommendation that imprisonment be used as a last resort for Indigenous persons has not been effectively implemented and Indigenous imprisonment rates remain at high levels (Cunneen and McDonald 1997, p. 9). Since 1987 the disproportionate imprisonment of Indigenous persons increased from 14.6 per cent (Biles and McDonald 1992, p. 91) to twenty-four per cent of the prison population in 2006—when Indigenous people made up only about 2.3 per cent of the Australian population (ABS 2006 census). In 2002, ten years after the RCIADIC's report was released, those assessing the implementation of the recommendations noted that

Indigenous people continued to be over-represented and to die in custody at very high rates. Stephanie Fryer-Smith (2002, p. 9) concluded that '[i]t is self-evident that the words of the Royal Commissioner remain as relevant in 2002 as they were in 1991'. This seems to be as true now as it was then: Indigenous people continue to account for more than 20 per cent of those held in custody. However, recent years have seen the introduction of some innovative justice alternatives— such as Indigenous courts and community justice groups—that address some of the RCIADIC recommendations, perhaps acknowledging if not yet effectively responding to the ill effects of dispossession on Aboriginal Australians.

This chapter maps out the conditions that provided for the development of these options. It builds on the history of the relationship between Indigenous people and colonial forms of justice (first described in Chapter 1), acknowledging that the criminalisation of Indigenous people's resistance to colonisation played a role in silencing criticism of the mass dispossession of Indigenous people (Blagg 2008, p. 2). It outlines their current status in the prison population. The chapter also briefly describes the role of the RCIADIC, noting relevant recommendations and how these articulate with some of the recent justice innovations—in courts and community corrections programs. It concludes by identifying the sentencing principles that have informed these interventions, using the concept of decolonisation (Blagg 2008; Cunneen 2001) to position them as a social and political response in the struggle against Indigenous disadvantage and marginalisation.

INDIGENOUS PEOPLE IN THE CRIMINAL JUSTICE SYSTEM

The responses of the Anglo-Australian criminal justice system to Indigenous people have varied historically. Cunneen (2007) distinguishes three periods: dispossession and war during the late eighteenth and nineteenth centuries; protection and segregation during the late nineteenth and early twentieth centuries; and formal equality since the 1960s. Rod Broadhurst commented in his study of Aboriginal imprisonment in Western Australia: 'Ironically with the grant of full citizenship rights to Aboriginal people in 1971 and the repeal of the paternalistic *Native Welfare Act*, an immediate consequence was a rapid rise in their level of incarceration' (1987, p. 154). Hogg (2001) reports that a census of NSW prisoners in 1971, a few years after the formal abandonment of 'welfare' policies and the abolition of the Aborigines Welfare Board, found there to be 213 Aboriginal prisoners out of a total population of just under 4000—approximately 5 per cent (NSW Bureau of Crime Statistics and Research 1972 in Hogg 2001, p. 367). The numbers identified as Aboriginal in NSW prisons in the first national prison census a decade later were much the same, but the trend over the 1980s and 1990s in New South Wales, in most other jurisdictions and nationally, has been an increase in the absolute numbers of Aboriginal prisoners, which has run ahead of the general upward trend in prison numbers. By 1999 Aboriginal prisoners constituted 20 per cent of the total Australian prisons' population (Hogg 2001, p. 367); in 2007, when Indigenous people constituted about 2.3 per cent of the population (see table 7.1 below, ABS 2000–2008), they made up almost one-quarter of the prison population. The growing rates of custody for Indigenous men and women in comparison to the general population are described in Table 7.1.

There is insufficient evidence to support a general claim that with the end of the 'protection' era, there was a simple transfer of Aboriginal people from administrative to penal forms of regulation (Hogg 2001, Finnane and McGuire 2001, Blagg 2008). The criteria and processes of containment and incarceration respectively are fundamentally different under the two systems. Historical changes in the second half of the twentieth century were mediated by not only localised factors, but also social and economic factors that impacted in particular ways on Aboriginal communities. Beginning in the 1970s, shrinking economic opportunities coincided with the removal of overtly racial mechanisms of segregation and control to make Aboriginal poverty and 'disorder' in the sites of contact more visible. This heightened white racial anxieties. Despite changes in government policy, these anxieties persisted and eventually found a voice in the rhetoric of law and order (Hogg and Carrington 1998; 2006). By the 1990s what had been seen as an 'administrative' problem was transformed into a criminal justice problem. Racial segregation gave way to policing through criminal justice procedures for growing numbers of Aboriginal people, and many of the social consequences of the former protectionist system were perpetuated rather than alleviated by the changing social arrangements.

TABLE 7.1 Custody rates for Indigenous people in comparison to the general population

Full-time custody (year)	All persons	Rate*	Indigenous persons	Rate	Indigenous male	Rate	Indigenous female	Rate
2008	26 885	164.7	6641	2201.6	6080	4160.6	561	361.0
2007	26 305	164.2	6430	2187.5	5847	4111.4	584	384.5
2006	25 169	160.0	6060	2116.2	5548	4006.0	512	346.2
2005	24 235	156.8	5664	2027.7	5185	3839.3	479	332.0
2004	23 281	151.7	5149	1888.9	4722	3596.0	427	202.7
2003	22 556	155.7	4757	1788.3	4380	3408.0	377	274.4
2002	21 490	144.0	4335	1785.9	3981	3407.4	354	281.0
2001	21 284	144.9	4168	1754.0	3814	3335.7	354	287.4
2000	20 659	142.6	3974	1713.7	3656	3278.1	319	264.7

Source: Australian Bureau of Statistics (2000–2008).
*All rates given are per 100 000 adult population.

Contributing factors

The factors contributing to the over-representation of Indigenous people—as victims and offenders—in the criminal justice system are complex. They include historical and structural conditions of colonisation, social and economic marginalisation and systematic racism, and the impact of specific (and sometimes quite localised) practices of criminal justice and related agencies (Cunneen 2001). Cunneen (2007, p. 149) lists key factors as:

- offending patterns (especially over-representation in offences likely to lead to imprisonment, such as homicide, serious assaults, sexual assaults and property offences)
- the impact of policing (in particular, the adverse use of police discretion, issues around police bail, and the availability and use of alternatives to arrest and of other diversionary options)
- legislation (especially the impact of laws giving rise to indirect discrimination, such as legislation governing public places or alcohol)
- factors in judicial decision-making (namely, bail conditions, the weight given to prior record and the availability of non-custodial options)
- environmental and locational factors (especially the social and economic effects of living in small, rural and remote communities)
- cultural differences (such as different child-rearing practices, the use of Aboriginal English and vulnerability during police interrogation)
- socio-economic factors (in particular, high levels of unemployment, poverty, lower educational attainment, poor housing and poor health)
- marginalisation (specifically drug, alcohol and other substance abuse, alienation from family and community)
- the impact of specific colonial policies (especially the forced removal of Indigenous children).

Cunneen draws attention to the effect of rural issues, including the concentration of poverty in particular areas, the lack of access to services and specific elements of the criminal justice system—like non-custodial sentencing options—that may not operate in rural areas (Aboriginal Justice Advisory Council undated). The NSW Legislative Council Standing Committee on Law and Justice (2006) inquiry into community-based sentencing options in rural and remote areas found that supervised bonds, community service orders, periodic detention and home detention were not available in many parts of New South Wales. For example, home detention has been operating for approximately fifteen years but is only available in the Sydney, Wollongong, Newcastle and Gosford areas. These sentencing options are generally employed at the heavier end of the sentencing scale, providing direct alternatives to the use of imprisonment. As a result, rural and regional courts are left with fewer alternatives to the use of imprisonment, and this particularly impacts on Indigenous people because they are more likely to live in rural and remote areas, to be before these courts and to be facing a term of imprisonment. Cunneen (2007) describes similar problems in Queensland, and explains that offenders receive either minor sentences, like unsupervised orders (and are thus potentially more likely to reoffend), or a harsher sentence of imprisonment. The failure to provide equitable services in rural and remote areas reinforces the over-representation of Indigenous people in the criminal justice system and in prison in particular.

Beyond these specific limitations of the criminal justice system, a range of social characteristics and problems that can be linked to offending behaviours have had negative consequences for Indigenous people (Cunneen 2007). These include:

- The relative youthfulness of the Indigenous population in comparison to the non-Indigenous population. This is important because we know that reported crime is likely to involve people in their late teenage to early adult years.
- Poorer educational outcomes, higher rates of unemployment, lower average household incomes and overcrowded, all of which are exacerbated by geographic remoteness. Some remote or rural communities, such as Palm Island, report overcrowding, with seventeen people per house. This can be associated with various social problems, including family violence.
- Poorer health outcomes, including the higher prevalence of certain diseases arising from inadequate housing and poor basic facilities.
- A comparatively large group in the medium- to high-risk drinking category (Bull 2007). Excessive alcohol consumption is associated with a range of health problems and interpersonal violence. It should be noted, however, that despite popular perceptions, a higher proportion of Indigenous people in remote communities do not consume alcohol (46 per cent) than non-remote Indigenous people (25 per cent) or non-Indigenous people more generally (16 per cent).

The crimes committed by Aboriginal offenders are overwhelmingly crimes of poverty, despair and defiance (Hogg 2001; Lincoln and Wilson 2000). Large numbers are drawn into the criminal justice net for crimes such as public drunkenness, swearing, damage to property, fighting and theft. In the National Aboriginal and Torres Strait Islander (NATSI) survey, 25 per cent of all respondents aged fifteen to forty-four reported having been arrested at least once in the previous five years. For men in this age group, it was almost 40 per cent. High recurrent contact, as much as offence gravity, contributes to high incarceration rates; of those who reported having been arrested in the NATSI survey, 57 per cent had been arrested more than once in the five-year period (ABS 1995, pp. 57–8 in Hogg 2001, p. 368). The first national police custody survey conducted in 1988 found that, of the Aboriginal persons detained in the course of a one-month period, 22 per cent were repeat custodies for that month (McDonald 1992). In the 1999 national prison census, for those who had been sentenced, about three-quarters of Aboriginal prisoners had a history of prior adult imprisonment compared with less than 60 per cent of the general prison population (ABS 2000). In 2004, 77 per cent of Indigenous prisoners had experienced prior imprisonment in comparison to 53 per cent of non-Indigenous prisoners (Healey 2007).

The Royal Commission into Aboriginal Deaths in Custody

During the early 1980s, the grossly disproportionate rate and number of Aboriginal deaths in police or prison custody created widespread community concern. The circumstances surrounding many of those deaths provided a catalyst for community activism and protest in all states and territories of Australia. Intense lobbying by groups like the National Committee to Defend Black Rights was supported by bodies such as Amnesty International. On 11 August 1987 then Prime Minister Bob Hawke announced that a Royal Commission into Aboriginal Deaths in Custody (RCIADIC) would be undertaken, and in January 1988 investigations into the deaths in custody of forty-four Aboriginal persons began. Those investigations continued for more than three years. During that period the mandate of the RCIADIC was expanded to incorporate a broad-ranging inquiry into Aboriginal involvement in Australian criminal justice. Ultimately, the circumstances of the deaths in custody between 1 January 1980 and 31 May 1989 of ninety-nine Aboriginal persons were examined. Commissioner Elliot Johnston QC produced a report with 339 recommendations that addressed matters of police and prison protocols and procedures, as well as more general recommendations aimed at tackling the underlying reasons for the high level of Indigenous involvement at all stages of the system. In addition, the RCIADIC also emphasised the importance of self-determination in countering the social and economic disadvantages that contributed to high rates of Indigenous contact with criminal justice agencies (Johnston 1991).

In many ways the RCIADIC represented an attempt by the non-Indigenous community to come to terms with the devastating impact that the criminal justice system has on Indigenous peoples. It was arguably the first time in Australian colonial history that the non-Indigenous community was made aware of the effects of the system on Indigenous communities. Moreover, it drew attention to the lived experiences of Indigenous persons who regularly confront acts of racism. That was the understanding of Royal Commissioner Johnston (1991, p. 20) who noted:

> I say very frankly that when I started upon my work with this Commission I had some knowledge of the way in which broad policy had evolved to the detriment of Aboriginal people and some idea of the consequences. But, until I examined the files of the people who died and the other material which has come before the Commission and listened to Aboriginal people speaking, I had no conception of the degree of pin-picking domination, abuse of personal power, utter paternalism, open contempt and total indifference with which so many Aboriginal people were visited on a day to day basis.

The RCIADIC carefully examined in separate reports the deaths and lives of each of the ninety-nine individuals who had died in custody between 1980 and 1989. It produced a damning archive, going beyond the usual forms of knowledge available in statistical collections. Hogg (2001) suggests that the degree to which most of these lives were documented in the records of state agencies, such as those concerned with education, child welfare, adoption, health and criminal justice, a degree to which 'few non-Aboriginal lives would be recorded' (Johnston 1991, p. 4), tells its own story about the relationship of many Aboriginal people to the state. The eleven-volume *RCIADIC: National Report (Final Report)* was released on 9 May 1991. Some of the key findings of Royal Commissioner Johnston, summarised in Volume One, were that:

○ It could not be asserted that abuse, neglect or racism were common elements in each of the deaths investigated. However, in many cases, 'system failures' or the absence of due care had contributed to the deaths.

○ Aboriginal people do not die in custody at a greater rate than non-Aboriginal people. However, Aboriginal people come into custody at a rate that is 'overwhelmingly different' from that of the general community. For example, Aboriginal people in Western Australia were forty-three times more likely to be in police custody, and twenty-six times more likely to be in prison custody, than non-Aboriginal persons.

○ Those Aboriginal people who died in custody were not atypical of the large numbers who have regular contact with the criminal justice system, the overwhelming majority being unemployed at the time of detention, desperately poor, ill-educated, alcoholic and of seriously poor health. The most significant cause of Aboriginal over-representation in the criminal justice system was the constantly disadvantaged position of Aboriginal persons within the broader society. The investigations had revealed that eighty-eight of the ninety-nine Aboriginal persons who had died in custody were men whose average age was thirty-two. In addition, of those ninety-nine persons:
  • Eighty-three were unemployed and the time of detention.
  • Only two had been educated to secondary school level.
  • Forty-three had been separated from their families as children by the intervention of the state, missions or other organisations.
  • Most had had early and repeated contact with the criminal justice system; seventy-four had been in trouble with the law before the age of twenty.
  • For half, the most common offences occasioning such contacts had been drunkenness and offences against good order; thirty-four had been detained for drunkenness just prior to their last custody.
  • Three-quarters came from remote, rural, fringe or small town communities (see generally Johnston 1991, pp. 35–55).

Royal Commissioner Johnston commented: 'An examination of the lives of the ninety-nine shows that facts associated in every case with their Aboriginality played a significant and in most cases dominant role in their being in custody and dying in custody' (Johnson 1991, p. 1). He concluded that the enduring legacy of British colonisation and post-colonial laws and practices was systematic socio-economic disadvantage, disempowerment and cultural fragmentation. It appeared that an inevitable consequence of that legacy was early, and repeated, contact by many Aboriginal persons with the criminal justice system (Fryer-Smith 2002).

Malcolm Smith: From the individual death reports of RCIADIC

SYNOPSIS

> The real horror story of Aboriginal Australia today is locked in police files and child welfare reports. It is a story of private misery and degradation, caused by a complex chain of historical circumstance, that continues into the present.

> Source: Gilbert (1978), p. 2.

The story of Malcolm Charles Smith illustrates the truth of Kevin Gilbert's words. It is the story of a life destroyed, not by the misconduct of police and prison officers, but in large measure by the regular operation of the system of self-righteous, heartless and racist destruction of Aboriginal families that went on under the name of protection or welfare well into the second half of the twentieth century.

AN ABORIGINAL DEATH IN CUSTODY

At 1.25 p.m. on 29 December 1982 Malcolm Charles Smith, an Aboriginal prisoner in the Malabar Assessment Unit (MAU) of the Metropolitan Reception Prison (MRP) at Long Bay, Sydney, went into a toilet cubicle and locked the door behind him. About half a minute afterwards, a piercing scream came from the cubicle. Prison officers rushed to the door and, when there was no response to their inquiries, knocked it off its hinges and found that the handle of an artist's paint brush had been driven through Malcolm Smith's left eye, so that only the metal sheath and hairs were protruding. He was quickly attended to by nursing staff and a doctor and transferred to Prince Henry Hospital, as an emergency case. Despite all possible care, he died at 11.41 a.m. on 5 January 1983.

No one at the MAU that day was at fault. Each officer was doing his or her duty in the normal way and had no reason to expect what would happen. When Malcolm inflicted the fatal injury on himself, the officers responded promptly and sensibly and can only be commended for the way they handled a most distressing incident. Equally, the medical attention which he subsequently received was beyond criticism.

AN ABORIGINAL LIFE IN CUSTODY

So much for *how* Malcolm died. Why did he die? Why was he in prison, seeking to pluck out his eye? The answer begins (depending on how long a perspective one takes), somewhere between 26 January 1788 and 5 May 1965. On the former day there commenced the European settlement that, in Rowley's phrase, was to mean 'the progress of the Aboriginal from tribesman to inmate'. It was to spread across the continent overwhelming people like the Paakantji, who occupied the rich hunter-gatherer habitat on the banks of the Darling, and the Ngiyampaa, their neighbours to the north-east. By the operation of massacre, individual killing, introduced diseases, destruction of food supplies, sexual exploitation, introduction of alcohol and dispossession from the land with which their whole life was entwined, these peoples were reduced to small remnants and many of them herded without regard to tribal affiliations into what were in effect concentration camps, although known as stations or 'missions', where they were denied civil rights in the name of protection and forced into a state of dependency in which many are still enmeshed. Whoever made the policies they enforced, it was usually the police that Aboriginals saw as the immediate agents of oppression.

Some bold spirits managed to maintain a precarious independence. Malcolm's parents, Gladys of Paakantji descent, who lost an arm in a shooting accident at 16, and her husband Joseph of Ngiyampaa descent, lived a roving fugitive life along the Darling between Ivanhoe, Menindee and Wentworth, travelling in horse-drawn vehicles and sleeping under tarpaulins, and supporting themselves by casual work on stations and fruit blocks, and by hunting and fishing, as their family grew to thirteen children. Always on the move, their constant concern was to escape the attentions of 'the welfare', and its agents the police, lest they suffer the fate of so many Aboriginal families and be forced to live on a reserve or have their children snatched away, often never to be seen again. Gradually they came to settle with related families at Dareton, near Wentworth, where irrigation farmers valued the easily accessible pool of casual labour. They lived in humpies built from discarded materials, where Gladys cared for her large family while Joe built a reputation as a reliable worker. Here disaster struck. Gladys died and despite the efforts of Joe and his elder daughters, 'the welfare' caught up with the younger children.

Immediately prior to 5 May 1965, the other date from which Malcolm's story may be commenced, he was a happy, healthy and free eleven-year-old, albeit grubby, living in a humpy, and truant from a school made unattractive by racial prejudice and irrelevance to his life. He was taken away from his family by police, cut off from his family, whom he did not see again until he was 19, and sent to Kempsey, over 1500 kilometres away on the coast, beyond the boundaries of their accessible world. When he finally rediscovered them at the age of 19, it was too late for him to start a normal life. The intervening eight years, mainly in despotic institutions of various kinds, had left him illiterate and innumerate, unskilled, and without experience of normal society. He had been taught a model of human life based not on mutual respect, cooperation, responsibility, initiative, self-expression and love, but on dominance and subservience, rigid discipline and conformity, repression and dependence, humiliation and fear, with escape or defiance as the only room for initiative. He had experienced the law as a system which gave him no rights, no representation, and no consideration, ignored the existence of his family, and treated him as having no place outside an institution.

Instead of being socialised into the family and kin network so important to Aboriginals, he had been 'socialised' to survive in institutional communities. He was to spend nine years of the remaining nine years eight months of his life in jails, where he found greater opportunities for freedom and privacy than he had known for the previous eight years in juvenile homes. In jail he was respected by staff and prisoners alike for his strong character, leadership, sporting prowess and artistic talent, and there he built his friendships and social relations. His five intervals of liberty, totalling only eight months, offered an environment with which he was ill-equipped to cope, and little opportunity for employment or constructive activity. The first two occasions lasted two or three months, the rest only a few weeks. All but the last ended as a result of petty theft or illegal use of a motor car. The society which had deprived him of the opportunity to grow up in a family and learn to live in a free community offered him no assistance whatever in adjustment or rehabilitation, but visited his every lapse with penal sentences. In many cases the sentences were extremely harsh.

Yet the bonds to his family formed in early childhood remained strong, and it was in a misguided attempt to assume the role of its protector that he committed his one serious crime, killing a man whom he believed to be ill-treating his sister. In jail he had assumed the role of protector of weaker prisoners, but in his inexperience of life outside jail, he so misjudged the situation that his distraught sister disowned him as a brother, and other members of his family gave evidence against him. Returned to jail, he was seen by his prisoner friends as a changed man, obsessed with religion he little understood and carrying a Bible he could not read. Burdened by guilt, he became psychotic and embarked on a series of self-mutilatory acts, culminating in his fatal third attempt to put out his eye in obedience to the Biblical text: 'If thy eye offend thee, pluck it out'.

His death is part of the abiding legacy of the appalling treatment of Aboriginals that went on well into the second half of this century in the name of protection or welfare. It is history, but history of critical importance today. It is history that few Australians know, and which our historians are only now piecing together.

Without a knowledge of it we cannot hope to understand Aboriginal/white relations today, for they are deeply moulded by that history. We will not understand the ill-suppressed hatred which many Aboriginals feel towards police, and their deep distrust of officialdom generally. We will fail to appreciate how many Aboriginal men and women there are now in the community carrying deep scars from that history, scars that prejudice not only their own lives but those of their children. We will run the risk that, as has happened so often, we will repeat the mistakes of the past.

The attempt to 'solve the Aboriginal problem' by the deliberate destruction of families and communities, which was the policy of the Aborigines Protection Board, and to some extent its successor, the Aborigines Welfare Board, not only wrecked individual lives but is seen by many Aboriginals as falling squarely within the modern definition of genocide. Few would openly advocate such policies today, but unless continuing positive steps are taken to understand and counteract them, there is a risk that long-standing racist attitudes will continue to influence the formulation and implementation even of more enlightened policies. In particular it is essential to stop treating Aboriginals as dependent people whose welfare is looked after by others who know better than they, and give them back the opportunities for self-reliance, independence and self-respect that were so cruelly taken away and denied them for most of the last two hundred years.

Source: Australian Royal Commission into Aboriginal Deaths in Custody and Wootten (1989).

As mentioned above, the final report by RCIADIC included 399 recommendations relating to: police; coronial inquiries; the public consumption of alcohol; bail; custody; government policy; courts; non-custodial sentences; education; family, identity, language and heritage; drugs and alcohol; and health. Numerous bodies have monitored the implementation of these recommendations, such as the Deaths in Custody Watch Committee in each state, the Australian Institute of Criminology (AIC) and the Aboriginal and Torres Strait Islander Commission.

The RCIADIC recommended that Australian governments reduce the rate of Aboriginal imprisonment; however, this has not occurred. Rates have risen steadily since 1991 (and continued into the new millennium), suggesting either that the operation of the criminal justice system is not easily adjusted by governments or that there is an unwillingness to act in ways based on affirmative action and counter the prevailing penal populism strategies (Dawes 2006). In October 2001 the AIC reported that in the decade 1990–2000 a total of 909 persons died in all forms of custody in Australia, 162 of whom (almost 18 per cent) were Aboriginal (Collins and Mouzos 2001; Williams 2001). The AIC also noted that a total of ninety-one persons had died in 2000 in all forms of custody compared with sixty-five in 1990 and eighty-five in 1999. The most frequent cause of deaths in custody was by hanging, as it has been for seventeen of the twenty-one years that such data have been collected. Young adult males feature disproportionately in the figures: in 2000 just under half of the deaths in custody were of persons aged between twenty-five and thirty-four. Seventeen (over 18 per cent) of the ninety-one persons who died in custody in Australia in 2000 were Aboriginal. Reflecting on these statistics, Fryer-Smith remarked: '[t]he conclusions are clear. Aboriginal people die in custody at a rate relative to their proportion which is totally unacceptable and which would not be tolerated if it occurred in the non-Aboriginal community' (2002, p. 9).

While nearly two decades have passed since the RCIADIC began, its general findings are still relevant. The problems that it made so public continue to beset Aboriginal communities. Aboriginal people continue to experience social and economic marginalisation, cultural isolation and disadvantage in every social sphere, and these problems have worked to maintain their massive over-representation in the criminal justice system.

INDIGENOUS JUSTICE PROGRAMS

In the 1990s, innovative programs that were introduced to respond to the RCIADIC recommendations tended to focus on the 'front end' of the criminal justice system through the creation of diversionary options for juvenile offenders, such as police cautioning and family conferences (Blagg 2008, see Chapter 9). While these successfully reduced the number of first and minor offenders entering the system, they also increased the opportunities for families and victims to participate in justice processes. Their main success, however, was among non-Aboriginal young offenders, who were more often the main beneficiaries of diversionary mechanisms. Initially, less attention was paid to the courts as a site of reform, despite recommendations that specifically focused on change in this domain. Those relating to criminal proceedings included:

Rec 100: That governments should take more positive steps to recruit and train Aboriginal people as court staff and interpreters in locations where significant numbers of Aboriginal people appear before courts.

Rec 104: In discrete or remote communities sentencing authorities should consult with Aboriginal authorities and organisations as to the general range of sentences which the community considers appropriate for offences committed within the communities by members of those communities. Further that subject to preserving the civil and legal rights of offenders and victims, such consultation should in appropriate circumstances relate to sentences imposed in individual cases.

Rec 108: That it be recognised by Aboriginal Legal Services, funding authorities and courts that lawyers cannot adequately represent clients unless they have adequate time to take instructions and prepare cases, and that this is a special problem in communities without access to lawyers other than at the time of court hearings.

Rec 96: That judicial officers and person who work in the court service and in the probation and parole services whose duties bring them into contact with Aboriginal people be encouraged to participate in an appropriate training and development program, designed to explain contemporary society, customs and traditions. Such programs should emphasise the historical and social factors which contribute to the disadvantaged position of many Aboriginal and non-Aboriginal communities today. The commission further recommends that such persons should, wherever possible, participate in discussion with members of the Aboriginal community in an informal way in order to improve cross-cultural understanding. (RCIADIC, <www.austlii.edu.au/au/other/IndigLRes/rciadic/national/rol5/5.html#Heading5>)

In the late 1990s justice innovations responding to these recommendations began to be introduced at the 'back end' of the system. Principal among these were community justice groups and various types of Indigenous sentencing courts.

Community justice groups

Community justice groups (CJGs) operate widely in Queensland and New South Wales: they represent a mechanism for grass-roots involvement in the local justice system and a means by which Aboriginal people can run their own justice processes. In 1993 the Queensland government established the Local Justice Initiatives Program as part of its response to the recommendations of RCIADIC. Its objectives included providing opportunities for Aboriginal and Torres Strait Islander (ATSI) input and participation in the rehabilitation of offenders, and sensitising the justice system to the needs and cultural values of these groups of people. Through this program, funds were provided for ATSI communities to develop local community-based strategies to address justice issues and to decrease ATSI people's contact with the criminal justice system. CJGs were the most common type of local justice initiative funded under the program. They are made up of elders and respected persons (they can include young people) from the various social or cultural groupings within each ATSI community.

The roles and responsibilities of CJGs vary both between and within communities over time, reflecting the changing nature of local circumstances and group priorities. They undertake a diverse range of activities, including mediation; counselling; community conferencing; crime prevention; working with police; addressing the cause of offending behaviour, such as truancy, alcohol abuse and domestic violence; supervising community-based orders; and assisting courts. An evaluation of pilot CJGs established in 1993 at Palm Island, Kowanyama and Pormpuraaw found that they focused on community development strategies designed to improve opportunities for young people, re-establish community authority and discipline based on the authority of community elders, and improving the relationship of the community with external agencies, such as the police, Children's Services, Juvenile Justice, Corrective Services and visiting magistrates (Chantrill 1998). (It concluded that the operation of these groups had effected significant reductions in juvenile crime and recidivism.) Chantrill (1998) suggested that the strength of the model lies in the fact that the operation of the groups is community driven. In his view these groups provided accountable and appropriate mechanisms based on their familiarity with local circumstances and the capacity to frame appropriate responses derived from knowledge of local resources and an understanding of how community arrangements can be given legitimacy and authority.

Currently, about forty CJGs operate in Queensland. In the 1990s CJGs initially used community norms and mechanisms of Indigenous social control in responding to crime, provided pre-sentence advice to judicial officers, visited incarcerated Indigenous people, and at times supervised offenders on community-based orders. Legislation in 2001 formalised their powers, requiring the court (whether it be the magistrates, district or supreme courts) to have regard to the views of community members in sentencing offenders (*Penalties and Sentences Act 1992* s9[2][o]). Legislation tabled in September 2002 created a new governance structure in remote Indigenous communities (*Community Services Legislation Amendment Act 2002*). CJGs were thus given a legislative basis, including rules for their establishment and membership, as well as new duties and responsibilities (Marchetti and Daly 2004).

Consistent with the Queensland strategy, the NSW Aboriginal Justice Agreement (Aboriginal Justice Advisory Council and Debus undated) explains that engaging local Aboriginal communities in the operations of the criminal justice system has significant potential to increase the level of confidence in the administration of justice, to provide more effective and appropriate outcomes from the justice system, and to reduce offending and repeat offending in Aboriginal communities. Local Aboriginal justice mechanisms also provide both a means by which Aboriginal victims of crime can address their problems and a way for Aboriginal communities to take an active role in their own governance. The justice agreement identifies Aboriginal CJGs as a key strategy for achieving these ends. In New South Wales, these groups deal with a large number of local issues in cooperation with police, courts, probation service, juvenile justice, such as developing crime prevention programs and activities. They may, for example:

○ work with police to issue cautions
○ establish diversionary options
○ support offenders when they are arrested
○ work with courts to help people get bail
○ provide advice to courts on defendants
○ manage court orders
○ develop local crime prevention initiatives.

Victoria has community justice panels that are similar to the CJGs. They resulted from a joint initiative of the Victorian Aboriginal Legal Service and the Victorian Government in 1987; they are currently funded and administered by Victoria Police. Indigenous panel members, who live in regional Victorian towns and cities, volunteer their time to work with criminal justice agencies to improve the treatment of Indigenous offenders. The panels take custody of Indigenous offenders, arrange their legal advice, liaise with the offender's family, and provide information about an offender's background and other relevant information to judicial officers at sentencing (Blagg 2008; Marchetti and Daly 2007).

INDIGENOUS COURTS AND CIRCLE SENTENCING COURTS

Indigenous people have been involved in sentencing at a local level in an ad hoc way for some time. Such participation has relied on the will and energy of local magistrates, prosecutory authorities and senior members of the Indigenous community. In some states, recent moves have allowed for more formal recognition of these procedures, and courts have shown themselves to be flexible enough to accommodate alternative justice strategies. Indigenous courts and circle sentencing courts have emerged as a means of responding to over-representation, the RCIADIC recommendations and Aboriginal justice agreements that recognise the need for partnerships between state government and Aboriginal organisations in the delivery of justice for Indigenous people. While these courts have different ways of operating, they share similar objectives: reducing Aboriginal over-representation in the prison system, providing credible alternatives to imprisonment, and reducing both offenders' failure to appear in court rates and the rate at which court orders are breached (Harris 2004; Marchetti and Daly 2004).

Since 1999 the number of Indigenous and circle sentencing courts established in Australia has been growing. Currently, Indigenous operate in South Australia (the Nunga Court), Victoria (Koori courts), Queensland (Murri courts), Northern Territory (community courts—while open to all, they are clearly modelled on the principles of the Aboriginal court) and Western Australia (Aboriginal community courts). Circle sentencing courts are available in New South Wales. These alternative justice forums are not universally available throughout each jurisdiction. For example, Koori courts operate in Melbourne and key regional Victorian centres; the availability of Murri courts in Queensland and circle sentencing courts in New South Wales is similarly restricted.

Indigenous sentencing courts do not practise Indigenous customary law; rather, they use Australian criminal laws and procedures when sentencing Indigenous people. The participation of Indigenous elders or respected persons is the key to the process. For example, Indigenous community representatives talk to defendants about their offending and assist judicial officers in sentencing. While Indigenous sentencing courts generally do not use traditional forms of punishment, 'they do give due recognition and respect to cultural considerations', such as respect for elders (Marchetti and Daly 2007, p. 421). Some courts will take into account an apology that has been given according to customary traditions, or banishment. Generally, however, the sentences imposed are within the bounds of mainstream criminal and sentencing law. There are limits (in some states and territories) on the types of offences that can be heard.

Jurisdictions vary in their approaches and the extent to which Indigenous people or groups are involved. Marchetti and Daly (2007) explain that because they emerged spontaneously without a written reference (except the global RCIADIC recommendations), these courts are literally Indigenous to the concerns of particular people and groups—usually local magistrates and Indigenous people— who believe that courtroom communication and procedures require modification for handling Indigenous cases. The key characteristics shared by various editions of Indigenous courts operating in each jurisdiction include:

- The offender must be Indigenous (or in some courts South Sea Islander) and have entered a guilty plea.
- The charge is normally heard in a magistrates' court, although this may change in the proposed Indigenous District Court in Ipswich, Queensland.
- The offence must have occurred in the geographical area covered by the court.
- The magistrate retains the ultimate power in sentencing the offender and sits at eye level to the offender, usually at the bar table rather than the bench, with a respected Indigenous person (elder) whose role varies by jurisdiction.

Some courts sit with one elder; others, with up to four. An elder's participation ranges from briefly addressing offenders about their behaviour to having a significant role in determining the sentence and monitoring the offenders' progress. Some courts try to ensure that the sex of the elder matches that of the offender, whereas others see 'all elders as being equal'. The degree of variation in the role of elders both across and within jurisdictions over time makes it difficult to generalise about their 'power' in the legal process; however, their power is advisory to the judicial officer who is ultimately responsible for the decision. Even if in custody, offenders sits at the bar table beside their solicitor; typically there is also a support person, such as a family member or partner, at the table. Once the charges have been read and defence counsel has responded, the offender and the support person are invited to speak directly to the magistrate about the offender's behaviour. People in the public gallery may also be asked to speak. The degree of informality adopted by the court varies by jurisdiction and magistrate, but generally much more time is taken for each matter than would be the case in a regular court. An important addition is the presence of Indigenous court workers who are referred to as Aboriginal justice officers, Aboriginal project officers or court liaison officers. Their role varies by jurisdiction. Some actively assist the prosecutor, offender and defence counsel to devise a sentence plan to present to the magistrate, some coordinate post-sentence follow-ups, while others mainly play a central backstage part. In some states, specific legislation has been passed to recognise and give effect to Indigenous courts, such as *Magistrates' Court (Koori Court) Act 2002* (Vic.). Other jurisdictions, such as Queensland, rely on general sentencing Acts to validate their procedural framework (see Marchetti and Daly 2007, pp. 438–40 for a useful comparative table).

It is possible to draw some clear distinctions between the different models of Indigenous courts. Marchetti and Daly (2004; 2007; also see Blagg 2008, pp. 127–30) differentiate between circle sentencing in New South Wales, which is based on Canadian models, and the Nunga and Aboriginal courts developed in South Australia. The NSW circle sentencing court is 'designed for more serious or repeat offenders and aims to achieve full community involvement in the sentencing process' (Mathews 2002, p. 1). It sits in a location that is more culturally appropriate to the offender and the Indigenous community than the local magistrates' court. While offenders are initially reviewed for suitability by the magistrate, it is the Aboriginal CJG that determines if the offender is acceptable for the court process (Potas et al. 2003). Participants sit in a circle that comprises four community elders, the magistrate, the offender, the offender's support people, the Aboriginal project officer, the victim and their supporters, the defence counsel and the police prosecutor. The court is closed, and permission from the magistrate and the elders is required before observers can watch the proceedings by sitting outside the circle. The magistrate prepares a document that describes the offence and relevant information about the offender's background. All participants in the court, including the offender, verbally respond to this written account. Through discussion, circle members develop an appropriate sentence plan for the offender. The circle reconvenes after a few months to assess the offender's progress (Potas et al. 2003). The court typically considers just one offender and convenes fortnightly. In contrast, the Nunga Court sits in a special courtroom in the Port Adelaide Magistrates' Court two to three times a month; eight to twelve people may be listed for sentencing each day. There is no process of vetting offenders at high risk of incarceration, and no pre-court deliberations on a sentence plan or a written report. It is an open court; people sit at eye level, but across several tables and not in a circle. There is greater informality and less reliance on legal actors than one would see in a regular courtroom, and more Indigenous court workers and groups are present on the day. In this way, it operates as an Indigenous court in a regular courthouse.

The Victorian Koori Court was established under the *Magistrates' Court (Koori Court) Act 2002*, with the objective of 'Ensuring greater participation of the Aboriginal community in the sentencing process … through the role to be played in that process by the Aboriginal elder or respected person and others' (*Koori Court Act* at 1[b]). Business is conducted at an oval table rather than from the bench. Offenders sit at the table beside their solicitor and are permitted to have a support person. Once the charges have been read and the defence counsel has responded, offenders and their support person are invited to speak directly to the magistrate about the offenders' behaviour; others in the spectators' area may also be asked to speak. The degree of informality adopted by the court varies by jurisdiction and magistrate. Importantly, there are attempts to incorporate Indigenous symbols and ways of conducting business—through modifications to the physical layout of the court, to make it less hierarchical and didactic, and through the introduction of the Aboriginal flag and Aboriginal artefacts into the court. Similar to the other Indigenous courts, the Koori Court relies on a close partnership between the presiding magistrate and elders. In the Aboriginal court system, elders play a prominent role; by articulating a set of Aboriginal values and principles, they introduce an additional dimension to the proceedings. Blagg (2008, p. 130) explains that while some offenders may successfully 'neutralise' censure by 'white fella' law, they may be less successful in neutralising the 'big shame' of censure by Indigenous elders. The court process is organised to involve Koori people. There is a focus on reintegration with the Koori community and family support as the key to change. Considerable time is spent on each case, which often includes rich detail (of a nature and degree that would not normally emerge in court) of the life and family history of the defendant. Emphasis is placed on linking Aboriginal offenders with Aboriginal community programs, employment services and drug and alcohol services.

PENOLOGICAL PRINCIPLES: THE POLITICS OF PARTNERSHIP

Indigenous justice practices share some similarities with those linked to therapeutic jurisprudence and restorative justice. Some scholars note that the shaming and healing elements of Indigenous sentencing courts are similar to the desired elements of restorative justice conferences. Others claim that Indigenous courts are problem-solving courts—or specialist courts with some problem-solving and therapeutic overtones—because they feature participation, coordination of service delivery and community involvement. At a general level there are similarities among these courts. All emphasise improved communication between legal authorities, offenders, victims and community members, using plain language and reducing some of the legal formalities. All emphasise procedural justice—that is, treating people with respect, listening to what they have to say and being fair to everyone. All suggest the value of using persuasion and support to encourage offenders to be law-abiding. All assume that incarceration should be used as a penalty of last resort. However, far less is said about the theoretical or jurisprudential underpinnings of Indigenous justice practices. Marchetti and Daly (2007) along with others, argue that Indigenous courts have a distinct theoretical jurisprudential basis that cannot be simply distilled from ideas about therapeutic jurisprudence of restorative justice. These other justice innovations lack the political dimension that is at the forefront of Indigenous sentencing courts and justice practices. Marchetti and Daly (2007, pp. 429–30) argue that Indigenous sentencing courts have the potential to empower Indigenous communities, to bend and change the dominant perspective of 'white law' through Indigenous knowledge and modes of social control, and to come to terms with a colonial past. With the political aspiration to change Indigenous–white justice relations, Indigenous sentencing courts in particular, and Indigenous justice practices generally, are concerned with groups based on change in social relations (a form of political transformation), not merely a change in the individual.

The objectives of Indigenous sentencing courts reach far beyond the correction and fair treatment of Indigenous offenders, although rehabilitation clearly remains a goal. They are about change. A significant driver in the development of these courts has been the activism of Indigenous people and organisations. In New South Wales the Aboriginal Justice Advisory Council 'explored the concept of circle sentencing and put a proposal in 2002 to the Standing Committee of the Criminal Justice System Chief Executive Officer to examine the development of a circle sentencing model for NSW' (Potas et al. 2003, p. 9). In Victoria, Koori courts were established as an initiative of the Victorian Aboriginal Justice Agreement—an agreement between Victorian state government departments and key Koori organisations (Blagg 2008). This contrasts with the movements for therapeutic jurisprudence (Chapter 6) and restorative justice (Chapter 9) that emerged in Australia mainly as a result of the efforts of government and judicial officers. The role played by Indigenous people and organisations in establishing Indigenous courts influenced their aims and practices in significant ways, even though the justice process remained within the scope of the mainstream non-Indigenous legal system; this foundation points to a political aspiration that is absent in other recent justice innovations. These courts and their proponents are concerned with rebuilding and empowering Indigenous communities by engendering greater trust and cooperation between Indigenous communities, court staff and Indigenous offenders, and by changing the way justice is achieved in the 'white' court system to better reflect Indigenous knowledge and values (Marchetti and Daly 2007, p. 441).

THINKING THEORETICALLY: THE DECOLONISATION OF JUSTICE?

'The relationships created between institutions of the nation-state and Indigenous people have been forged within the contexts of a colonial political process and a colonial 'mentality'. Those processes have relied on treating Indigenous people as people to be excluded from the nation-state. Particularly in the more recent period, criminalisation has played an effective role in the process. Ultimately self-determination is thus directly linked to a process of decolonisation: both decolonisation of institutions and decolonisation of the colonial construction of Indigenous people as 'criminals'. (Cunneen 2001, p. 3)

How can we understand these innovative practices as a means of delivering justice while—at the same time—responding to the very real problem of high rates of Indigenous offending? To fully appreciate the principles expressed and applied in these emerging social institutions, it is necessary to briefly revisit our history of colonisation and punishment and consider its significance in relation to Indigenous Australians.

As mentioned in Chapters 1 and 2, penal institutions and practices underwent a significant reconfiguration in the nineteenth century. Penal welfarism notions of fault and proportionality were articulated with institutional differentiation aimed at scientifically categorising various forms of deviance and pathology as a means of allocating offenders to appropriate domains of technical expertise. Penal severity was moderated by a concern for correction, normalisation, integration and optimal social functioning. Penal incarceration took its place at the end of a continuum of measures of social government, most of which functioned to shepherd and regulate the family and those institutions that surrounded it, such as the school, medicine, public health, welfare and organised recreation (Hogg 2001). From the end of the nineteenth century, the welfare–penal institutions focused on Aboriginal families and communities; however, they tended to invert the logic of social governance and control being applied more generally. Aboriginal people were to be integrated or socialised into Australian society not by policing, supporting and augmenting the Aboriginal family, but by its destruction. The Aboriginal family and community were cast as the enemy of social order and civilised values, the principal means by which Aboriginality and culture were reproduced, and thus something that had to be eliminated.

Russell Hogg (2001) argues that the protection and segregation policies of the nineteenth and twentieth centuries may have insulated Aboriginal people to a degree against criminalisation and penal incarceration; however, the surveillance, control and forms of institutional treatment they provided for often amounted to the same thing. Local studies and scattered records indicate that the regimes of administrative segregation were employed in some places as an alternative to prosecuting suspected Aboriginal offenders before the ordinary criminal courts or as an adjunct to penalty (Finnane and McGuire 2001). When these administrative measures were removed in the 1960s, Aboriginal communities were suddenly subject to the full force of markets, legal institutions and pressures in environments that generally remained deeply hostile to Aboriginality. The social control and support that commonly underpin and surround 'law abiding citizens'—stable family relationships, property ownership, education, employment and so on—was almost totally lacking because it had been the purpose of earlier segregation policies to destroy it. Taking this into account, it is perhaps not very surprising that, for Aboriginal communities, administrative segregation in the 1960s gave way to penal incarceration for so many of their members (Hogg 2001). Current rates of contact with the criminal justice system exacerbate the existing high levels of poverty and unemployment among those directly affected, as well as their families and communities, many of whom can expect at any given time to have a substantial proportion of their young adult men (a fifth to a quarter) under some form of detention or otherwise caught up in the criminal justice system. High Aboriginal incarceration rates perpetuate for communities, as well as for the individuals incarcerated, some of the effects of civic and economic disenfranchisement that were formerly produced by segregationist laws.

However one traces the precise aetiology of Aboriginal offending, criminalisation and incarceration, the historical role of protection and welfare institutions in the production of carceral careers of Aboriginal people is undeniable. In seeking to erase Aboriginality, they set out to destroy rather than cultivate the forms of social authority that would inhibit offending and protect against criminalisation. In this context Indigenous justice initiatives—stimulated by the RCIADIC—can be seen as a response to devastating effects of colonisation for Aboriginal people, which had the effect of dismantling Indigenous cultural and social arrangements that worked to regulate behaviour (and potentially offending). In Queensland the Local Justice Initiative Funds were provided to develop local community-based strategies to address justice issues; the CJGs that were funded consisted of elders and respected persons and worked to re-establish community authority and discipline based on the authority of community elders. They have helped to improve the relationship between Indigenous people and government agencies, by providing either a direct role for the community in the rehabilitation of offenders or a means by which the community can have a say in how the state proposes to rehabilitate an offender. Aboriginal communities can therefore take on an active role in their own government.

Indigenous courts similarly rest on close partnership between state and community authority figures—that is, magistrates and Indigenous elders. The court processes are organised to involve Aboriginal people. For example, the NSW *Equality Before the Law Bench* book (Judicial Commission of New South Wales 2006, p. 2205) explains that circle sentencing enables 'full Indigenous input from Indigenous elders, provides a culturally appropriate way of discussing sanctions and therefore (some) self-determination, while at the same time meeting the requirements of Australian law in relation to the type of sentence imposed.

It is also delivering successful results in terms of recidivism'. There is a focus on reintegration with the community and family support as the key to change. Considerable time is spent on each case, taking into account the rich detail of the life and family history of the defendant. Emphasis is placed on linking Aboriginal offenders with Aboriginal community programs, employment services and drug and alcohol services. The court's work is not about 'processing' a case or 'finalising a file' but about learning more about the offender and the offence and making the effort to develop an appropriate response.

Blagg suggests that the various types of Indigenous courts can reduce the sense of estrangement that many Aboriginal people feel when confronted by the non-Aboriginal justice system. A lack of understanding of cultural issues in court raises some considerable difficulties for Aboriginal people, as one Aboriginal person told the Law Reform Commission of Western Australia:

> White man doesn't understand the black man law. There is no understanding of Customary Law protocols. Presentence and Court reports should include cultural matters, such as the significance of avoidance relationships. Lack of understanding of these avoidance principles sometimes causes Aboriginal people to break their law and get punished when they return to the community and even while a trial is going on. The trial itself creates situations where law is broken. For example, where a mother-in-law testifies about a son-in-law, people coming into Court who have avoidance relationships and are forced to sit or stand with each other. (Community consultation Pilbara in Blagg 2008, p. 128)

Traditional courtrooms are spatially, culturally and linguistically non-Indigenous—there are no Indigenous cultural points of reference, and they are presided over by authority figures to whom Indigenous people usually cannot relate and with whom they have little or no connection. Aboriginal people maintain that the alienation that many experience in the system is a factor in the high rates of repeat contact with the system and the failure to attend court and to comply with court orders. In a physical sense the Aboriginal courts attempt to incorporate Indigenous symbols and ways of conducting business—through modifications to the layout of the courtroom.

Clearly the justice processes described above are focused on the rehabilitation not only of offenders but also of the institutions of the criminal justice system itself. They seek to reshape the relationship between Indigenous peoples and these institutions. Offenders are to be rehabilitated through reviving relationships within Indigenous communities shaped through cultural practices and beliefs. Criminal justice institutions are to be reformed through partnership—not colonisation. For example, Indigenous people resist the idea that customary law should be adopted into 'white' law because this would simply be a variation on the theme of colonisation, where Indigenous people lose control of their laws (an important aspect of their lives) to the dominant culture. Taking this into account, it is arguable that the innovations described in this chapter have the radical ambition of reshaping the structural relations of criminal justice. This project is ambitious and far from complete, and Indigenous justice mechanisms will no doubt remain a site of ongoing struggle and tension as institutions work out how best to acknowledge and engage with the cultural practices of the original inhabitants of Australia.

CONCLUSION

Since colonisation, the experience of justice for Indigenous people has starkly contrasted with responses to other Australians. From the outset, British law failed to protect their interests when it ignored traditional rights to land. Any resistance was met by a system of harsh and differentiated justice. The promise of equality with the grant of full citizenship rights to Aboriginal people in 1971 did little to alleviate the devastating effects of colonisation. An immediate consequence was a rapid rise in their level of incarceration as Indigenous people were funnelled into the criminal justice system through a more direct route. The lived experience of these people—the environmental and locational factors shaping life and service delivery in rural and remote locations, patterns of policing and offending, legislation, factors in judicial decision-making, cultural difference and marginalisation— all contributed (and continue to contribute) to their over-representation in the Australian justice system and their incarceration at disproportionately high rates. Such high rates translated into an alarming number of Aboriginal deaths in custody; the RCIADIC inquiry marked the first acknowledgement and attempt by the non-Indigenous community to come to terms with the devastating impact that the criminal justice system has had on Aboriginal lives.

The Indigenous justice innovations—community justice groups, circle sentencing and Indigenous courts—were introduced in response to RCIADIC recommendations. Their practices clearly share some similarities with those linked to therapeutic jurisprudence and restorative justice. For example, the shaming and healing elements of Indigenous sentencing courts are similar to the desired elements of restorative justice conferences, while attention to therapeutic outcomes though participation, coordination of service delivery and community involvement align them with problem-solving courts. At a general level there are similarities among these courts. All emphasise improved communication between legal authorities, offenders, victims and community members, using plain language and reducing some of the legal formalities. All emphasise procedural justice—that is, treating people with respect, listening to what they have to say and being fair to everyone. All suggest the value of using persuasion and support to encourage change in offenders. All assume that incarceration should be used as a penalty of last resort.

The distinguishing features of Indigenous sentencing courts and other justice practices reach far beyond the correction and fair treatment of offenders. They are about change. The Indigenous justice processes are focused on the rehabilitation not only of offenders but also of the institutions of the criminal justice system itself. They seek to reshape the relationship between Indigenous peoples and these institutions. So this chapter has been a story of rehabilitation—but not just by conventional means. All the regulatory mechanisms of Aboriginal culture that might have assisted in the governance of the population were systematically dismantled by first the colonial state and then the welfare state. Through the reconfigured idea of rehabilitation in these new practices, Indigenous people themselves seek to resuscitate and revive their own cultural institutions of control through innovative and active relationships with post-colonial institutions of justice.

Responding to domestic violence: Special pleas and specialist courts

INTRODUCTION

In 2006 Toni Makkai, then Director of the Australian Institute of Criminology, noted that the reasons why individual offenders engage in criminal activity are numerous and varied (in Payne 2006). She pointed out that three key priority areas have emerged in recent years—reducing crime related to drug dependence and mental health, the over-representation of Indigenous offenders and the incidence of domestic violence. Moreover, policy-makers and criminal justice practitioners have responded to these priority areas in part through the development of specialist courts designed to tackle specific problem behaviours and associated issues. While each of these specialist court programs shares the same overall aim of reducing reoffending, they nevertheless have significantly different structures as they attempt to deal with very different problems. The preceding two chapters of this book considered how drug courts and Indigenous justice programs respond to crime and deliver punishment. This chapter is focused on the last of the problem areas identified by Makkai—that is, the contribution made by the addition of domestic violence courts, and the programs they represent, to the Australian criminal justice system.

As with drug courts, domestic violence courts have been a controversial addition to the Australian justice system. While evaluations demonstrating that they achieve reductions in offending are yet to be produced, participants in the process express high levels of satisfaction in comparison to usual criminal justice approaches to family and intimate partner violence. Unlike Indigenous justice programs, the development of domestic violence courts does not respond to recommendations of a ground-breaking royal commission. This does not suggest that domestic violence is not a significant problem: crime statistics describe alarming rates of violence among men and women who are or have been intimate partners. Analysts consistently note that women are more likely to know (have some relationship with) their attacker than men, and that they are more likely to be assaulted in private than in a public space. This pattern of victimisation indicates that women are often vulnerable in the 'safety' of their own home. Men are also subject to victimisation; however, less information is available on the dimensions of this type of violence. Research on intimate partner violence suggests that the relations involved are complex and simple victim–offender dichotomies are an inadequate means of understanding the dynamics.

Most investigations of domestic violence are focused on the problems of policing. In contrast, this chapter is focused on the ways we have responded to domestic violence after arrest and conviction. It begins by outlining the problem, describing trends in relation to offenders and victims. A frequent critique of relevant scholarly work is that the focus is on men as offenders and women as victims. There are good reasons for this. While current vigorous debate considers the relative experience of relationship violence by men and women, with some arguing that figures from general population surveys are roughly similar (Fergusson et al. 2005; Johnson 2005; Mouzos and Smith 2007), there is agreement that when it comes to the types of violence visible in hospital emergency departments, women's refuges, police statistics and in courtrooms, men are predominantly the perpetrators and women are greatly over-represented as victims (Fergusson et al. 2005). Nevertheless, some women do come to the attention of the criminal justice system for violence-related matters. When it comes to intimate partner violence, a small amount of literature describes battered women's syndrome, which seeks to acknowledge the context of this type of violence. In the interests of providing a thorough consideration of how the criminal justice system treats domestic violence, this chapter briefly reviews how courts in Australia have engaged with this concept. It then moves on to consider the recent introduction of specialist courts and their programs that tend to focus on men as offenders and women and children as victims. It concludes by assessing the principles of punishment underpinning these responses and links them to theoretical ideas. It the course of this analysis it becomes clear that feminist critiques have been (and continue to be) important because they both helped put domestic violence on the public agenda and continue to influence how we respond to this pressing problem.

THE PROBLEM WITH DOMESTIC VIOLENCE
The gendered experience of interpersonal violence

The 2005 national Personal Safety Survey (PSS) (ABS 2005) delivered some alarming information on the experience of violence by members of the general Australian population. In the twelve months prior to the survey period, 10 per cent of men and almost 5 per cent of women experienced physical violence[4]. The overall experience of physical assault for these men and women was different, however: 65 per cent of men and 15 per cent of women were physically assaulted by a male stranger, while 31 per cent of women and less than 5 per cent of men were physically assaulted by a current and/or previous partner. Of those men who had been physically assaulted since the age of fifteen, almost two-thirds were assaulted by a stranger, whereas over half of the corresponding group of women had been assaulted by a current and/or previous partner. People who experienced violence from their current partner were more likely to experience physical rather than sexual violence. Since the age of fifteen, more than twice as many women as

---

4   Physical violence includes any incident involving the occurrence, attempt or threat of physical assault. Physical assault involves the use of physical force with the intent to harm or frighten. An attempt to inflict physical harm is included only if a person believes it is likely to be carried out.

men experienced current partner violence, and both men and women were more likely to have experienced violence from a previous partner than from a current partner. More than three times as many women than men experienced violence from a previous partner.

Ultimate forms of violence: Intimate partner homicide

When it comes to the most extreme form of physical violence — homicide — trends are contrary to public perceptions that we are most at risk of being murdered by a stranger. Homicides in Australia and elsewhere are more likely to involve people who know one another: friends, acquaintances and family members. In Australia almost two in five homicides occur between family members, with an average of 129 family homicides each year. The majority of family homicides occur between intimate partners (60 per cent), three-quarters of which involve males killing their female partners. On average, twenty-five children are killed each year by a parent, with children under the age of one at the highest risk of victimisation. The less common types of family homicide include children killing their parents (twelve incidents per year) and homicide between siblings (six per year) (Mouzos and Rushforth 2003).

Most domestic violence occurs within the privacy of the home (ABS 2005). According to the PSS (ABS 2005), four out of five intimate partner homicides occurred in a private dwelling, with almost two in five occurring between partners with a known history of domestic violence. The majority (70 per cent) took place in the evening or early morning (between 6 p.m. and 6 a.m.) and on a week day.

When the motive for intimate partner homicides is examined, more than half stemmed from a domestic altercation between the victim and the offender; slightly less then three in ten were believed to arise from jealousy, desertion or the (actual or pending) termination of a relationship (Mouzos and Rushforth 2003). Intimate partner conflict can have deadly repercussions for other family members. Research on child deaths in New South Wales reported that family breakdown was a precipitating factor in almost one in five filicides (Lawrence and Fattore 2002), and Wallace (1986, p. 157) identified both marital conflict and violence as the common themes running through other family homicides and particularly in-law killings (Mouzos and Rushforth 2003).

Intimate partner violence in criminal justice populations

Mouzos and Smith (2007) found the level of intimate partner violence among a group of police detainees (49 per cent, $n = 1597$) was much higher than that in general population surveys. A higher percentage of female detainees than male detainees reported experiencing at least one incident of physical confrontation with an intimate partner over their lifetime. Female detainees were more than five times more likely than male detainees to report that their intimate partner had been arrested for an incident related to domestic violence. Similarly, male detainees were more likely than female detainees to report that they themselves had been arrested for an incident related to domestic violence. Of the detainees who were involved in partner violence, two-thirds of males and three-quarters of females reported being both victims and perpetrators of partner violence. The percentage of those who were victims of domestic violence was similar for men and women, whereas males were more likely to be perpetrators only. Mouzos and Smith's analysis revealed that female detainees generally experience more partner violence in their lifetime than males. When risk markers for involvement in partner violence were examined, the results from the multivariate analysis indicated that the gender of the detainees was not a significant predictor of intimate partner violence. Risk factors were arrest in the past twelve months, dependency on drugs, dependency on alcohol, having dependent children at home and experience of physical abuse as a child.

Mouzos and Smith (2007) caution that the results found in relation to this group may not be applicable to either the whole offender population or the general population; however, they do suggest that they indicate that differing levels of intervention are required to address the issues of violence and drug use for persons who come into contact with the criminal justice system. Within the family, early intervention could focus on identifying those at risk of abusing their children and partners and providing them with adequate support and positive alternatives to violence to enable them to cope with the stresses associated with parenting and relationships. Early signs of drug and alcohol dependency should also be addressed. Outside the family, early intervention could focus on diverting first offenders into suitable programs to address the possibility of their reoffending and becoming regular offenders.

RESPONDING TO WOMEN AS OFFENDERS: BATTERED WOMEN'S SYNDROME

As discussed above, a significant proportion of homicides in Australia occur within families, often against a background of domestic violence. While it is more common for women to be killed by a violent partner than to kill, some women fight back, thereby blurring any neat distinction between victim and offender. In 1999–2000 there were seventy-one spousal homicides in Australia (including current and separated legal and de facto spouse, sexual intimate, boyfriend, girlfriend and same-sex relationship), which accounted for approximately 20 per cent of all homicides. Women committed roughly one-quarter of spousal homicides (Mouzos 2001, p. 3). In approximately 24 per cent of intimate partner homicides in Australia in 2003–2004, one or typically both partners were Indigenous, yet Indigenous people make up 2.4 per cent of the Australian population (Mouzos 2005, p. 14); Indigenous women are substantially over-represented as both victims and offenders within the criminal justice system. Criminalised women commonly have a background of having been abused, and the proportion reporting abuse is typically higher for Indigenous women. Research undertaken by the Aboriginal Justice Advisory Council with Aboriginal women in NSW prisons found that 70 per cent of respondents had been sexually abused as children and that approximately 80 per cent had been victims of 'domestic/family violence' as adults: 'the figures suggest that many Aboriginal women in custody were victims of violence offences long before they were "offenders" themselves' (Lawrie 2002, p. 52).

Intimate violence has long been recognised as a context in which the boundaries between victim and offender may be blurred. Battered women who resist their abuser or retaliate are at risk of being seen as the aggressor and of being criminalised, while at the same time having their victimisation obscured or denied (Stubbs and Tolmie 2008). Women who kill in response to domestic violence have historically faced great difficulty in having courts recognise their victimisation and the full context of their offence. Feminist criminologists have drawn attention both to the blurred distinction between victim and offender and to the shortcomings of theoretical and empirical work that sets up a simple dichotomous construction of victim and offender (or agent). They argue that, for battered women (and for some other offending women), 'victimisation and agency are false dichotomies; both fail to take account of the women's daily experiences of oppression, struggle, and resistance within ongoing relationships' (Schneider 1992, p. 549 in Stubbs and Tolmie 2008, p. 142). According to Schneider, the challenge has been to connect 'the general' to 'the particular', to contextualise women's offending with reference to a structural approach to understanding battering, grounded in the particular circumstances of each offender:

> ... the problems that battered women face are viewed in isolation; they are rarely linked to gender socialisation, women's subservient position within society and the family structure, sex discrimination in the workplace, economic discrimination, problems of housing and a lack of child care, lack of access to divorce, inadequate child support, problems of single motherhood, or lack of educational and community support. The focus is all on the individual woman and her 'pathology' instead of on the batterer and the social structures that support the oppression of women and that glorify or otherwise condone violence. (Schneider 2000, pp. 72–3)

When it comes to responding to intimate partner violence, social context is therefore important because it promotes a more complete understanding of the women's actions. According to Stubbs and Tolmie (2005; 2008), it is unlikely that the behaviour of women charged with offences committed in response to domestic or family violence will be fairly assessed if this aspect of offending is not understood and taken into account. For example, they explain that failure to understand social context is a major obstacle in raising 'self defence' as a defence in court; it may also impact on other possible defences, the exercise of pre-trail discretion and sentencing. Feminist work has typically emphasised self-defence because it offers the potential to acknowledge both the structural realities of many battered women's lives and the circumstances surrounding their killings. It has stressed that because self-defence is about judging whether the accused woman's response to her circumstances was reasonable, those circumstances must be made intelligible to the court. Moreover, it is the only defence that offers vindication of the defendant's actions and results in an acquittal. By contrast, provocation and diminished responsibility result in a manslaughter conviction, which is based on a concession to human frailty or mental incapacity rather than the social and situational context.

Battered women's syndrome (BWS) is a concept that was introduced in the United States in the 1970s. Operating within an equal rights framework, BWS is as a feminist strategy to assist women charged with killing a violent abuser/partner in arguing self-defence by bringing their social context to the attention of the court (see Caven 2003; and Easteal 1991 for a definition of BWS and further discussion of its use in the Australian courts). Early decisions in the United States and Canada accepted BWS evidence and offered hope that courts were becoming responsive to feminist arguments that challenged the gender bias inherent in self-defence (and other defences), where women typically face different circumstances from men but have been judged against a benchmark derived from men's experiences. In practice, however, BWS has usually not been understood as a means to explain the social context of the defendant's actions and has been largely unsuccessful in reshaping self-defence law to better reflect the circumstances of battered women who kill to protect themselves or their children. Instead of explaining why the behaviour was reasonable given the circumstances, BSW has commonly been used in a way that frames those circumstances subjectively rather than objectively. It has been used primarily to describe and justify the defendant's perceptions, often cast as individual pathology by, for example, suggesting that a woman's inability to leave a relationship stems from personal inadequacy. Such an individualised focus tends to confuse notions of choice with agency, whereby the woman's belief that she has few choices available to deal with ongoing violence is rendered irrational or distorted (Hudson 2002, p. 43). Expert psychiatric or psychological evidence typically used in BSW cases, combined with the labels 'syndrome' and 'learned helplessness', reinforces individualised understandings of battered women's behaviour in ways that conform to narrow stereotypes of helplessness.

Stubbs and Tolmie (2008; 2005) argue that adopting this individualised focus fails to acknowledge structural patterns and trends; as a result, systemic gender and race inequalities are commonly rendered invisible. They propose that BWS may be even more problematic as a defence strategy for Aboriginal or other racialised women. The marked over-representation of Indigenous women in intimate homicides emphasises the need for any analysis of the legal response to these cases to recognise the contribution made by the intersecting social factors, which include gender, race and disadvantage. Instead, testimony about BSW is often heard as a kind of special pleading consistent with an exercise of compassion, rather than as an explanation of systemic inequalities faced by many women.

Battered voices

Below are stories that represent the voices of many people who have been affected by violence and gather through the consultation process of the Aboriginal and Torres Straight Islander Women's Task Force on Violence (Robertson 2000).

Over the years it was the same every pay day, any day he could get money … six or seven nights a week. Mostly it was my money. I couldn't stay in the house or he'd have killed me for sure. I'd run away or get into the car and drive. I'd sleep in the car or on the beach with the homeless people. Then I'd go back into the house in the morning and shower and go to work and pretend nothing was happening to me.

To add to my problems my eighteen year old daughter returned home. Instead of having another woman for a companion, I now had two alcoholics on my hands … and a drug addict. Then I found out her father was supplying her. I had them both abusing and fighting me. My only option was to kill him or to do something in my job … that resulted in me getting six years but it got me away from the violence. Being locked away was the first peace I'd had in years. With all my troubles I never considered suicide. Never even thought about it.

This time he came home drunk and I'd only just started to get tea ready. He picked up the saucepan of boiling potatoes and tipped it all over me and then started bashing me with the heavy saucepan. He smashed me right across the face and then started belting me around the shoulders and wherever he could hit because I was trying to get away and screaming for someone to help me. Blood was pouring from my face. He had me by the hair trying to rip it out by the roots. No one came to help me. They all stood outside trying to get a good look through the door. But someone at least called the police and they took me to hospital. I couldn't see out of my eyes for days and I was scalded all down one side …

He came to visit me in hospital and cried and said he was sorry. Like a fool I went home and every night in bed, he'd warn me what he would do to me if I tried to run away. I'd lie there wondering where I could go for help. I didn't know where to even start. I was terrified. And it happened again. And it did … lots of times. Still I was too scared to leave. Twice I overdosed and another time I slashed my wrists but he'd say he was sorry and call for me at the hospital. I just went home with him because I was too frightened to ask for help. You don't know how relieved I was when he went to jail. My big worry now is where do I hide when he comes out? I don't have anywhere to go and I know it'll all start again but this time it will be worse because he's going to want to get even. He's going to make me pay for this. I might have to pay with my life.

Source: Roberston (2000), pp. 87–8.

RESPONDING TO WOMEN AS VICTIMS: DOMESTIC VIOLENCE COURTS AND PROGRAMS FOR MEN

Since the 1980s the central policy tenet in Australia and other industrialised Western countries has been that domestic violence is a crime and that legally enforceable safety and protection of victims is to be provided. Despite this formal acknowledgment, the responses of criminal justice agencies have continued to attract criticism. In the past they have often failed to treat family, and especially domestic, matters seriously. Even though changes in policy explicitly defined domestic violence as a crime, low charge and conviction rates suggested it was still not considered as such; moreover, there was (and continues to be) insufficient systemic case coordination within and across criminal justice agencies. Police have been condemned for inadequate initial responses, lack of appropriate action or intervention, and lack of victim follow-up and referral. Victim witnesses have been reluctant to attend court. Prosecutors have poor understandings of the complexities and sensitivities of the offence and its context; bail determinations have lacked appropriate conditions and the enforcement of bail and protection orders has been unreliable. Police attendance and intervention at both single and repeat domestic-violence incidents tends to be informed by a perception of the incident as a one-off incident or offence. Little consideration is given to the nature of the experience as a course of conduct—that is, the social and historical context of offending. Courthouses have not been designed to facilitate the comfort and safely of victim witnesses. Attitudes expressed both from the bench and by prosecutors and police officers have been at times unhelpful and inappropriate. Sentencing options are ineffective in reducing repeat offending, do not provide for victim input and pay insufficient attention to compliance with court orders (Holder 2001; Stewart 2005).

TABLE 8.1   Domestic violence courts in Australia

State	Year introduced	Program	Core components
Australian Capital Territory	1998	Australian Capital Territory Family Violence Intervention Program	Responds to domestic violence, child abuse and elder abuse through an approach that involves: • pro-arrest, pro-charge and presumption against bail • early provision of support for victims • pro-prosecution • coordination and case management • rehabilitation of offenders
South Australia	1999	Adelaide (Central Violence Intervention Program—CVIP) Elizabeth (Northern Violence Intervention Program—NVIP)	• Advice about making protections orders • Services for men to address violent/abusive behaviour • Facilitates access to services for women and children

(Continues)

TABLE 8.1 Domestic violence courts in Australia (*continued*)

State	Year introduced	Program	Core components
Victoria	2005	Family Violence Court Heidelberg (outer metropolitan) Ballarat (regional Victoria)	• One-stop-shop approach to offenders and victims • Integrated response from legal and support services • The court deals with: o intervention/protection and counselling orders o civil personal injury claims o family law and child support matters o summary criminal proceedings o committal proceedings for indictable charges o compensation and restitution cases
New South Wales	2005	Wagga Wagga (regional New South Wales) Campbelltown (outer metropolitan)	Integrated response to domestic violence: • improved police response to reported incidents • early support and information for victims • provision of counselling and support services for women and children • offender treatment/education program integrated with women's and children's programs
	1996	33 women's domestic violence court advocacy programs supporting women at 64 courts in domestic violence matters	Applications for protection orders
Queensland	1999	No specialist domestic violence court, but court support services are available in magistrates courts throughout the state	• Community-based integrated response to domestic violence • Court support services provide information support and assistance to people affected by domestic and family violence in relation to a domestic violence order, including support people in the Magistrates Court during a domestic violence matter • Some services provide information to both men and women on domestic and family violence matters; others only support women
Western Australia	1999	Joondalup Family Violence Court Rockingham Family Violence Court Fremantle Family Violence court Perth Family Violence Court Midland Family Violence Court	• Joondalup Family Violence Court was the first of these; it was based on the South Australian Northern Violence Intervention Program (NVIP), which adopts an inter-agency case-management approach to the supervision of offenders and support of victims • Geraldton Alternative Sentencing Regime focuses on rehabilitation of offenders with substance abuse, domestic violence and other offending related problems

(*Continues*)

TABLE 8.1 Domestic violence courts in Australia (*continued*)

State	Year introduced	Program	Core components
		Armadale Family Violence Court Geraldton Court (regional Western Australia)	• The court requires both parties to enter into a behavioural contract to participate in the Roads to Healing Program and protection orders may be amended to allow them to attend together
Tasmania		No specific domestic violence court, but infrastructure and legislation changes	Changes provide for: • pro-arrest, pro-prosecution policing and a victim safety response time for Tasmania police • courts to expedite domestic/family violence proceedings • funding for statewide court support services • funding for additional services for child witnesses and for counselling and support for adult and child victims • family violence offender intervention programs, delivering rehabilitation for suitable offenders as a sentencing option • accommodation of offenders ordered from the family home
Northern Territory		No specialist domestic violence court program	

In the context of these failings, as well as other emerging justice innovations in criminal courts (described in Chapters 6 and 7) and in line with developments for addressing domestic violence in many overseas jurisdictions, most Australian states and territories over the last decade have established, or are in the process of establishing, specialist domestic violence courts. They exist either as divisions of existing magistrates courts or as specially convened courts on particular court sitting days, operating with special procedures and protocols and ideally improved professional practice. By removing domestic violence cases from the mainstream day-to-day court processes, identifying them and tagging them for specialist legal processing and expedition, these courts aim to improve victims' experience of the legal system and, more often than not, use their powers to direct offenders into treatment (Payne 2006).

The rationale behind the establishment of specialist domestic violence courts recognises that problems resulting from this type of violence are complex. Any effective response is likely to involve intervention by agencies that can provide an array of culturally appropriate services to victims and their children. In general, specialist domestic-violence courts differ from other problem-solving courts in that they consider evenly the safety of victims and ways to ensure offender responsibility and accountability; they are frequently described in the literature as victim-centred, with a primary focus on victim protection (Goldberg 2005). This makes them different from other specialist courts, such as drug or Indigenous courts, in which offender well-being is clearly the issue. Some court-based initiatives seek to create a one-stop-shop intake centre, which co-locates justice and victims' support personnel (for example, the Collingwood Neighbourhood Justice Centre, which is discussed in Chapter 2). Others provide specialisation through prosecutors and judges and reviewing the physical location and layout of courts.

The sentencing process

As with drug and Indigenous courts, the judge or magistrate (depending on the jurisdiction) has an expanded role in domestic violence courts. This involves a departure from standard judicial practice. Judicial officers engage with the broader community—often through court users' forums, case management and interagency meetings—to develop an understanding of the realities and limitations of service provision to victims, children and offenders so that they can sentence appropriately and make appropriate orders. Their role is therefore more interactive: they are likely to adopt a more inquisitorial style by asking questions from the bench to better inform the course of action to be taken. In sentencing, specialist domestic-violence court judges or magistrates weigh up the issues involved in domestic violence and balance these with the safety and needs of the victim and the family. Sentencing options can include:

- imprisonment, including periodic detention
- post-imprisonment attendance at court for review and setting of conditions of parole and/or orders
- a suspended sentence with supervision, pending progress reports and outcomes of participation in a perpetrator program
- a bond with conditions, including attendance at a perpetrator program and supervision, pending progress reports and outcomes of participation in the program
- fines and appropriate community service orders
- home detention with monitoring and supervision (Stewart 2005).

Sentence discounting is a common feature of courts where defendants enter a guilty plea; the earlier the plea, the greater the discount. Upon conviction, magistrates have been urged to make a protection order if one is not already in existence. In the Australian Capital Territory, on a plea of guilty and on conviction by the court and at the discretion of the court, offenders may be ordered for assessment prior to sentencing for suitability and eligibility for entry into a treatment or education program as a condition of probation or parole following release from prison. Alternatively, in South Australia, participation in a program is a condition of bail and sentencing takes place after completion or withdrawal from that program. Assessment for suitability is based on: appropriateness of the referral, some indication of contrition and responsibility for the offence (not necessarily a guilty plea), a commitment to participate in the program as a whole, and satisfaction of a range of other criteria pertaining to such issues as language, mental health and/or drug and alcohol abuse or dependence. The results of assessing suitability and eligibility are provided to the court as part of pre-sentence reporting.

In a number of models the function of assessing eligibility and suitability for inclusion in perpetrator treatment may be provided by community corrections or probation services. It is not common for perpetrator treatment to be provided by these services; it is more often provided by the private sector. For example, in the Australian Capital Territory, a probation officer assesses the offender as eligible while the program provider (such as Relationships Australia, under contract to the Department of Corrections) makes the assessment for suitability. The program is both one of the sentencing options available and one of the 'management' options available to a probation officer. By way of contrast, in New South Wales, the Probation and Parole Service of the Department of Corrective Services actually provides the treatment program for perpetrators in the domestic violence courts (which operate in Campbelltown and Wagga Wagga). Compliance with orders or conditions imposed on the defendant by the court are monitored and reported back to the court by the probation service in the form of progress and final reports on completion of a program or on non-compliance with orders and conditions. Prosecution of breaches of probation and parole are initiated by probation and parole officers. This is significant because corrections departments had been until recently absent from the arena of domestic violence service provision. Specialist courts have brought them into the process through the management of offenders, extending the role of corrections agencies to ensure the safety of victims and their families and broadening their focus to the community at large.

Perpetrator treatment programs

Approaches to intervention with perpetrators are based on differing theoretical explanations for their abusive, violent and controlling behaviour. These perspectives in part reflect different emphases on different levels of intervention. Individual perspectives focus on understanding the particular characteristics of men who are violent towards their partners. The literature here is divided between two perspectives: one compares domestic violence perpetrators to men who are not violent in their intimate relationships, while the other seeks to develop typologies of domestically violent men (Johnson and Ferraro 2000; Johnson 2005). Alternatively, systemic theories of intimate partner violence focus on the patterns of interaction between couples and involve intervention with the man and woman as a couple (see Fergusson et al. 2005). Such approaches have attracted criticism because: couples counselling may jeopardise the woman's safety by making her vulnerable to retaliation through disclosures made in the therapy situation; it implies that the problem is mutual and that, as a contributor, the woman is expected to change; and the focus is on saving the relationship rather than addressing the violence and coercive control exercised by the perpetrator (Lipchik et al. 1997). Lipchik and colleagues (1997) argue that there should be a place for conjoint therapy in a coordinated inter-agency response to domestic violence because many couples 'continue in the relationship despite the best efforts of police, prosecutors, shelters and advocates', and because there is as yet little evidence of the effectiveness of perpetrator groups, which are the most popular form of intervention. Over the last decade a number approaches that attempt to address the concerns and risks of conjoint therapy have been described in literature (see Laing 2002; Mouzos and Smith 2007). Because of the focus of this book and space limitations, these approaches will not be discussed in any detail here. A third approach—the socio-political perspective—has arguably been the most influential both in the context of Australian programs aimed at preventing domestic violence more generally, and in the development of relevant specialist courts in this country more specifically.

In her extensive review of the effectiveness of programs for perpetrators of domestic violence, Laing (2002) summarises the socio-political perspective. First, approaches from this perspective seek to understand domestic violence at a social or group level rather than at the level of the individual man. 'Instead of examining why this particular man beats his particular wife, feminists seek to understand why men in general use force against their partners' (Bograd 1988, p. 13). Second, because domestic violence is a common event (ABS 2005), the focus is on the social conditions that support it, not the identification of the characteristics of a small 'deviant' group of men. Third, concepts of gender and power lie at the foundation of this perspective. As a social group, men have greater power than women and violence is an important means of maintaining this dominant position. Rather than being a 'safe haven', 'the family as a social institution mediates between oppression at the broadest social level and the personal relationships of intimate adult partners' (Bograd 1988, p. 14). From a socio-political perspective, violence against women can therefore only be understood in its social context:

> Men are violent to their women partners in a wider context of family, friends and the general cultural and institutional settings in which such behaviour and accompanying attitudes are more or less condemned or condoned. The messages and responses are often mixed and ambivalent, showing support for men's authority over wives, boundaries of 'appropriate' behaviour for women in the role of wife, and more or less tolerance for the use of violence under certain circumstances. Sanctions for the use of violence are often weak or non-existent and men incur few if any costs for its use. (Dobash et al. 2000, p. 13)

However, there is no consensus from the socio-political perspective on the most appropriate response to violent men. Some advocates strongly oppose intervention with individual men, whereas others argue that a socio-political explanation for violence can be incorporated into work with these men as part of the larger process of social change. From this latter viewpoint, work done with men who use violence must address the social context of gendered inequality. Pro-feminist or gender-based group work has been the most common response to working with men who use violence in their intimate relationships (Laing 2002).

Gender-based cognitive behaviour groups

Socio-political perspectives on domestic violence have resulted in the development of a specialised type of group-work intervention, commonly termed gender-based cognitive behaviour group work. In these groups, an emphasis on social context results in a focus on the education of men about gender inequality and the tactics of power and control in relationships. Stopping the violence, abuse and controlling behaviours is the goal of intervention rather than providing a therapeutic response to the man's individual psychological problems, such as low self-esteem or poor impulse control.

The notion of the man accepting responsibility for the abuse, for its effects and for stopping violence and controlling behaviour is central to this form of intervention. Key characteristics include:

○ These groups do not stand alone as an adequate response to domestic violence; they are one part of a coordinated community response, involving at a minimum the criminal justice system and services for abused women.

○ The safety of women and children is the primary goal.

○ It is vital that the program used is accountable and transparent to women's lived experience of domestic violence.

○ In contrast to the norms of conventional therapeutic encounters, the confidentiality offered to participants is limited, with the program given permission to contact partners and the criminal justice system to ensure victims' safety and offender accountability.

○ The groups are respectful. In Australia, the work of Jenkins (1990) and White (1989) has been influential in developing approaches that respectfully invite men to address their violent behaviour as the focus of work, but without unproductive confrontation. Based on narrative therapy (White and Epston 1989), these Australian developments contrast with some of the 'educational' group-work approaches developed in North America (Laing 2002, p. 4).

Despite a lack of conclusive evidence on the efficacy of any of these criminal justice interventions, many commentators agree that it is the combined effect of the activities of the criminal justice agencies that maximises impact, rather than the isolated action (for example, arrest) by one agency (for example, the police). Process evaluations have indicated high rates of victim satisfaction; and in relation to recidivism, recent studies have explored whether the combined effect of the various criminal justice interventions have more effect together than singly (Laing 2002). Indeed, Steinman (1990), Syers and Edleson (1992), Jaffe et al. (1993) and Dobash and Dobash (1997) have all found that the combination of arrest, prosecution and court sanctions, such as perpetrator programs, was more likely to end repeat violence than other combinations of criminal justice actions. Moreover, Steinman (1990) found that police actions that were not coordinated with other sanctions led to increased violence.

PENOLOGICAL PRINCIPLES: PUNISHMENT AND PROTECTION

Holder (2001, p. 2) explains that criminal justice performs a function that not only is instrumental in enforcing legal and social norms, but also is highly symbolic. Criminal law is a powerful agency of public disapproval and reprobation. The criminal justice system purports to deliver justice, uphold citizens' rights and protect the vulnerable. For victims of domestic violence and their advocates, criminal justice interventions are one means of society delivering concrete meaning on these terms. They also provide one of the few mechanisms available to victims for actually stoping violence. The first part of Holder's statement clearly echoes the just deserts principles of punishment described in Chapter 2—that sentences should communicate official censure or blame, the communication being chiefly to the offender but also to the victims and the society at large. In the late 1980s the Australian Law Reform Commission (ALRC) explained that with the adoption of just deserts in Australia, the primary emphasis was on 'just deserts for the offender and reparation for the victim'; however, '[d]eterrence, rehabilitation and incapacitation should still be relevant but given a lesser priority' (ALRC 1987, p. 17 in Brown 1998, p. 383). While it is clear that just deserts and victim reparation (or at least victim safety) are key considerations in the deliberations of domestic violence courts, prevention constituted through deterrence, rehabilitation and incapacitation are of no lesser concern.

In a discussion paper reviewing the introduction of domestic violence courts to Australia, Stewart (2005, p. 7) explains that the aims of these specialist courts include:

- best practice in policing and prosecuting domestic violence offences
- expedition of cases
- information, support, advocacy and services for victims of domestic violence and their children
- safety for victims and their children as the primary outcome
- safety for victims at court
- validation and empowerment of victims and their children
- responsibility and accountability for domestic violence to be accepted by offenders
- reduction and prevention of domestic violence.

The desired outcomes of achieving these aims are broadly an increased level of awareness of domestic violence within the community and agencies that respond to it, and more specifically a heightened awareness in offenders and victims that action will be taken if an offence is reported to the police. These objectives are about both censure and deterrence. Beyond these, other hopes for domestic violence courts are increased rates of reporting offences and a lessened rate of victims' withdrawal from proceedings. Higher standards of professional behaviour have been achieved through proactive policing and improved investigation methods in domestic violence offences. Ideally, this translates into: increased rates of guilty pleas and convictions (due in part to better evidence and brief preparation); increased rates of prosecution of domestic violence offences; decreased rates of withdrawal of charges; higher levels of safety for victims of domestic violence and their children; and more appropriate protection orders, which are tailored to victims' circumstances. It is also expected that the coordinated criminal justice response will enhance inter-agency cooperation, improve the quality of service delivery and result in greater accountability and a more consistent approach to domestic violence. These system changes, along with discounts for (early) guilty pleas, are consistent with indicators described in relation to managerialist rationalities outlined in Chapter 2.

Reduction and prevention are not only achieved by deterrence; victim services promoting safety and offender programs addressing behavioural change are also key components of the integrated response. Domestic violence courts lend support to Finnane's claims regarding the emergence of victims as a chief consideration in the criminal justice debate and policy in recent years. Generally, the profile of victims has been highlighted by criminal justice system practices that are shaped by principles of restorative justice and communitarianism. Indeed, the victim-centred nature of the aims and outcomes described above, along with the aspiration that responsibility and accountability for domestic violence be accepted by offenders, suggests that these courts are shaped by these principles. Alternatively, the provision for treatment both in the form of perpetrator programs and counselling for victims indicate some therapeutic intent.

There is no clear agreement in the literature regarding the fundamental principles underpinning the operation of specialist domestic-violence courts. According to Stewart (2005), discussion centres on the application of therapeutic jurisprudence to criminal determinations, and argues that the establishment of specialist domestic-violence courts is a further and logical application of the doctrine. Therapeutic jurisprudence focuses on accountability of the offender and rehabilitation (Phelan 2003). Goldberg (2005) describes therapeutic sentencing as addressing the revolving-door syndrome and giving hope of change and positive outcomes in an inclusive and non-coercive manner. She states that offender accountability is the primary focus, along with safety of the victim, and that the rehabilitation of the offender is secondary to these (2005, p. 25). Hannam (2003) points to the negotiation with the offender over bail and probation conditions as a means of encouraging compliance through remand, with regular reviews and lengthy adjournments to give defendants chances to demonstrate reform. In describing her observations of therapeutic jurisprudence in action in a New York specialist domestic violence court, she emphasises the positive therapeutic effect on victims—particularly as a result of their access to an array of support services and early intervention.

Restorative justice is often mixed up with therapeutic jurisprudence— that is, there is a blurring of the two theoretical concepts—though their court practices are distinctive (see Marchetti and Daly 2007 for a clear presentation of the differences). Restorative justice is described as 'placing an equal focus on the offender, the community and the victim … the goal of sentencing is to repair the harm to the offender, victim and the community, restore offender accountability to the other stakeholders and encourage community responsibility for responding to crime' (Phelan 2003, p. 6). Alternatively, the concept of problem-solving courts is also mentioned in discussion around domestic violence courts. Problem-solving courts signify the recognition by governments and the judiciary of their 'failure … to solve problems of quality of life crimes' and that persistent problems might be dealt with in such a way as to effect more lasting benefits to victims, the community and offenders (Feinblatt and Denckla 2001). Courts have modified their practices to accommodate offenders whose criminality is deemed to be caused by their disadvantage and for whom imprisonment is unlikely to lead to ongoing positive outcomes for anyone—the offender, the victim or the community (Stewart 2005).

The view that there is merit in the application of restorative or problem-solving approaches in criminal proceedings involving victimless crime, petty property offences and other infringements has been accepted by policy-makers. However, vigorous debate surrounds whether or not these approaches can be applied when addressing crimes of violence against a person. Feminist legal scholars and the community of women who struggled throughout the 1970s, 1980s and 1990s (and are still struggling) to ensure that domestic assault is recognised, named and dealt with as a crime argue against the use of restorative justice practices in which the direct victim of the offence participates in the sentencing process (Petrucci 2002). Personal violence, including sexual violence, committed within the context of an intimate or family relationship is complex; the position of power of the offender over the victim distorts, even negates, the purpose and process of a victim participating freely in conferencing for sentencing in a restorative justice framework.

Stubbs (2002; see also Busch 2002; Daly 2002a) clearly highlights the risks of restorative justice in this context. Strang and Braithwaite (2002) explain that the features of restorative justice reflect its development in the terrain of juvenile justice, where the focus on the discrete past incident and it alone was part of a strategy for avoiding the pathologising of young people and averting net widening. When it comes to domestic violence, it is the argument of Stubbs and other feminists that the nets of social control need to be widened. With restorative justice for young offenders, one of the benefits that victims report is that they leave the process no longer frightened of their assailant. Victims typically learn that they were not specifically targeted but were chosen more randomly. It is problematic to assume that this is the case for all victims. As advocates of restorative justice, Strang and Braithwaite admit their failure to think about the contextual specificity of domestic violence. In such cases, victims are not chosen at random, are likely to be re-victimised, and in most cases are objectively in fear of someone with the physical and other resources to dominate them. Restorative justice is theorised as a response to a discrete past event as opposed to an ongoing course of conduct, like domestic violence. In the restorative process, great significance is invested in an apology. This assumes a certain level of trust between the parties: that an apology will be offered genuinely and accepted in good faith. Yet, as Stubbs (2002) points out, often there is little basis for trust since domestic violence is commonly characterised by repeated offending and apology. Domestic violence perpetrators often are adept at using apology to manipulate their partners and others. Furthermore, it is very difficult to empower women to make their own undominated choices through an institution like restorative justice when the contextual fact of the matter is that they will refuse to make choices other than those in the interests of their children—children perhaps who love a father who batters their mother. (For a more detailed feminist critique of restorative justice, see Daly and Stubbs 2006.)

THINKING THEORETICALLY: FEMINISM AND ITS DISCONTENTS

The recognition of domestic violence as a serious social problem is an achievement of second-wave feminism, a social movement originating in the late 1960s and early 1970s. Feminism applied a socio-political framework to understanding domestic violence, a vastly different perspective from the (then) prevailing medical model that saw the causes of domestic violence as lying within the pathology of the individuals involved. In the political lobby for equal rights for women internationally and nationally, domestic violence was recognised as one of the most powerful tools of the oppression and subordination of women. Awareness of this shifted private relations into the public sphere so that women need no longer bear the shame and suffering in silence and in private. A range of initiatives were developed and eventually funded by governments to acknowledge the problem and to attempt to enable women to live safely and without fear. Women's refuges were an important development for women and their children made homeless by violence, but these provided only short-term solutions. Feminists, who through the refuge movement began the modern movement against domestic violence, provided a template for change. While they responded to the needs of individual women for safety and support, they linked this work to the need for change at the broader societal level. They focused on gender inequity, the attitudes that support it and the legal and institutional changes necessary to name domestic violence as a crime, to hold men accountable and to make services responsive to women's needs for safety.

These objectives are clearly evident in feminist pleas for the recognition, and accounts of the failures, of the concept of BWS as a response to women who resist violence with violence, as well as the form of programs offered through domestic violence courts in this country (in particular perpetrator treatment programs). The traditional criminal justice response views episodes of domestic violence in isolation. More often than not, courts position violent responses as a single event; this obscures any preceding victimisation and works to reinforce a false dichotomy between victim and offender, thereby failing to take into account the daily experience for some women of oppression, struggle and resistance. The objective of promoting the concept of BWS was to highlight the significance of the broader social context of intimate partner violence, with a view to facilitating a more complete understanding of women's actions.

The significance of social context is also at the heart of programs for perpetrators delivered through domestic violence courts, which explicitly aim at a practical level to hold men accountable and ensure the safety of women and their children. The socio-political perspective shaping these programs seeks to understand domestic violence at a social or group level rather than at the level of the individual man. Instead of trying to understand why a particular individual man beats his wife, the focus is on the way men in general use force against their partners. This orientation shapes the form of gender-based cognitive behaviour groups that seek to educate men about gender inequality and the tactics of power and control employed in relationships. The significance of social context is also borne out when it comes to the acknowledged limits/failure of restorative justice in the domestic violence court environment: its inability to engage with the contextual specificity of domestic violence and to recognise that it is rarely a discrete event—victims are not chosen at random—and that any apology is highly unlikely to have any healing effect.

CONCLUSION

Domestic violence is a significant social problem. Unfortunately, it is a common experience for many people, with sometimes deadly consequences for those involved. In the past, criminal justice agencies have been judged as inadequate in their responses to this type of crime. Charge and conviction rates have remained low despite the introduction of policy that clearly defines domestic and family violence as a crime. There has also been poor coordination of cases within and across criminal justice and service provider agencies. This tends to be the result of a tendency to view instances of domestic and family violence as isolated events. Police and other key actors in the criminal justice system have failed to recognise and respond to the complex social and historical aspects—the context—of this type of offending behaviour.

Recent attempts to address this short-sightedness have varied in their approach and success. The introduction of the idea of battered women's syndrome (BWS) was a feminist strategy to assist women charged with killing a violent partner in arguing self-defence by bringing their social context to the attention of the court. Despite this original intent, BWS has more commonly been used in Australia and overseas in a way that frames the circumstances of violence and retaliation subjectively rather than objectively. It has been used primarily to describe and justify the defendant's perceptions, often cast as some kind of individual weakness or deficit. Programs responding to the more common occurrence of male offending have also focused on the significance of the social context of violence against women. Perpetrator treatment programs delivered in domestic violence courts in this country are developed from a socio-political perspective that focuses on the systemic nature of gender inequality and the tactics of power and control in relationships. While it is clear that offender responsibility and victim safety are key considerations in the deliberations of domestic violence courts, prevention through offender programs addressing behavioural change is a main component of the integrated response.

Both these contemporary criminal justice responses aim to achieve an increased level of awareness of domestic violence within the community and agencies that respond to it. Both programs are delivered from a socio-political perspective that draws attention to the systemic nature of gender equality. Pleas that rely on BWS and domestic violence courts can be understood as more or less effective strategies for achieving systematic change: they work to alter attitudes and, more specifically, to reconfigure key legal and institutional structures. Like Indigenous justice initiatives, they are about change—challenging and changing structural and institutional dimensions of society that shape and maintain community attitudes to violence against women and the violent behaviour of men.

Restitution

PART 4

Youth justice and group conferencing: Restoration and restitution

INTRODUCTION

We began our practical investigation into the principles of and ideas about punishment and sentencing by exploring the idea of risk. Part 2 focused on the concept of risk and considered how ideas about punishment are linked to concepts of dangerousness and risk (Pratt 1997; Pratt and Brown 2000). The key theme in Part 3 was rehabilitation, exploring the recent introduction and seeming proliferation of various types of problem-solving courts that tend to blur boundaries between sentencing, punishment and correction. Such courts involve preventive partnerships (Garland 2001) with treatment service providers in the community; and (with the exception of a concern for safety in domestic violence courts) they are not so much concerned with victims or vulnerable situations, but intensely focused on treating or changing the offender. This final part of the book, which deals with restitution, positions offenders as opportunistic. Individuals who are the subject of the interventions and responses discussed here are not understood as poorly socialised misfits in need of assistance; instead, they are seen as illicit, opportunistic consumers who lack a strong moral compass or any effective internal controls, aside from a capacity for rational calculation and a will to pleasure (Garland 2001; Lynch 2005). Chapters 9 and 10 explore how interventions driven by the principle of restitution rely on the capacity of the offender to make 'the right' choices once made aware of the consequences of their behaviour and strategies that seek to govern crime though the manipulation of interests and the promotion of mechanisms of self-regulation. We will see how youth conferencing and fines, together with the recent anti-hooning legislation, can be understood as exemplars of neoliberal governmental approaches to crime (Bottoms 2003; Braithwaite 2000; Rose 2000) that largely govern by altering criminogenic situations rather than seeking to significantly change or retrain the offender.

The subject of this chapter—youth justice conferencing—offers an approach to offending that contrasts starkly with some recent and fairly controversial proposals for addressing crime committed by young people. In Australia these have included youth curfews (Morris et al. 2007) and mandatory sentencing of repeat offenders, which work to incapacitate through containment (or simply clearing young people, as a group, out of the way). Youth justice conferencing (YJC) is a program based on restorative justice principles. It is described as a problem-solving approach to offending that aims to balance the needs of young people, victims and the community by encouraging dialogue between individuals who have offended and their victims (Department of Human Services 2007). This response to young offenders was folded into the new forms of juvenile justice legislation enacted during the 1990s, which frequently positioned diversion (in the form of police cautioning and family conferences) at one end of the justice model punishment continuum (Polk et al. 2003). Advocates of restorative justice often promoted YJC as an antidote to the potential problems of retributive justice associated with just deserts reforms. Daly (2002a; see also Braithwaite 2002) points out, however, that this advocacy relies on a false dichotomy between ideas of restorative and retributive justice that tends to portray each of these approaches as respectively good or bad. Indeed, as we shall see, an examination of the objectives of conferencing described in legislation reveals that, in practice, conferencing is perhaps not as benevolent as its supporters would have us believe; moreover, it is intended to achieve many of the outcomes more often associated with just deserts.

This chapter reviews the introduction of YJC as a response to young offenders in Australia. It positions conferencing in the realm of penalty because, like the other forms of innovative justice discussed in Chapters 6 to 8, youth conferences are not adjudicative. In general, these processes have only been applied to those offenders who have admitted to an offence. Conferencing deals with the penalty (or post-penalty) phase of the criminal process for admitted offenders—not the fact-finding phases (Daly 2003). The chapter begins with a brief sketch of the history of youth justice responses in Australia. This is followed by a description of the current form of YJC processes available in all Australian states and territories. As a relatively new justice response, conferencing has been subject to extensive evaluation, which indicates its failure to clearly demonstrate any significant reduction in recidivism; however, other claims have been made about the value of the process. In the final part of the chapter, the expectations and outcomes of conferencing are critically addressed in the context of ideas of restoration and restitution as rationalities for justice. We will also explore how key social theories help us to understand the possibility of conferencing and its relationship to punishment in contemporary Australian society.

A BRIEF HISTORY OF RESPONSES TO YOUNG OFFENDERS

From the start of transportation, the problem of how to manage young people has troubled governments; a significant number of convicts sent to Australia were under the age of seventeen (Wundersitz 1996). Initially, young offenders were treated in much the same way as adults: they were assigned to work gangs, held in prison, and on occasion boys as young as fifteen were hanged. For example, Seymour (1988) reports that in 1896 in Victoria two children aged five and seven were imprisoned in Pentridge Prison when their parents failed to pay a fine resultant from their children's assault on another child. During the nineteenth century, separate provisions and institutions designed to address the needs of young people began to emerge. These included reformatories for those who broke the law and industrial schools for the neglected (see Chapter 2). A series of reforms also developed that allowed children to be dealt with by lower criminal courts rather than being brought before the Supreme Court for trial by jury. At the end of the century, South Australia[5] established a separate court for children and other states followed this lead by establishing their own juvenile courts in the early years of the twentieth century.

The 'child saving movement' was one element motivating the development of a separate children's court system. Its founding belief was that offending children should not be dealt with as criminals but as persons who, because of their immaturity, needed help and guidance to become good citizens. The 'child savers' argued that the court's role should be similar to that of a 'caring parent': it should seek 'to save the child rather than punish the criminal' (Seymour 1988, p. 71). To achieve this, the court needed to shift its focus: rather than responding to the offence, it should concentrate on identifying and then treating the underlying cause of the child's offending behaviour. The child would be saved from a life of crime and turned into a decent member of society (Wundersitz 1996, p. 117). The child saving approach became known as the 'welfare model' of justice, which dominated the Australian youth justice system until the 1970s and 1980s.

From as early as the 1920s, criticism of the child saving or welfare model of youth justice surfaced from time to time in Australia. Key concerns included whether the court should relinquish control over sentence duration and whether it should place greater emphasis on punishment or rehabilitation; however, it was not until the 1960s and 1970s that serious challenges emerged (see Chapter 2). The law-and-order lobby argued that the welfare approach was too lenient; that by placing emphasis on the needs rather than deeds, the system failed not only to hold young people accountable for their criminal acts but also to provide adequate protection for the community. Escalating youth crime rates were cited as evidence of the failure of rehabilitation to reform young offenders, and therefore fuelled demands for a return to a just deserts approach in which the punishment more closely fits the crime (O'Connor 1997). Civil libertarians also rejected the welfare model because it gave the state too much discretion when intervening in the lives of young people. Placing children under the care of the state for indeterminate periods allowing for rehabilitation often meant that young offenders were subjected to longer and harsher outcomes than would have been the case for adults. These critics argued for the abolition of indeterminate sentencing, greater proportionality between crime and punishment, and guaranteed access to the full range of legal rights traditionally available to adult accused.

False Dichotom
resonitive 176-8

In response to these attacks, in the late 1970s a process of re-evaluation of the youth justice system began in Australia. The 1980s and early 1990s saw a movement away from the welfare model to more formal and predictable justice

---

5   There is debate whether the (then) colony of South Australia, or the city of Chicago in the United States, was the first jurisdiction to commence operations of separate courts for children (Blackmore 1989).

for children based on just deserts and due process. By the late 1990s all Australian states had introduced legislation based on what is referred to as the 'justice model' (O'Connor 1997). Its emphasis on due process rights secured support from the legal profession and those who objected to the welfare model's disregard of these rights. At the same time, a more direct correlation between punishment or just deserts and behaviour satisfied both police and law-and-order lobbies who saw the welfare model as too permissive. The success of the justice model lay in its popular appeal. Despite its rapid adoption, the model has nevertheless been subject to criticism regarding flaws in deterrence theory: an over-reliance on the court to remedy injustices, a lack of attention to the biases inherent in the criminal justice system, and disregard for the reality of the lives of child offenders. Ian O'Conner (1997) explains how the shift in Australia towards just deserts was subsequently overtaken by the introduction of YJC (also known as family group conferencing, or FGC).

AUSTRALIA AS A LEADER IN RESTORATIVE JUSTICE AND YOUTH JUSTICE CONFERENCING

Over the past two decades, Australia and New Zealand have been world leaders in the development and implementation of YJC programs. The rise of conferencing as a justice option in Australia was largely influenced by developments in New Zealand, where conferencing emerged in the 1980s in the context of Māori political challenges to the welfare and criminal justice systems. As a response, decision-making practices were invested with Māori cultural values, family groups (*whānau*) came to have a greater say in what happens, venues were to be culturally appropriate, and justice processes accommodated a mix of culturally appropriate practices (Maxwell and Morris 1993). In 1989 the *Children, Young Persons and their Families Act*, which introduced family group conferencing, was passed. New Zealand was therefore the first country to provide a statutory basis for conferencing. The legislation sought specifically to avoid the pitfalls of justice and welfare models of justice by:

O responding to the over-representation of poor, working-class and Māori and Pacific Island Polynesian children in the youth justice system
O responding to the problems experienced by victims of crime
O minimising reliance on criminal prosecution and fostering diversionary measures to resolve crime
O strengthening the role of family and the traditional family group for Māori and Pacific Island Polynesian children
O protecting children during police investigations (O'Connor 1997).

In New Zealand, conferencing is used not only as a diversion from court but also as pre-sentencing advice to the youth court for most serious cases.

Unaware of the events leading up to the New Zealand legislation, Australian criminologist John Braithwaite wrote *Crime, Shame and Reintegration* (1989), in which he argued for the development of criminal justice processes that increased the likelihood of the reintegrative shaming of offenders, rather than stigmatic shaming. The link between Braithwaite's concept of reintegrative shaming and New Zealand conferencing was first made in 1990 by John MacDonald, who was then an adviser to the NSW police service (Daly and Hayes 2002). MacDonald suggested that New South Wales adopt features of the New Zealand conference model, but that it be located within the police service. A pilot scheme of police-run conferencing was introduced in Wagga Wagga in 1991 to provide an 'effective cautioning scheme for juvenile offenders' (Moore and O'Connell 1994, p. 46). The rationale for placing the administration and operation of the scheme in the hands of the police rather than the welfare department, which was the case for conferencing in New Zealand, was that it would render conferencing 'more truly diversionary' (Moore and O'Connell 1994, p. 50).

Throughout the early 1990s, vigorous debate in Australia centred on the relative merits of police-run (Wagga Wagga model) and non-police-run (New Zealand model) community conferencing. In addition to New South Wales, other states—including Tasmania, the Northern Territory and Queensland— trialled police-run conferencing. In 1994, South Australia was the first Australian state to enact legislation that provided for family group conferencing (following the New Zealand model). This was consistent with its long history of innovation in juvenile justice (Wundersitz 1996). Since that time, all remaining Australian states and territories have introduced diversionary legislation for young offenders that includes restorative justice conferencing based on this model. In the Northern Territory, Tasmania and the ACT, conferencing run by police along Wagga Wagga lines coexists with systems that refer offenders to a community conference through the courts (and corrections). Regardless of its configuration, conferencing is only one component in a hierarchy of responses to youth crime. The overarching goal in legislative frameworks is to keep juveniles out of the formal system as much as possible.

In each jurisdiction the practical characteristics of conferencing can vary in relation to where conferences are located in the progression of discretionary decision-making, where they are housed organisationally and the kinds of offences that are, or can be, conferenced (Daly and Hayes 2001; Polk et al. 2003). For example, Western Australia tends to conference a high volume of less serious cases, including traffic offences. This contrasts with South Australia, which has no specifically prohibited offences: it conferences a high volume of cases and uses conferences in serious offences, including sexual assault. Variation also exists in relation to the length of time allowed for completing an outcome and the upper limits on what outcomes might require. For example, South Australian provisions allow for the highest maximum number of community service hours (that is, 300 hours) in Australia.

Youth justice conferencing: What is it?

Despite some organisational differences, conferences in Australia and New Zealand are similar in a number of ways. Typical participants include the convenor, a police officer (either the arresting officer or a representative), the offender(s) (who, as a condition of attending, must admit to the offence), the victim(s), and support people for the offender(s) and victim(s). Once the wrongdoing is admitted, offenders and their family are asked who they would like to attend the conference as supporters; the victim is also asked to nominate supporters to attend. The conference is a meeting of these two communities of care. Ideally, it takes place in a context of compassion and understanding, as opposed to the more adversarial and stigmatising environment associated with the youth court (Daly 2002b).

Drawing on observational research, Hayes (2006) explains that conferences usually last approximately sixty to ninety minutes and progress through three phases: introduction, storytelling and agreement negotiation. Convenors (or coordinators) open conferences with general introductions and a summary of what the conference is expected to achieve and what participants are expected to do. Considerable preparation for conferences occurs before they are convened. This is extremely important in both helping participants understand their roles in the conference and establishing realistic expectations (Braithwaite 2002). Following introductions and the orientation summary, attending police officers are asked to read out official details of the offence. Offenders are then asked to account for their behaviour (to 'tell their story'). They are asked to describe how they came to be involved in the offence, to acknowledge the harm they have caused victims, as well as the pain and embarrassment they have caused parents and other supporters, and to say sorry. Hayes (2006) describes how offenders are often demonstratively remorseful. Next, victims are asked to describe the impact of the offence. The emphasis of the victim's story is on how the offence affected them emotionally, physically and materially. Such accounts are intended to move offenders, who may otherwise be indifferent to the harms they have caused, and to draw out an apology as part of the processes of reconciliation and repair. Supporters are then invited to comment. Before moving to the final phase of negotiating the agreement, convenors return to offenders, asking how the victims' stories make them feel. Frequently offenders admit that victims' descriptions made them more aware of the effects of their behaviour and many, at this point, offer apologies to their victims. The conference ends with a discussion of what the young person can do to make amends for the offence (the agreement); all participants are encouraged to provide suggestions. Common agreements include a verbal and/or written apology, attending counselling sessions, performing some work for the victim or the community, or monetary restitution.

Conferencing advocates claim that asking offenders to confront the consequences of their wrongdoing—and talking them through in the presence of those who have suffered them—has a variety of benefits for the offender, namely taking responsibility, experiencing remorse and offering practical help and apology to the victim and the community to right the wrong (Braithwaite 2002, p. 26). Not all conferences achieve their intended aims or can be judged to be successful. Daly (2003) highlights the gap between what conferences aim to achieve and what they achieve in practice. The outcome may be feelings of mutual goodwill, repair and reconciliation; however, offenders can remain belligerent and unapologetic and victims angry and unmoved. While conference dialogue hopefully promotes reintegrative shaming, it may alternatively work to stigmatise and censure (Hayes 2006).

Outcomes: Fairness and offending

According to Hayes (2005), the main aims of restorative justice conferencing — meeting the needs of victims, holding the offender accountable, reparation and restoration — have guided much of the empirical research on youth conferencing processes and outcomes. He notes that preventing future offending has never been a key aim of restorative justice and explains the advocates' claim that if restorative justice can achieve these key aims, young offenders will be less likely to reoffend. Indeed, some have suggested that restorative justice initiatives such as conferencing should not be assessed in terms of reductions in recidivism because there are other important outcomes for both offenders and victims, such as repairing victims' sense of loss and giving offenders a chance to make amends. Nevertheless, when policy-makers invest in these justice programs, they want to know if they can affect offending behaviour and understand how the process of conferencing is linked to recidivism.

There is a large degree of consistency in research findings from around Australia and overseas that shows participants — both victims and offenders — are largely satisfied with restorative justice conference outcomes and feel they are treated fairly and respectfully. That is, participants experience a high degree of procedural justice. For example, Strang et al. (1999) reported results for the ReIntegrative Shaming Experiments (RISE) project in Canberra, where admitted offenders were randomly assigned to court and conference.

RISE

The ReIntegrative Shaming Experiments (RISE) were a landmark study conducted by the Centre for Restorative Justice at the Australian National University between 1995 and 2000. They made up a unique project that focused on justice processes in the Australian Capital Territory. It examined conferencing in Canberra, based on the 'Wagga Wagga model' of police-run conferences. An experimental research process that randomly assigned 1300 cases to a conference or a court hearing was used to compare and assess the effectiveness of each procedure for certain kinds of offences. The effects of standard court processing were compared with those of

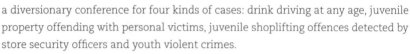

a diversionary conference for four kinds of cases: drink driving at any age, juvenile property offending with personal victims, juvenile shoplifting offences detected by store security officers and youth violent crimes.

Critics at the time argued that shaming conferences were a soft option. The experience of offenders suggested otherwise. Conferences often involved over an hour of critical examination by family, friends, victims or community representatives sitting in a private room at a police station. They were emotionally intense discussions of what the offender did, whether the offender is sorry, and how the offender can repair the harm caused by the crime. For drink drivers, the average court case in the study takes six minutes, while the average conference takes eighty-eight minutes. For young offenders, the average court case takes thirteen minutes, while the average conference takes seventy-one minutes (Sherman and Strang 1997).

The researchers relied on the randomised clinical trial approach used in medicine, education and other fields to reach their conclusions about the comparative effects of court and conferences. They argued that this approach virtually rules out other explanations for any differences between the two groups other than the treatment they received. Across the four experiments, very different results emerged for each of the different offence categories. The substantive conclusion of RISE was that restorative justice can work and even reduce crime by violent offenders; however, there is no guarantee that it will work for all offence types.

These authors concluded that, compared with those offenders who went to court, those going to conference had experienced higher levels of procedural and restorative justice and an increased respect for police and the law. Compared with victims whose cases went to court, conference victims had higher levels of recovery from the offence. While conference victims also experienced high levels of procedural justice, they could not be compared with court victims who rarely attend court proceedings. The South Australia Juvenile Justice (SAJJ) project (Daly et al. 1998; Daly 2001) on conferencing similarly reported very high levels of procedural justice registered by offenders and victims. Daly (2001, p. 169) explained that to items such as 'were you treated fairly', 'were you treated with respect', 'did you have a say in the agreement' 80 to 95 per cent of victims and offenders said that they were treated fairly and had a say. Procedural justice scholars argue that when citizens perceive a legal process as fair, when they are listened to and treated with respect, there is an affirmation of the legitimacy of the legal order and this helps to reduce future offending.

The relatively recent introduction of restorative justice conferencing in Australia has meant that opportunities to assess long-term behavioural outcomes for young offenders have been limited. Reoffending has been assessed in the Australian Capital Territory (Sherman et al. 2000), New South Wales (Luke and Lind 2002), South Australia (Hayes and Daly 2003) and Queensland (Hayes and

Daly 2004). Hayes (2005) summarises the results of these studies as follows. In the Australian Capital Territory, researchers working on the RISE study followed offenders arrested across four offence categories—violent offences, drink driving, property offences and shoplifting—randomly assigned to either a police-run conference or court for twelve months. Results suggested that conferences may be more effective in reducing further offending for young violent offenders. This was not true for the other categories. Violent offenders randomly assigned to conferences had a significantly lower rate of post-assignment reoffending compared with violent offenders assigned to court. For drink-driving offenders a very small increase in detected reoffending was found for those attending a conference relative to court.

In New South Wales, Luke and Lind (2002) conducted a retrospective analysis of several thousand first offenders (those with no prior proven court appearance) who went to conference or court from 6 April 1997 to 5 April 1999. They compared post-intervention offending for three groups of offenders: offenders in court during the twelve months before the introduction of conferencing; offenders in court during the first twelve months of conferencing; and offenders in conference during the first twelve months of operation. Records for first offenders were chosen to control for the effects of prior offending. After making several comparisons between the conference and the court groups, Luke and Lind (2002) concluded that conferencing produced a 15 to 20 per cent reduction in predicted risk of offending.

In South Australia, Hayes and Daly (2003) analysed data collected for the SAJJ project (Daly et al. 1998; Daly 2001) to examine how features of family conferences, as well as offender characteristics (age, gender, race and prior offending), relate to future offending behaviour. They aimed to investigate the aspects of conferences that could predict reoffending over and above those variables known to be linked to lawbreaking and its detection: past offending and social marginality. Drawing on observations of eighty-nine conferences and the offending history data for the primary offenders in these conferences, they found prior offending, sex and race to be highly predictive of post-conference offending. Beyond these variables, however, they also found that when young offenders are observed to be remorseful and when the conference decision-making about outcomes was observed to be consensual, reoffending was less likely. These results were consistent with findings reported by Maxwell and Morris (2001). Similar results were also obtained in Queensland, where Hayes and Daly (2004) followed 200 young offenders over three to five years following their youth justice conference. Their findings indicated that offender characteristics such as age, gender and prior offending remained highly predictive of future offending. In contrast to the South Australian results, no features of conferences were associated with future offending.

Hayes (2005) concludes that results of research on conferencing and reoffending conducted in Australia are mixed but show that restorative conferences have the potential to reduce crime; research conducted overseas presents a similar picture. While there is some consistency in how studies have measured process features like restorative and procedural justice, when reoffending is measured there is more variation in how it is conceptualised and measured. He suggests that the differences in how reoffending has been measured across studies contributes to the variable outcomes observed. Another source of variation is the type of restorative justice program being evaluated. It is important to remember that restorative justice encompasses a broad array of new justice practices. These include mediation, circles, peacemaking, reconciliation and conferencing (Braithwaite 2002). It is also important to remember that, even when attention is focused on one form of restorative justice process—for example, youth justice conferencing—there is substantial variation from one restorative event to the next. Offenders come to conferences with a range of experiences, victims come to conferences with different orientations and expectations and not all conferences achieve the stated aims of restoration and reintegration.

PENOLOGICAL PRINCIPLES: RESTORATION OR RESTITUTION

As we have seen, YJC is promoted as an opportunity for restorative justice and as an enlightened response to offending. However, restorative justice is difficult to define. As an idea it has been very popular with governments; as a term it has been used to describe a wide range of programs and policies (Marchetti and Daly 2007). As yet there is little empirical work establishing the 'restorative' nature of such processes. From a review of many lists of core features of restorative justice, Daly concludes that the common elements include: 'an emphasis on the role and experience of victims in the criminal process; involvement of all the relevant parties (including the victim, offender and their supporters) to discuss the offence, its impact and what should be done to "repair the harm"; and decision-making carried out by both lay and legal actors' (2002b, p. 58). She notes that while definitions and lists of core elements of restorative justice vary, all display a remarkable uniformity in defining restorative justice by reference to what it is not—and this is retributive justice (Braithwaite 2002).

By situating restorative justice (as expressed in conferencing) in opposition to retributive justice, advocates assume that the practice of conferencing should exclude elements of retribution. However, Daly (2002b) rightly points outs that the conferencing process is far more flexible, drawing on some elements of retributive justice (seeking censure for past offences), of rehabilitative justice (asking what shall be done to encourage future law-abiding behaviour) and of restorative justice (asking how offenders can make amends for what they did to their victim). A cursory review of the objectives expressed in the statutory basis for the delivery of youth conferencing in Australian states and territories confirms this assessment. Table 9.1 lists the objectives defined in the legislation for each Australian jurisdiction and maps the diversity of ends sought.

TABLE 9.1 Principles and objectives

Northern Territory *Youth Justice Act 2005* s3 and s4 Part 6, Division 1, Section 84 (Previously *Juvenile Justice Act 1997 as amended in 1999*)	Western Australia *Young Offenders Act 1994* s7 and s24 (1993 non-statutory)	Tasmania *Youth Justice Act 1997* s4 and s5 Part 2, Division 3 (proclaimed in 2000) (1994–1999 non-statutory)
Section 3 • Providing appropriate treatment punishment and rehabilitation Section 4 • Holding offenders accountable and encouraging acceptance of responsibility for behaviour • Acknowledging the needs of offenders and providing the opportunity to develop in socially responsible ways • Custody should be a last resort and for the shortest period of time • Taking account of the age and maturity of the offender and maintaining the same rights and protection afforded to adults in similar circumstances • Making offenders aware of their obligations under the law and the consequences of breaking the law • Dealing with offenders in a way that allows them to be reintegrated into the community • Balancing the needs of the young offender, the rights of the victim and the interests of the community • Preserving and strengthening family relationships • Avoiding unnecessary withdrawal of offenders from families and education or employment	Section 7 • Treating young people fairly • Encouraging young people to accept responsibility for their conduct • Not treating young people more severely than adults • Protecting the community • Providing victims with the opportunity to participate • Encouraging responsible adults to fulfil their responsibilities • Consideration should be given to dealing with an offence without judicial proceedings (diversion) • Custody should be a last resort, as short as possible and in a suitable facility • Providing an opportunity to develop a sense of social responsibility • Dealing with young people within an appropriate timeframe • Fostering the ability of the family group to develop their own means of dealing with offending by their young persons	Section 4 • Making offending youth aware of their rights and obligations • Receiving appropriate treatment, punishment and rehabilitation • Enhancing the roles of guardians, families and communities in minimising punishment and managing and rehabilitating young people who have committed crimes • Promoting factors that enhance a youth's acceptance of responsibility • Being culturally appropriate and enhancing cultural identity • Ensuring that an offence is dealt with taking into account the youth's social and family background and their capacity for acceptance of personal responsibility Section 5 • Encouraging the youth to accept responsibility for their behaviour • Not treating young offenders more severely than adults

(Continues)

TABLE 9.1 Principles and objectives (continued)

Northern Territory *Youth Justice Act 2005* s3 and s4 Part 6, Division 1, Section 84 (Previously *Juvenile Justice Act 1997 as amended in 1999*)	Western Australia *Young Offenders Act 1994* s7 and s24 (1993 non-statutory)	Tasmania *Youth Justice Act 1997* s4 and s5 Part 2, Division 3 (proclaimed in 2000) (1994–1999 non-statutory)
• Acknowledging offenders' sense of racial, ethnic or cultural identity and providing the opportunity to maintain it • Providing victims with the opportunity to participate in the process of dealing with the young offender • Encouraging adults to fulfil their responsibility for the care and supervision of young offenders • Making and implementing decisions within a timeframe appropriate to the young offenders' sense of time • Providing opportunities for young offenders to develop a sense of social responsibility and to develop in beneficial and socially acceptable ways • Involving the community of Aboriginal young offenders • Programs should be culturally appropriate, promote health and self respect, foster a sense of responsibility, and encourage attitudes and skills that will enhance the social potential of young offenders • Dealing with the matter by means other than criminal proceedings, unless public interest requires otherwise • Conducting proceedings separately from those in relation to adult offenders	Section 24 Where there is no well-established pattern of offending, principles include: • Avoiding exposure to further offending • Encouraging and helping the family • Offering fair and consistent treatment of the offender and in proportion to the seriousness of the crime	• Protecting the community • Giving victims the opportunity to participate in the judicial process • Involving guardians in taking responsibility for and participating in decisions and sanctions • Custody should be a last resort and for shortest possible time • Providing an opportunity for the development of a sense of social responsibility and youth development in beneficial and socially acceptable ways • Preserving and strengthening family relationships • Punishment should be appropriate to age, maturity, offending history and cultural identity of youth • Providing compensation and restitution to victims • Preserving and strengthening family relationships • Not interrupting education and employment

New South Wales *Young Offenders Act 1997* s34 (1991–1997 non-statutory)	Australian Capital Territory *Crimes (Restorative Justice) Act 2004* s6 (1995–2005 non-statutory)	Queensland *Juvenile Justice Act 1992 as amended in 1996* Schedule 1 (1995–1996 non-statutory)	Victoria *Children Youth and Families Act 2005* s362, s415	South Australia *Young Offenders Act 1993* s3
• Promoting acceptance of responsibility by the child • Strengthening the family of the child • Providing the child with developmental and support services to assist in overcoming offending and becoming fully autonomous • Enhancing the rights and place of victims • Being culturally appropriate where possible • Having due regard to victims' interests • Promoting the development of the child within their family or family group	• Enhancing the rights of victims by providing restorative justice • Empowering victims to make decisions about how to repair the harm • Establishing a system of restorative justice, bringing victims, offenders and their supporters together in a safe environment • Giving the interests of victims high priority in the administration of restorative justice • Enabling access to restorative justice at every stage of the criminal justice process	• Protecting the community • Upholding the rights of the young offender • Treating those involved in the juvenile justice process with respect and dignity • Protecting the young offender during an investigation or proceedings • Diverting the young offender from the criminal justice system unless the nature of the offence and their criminal history indicate proceedings should be started • Ensuring proceedings are fair, just and timely • Providing the young offender with the opportunity to participate • Holding young offenders accountable and encouraging acceptance of responsibility for behaviour • Providing an opportunity for the young offender's development in responsible beneficial and socially acceptable ways • Preserving and strengthening family relationships	Section 362 • Preserving and strengthening family relationships • Maintaining education, training or employment • Minimising stigma to the child • Considering the suitability of the sentence • Ensuring the child bears responsibility for breaking the law • Protecting the community

Section 415 • Increasing the child's understanding of the effect of their offending on the victim and the community • Reducing the likelihood of the child reoffending | • Providing care, correction and guidance for young offenders to develop as responsible and useful members of the community and realise their potential • Developing awareness of obligations under the law and the consequences of breaking the law • Protecting the community • Imposing sanctions with regard to their deterrent effect, balancing the protection of the community and rehabilitation of the offender |

(Continues)

TABLE 9.1 Principles and objectives (continued)

New South Wales Young Offenders Act 1997 s34 (1991–1997 non-statutory)	Australian Capital Territory Crimes (Restorative Justice) Act 2004 s6 (1995–2005 non-statutory)	Queensland Juvenile Justice Act 1992 as amended in 1996 Schedule 1 (1995–1996 non-statutory)	Victoria Children Youth and Families Act 2005 s362, s415	South Australia Young Offenders Act 1993 s3
• Taking the least restrictive form that is appropriate	• Enabling agencies that have a role in the criminal justice system to refer offences for restorative justice	• Providing the victim with an opportunity to participate • Supporting parents to take responsibility for the care and supervision of the young offender • Making and implementing decisions within a timeframe appropriate to the young offender's sense of time • Considering young offender's age, maturity, cultural and religious beliefs and practices in decisions • Involving the community of Indigenous offenders • Providing programs and services that are culturally appropriate, and promote health and self respect • Providing young offenders with access to legal and other support services • Responding in ways allowing for reintegration into the community • Custody should be a last resort, for the least amount of time justifiable and in a facility suitable for children which provides a safe and stable living environment, and fosters and maintains contacts with the child's family and community	• Negotiating an outcome plan that is agreed to by the child • Assisting young offenders to take responsibility and make reparation for their actions	• Providing compensation and restitution for victims • Preserving and strengthening family relationships • Avoiding withdrawal from the home, education or employment • Preserving a youth's sense of racial, ethnic or cultural identity

For example, the Australian Capital Territory legislation explicitly focuses on restorative justice and responding to victims. While acknowledging the importance of strengthening families, other jurisdictions clearly highlight elements of the justice model (accountability, procedural justice, rights of the child, responsibilisaton, compensation and restitution). Queensland, Western Australia and Tasmania express concern for community safety. In Tasmania, New South Wales and the Northen Territory, the residue of rehabilitation clearly remains. One of the Objects listed in Section 3 of the Northern Territory Act is 'to ensure that … young offenders are given appropriate treatment, punishment and rehabilitation'.

Daly (2002b) suggests that the advocacy literature is perhaps too focused on 'repairing the harm', 'healing those injured by the crime' or 'reintegrating offenders', passing too quickly over the crucial phase of 'holding offenders accountable', which is the retributive part of the process. As a result, restorative justice is more often portrayed as a set of ideals about justice that assumes a generous, empathetic, supportive and rational human spirit. It assumes that victims can be generous to those who have harmed them, that offenders can be apologetic and contrite for their behaviour, that their respective 'communities of care' can take an active role of support and assistance, and that a facilitator can guide rational discussion and encourage consensual decision-making between parties with antagonistic interests. These ideals can be very difficult to achieve in practice. In the SAJJ project, for example, research found that compared with high levels of perceived procedural justice commonly reported in research, there was relatively less evidence of restorativeness (Daly 2002b; Hayes 2005; 2006). The measures of restorativeness used in this research mapped the degree to which offenders and victims recognised the other and were affected by the other; they focused on the degree to which there was positive movement between the offender and victim and their supporters during the conference. According to Strang (2002 and others; Hayes 2006), in the aftermath of crime, what victims want is 'symbolic reparation, primarily an apology'. Daly (2006) argues that they want more than this: they want vindication for the wrong done to them, and they want the offender to stop harming and hurting them or others. A sincere apology may be a start, but we might expect most victims to want more. She cites Cretney and Davis who suggest that a 'victim has an interest in punishment not just restitution or reparation, because punishment can reassure the victim that s/he has public recognition and support' (1995, p. 178 in Daly 2006, p. 139).

The SAJJ project explicitly explored the process of apology. Young offenders were asked why they decided to say sorry to victims: 27 per cent said they did not feel sorry but thought they would get off more easily if they apologised, 39 per cent said they apologised to make their family feel better, and a similar percentage said they felt pushed into it. However, when asked to identify the main reason for saying sorry, more than 60 per cent said they really were sorry. When victims were asked about the apology process, most believed that the offender's motives for apologising were insincere. Just over half thought that the young person said sorry either to get off more easily or because they were pushed into it; 27 per cent believed that the main reason why youth offenders apologised was because they really were sorry. Explanations for this apparent perceptual dissonance between these groups might include the differing orientations of offenders and victims to the conference process, as well as variations in what they hope to achieve. Moreover, because the stance of empathy and openness to 'the other', the expectation of being able to speak and reflect on one's actions and the presence of new justice norms (or language) emphasising repair are novel cultural elements for most participants, they may not know exactly how they should behave (Daly 2003).

In short, very often conference participants do not fully understand the idea of restorative justice. Unlike interactions with the police in the street or station, or interactions with lawyers and judges in the courtroom—for which many images are available in popular culture—most people do not have much of an idea of what this type of justice looks like, how they are to act in it or what the optimal result is. Despite the lack of cultural referents, they are expected to come into a room, know what to say and be 'appropriately' affected by the encounter. Because conferences are confidential affairs, there is little public knowledge of the process. This means many young people and their parents do not know what is expected of them. The potential for restorativeness, for example, is greater when participants—and especially offenders—have taken the time in advance to think about what they want to say. Over half the young people interviewed as part of the SAJJ project had not thought about what they would say to the victim. While most knew that a conference was different from a court proceeding, they adopted a similar posture towards both: it was a place they have been made to go because they have done something wrong (and been caught) (Daly 2003). Few saw the conference as an opportunity to take an active role in speaking to a victim. Most were not there to 'repair the harm', but to answer questions in the hope of not receiving too many hours of community service or a good behaviour bond. Most did not think in terms of what they might offer victims, but what they would be made to do by others. In practice, the young people seemed to be as, if not more, interested in repairing their own reputations than in repairing the harm to victims. Among the most important things that the victims hoped would occur at the conference was for the offender to hear how the offence affected them, but half of the offenders reported that the victim's story had no effect or only little effect on them (Daly 2002b).

A factor undermining the restorative potential of YJC is perhaps the assumption made by advocates that everyone has the requisite skills and desire to participate. However, as Daly (2003) thoughtfully points out, effective participation requires a degree of moral maturity and empathetic concern that many people, especially young people, may not possess (Mill 1859/1975, pp. 15–16; Hindess 2001, p. 101). 'Restorativeness cannot be forced or scripted in the way that fairness can. It works with emotions and feelings, with anger and shame, with feeling harmed and feeling bad. Fairness works with established roles and procedures, and at times with deceit—e.g. when judicial officers and police officers must appear to be fair, polite and respectful towards offenders even when they have low opinion of them' (Daly 2003, p. 234). She concludes that there are limits to the idea of restorative justice that stem from organisational constraints on what can be achieved and from the popular understandings of what 'getting justice' means to people. 'It will take time for people to become familiar with new justice scripts and social relations in responding to crime; and there will be variation in people's capacities to enact and read the scripts' (Daly 2003, p. 235).

THINKING THEORETICALLY: YJCs AS RITUALS OF RESPONSIBILISATION

The significance of saying 'sorry'

It is widely acknowledged that John Braithwaite has been very influential in the promotion of the concept of restorative justice not only in Australia but also internationally. The link between his concept of reintegrative shaming and the introduction of YJC into Australia was noted above. In *Crime, Shame and Reintegration* (1989) Braithwaite provides a summary of his theory (pp. 98–104). He explains that the key components include interdependency, communitarianism and (reintegrative) shaming. He describes interdependency as a condition in which individuals are dependent on others to achieve valued ends and others are dependent on them. Communitarianism is defined as a societal condition in which individuals are densely enmeshed in interdependencies that have the special qualities of mutual help and trust; he emphasises the need for mutuality of obligation in interdependency. By shaming, Braithwaite refers to all social processes of expressing disapproval that have the intention or effect of invoking either remorse in the person being shamed or condemnation by others who become aware of the shaming. This normative and moralising aspect of shaming is a contemporary analogue of Durkheim's view of punishment as symbolic: a ritualised expression of social values and the controlled release of psychic energy. For Durkheim, punishment was a useful reaction against violators of the conscience collective—likewise the community conference ideally works to demonstrate the material force of social values and restore collective confidence in the integrity and power of the moral order. As a ritual of punishment, it is directed less at the individual offender than the impassioned onlookers (victims, their supporters and the supporters of the offender) whose values and security have been challenged by the offender's actions. It works as an instrumental means of channelling the energy of outraged sentiments into a socially binding ritual of moral affirmation, ultimately signified in the apology.

Unlike purely deterrent punishment, shaming sets out to moralise with offenders; to communicate reasons for the evil of their actions. Most shaming is neither associated with formal punishment nor perpetrated by the state, though both shaming by the state and shaming with punishment are important types of shaming. Most shaming is by individuals within interdependent communities of concern. Reintegrative shaming is shaming followed by efforts to reintegrate the offender back into the community of law-abiding or respectable citizens through words or gestures of forgiveness or ceremonies to decertify the offender as deviant. Shaming and reintegration do not occur simultaneously but sequentially, with reintegration occurring before deviance becomes a master status. It is shaming that labels the act as evil while striving to preserve the identity of the offender as essentially good—in the Christian tradition of 'hate the sin and love the sinner' (Braithwaite 1989, p. 101). Reintegrative shaming can be harsh. It is not distinguished from stigmatisation by its potency, but by a finite rather than open-ended duration that is terminated by forgiveness and by efforts to maintain bonds of love or respect throughout the finite period of suffering shame.

Braithwaite sees conferencing, including YJC, as an opportunity for reintegrative shaming. With Mugford, he portrays the process as a ceremony of reintegration and explains what he means by this by turning Garfinkel's (1956) work on the 'conditions of successful degradation ceremonies' on its head. Braithwaite and Mugford (1994) investigate whether the same kind of social structures and socio-psychological processes that Garfinkel links to rituals of degradation are at work here, but in different combinations and directed to different ends. According to Garfinkel, degradation ceremonies consist of communicative work that names an actor as an 'outsider', that transforms an individual's total identity into an identity 'lower in the group's scheme of social types' (1956, p. 420), or a deviant identity (Goffman's mortification of the self might be another example, see p. 126). Criminal trials are an example of status degradation ceremonies and this view of them became a central idea in the sociology of deviance, especially among labelling theorists (Becker 1963; Schur 1973). Labelling theory has been at the foundation of programs designed to divert offenders and particularly young offenders from the criminal justice system—the origins of youth conferencing (such as in Wagga Wagga; see p. 179) and its relationship to diversionary options described in legislation are testaments to this heritage.

However, Braithwaite and Mugford argue that the labelling approach is too simplistic, exaggerated and overly deterministic (1994; Braithwaite 1989). Most young people labelled as delinquents never go to jail as adults. While the labelling theorists did useful empirical work that refocused responses to offending and punishment away from institutionalisation, their work was narrowly focused on front-end processes that certify deviance. They envisaged individuals as having 'total identities'. Braithwaite and Mugford (1994) reject this totalising approach and replace it with the notion that people are made up of multiple identities—for example, son, brother, footballer, student—many (or most) of which involve normatively conforming behaviour. They propose that this move allows us to recast the interest in transformation ceremonies, 'asking questions as much about ceremonies to decertify deviance as to certify it' (1994, p. 142). While degradation ceremonies are about the sequence disapproval–degradation–exclusion, they argue that reintegration ceremonies are about the sequence disapproval–non-degradation–inclusion. In a reintegration ceremony, disapproval of a bad act is communicated while sustaining the identity of the actor as good. Shame is transmitted within a continuum of respect for the wrong-doer. Repair work is directed at ensuring that a deviant identity (one of the actor's multiple identities) does not become a master status trait that overwhelms other identities. Communicative work is directed at sustaining identities—like daughter, student, promising footballer—in preference to creating master identities—like delinquent/young offender. Practically, this condition of successful reintegration is accomplished by having the offender's responsible self disassociate from the irresponsible self. Apology is identified as the standard device for accomplishing this, as Goffman pointed out:

> An apology is a gesture through which an individual splits himself into two parts, the part that is guilty of an offence and the part that disassociates itself from the delict and affirms a belief in offended rule. (1971, p. 113 in Braithwaite and Mugford 1994, p. 150)

Although not an essential part of the YJC process (perhaps because of the impossibility of scripting a 'sincere' exchange), apology has repeatedly been identified as a key restorative facet of this justice process. Braithwaite argues that for informal justice to be restorative, it has to be about restoring victims, offenders and communities. Bottoms (2003) points out that communities always consists of individuals in relationships; those relationships take place within social structures and cultural contexts. From a sociological perspective, he proposes that community restoration is about 'a restoration of prior social relationships in a community, within an understood structural and normative frame'. Bottoms systematically lays out a plausible argument that the apology (followed usually by some restitution) is a generative social mechanism that can potentially lead to the restoration of prior social relationships in a community. He draws on Tavuchis' (1991) discussion of the ideal typical apology, where the parties already have some kind of relationship, even if that relationship is, at a personal level, tenuous and indirect. A social norm is violated and a 'moral imperative' compels the wronged person to take note of that breach and to call for an apology. The call for the apology has the effect of simultaneously:

○ drawing attention to the prior shared social relationships and understandings within the community

○ emphasising that the act complained of is a departure from the accepted positive morality of the group, and cannot be ignored if the legitimacy of the relevant moral rule is to be upheld

○ looking forward to a social situation in which, after the apology has been offered, there will potentially be a restoration of a prior state of relations between the parties within the community more generally.

In other words, both prior social relationships in the community and the accepted positive morality of the group are deeply embedded as background characteristics (or part of the framework) of the ideal typical apology (Bottoms 2003, p. 94).

Bottoms introduces a caveat. He asserts that the conditions for restorative justice through apology rely on two assumptions: first, that we are speaking of the ideal typical apology; and second, that the victim and the offender are part of the same social/moral community (although perhaps with only a tenuous or indirect relationship). Citing Hann (2000, p. 14 in Bottoms 2003, p. 98), he points out that reconciliation is 'especially important where the contesting parties have necessarily to continue … to be part of a continuing community in everyday life'; by definition, this consideration is much less relevant for 'unrelated' (or unlinked) parties than for 'related' parties. In 'unrelated' cases, the linkage to the social/moral attachments and structures in society is necessarily weaker, making dispute settlement procedures hard to convene and any settlements reached harder to enforce. The implication here is that where the offender and victim are not part of the same social/moral community, the genuine apology—and the social mechanisms of reconciliatory justice more generally—may be much harder to orchestrate. This raises important questions about how restorative justice mechanisms might work in the anonymous urban societies of the contemporary world. A key consideration is that while some element of 'community' can be built around almost every single person, that 'community' might or might not be a strong enough social, structural base to make the social mechanisms of restorative justice work effectively. According to Bottoms, if this is correct we should expect mixed results from empirical work on restorative justice—for example, with apologies sometimes being received as sincere and sometimes not; sometimes a real meeting of hearts and minds among the participants, sometimes not; and so on. Indeed, this is exactly what current Australia research seems to show (Hayes 2006; Daly 2003).

YJCs and the regulatory state

On a broader level we might also wonder about the place of restorative justice in a global context, where punishment is often understood in terms of the 'new penology' that is shaped by managerialist concerns (see Chapter 2). On this horizon, restorative justice practices that are characterised by a localised focus, informal processes, lay participants and very little use of late modern devices (such as risk assessment profiles) seem to be out of place.

Bottoms (2003) usefully speculates on how we might understand the apparently anomalous appeal and growth of restorative justice in contemporary societies. First, he points to Kamenk and Tay's (1980) work that identifies three ideal types of law:

- gesellschaft law—enshrining basic legal rights and freedoms for individuals (Human Rights Acts)
- bureaucratic administrative law—such as risk-based legislation on parole release or the community-based monitoring of sex offenders
- gemeinschaft law—expressed in provisions for restorative justice conferences for certain categories of persons who have admitted offences.

Kamenk and Tays' analysis argues that while bureaucratic administrative approaches might be prioritised at the end of the twentieth century, there seems to be in modern legal arrangements a desire for gemeinschaft-type approaches expressed in policies that could help to provide at a minimum 'a certain humanising cosmetic for bureaucratic practice' (1975, p. 142 in Bottoms 2003, p. 102). Second, Bottoms suggests that, sociologically speaking, the restorative justice movement can unquestionably be read as part of the victimological turn in criminal justice policies in many jurisdictions since the 1960s (see Chapter 2). Third, it has gained part of its strength from the perceived deficiencies of the courts, which he argues are more fully exposed in consumer-oriented societies (late twentieth and early twenty-first centuries) characterised by demands for enhanced accountability of professionals (who are no longer afforded that automatic deference that they once were); and, on occasion, demands for lay participation in decision-making. The growth of restorative justice appears to fit well with these sociological trends since it typically uses primarily lay and participatory forums and tends to have suspicion of professionals. Fourth, all the jurisdictions that have led the introduction of restorative justice practices have in common the presence of a minority group of a significant size (New Zealand, Australia and Canada, for example) that has over time become alienated from the official criminal justice system in light of a colonialist or quasi-colonialist history. In each case, restorative justice processes now seem attractive to policy-makers as a way of trying to heal past conflicts and wrongs and to incorporate greater awareness of different cultural traditions into the criminal (and especially juvenile) justice systems. This inclusion draws on two important features of restorative justice: the reconciliatory element in the restorative justice philosophy and the element of 'normative clarification' sometimes present in restorative justice-style forums. However, the normative clarification dimension has its own dangers in situations of seriously contested legitimacy because the official policy-makers' gesture of setting up restorative justice processes—within a state formation still dominated by the previous majority group—can easily be attacked as being insufficiently aware of cultural differences and the depth of the 'legitimacy deficit' that the majority community's past actions have engendered. This is a problem certainly experienced in Australia in relation to Indigenous justice (see Chapter 7).

A final explanation comes again from Braithwaite (2000) who explains the rise of restorative justice in terms of a shift from Keynesian politics (associated with the welfare state) to regulatory politics (Bottoms 2003). The metaphorical representation of this change is a distinction between two possible approaches to the exercise of state power in society described in terms of 'rowing' (similar to a rowing boat, the state does the principal work) and 'steering' (like a coxswain, the state provides direction while the rowing is done by others, notably private firms, voluntary agencies and local communities). This shift has involved not only massive privatisation of former state functions—from nationalised industries to policing and prisons—but also a pattern of insisting that individuals and groups should make provision for their own welfare (a process sometimes described as 'responsibilisation') (Dean 1999; O'Malley 1992; 2001; Rose 1999). In withdrawing from previous rowing functions, the state has frequently set up 'regulators' whose role is to ensure that the public interest is protected; hence the state offers a strong steering guideline to markets and civil society in the new regulatory state. From this perspective, contemporary restorative justice procedures—where typically people are asked to settle their own conflicts under the guidance of a state-appointed mediator or chairperson—can be viewed as an 'important manifestation of the new regulatory state in criminal justice' (Braithwaite 2000, p. 227 in Bottoms 2003, p. 107). Bottoms argues that while Braithwaite's account helps us to understand the revival of some restorative justice-style practices in contemporary societies, it is less successful in explaining the anomaly of the rise of restorative justice in the predominantly managerialist and control-oriented penal systems of contemporary Western societies (since any of these developments look distinctly like state rowing). Developing Braithwaite's argument, Bottoms suggests we see criminal justice in the era of the regulatory state as having a dual focus: a coercive, rowing-based, risk-focused state criminal justice system for more serious and persistent criminality, and a delegation to local communities of the process of dealing with non-persistent low-level criminality (see Chapter 1).

CONCLUSION

Youth justice has long been a field of innovation. The late nineteenth-century view that offending children should not be dealt with as criminals but as persons who, because of their immaturity, need help and guidance to become good citizens paved the way for the introduction of separate courts and programs of rehabilitation. Throughout the twentieth century these changes were increasingly linked to welfare models of justice that focused on needs rather than deeds. By the end of the century the failure of this approach to reduce offending behaviour and to hold young people accountable for their criminal acts fuelled demands for a return to just deserts approaches. Critics called for an end to indeterminate sentencing, greater proportionality between crime and punishment, and guaranteed access to the full range of legal rights traditionally available to adult accused. All Australian jurisdictions re-evaluated their systems of youth justice and introduced reform based on principles of just deserts and due process. This reorientation quickly became the subject of complaint regarding the flaws in deterrence theory, an over-reliance on the court, a lack of attention to the biases inherent in the criminal justice system, and a disregard for the lived experiences of young offenders. Youth justice conferencing was introduced in this context as a remedy to the limits of just deserts. Conferences involve a meeting of two communities of care, in which offenders are asked to confront the consequences of their wrongdoing. Talking through these consequences in the presence of those who have suffered ideally ensures that offenders take responsibility for their actions, experience remorse and offer practical help and an apology to the victim and the community to right the wrong (Braithwaite 2002, p. 26).

This outcome is understood in terms of the principle of restorative justice, which is often defined by a differentiation from retributive justice. By nature—an emphasis on the role and experience of victims, involvement of all relevant parties, and decision-making by lay and legal actors—the outcomes of conferencing, however, are more flexible, drawing at times on both retributive and rehabilitative ideas. Nevertheless, as Christie (1977) explains, any concern for rehabilitation is framed not in terms of reforming the offender. Reducing recidivism is not a primary consideration; rather, rehabilitation matters only in so far as it helps the young offender's capacity to offer meaningful restitution to the victim. The apology plays an important symbolic role in this process. It draws attention to prior shared social relationships, acknowledges that the act is a departure from accepted group norms and promises the possibility of restoration—where contesting parties necessarily have to continue to be part of a community in everyday life. Given this localised communitarian requirement, youth justice conferencing perhaps seems out of place given the fragmented relations of late modernity, but it does makes sense through its ability to address the victimological turn; to respond to the perceived deficiencies of the courts, demands for professional accountability and participatory decision-making, the decolonisation of justice and the neoliberal privatisation of former state functions and insistence that individuals and groups take responsibility for their own welfare and security.

10

From fines to forfeiture

INTRODUCTION

In the early twenty-first century, a new road problem referred to both colloquially and in some official forums as 'hooning' is grabbing headlines in the media. Despite the ability of pre-existing law-enforcement provisions to address this particular style of traffic offence, most jurisdictions (that is, in Australia and New Zealand) have felt it necessary to introduce 'tough' new legislation to address it. In a familiar 'law and order' auction style, states and territories have begun boasting that they have 'some of the harshest penalties in the country dealing with the sort of anti-social behaviour that blights many neighbourhoods' (Government of South Australia 2008). In contrast to the earlier traffic regulations, which were justified by the governmental imperative of protecting life and limb, the perceived need for 'anti-hooning' or 'boy racer' (New Zealand) laws are more often linked to 'anti-social' and 'loutish' behaviour; the threat of loss of life seems to have been overtaken by issues of annoyance, nuisance and lack of amenity (Fuller 2007).

At their strongest, anti-hooning laws provide for the forfeiture of vehicles and ultimately imprisonment. In Australia until recently, this type of draconian penalty was considered to be appropriate for only the most serious types of traffic offences—usually committed by recidivist drink drivers—not for activities that were considered to be more of a nuisance than a serious danger (Staysafe 35 1997, p. 15). Critics protested that the confiscation of a vehicle would result in unacceptable hardship for the offender or their family (Jarred 2002). More generally, such a tough response seemed out of step with neoliberal principles of government founded on respect for private property and individual rights.

This chapter explores the conditions that have subsequently provided for the introduction of these previously controversial laws in all states and territories. It begins by outlining the problems that they are intended to address—that is, by defining hooning. The provisions of the laws are described and the value of vehicle forfeiture as a penalty is assessed in relation to principles of punishment. The chapter concludes by considering how anti-hooning laws work by locating forfeiture as a governmental response to a particular type of offending behaviour.

THE PROBLEM OF HOONING

It is difficult to find a definition of hooning in the general criminological research literature. This is probably because the terms *hoon* and *hooning* are Australian colloquialisms. The *Macquarie Dictionary of New Words* describes hoon as an Australianism, with the earliest citation found in Xavier Herbert's *Capricornia* (1938). According to Herbert, a hoon was 'that sort of flash person who fangs their car around for amusement' (in Fuller 2007, p. 124). His definition is consistent with those expressed in more contemporary examples of popular culture. For example, an Australian automotive website described a hoon as:

> The slightly rebellious, sun-glass clad, ever so cool dude, usually spotted behind the wheel of something special, his arm mysteriously jutting out the window, usually with a smile a mile wide—he has an abnormally heavy right foot and it is believed gasoline flows freely in his veins. ('Hoon Auto Gear—Australia', <www.hot-rod.com.au/links/members.htm>, accessed 18 March 2009)

The Australian media is a little less complimentary in its portrayal of drivers involved in hooning as young males who drive high-performance or 'souped-up' cars, rev big engines, play loud music and travel with groups of 'testosterone-addled chums' (for example, Altman 2006; Johnson 2007; Penberthy 2004; Russell and Cooke 2006 in Leal et al. 2007, p. 5). While from the perspective of the Queensland Polices Service (QPS), a hoon is:

> a person who performs hooning activities such as organised illegal street racing, in vehicles that are often defective and unroadworthy. 'Hooning' involves a number of illegal activities with vehicles, including travelling at high speeds, street racing, burnout offences and playing loud music from car stereos. Hoons tend to congregate in groups where they network and organise locations to commit the offences. (Folkman 2005, p. 2)

Recently, the term *hoon* has started to appear in more scholarly forums. Researchers (Armstrong and Steinhardt 2006; Leal et al. 2007) from the Centre for Accident Research and Road Safety—Queenland (CARRS-Q) explain that it refers to 'antisocial driving behaviours such as illegal street racing, burnouts, donuts, drifting, unnecessary speed or acceleration, speed trials and even cruising' (Leal et al. 2007 p. 2). Illegal street racing is described as highly organised or spontaneous in nature. Highly organised illegal races are usually staged at night in industrial areas, with start and finish lines marked a quarter of a mile apart (the traditional distance for drag races) (Leigh 1996). Alternatively, they may be staged in the middle of a highway or other large multi-laned road by using rolling road blockades. In contrast, spontaneous illegal street racing refers to impromptu, one-time races between strangers; for example, drivers stopped at traffic signals on a straight stretch of double-laned road may race, with the traffic signals providing the race start. Alternatively, according to Leal and colleagues (2007), the label *hoon* is used more generally to refer to car enthusiasts, drivers of modified vehicles or young drivers. However, their research demonstrates that those involved in the car-enthusiast scene are not a homogeneous group; that there are a number of subgroups, some of which are perhaps less deserving of police attention than others.

Hooning around

According to the QPS, the activities that hoons typically engage in that constitute antisocial driving behaviour are often enforceable offences. They include:

O Burnouts: Wilfully driving a vehicle in a way that causes the tyres or a substance (like oil) poured onto the road surface, or both, to smoke when the drive wheels lose traction with the road surface.

O Lapping: Driving at a very slow speed repeatedly around a number of predetermined streets. The predominant complaint is the loud volume of sound systems in vehicles during lapping.

O Street racing: When two or more vehicles are side by side or in very close proximity to each other and then simultaneously and rapidly accelerate to a higher speed. It is a test of acceleration, and a conviction requires evidence of a starting and finishing point but not of any speed in excess of the speed limit being attained. Races predominantly occur on multi-lane arterial roads within the built-up areas and on the motorways and highways.

O Road blockades: Where vehicles, travelling on multi-lane roadways, slow down to speeds well below the prescribed speed limit to allow vehicles at the front of the blockade to commit street-racing offences from a rolling start.

O Speed trials: Any attempt to establish or break any vehicle speed record of any description on a road; or any trial of any description of the speed of a vehicle on a road; or any competitive trial of any description designed to test the skill of any vehicle or driver or the reliability or mechanical condition of any vehicle on any road.

O Drifting: When a vehicle approaches a corner or intersection at relatively low speed and is then rapidly accelerated through the corner, causing the rear of the car to slide out and the tyres to slip on the roadway and screech.

O Parking up: When hoons gather in large numbers, look at each others' cars, network and arrange illegal behaviour (Folkman 2005, p. 3).

Demographics: Who are hoons?

Early Australian research on illegal street racing identified participants as young men, with the majority between the ages of sixteen and twenty-five (Leigh 1996). More recent research suggests that this profile is still accurate (Leal et al. 2007), although the number of females attending events is increasing (Armstrong and Steinhardt 2006). Anecdotal police accounts identify hoons as stereotypically male, aged between seventeen and twenty-five, of low income and a blue-collar worker or unemployed; however, they also include 'wealthy Asian students, young women and relatively wealthy middle aged business men' (Folkman 2005, p. 2). Researchers and participants describe street racing as transitory activity, with most people racing for only two or three years. Non-Australian research concludes that illegal street racing and social meets are associated with criminal activity (Armstrong and Steinhardt 2006). In contrast, Leigh (1996) reported that drivers in the Sydney street-racing scene were largely mainstream citizens who have an active interest in motor sports. Many were employed on a full-time basis as mechanics or in other trades, while others were involved in full-time education at high school or TAFE colleges. Higher rates of participation in employment and education (in relation to peers) were linked to the expense of street racing. Some respondents spent between ten and twenty-five thousand dollars on their vehicles and several thousand dollars in fines for traffic offences and vehicle defect notices. In Leigh's study, although the racers recognised that their activities were illegal, most had not abandoned many of society's traditional goals or the conventional means of attainting these goals. They engaged in little associated crime, drug use, drunkenness or gambling, and tended not to conceal their activities from family and friends. Some brought interested friends and family along to watch events, or recorded races so that they could be viewed at home. There was little social stigma among the group—participation was more about status.

Cars and hooning

Typically, a hoon drives a car that is ten years old or older, but many drive late model expensive cars. In Queensland, the most predominant types of vehicles are Holden and Ford sedans or high-performance Japanese models. Modifications of both a legal and illegal nature are often made to Holdens and Fords to enhance performance. A number of Japanese models are imported and can be purchased for under $20 000—such as Sylvia; no modifications are required because they are already high performance. Not all people with modified vehicles are guilty of illegal hoon behaviours (Folkman 2005, p. 2, see also Leal et al. 2007 p. 12).

PENALTIES FOR TRAFFIC OFFENCES

When a traffic offence is detected, a range of possible penalty options are available to police: no action, verbal or written warning, fixed penalties (fines, licence suspension, impounding vehicles), prosecution or arrest. The use of verbal and written warnings is linked to the importance of fairness of enforcement, the need to educate drivers as opposed to punishing them and the potential increase in police efficiency due the time saved in offence processing. A large proportion of road users are often unaware that they have committed an offence owing to lack of local knowledge or poor attention to the road environment. In such cases, researchers suggest that there may be greater merit and fairness of punishment in issuing a warning to these offenders; more severe penalties should be reserved for road users who blatantly breach traffic laws (Zaal 1994).

The most common type of traffic violation penalty is the use of fixed amount fines. These are useful because they provide a means of relating penalty severity to the type of traffic offence committed, needed income for the implementation of enforcement-based countermeasures, and a meaningful deterrent because financial punishment means that offenders have less disposable income for other purposes. Fines can increase the efficiency of offence-processing tasks because they are simple to administer and reduce the workload of the legal system—for example, the State Penalties Enforcement Registry (SPER), which is responsible for the collection and enforcement of unpaid infringement notice fines and court-ordered monetary fines issued in Queensland. On the downside, fines are usually set in relation to other criminal offences and efforts to increase deterrence by substantially increasing fine amounts (for what are often viewed as relatively minor misdemeanours) may undermine other aspects of the criminal justice system. As a result, fines are usually quite low in relative terms and may convey the message to road users that a certain level of illegal driving behaviour is affordable.

Point demerit schemes are used as a means of linking road user behaviour to penalty severity. Such schemes involve the allocation of points to various types of traffic offences. When a driver accumulates more points, usually within a specified time limit, than the maximum number permitted, automatic licence suspension results. Point demerit schemes allow road users to make a certain number of errors before more serious penalties are incurred. They have been introduced as a means of differentiating between different types of road users and as a way of providing a regulated deterrent threat to those road users who consistently violate traffic laws.

Dingle (1985 in Zaal 1994, p. 27) identified three main types of road user groups and the effects that the points demerit scheme has on the driving behaviour of each group. The first are those who adhere to the traffic rules and therefore rarely receive a traffic offence notification. For these drivers, the points system has no direct impact on driving behaviour, but provides a minimum level of deterrence and influences them to maintain a good driving record. The second are those who usually adhere to the traffic laws but occasionally commit some form of minor traffic offence; they will usually only acquire a small number of points at any one time. For these drivers, the system provides an incentive to modify their driving behaviour to avoid obtaining additional points and risk the chance of receiving a more severe penalty. The third are those who consistently violate traffic rules. These drivers are most affected by the points system by quickly approaching and in many cases exceeding the maximum number of points allowable. Behaviour modification occurs only when licence suspension becomes a real possibility. Drivers in this third group may exceed the maximum allowable number of points several times before more lasting behaviour changes occur.

Licence suspension is often regarded as the 'teeth' of traffic enforcement systems. Historically, it has been the ultimate sanction and was administered as the last resort in attempts to deal with high-risk or problem drivers. In recent years, it has become one of the principal sanctions for dealing with drink-drivers and has been shown to be an effective countermeasure with a high deterrent effect (Ross 1991). Licence suspension is administered for two reasons: punishment and safety. As a punitive measure, licence suspension is assumed to work as both specific and general deterrents. As a specific deterrent, it punishes the drink-driver by removing the privilege of driving, thereby reducing the likelihood of subsequent drink-driving behaviour when the privilege is reinstated. As a general deterrent, the threat of licence suspension is believed to decrease the likelihood of drink-driving because drivers are not prepared to risk the chance of losing the privilege of driving. As a safety measure, the use of licence suspensions ideally has the benefit of removing the high-risk driver from the road, preventing them from being a danger to themselves and other road users. According to Zaal (1994), licence sanctions have a greater deterrence potential because when they are administratively applied, they are more certain and swift than traditional sanctions that depend to a large degree on the criminal justice system for their application.

As the most severe of driving sanctions, imprisonment is an integral component of many deterrence-based strategies targeted at potential and convicted dangerous drivers. Recently it has been joined by the confiscation of the vehicles. This latter measure does not completely stop the amount of illegal driving; however, it does make it more difficult because drivers must obtain another vehicle to drive and as a result the overall frequency of such behaviour is reduced. It has become a key response to the types of hooning behaviours referred to above.

Punishing hoons

The most commonly reported strategy used for policing illegal street racing has been the issuing of vehicle defect notices. In his Sydney study, Leigh (1996) explained that if a large number of such notices were issued in a weekend, attendances at such races over the following weeks were reduced. Most of Leigh's participants had incurred significant fines for traffic offences and defect notices. One interviewee estimated that he had paid 'about 5K' to the police over four years of racing; nevertheless, he identified himself as 'one of the luckier ones'.

Staysafe 35 (1997), the report of a joint NSW parliamentary committee, confirmed the significance of this style of enforcement for policing activities referred to as 'hooning'. In terms of vehicles used for illegal street racing, witnesses described how combined police, Roads and Traffic Authority (RTA) and Environment Protection Authority (EPA) operations were set up at or near known meeting places, where large numbers of young drivers congregate with their vehicles. During these combined operations, police typically directed the driver of a vehicle suspected of being defective to present the vehicle at a RTA/EPA inspection site within a specified time (usually fifteen to twenty minutes).

The RTA provided information to the joint parliamentary committee regarding these combined operations:

- Operation Hoon 1 on 28 July 1996 resulted in forty defective vehicle notices being issued.
- Operation Hoon 2 on 4 September 1996 resulted in fifty-two defective notices.
- Operation Beachfront on 13 October 1996 resulted in seventy-one defective vehicle notices being issued.

The submission indicated that the types of vehicles identified as unroadworthy were not generally vehicles that could be regarded as enthusiast/street machines. The majority were standard or neglected vehicles, or those with minor modifications (Staysafe 35 1997).

More recently Folkman (2005), a Queensland police officer, referred to the use of defect notices as a continuing method of enforcement at large gatherings of 'hoons' in industrial estates and car parks. 'Vehicles can be simply defected, which has the tendency to disperse the group' (p. 11). Jarred (2002) cited press reports of a scene in Sunnybank, Queensland, in mid-January 2002, where police descended on a large gathering of car enthusiasts and issued twenty-four defect vehicle notices. The weekly gatherings in this location were reported to involve up to 300 vehicles and 500 people. Armstrong and Steinhardt's (2006) study that interviewed car enthusiasts to explore their experience of policing and attitudes to new anti-hooning legislation identified the practice of issuing defect notices as a key concern. Problems that were identified related to the consistency of policing and information availability. While the group had no problems with being booked for clearly dangerous modifications, they expressed annoyance with the application of fines and demerit points for technicalities. A loss of licence due to a defected vehicle was considered a major concern, outweighing any other single issue, as one interviewee complained: 'I don't have a problem with like say your rear tyres are lowered, sure that can be really dangerous especially if it is wet, if I have illegal tread depth, and a coppa fined, wouldn't have a problem with it, the issue I have is if you have no water in your washer bottle, or having no H pattern on your gear stick, you know how it has got the gears written, they defect you for that' (Armstrong and Steinhardt 2006, p. 41).

The problem of inconsistency in police discretion was highlighted in regard to the defect notices issued. For instance, participants recounted several instances of being cleared of any defects only to be picked up by a different officer on a different occasion. The timing and appropriateness of defect notices as an enforcement strategy was also brought into question by the groups. Participants reported how 'defect stations' had been set up around charity cruises and on exiting legal track race days. A number of participants voiced concerns that they were being targeted, even when they were partaking in organised and approved legal activities. One participant said: 'I just wish they wouldn't target us so much, like after every motor sport event, after every single drifting event that I have ever been to out there, there's always been a radar and defect station on the way home, it's ridiculous' (Armstrong and Steinhardt 2006, p. 41). The group felt that car enthusiasts were the primary focus of new anti-hooning legislation. It was argued that if the vehicles of the whole community, of all ages and types, were scrutinised to the same level as that of the modified car community, the legislation would not be so easily accepted.

Anti-hooning legislation

In New South Wales the *Traffic Amendment (Street and Illegal Drag Racing) Act 1996* was the first legislation of its kind. It was drafted to provide the NSW police service with the power to confiscate the vehicles of any persons engaged in such illegal activity. The provision of this power was designed to address the apparent failure of existing laws and punishments to effectively dissuade offenders from repeatedly participating in 'illegal racing on public streets, burnouts, doughnuts and other dangerous practices' (Staysafe 35 1997, p. 8). Then Minister for Police, Paul Whelan, described it as 'innovative legislation', providing 'new powers which allowed the police to impound any motor vehicle used for unlawful street racing, either on the spot or if circumstances require at a later date' (Staysafe 35 1997, p. 8). The courts could also order a vehicle to be impounded. When impounded, the vehicle was to be taken by either police officers or a contractor to a holding yard. It could be impounded for a period up to three months (at the owner's expense) for a first offence. If the person was convicted of a subsequent offence, the court would have the power to order the forfeiture of the vehicle—that is, it could be lost to the owner permanently.

During debate on the Act in its draft form in 1996, parliament acknowledged that confiscation as a punishment appeared somewhat anomalous when compared with fines and other punitive measures for other road traffic offences. Nevertheless, the argument that individuals involved in this specific activity would be more influenced by the threat of vehicle confiscation than any other punitive measure was accepted. As a safeguard, the Act included a sunset clause that provided for a review of the operation of the Act after six months, and required both houses of parliament to resolve to continue the operation of the Act. The Staysafe Parliamentary Committee conducted hearings with representatives of those most directed affected by the Act: the NSW police service, the RTA, members of car clubs and road safety experts. It concluded that 'the Act … and the threat of vehicle confiscation it provides, has successfully broken up large and regular congregations of car enthusiasts engaging in illegal, dangerous and disruptive activities such as racing and performing burnouts' (Staysafe 35 1997, p. 4). The Staysafe Committee formed the view that the Act should be confirmed, with minor amendments, and reviewed again in the next two to three years. At the time, no other Australian state had specific legislation that allowed the impoundment and forfeiture of motor vehicles. Although no specific Acts in other states addressed illegal street racing, police powers to seize motor vehicles used for illegal street racing were available through more general provisions. For example, under the *Crimes (Confiscation of Proceeds of Crime) Act 1988* (Vic.), motor vehicles seized from a convicted offender were subject to forfeiture—and the use of these vehicle forfeiture provisions was linked to reduction in illegal racing (Jarred 2002).

In 1999 the principal pieces of legislation in New South Wales that addressed hooning behaviours (namely, street racing and burnouts) became the *Road Transport (Safety and Management) Act* (NSW). This legislation provided for the offences of:

○ promoting, organising or taking part in unauthorised racing or speed trials on any road or related area
○ burnouts (where a vehicle loses sustained loss of traction with the road surface)
○ driving that is negligent, furious, reckless or menacing.

The *Road Transport (General) Act 1999* (NSW) provided the authorities with powers of:

○ removing and impounding of motor vehicles used in such offences
○ impounding or forfeiture on findings of guilt or admission
○ search warrants for motor vehicles used in unauthorised racing, speed trials, burnouts or any similar offences
○ suspension of licence for a period of fourteen days
○ immediate suspension of licence in certain circumstances by police
○ suspension of driving privilege in New South Wales of a person who does not hold a NSW licence.

Imprisonment (Jarred 2002) was introduced as a sanction for: driving negligently resulting in death or causing grievous bodily harm; driving behaviour determined to be furious, reckless or at a speed or in a manner that is dangerous to the public; or driving that is intentionally or deliberately menacing to another person (manifest in a threat to personal injury or to damage property).

Legislation adopted by the Australian Capital Territory in 1999 and Queensland in 2002 mirrored that introduced in New South Wales. The *Road Transport (Safety and Traffic Management) Act 1999* (ACT) provided for offences such as negligent driving; furious, reckless or dangerous driving; and menacing driving. A further amendment soon after its enactment included provisions addressing racing, speed trials and records, burnouts and for the seizure, impounding and forfeiture of motor vehicles in certain circumstances. In Queensland, amendments to the *Police Powers and Responsibilities Act 2000* gave police the power to impound the vehicles of drivers committing prescribed hooning offences, including: dangerous operation of a motor vehicle; careless driving of a motor vehicle, racing and speed trials on roads; and wilfully starting a vehicle, or driving a vehicle, in a way that makes unnecessary noise or smoke. Among other sanctions imposed (including fines, demerit points and licence disqualification), the vehicles of drivers so charged could be impounded for forty-eight hours for a first offence, three months after a second offence within three years, and forfeited to the state after a third offence within three years.

In 2004 the Tasmanian *Police Offences Amendment Bill* and the Western Australian *Road Traffic Amendment (Impounding and Confiscation of Vehicles) Act* set out stipulations similar to those described in the Queensland legislation. The South Australian *Statute Amendment (Misuse of Motor Vehicle Act)*, or the 'hoon drivers' legislation, created two new summary offences relating to the driving of a vehicle in a public place that involves any 'competitive trial to test drivers' skill' or the sustained wheel spin [s66(2)(a–d)]. Penalties included impounding and forfeiture. While the Act had some safeguards against abuse, the impounding and possible forfeiture of a vehicle were seen by critics as dramatic responses to a misuse of a motor vehicle (Williams 2006). The Northern Territory similarly introduced anti-hoon legislation that provided sanctions for antisocial driving practices, such as burnouts and road races. The legislation provided for the confiscation of vehicles of repeat offenders (Territory Roads 2004).

In 2006 amendments to the *Road Safety Act 1986* brought Victoria into line with other states by introducing provisions modelled on those available in the jurisdictions described above. Police were given the power to immediately impound or immobilise a car driven by a person who they reasonably believe has committed a hoon-related offence, and to seize the vehicle for forty-eight hours either through impoundment or by way of on-site immobilisation. The penalty for second hoon-related offences committed within three years is vehicle impoundment for up to three months, and a third or subsequent offence inside three years could result in the vehicle being permanently forfeited to the Crown. According to the then Minister for Police and Emergency Services, Tim Holding, it was 'three strikes and the vehicle's out: sold by the State of Victoria, which will keep the proceeds'. He warned that the family car was not exempt from impoundment or permanent confiscation, so parents should ensure that their children did not engage in hoon driving behaviour. 'Authorities have the power to impound, immobilise or confiscate any vehicle involved in a hoon act, regardless of whether or not the driver is the registered owner' (Department of Police and Emergency Management 2006).

While the provision that vehicles could be impounded regardless of whether or not the driver is the registered owner was not included in the earliest versions of anti-hooning legislation, it nevertheless became a feature of provisions in jurisdictions that subsequently adopted this style of legislation. From the outset in Tasmania the police information about anti-hoon legislation warned that: 'It doesn't matter if the car you are driving at the time of the offence is yours or not' (Tasmania Police 2008), while in 2008 Paul Holloway, the South Australian Minister for Police, boasted that amendments that strengthened that state's provisions 'were some of the harshest penalties in the country' (Government of South Australia 2008). The new legislation allowed police to immediately home-clamp or impound an offender's vehicle for up to seven days, and to apply to the courts to extend that period to ninety days. Moreover, the Minister warned that the family car was not exempt from being impounded, and the police have the power to impound a vehicle involved in hoon activity regardless of whether or not the driver is the registered owner. As with the Victorian case above, parents were urged to ensure their children do not become involved in hoon behaviour.

Adding to what seems to be an emerging new category of 'law and order' auction, the NSW parliament in 2008 toughened penalties through the Road Transport Legislation Amendment (Car Hoons) Bill. The penalty for street racing was increased to $3300 for a first offence and to $3300 or nine months imprisonment, or both, for a second or subsequent offence. The aim was to provide a more effective deterrent to hoons who persist in committing street-racing offences through the threat of a jail term for a second offence. The criteria defining a burnout were expanded and the penalties doubled (to ten penalty units or $1100). Previously, aggravated burnouts were defined as burnouts committed with the knowledge that a flammable liquid was on the road. The 2008 legislation expanded the definition to include repeated burnouts, long and loud burnouts that disturb community amenity, burnouts that endanger public safety and burnouts that are committed as part of a group activity. All these factors now contribute to the severity of a burnout, and as such to the severity of the penalty. The penalty for aggravated burnout was increased to $3300 for a first offence and $3300 and up to nine months imprisonment, or both, for a second or subsequent offence. Aggravated burnouts were described in the parliament as the 'worst types of hoon behaviour'. The objective was to address those people who deliberately do long, noisy burnouts down public streets or as part of an illegal street race (Sharpe 2008).

The new provisions allow the police to immediately suspend the licences of people charged with street racing and aggravated burnouts at the roadside. Drivers convicted of an aggravated burnout offence can be disqualified from driving for twelve months. This was already the case for people convicted of a street-racing offence. New penalties are focused on the groups of friends and associates that may gather to watch, or urge others on, or who take photographs or film to glamourise the activity. The 2008 Bill introduced offences for willingly participating in a group activity involving burnouts; viewing, organising, promoting or urging any person to participate in any group activity involving burnouts; and photographing or filming a motor vehicle doing burnouts for the purpose of using the photographs or film to promote or organise group activity involving burnouts. The penalties for spectators are the same as for drivers: $3300 for a first offence and $3300 or nine months imprisonment, or both, for a second or subsequent offence.

In New South Wales, when offenders use their own vehicle, it can now be impounded or clamped for three months for a first offence, and forfeited to the Crown for a second or subsequent offence. A vehicle that is forfeited may be sold or given to the RTA to be used for crash-testing or education programs. Clamping is said to provide offenders with a daily reminder of the consequences of their actions, and to show their neighbours exactly what they have been up to. Restrictions have been placed on the court's discretion to reduce, commute or dispense with a period of confiscation or forfeiture in cases of extreme hardship only; penalties cannot be reduced because of inconvenience. Difficulty carrying out employment or in travelling to or from a place of employment, business or education is not considered sufficient to constitute extreme hardship. Where a driver is found guilty in someone else's vehicle, sanctions can now be placed on the registered owner of that vehicle—the hardship clause is similarly applied: '[v]ehicles will not be returned because of weak excuses, or because they suddenly have to find alternative means of carrying out their day to day life' (Sharpe 2008). The RTA can issue the registered operator with a suspension warning notice that additional sanctions will apply if any vehicle owned by them is used in the commission of a further street racing or aggravated burnout offence within five years of receiving the warning. Vehicle registration can be suspended for up to three months.

South Australian Government media release

'The Government's message … is simple. If you drive like a hoon, you'll get caught and you'll lose your car, and with the introduction of these new laws you'll lose your car for even longer.'

Members of the public continue to play an important role in catching these 'hoons' by reporting this type of irresponsible driving to SAPOL's Traffic Watch. Following are two examples of the stupid behaviour of hoon drivers, and how assistance from the public has helped Police impound two hoon cars.

EXAMPLE 1

A 21-year-old male was detected on four occasions for breaches of the *Misuse of Motor Vehicle* legislation (and other road traffic offences) on 19 June, 24 June, 22 August and 18 September 2006 in Port Pirie.

On 19 June he was observed by a member of the public excessively spinning the rear wheels of his vehicle, doing a 'huge burnout', which left about 10 metres of tyre marks on the road. The male was reported and his vehicle impounded for 48 hours.

On 24 June, he was observed by police [to] excessively spin the rear wheels of his vehicle for about 15 seconds and produce large clouds of smoke. The driver was arrested and his vehicle impounded.

On 22 August he was seen driving the same previously defected vehicle by police, and when attempting to stop the vehicle police were engaged in a pursuit with the driver. During this pursuit the driver accelerated at speed causing a sustained wheel spin. The male was reported and his vehicle impounded.

On 18 September 2006 the driver was observed by a member of the public reversing out of a driveway, engine revving loudly, tyres screeching and large cloud of smoke around the vehicle. This member of the public observed two distinct black tyre marks on the road and notified police of the vehicle details. Shortly afterwards police observed this vehicle driving towards them, where the vehicle was stopped and the male driver arrested. The vehicle he was driving was examined and found to be a Mitsubishi Colt, which had been modified extensively to include a V8 253 engine. Part of these modifications included removal of the air cleaner so that the engine would not show from the outside, modification of the steering and braking system, which made the handbrake and rear brakes inoperative and the placement of the battery in the boot. He was arrested and this vehicle was impounded.

A forfeiture order for the vehicle involved ... was issued 9 October 2006 by the local Port Pirie Magistrates Court for the vehicle to be impounded for a period of 3 months.

EXAMPLE 2

On Tuesday 5 September 2006 a member of the public saw two sedans travelling at about 100 kilometres per hour along Actil Avenue, Woodville. Both vehicles were then seen to execute a U turn and in doing so, the witness heard wheels on both vehicles screeching and saw grey smoke coming from the tyres of both vehicles. The screeching lasted for about five seconds. There were numerous people in the vicinity, including school children playing sport nearby. Police were called and spoke to the drivers of both vehicles. Police immediately seized both vehicles for a period of 48 hours and reported both drivers for traffic offences that include Misuse Motor Vehicle—Sustained Wheel Spin (S44B (3) 2 RTA). Two other members of the public supported observations of the driving of both vehicles.

The following table provides a breakdown of offences (according to SAPOL's data for the first six months of the financial year):

TABLE 10.1 Breakdown of offences

Type of offence	2005/06	2006/07
Race or speed trial	66	51
Sustained wheel spin	328	337
Engine or tyre noise	120	96
Drive on park or garden	44	48
Unknown	7	2
Total	565	534

Source: News Release, Government of South Australia, Hon. Paul Holloway, Minister for Police, Thursday 8 February 2007, <www.ministers.sa.gov.au/news.php?id=1227>.

PENOLOGICAL PRINCIPLES: MANAGERIALISM, DETERRENCE AND INCAPACITATION

The rise of managerialism in both the public sector and criminal justice has been well documented, with increased attention to the three Es of economy, efficiency and effectiveness. Recent years have seen the growing influence of economic considerations on the shape of penal systems. One example of this is the expanded use of infringement notices (on-the-spot fines) that allow offenders to discharge their liability by paying a fixed sum without having to attend court. Zdenkowski (2000) points to the problems with these types of penalties, citing the scope for the inconsistent use of such remedies, potential for anomalies and capricious justice, the erosion of due process and the reduced accountability because of invisibility, and lack of deterrence. These are all issues when it comes to traffic offences.

Fines are the most common penalty and provide a meaningful deterrent if the risk of apprehension is high; they also increase the efficiency of offence processing because they are simple to administer. However, efficient punishment does not necessarily result in effective punishment. Many drivers are undeterred and continue to speed or commit other traffic offences, seeing the fine as little more than one of the costs of driving. Moreover, respondents in Armstrong and Steinhardt's (2006) study of car enthusiasts clearly highlighted problems in relation to police discretion and the inconsistent application of this type of penalty when it comes to defect notices. Licence suspension is another administrative penalty that addresses high-risk or problem drivers. Working with point demerit schemes, licence suspension acts both as a punishment and a safety strategy. As a punishment, the loss of licence acts as specific and general deterrents; as a safety strategy, it works to remove dangerous drivers from the road. Licence sanctions have greater deterrent potential because when they are administratively applied, they are more certain and swift than traditional sanctions that rely on the criminal justice system for application.

Less common, and perhaps more extreme, punishments for traffic offences include the confiscation or forfeiture of vehicles and imprisonment. These forms of penalty are the 'muscle' of anti-hooning legislation. Like other traffic law-enforcement practices, this legislation relies to a large degree on the principle of deterrence (along with elements of managerialism and incapacitation). Indeed, the utilitarian concerns for 'the overall happiness of everyone' (more often translated into the greatest good for the greatest number) we first encountered with Bentham's moral philosophy is clearly expressed in the following quotation from the Second Reading of the Road Transport Legislation Amendment (Car Hoons) Bill 2008 in the NSW parliament:

> The *hoon activity of a few should not be allowed to disturb the peaceful enjoyment of the many*; nor should it be allowed to put other road users at risk of serious injury or death. This Bill toughens the penalties for street racing and aggravated burnouts to provide more appropriate sanctions and a more effective deterrent. The Bill targets the drivers, the vehicles used to commit the offences, the vehicle owners who let hoons use their vehicles and the participants who actively encourage hoon behaviour. It sends a clear message to the community that hoon behaviour is not acceptable and will not be tolerated. (Sharp 2008)

According to Bentham, punishment 'in itself is evil' and 'ought only be admitted in as far as it promises to exclude some greater evil', namely the suffering resulting from the commission of further offences. The main benefit was expected to flow from the effect of punishment on the actions of people besides those undergoing it—on the community. Punishment would achieve this by altering the balance between pain and pleasure as seen as by potential offenders. Bentham regarded the prevention of future offences by example as fundamental. He argued that reform and incapacitation were important but secondary, affecting only 'the comparatively small number of individuals, who having actually offended, have moreover actually suffered for the offence'. Example, on the other hand, affected 'as many individuals as are exposed to the temptation of offending; that is ... all mankind' (Bentham 1843/1995, p. 174). Beyond this, Bentham's emphasis on example indicated a willingness to punish an individual according to the social consequences that would follow; it could justify excessive punishment or the punishment of an innocent person if this would prevent future offending.

A key concern relating to anti-hooning provisions is their tendency to excess, to be out of kilter with other law-enforcement sanctions. In the Queensland context, a spokesperson for the RACQ—while acknowledging that there were some areas of the state that were experiencing 'problems with outlandish driver behaviour'—expressed the view that the proposed legislation might contain penalties that were greater than the offences warranted. This criticism was echoed by the Council of Civil Liberties whose representative argued that legislation that existed prior to the amendments was sufficiently strong to deal with such behaviour. A spokesperson for the peak representative body Youth Affair Network of Queensland criticised the proposed legislation on the basis that it would unfairly discriminate against young people (Jarred 2002). These submissions were consistent with the view of Dr Michael Henderson, a consultant described as an 'eminent road safety researcher' in the NSW Staysafe 35 inquiry. He said:

> As a road safety person I cannot accept the validity of using this type of *draconian* penalty for an offence which overtly does not have a very dangerous effect. Clearly there is a hazard, but so has jet skiing and hang gliding and whole host of other things. But clearly it has a high nuisance effect.
>
> If we want to put aside the option of using these kinds of *draconian* penalties for persons who are a serious threat to mankind, such as drink drivers, I think we lose something by using this type of penalty for essentially what is a nuisance activity. (Staysafe 35 1997, p. 15, emphasis added)

From Bentham's deterrence perspective, this type of exemplary punishment might be justified by positive social consequences. This was implied in the submission of another expert witness. Christopher Ford, Director (Road Safety and Traffic Management) of the RTA, commented: 'You might recall my earlier comment, that while I considered the empowerment to be fairly *draconian*, I would be sure it would be effective' (1997, p. 11, emphasis added). At the conclusion of its investigations the Staysafe committee formed the view that the Act should be confirmed and the provision should continue to operate. On balance it found 'no negative effects other than those intended' (1997 p. 5). The bulk of the evidence presented indicated that the Act had produced positive effects. Three hundred and eight-four offences were detected and 136 vehicles impounded in six months of review following the initial introduction of legislation. Police service evidence suggested that the Act and the threat of confiscation had directly led to the reduction of what were regular large gatherings of car enthusiasts engaging in activities prohibited by the Act.

Other aspects of more recent legislative provisions might also be categorised in terms of this style of deterrence and the exemplary punishment of the innocent, including parents and families, vehicle owners and spectators. According to South Australian, Victorian and Tasmanian legislation, for example, the police have the power to impound a vehicle involved in hoon activity regardless of whether or not the driver is the registered owner. The South Australian police minister warned that the family car was not exempt from impoundment or permanent confiscation, so parents should ensure that their children did not engage in hoon driving behaviour. The recent NSW amendments also introduced penalties for vehicle owners who were not the driver when the alleged offence occurred. Moreover, the 2008 Bill introduced offences for willingly participating in a group activity involving burnouts; viewing, organising, promoting or urging any person to participate in any group activity involving burnouts; and photographing or filming a motor vehicle doing burnouts for the purpose of using the photographs or film to promote or organise group activity involving burnouts. Harsh penalties matching those directed at drivers—including imprisonment—can therefore be applied to those standing on the sidelines.

Paradoxically, such excessive or harsh response can actually be counter-productive in terms of deterrence. The success of enforcement is dependent on its ability to create a meaningful deterrent to road users. To achieve this, the primary focus should be on increasing surveillance levels to ensure that perceived apprehension is high. Once this has been achieved, increasing penalty severity and the quick and efficient administration of punishment can further enhance the deterrent effect. However, Nichols and Ross (1990) argue that the criminal justice system may hinder the effectiveness of penalty severity as a deterrent. The more severe the penalty administered, the more legal representations usually required. This may, in turn, lead to delays in receiving punishment and even uncertainty about receiving any punishment at all. This punishment delay can compromise all other aspects of the deterrence threat. They explain that policies based on increasing the certainty and the swiftness of punishment have a greater deterrent impact than those based upon severe punishments.

Finally, the confiscation and forfeiture provisions not only work as deterrence but also have a clear capacity for incapacitation. Unlike the examples of preventive detention discussed in Part 2 of this book, here incapacitation achieves its goal of removing the opportunity for crime by impounding the vehicle (an object) rather than the offender. This can be explained in terms of how the offender is understood. In Chapter 2, those who were detained were seen as risky and dangerous, and not suitable for correction; in this chapter, however, offenders are understood as (immature) rational actors who have a capacity to calculate the costs and benefits of their actions, who will ultimately become amenable to strategies that seek to govern crime though the manipulation of interests and the promotion of mechanisms of self-regulation (Garland 2001). The limited risk of the offender is apparent in their continued liberty and potential to access other vehicles. Confiscation and forfeiture remove the vehicle in the hope that in its absence the young (male) offender will develop mechanisms of self-regulation and will grow out of the offending behaviour through processes of normal development. Only in cases where this fails to occur is imprisonment of the offender (now seen as risky) the option of last resort.

THINKING THEORETICALLY: JUSTIFYING DRACONIAN PENALTY

A Queensland Parliamentary Library Research Brief that explored in 2002 the potential for the introduction of anti-hoon legislation in that state is titled 'Police Powers and Responsibilities and Another Act Amendment Bill 2002: Confronting bad and nuisance road behaviour'. The preface to the paper (appearing as a lone statement on the title page) explains that the Bill is 'primarily aimed at *clamping down on loutish behaviour* involving motor vehicles on public roads. Behaviour such as burnouts, street racing and using loud sound systems is specifically targeted'; and the introductory section begins by stating that: '[t]he intention is to grant greater powers to police to deal with deliberate driving behaviour that is *annoying* and *perhaps dangerous* to other road users and/or nearby residents' (emphasis added). It is difficult not to conclude that the message repeated in these opening remarks is that the problem to be addressed is judged in value terms to be 'bad', 'nuisance', 'loutish', 'annoying' and only 'perhaps dangerous'. Indeed, the body of the paper goes on to describe it as 'the flamboyant manoeuvres of some car enthusiasts' that are exemplified by the comments of a local government councillor who explained: '[i]f these kids were just getting together to look at the cars, there would not be an issue. The problem is the danger involved in doing spin-outs, doughnuts and the rest of the sideshow' (Jarred 2002, p. 2). A Sunnybank resident provided more detail about the nature of the danger, describing gatherings that had been occurring on a weekly basis for about six months:

> They park on both sides of the street and in every available parking space. They slowly rev up and down the street for hours. Not only is it highly dangerous, but it is very intimidating, they are all leaning against the cars, alarms are going off, car horns are going, and engines are revving.

> They appear to have a system in place that warns of any imminent arrival of police.

> It would be wonderful if they took it in turns to meet outside their own homes and completely disrupt the neighbourhood with noise. (Jarred 2002, pp. 2–3)

According to Fuller (2007), the practice of street racing and, to a lesser extent, cruising can appear dangerous and even sinister; however, the statistical evidence indicates (as Henderson suggests) the reality is otherwise. Fuller argues that the percentage of so-called hooning accidents in Queensland in the context of all accidents is insignificant. Based on Armstrong and Steinhardt's (2006) study that discovered that for the targeted age group of twelve to twenty-four there were 169 hooning-related accidents involving injury and property damage in the period 1999–2004, and the publicly provided road safety statistics from the Queensland Road Safety Authority (Queensland Transport 2005 in Fuller 2007) that indicated that there were over 100 000 accidents in Queensland in the period 1999–2003 (six years compared with five), he calculated that hooning accidents represented roughly less than one-quarter of 1 per cent of the total number of recorded accidents. Fuller points out that this is not how things are portrayed in the media or political rhetoric. On his account, as a road safety problem hooning is simply not that dangerous. Fuller positions responses to behaviour described as hooning as a 'moral panic'. The regulatory drivers are reflected in the way the police (Folkman 2005, pp. 3–4), and as we have just seen parliamentary researchers (in Queensland), represent the 'severity' of the hoon issue as a function of complaints and then accidents. Fuller argues that the politics of anti-hoon legislation is more concerned with the threshold of public attention than actual governance. He concludes that '[b]y making hoons a road safety problem and writing them of as a danger—potential killers—the government did not have to consider the more complex social and cultural questions about who these so called hoons actually were' (2007, p. 133).

In contrast to Fuller's view, it is possible to argue that anti-hooning legislation is able to take the form that it does precisely because there is a sense of (exactly) who these drivers are. The introduction of anti-hooning legislation can be interpreted from a governmental perspective that understands the possibility of these provisions in the context of neoliberal rule. While some recent accounts of neoliberal government have been preoccupied with the implication of the liberal belief that members of the population are naturally endowed with a capacity for autonomous self-directed activity (Rose 1999; Dean 1999; O'Malley 1992; 2001 for example), in the past liberal political reason has been as much concerned with paternalistic rule over minors and adults judged to be incompetent as it has been with the government of autonomous individuals (Hindess 2001). Governmental action has been based on the assumption that although individuals may be naturally endowed with a capacity for autonomous action, this does not mean that the capacity will always be fully realised in practice. The capacity for autonomous action was usually understood from historical and developmental perspectives, suggesting that an extended period of education and training is required before it can be realised in an individual and that it will be well-established among *adult* populations only in relatively civilised commercial societies.

Hindess (2001) considers how liberal political reason has dealt with the problem of governing those it identifies as being less than fully autonomous. He argues that it is possible to distinguish three broad types of response—these help us to understand the form of penalties for traffic offences and hooning:

1   Some people—the hopeless cases—are so far from acquiring the relevant capacities that they should simply be cleared out of the way. This is achieved through the imprisonment or incapacitation of the offender.

2   The capacity for autonomous action can be developed in a population only through compulsion and the imposition of more or less extended periods of discipline. The treatment of deviant members of civilised populations is founded on the belief that the problem arises from the relaxation of discipline and the corruption of manners. The only remedy is to break the bad habits and establish better ones in their place, which is achieved through forfeiture and confiscation, and the incapacitation of the vehicle.

3   In relatively civilised populations, many of those who lack the capacities required for autonomous action do so largely for what might be considered external reasons—like inadequate education—so the role of government is to facilitate the development of their capacities by establishing a benign and supportive social environment. The implication here is that the improvement of many individuals within an already improved population should be brought about with only limited resort to authoritarian means: deterring offenders through graduated sanctions of point demerit systems and fines that rely on offenders' calculated compliance (Hindess 2001, pp. 101–7).

Those engaging in behaviour associated with hooning have been identified as mainly young men, with the majority between the ages of sixteen and twenty-five. Such behaviours, like street racing, have been described as transitory activities, with most people racing for only two or three years. Acknowledging these demographic and developmental characteristics, Leal et al. (2007) suggest that hooning could be viewed as part of the mainstream young-driver problem. This assessment is consistent with results from Armstrong and Steinhardt's (2006) interviews with car enthusiasts, which differentiated between 'enthusiasts' and those who are involved in the antisocial element of activities or 'hoons' (see also Leigh 1996). The car enthusiasts they interviewed identified a problematic element considered to be no more than a small group (of hoons), constituting approximately 10 per cent of the entire population, that would be present at a venue or event on a particular night. They distanced themselves from this subgroup, preferring to identify themselves as car enthusiasts. Beyond this disassociation, however, there was a ready acknowledgment that 'because someone may currently not be a socially responsible member of the scene that this will not always be the case' (Armstrong and Steinhardt 2006, p. 40). Participants noted how younger members of the scene, including themselves some years ago, were more prone to taking part in inappropriate or illegal behaviours.

In short, the problem behaviour has been constituted as something characteristic of mainly (a few) young men who eventually 'grow out of it'. In terms of liberal rule, these 'hoons' are yet to develop 'suitable habits of self government' and 'anti-hooning legislation' is intended to work to strategically govern these young persons who are not yet 'in the maturity of their faculties' (Mill 1859/1975, pp. 15–16). The forfeiture or confiscation of vehicle (incapacitation through the removal of the vehicle), and the point demerit system for that matter, provide various windows and levels of disciplinary intervention, allowing for the development of autonomous self-rule. In contrast, imprisonment, the ultimate sanction—incapacitation through the removal the offender—is reserved for the hopeless few. Of course, the problem with such programs of government is the difficulty of getting them to work as intended (Rose and Miller 1992, p. 185); techniques invented for one purpose may find their governmental role for another. While formal evaluations of this punitive response to problem drivers are yet to be produced, reports in the media have highlighted some of the ways that the legislation has been used. Queensland's *Courier Mail* reported the confiscation of a B-Double truck north of Brisbane because the driver, in his forties, did not have the right class of licence (Ironside 2008), while a tourist bus (full of prospective whale watchers) driven by a woman also in her forties was similarly impounded in Hervey Bay (Dickinson 2008). These uses raise questions beyond the scope of this chapter, and it is perhaps needless to say they are clear evidence of the legislation being coopted for purposes beyond the stated aim of 'clamping down on loutish (and annoying) behaviour'.

CONCLUSION

Punishments responding to problem traffic behaviour—like speeding—were introduced in the face of increasing road death and injury tolls. Effective interventions have tended to rely on the utilitarian principle of deterrence operationalised through graduated systems of penalty, such as point demerit schemes and licence suspension. The key mechanism for behavioural modification is the driver's own rational calculation of the costs and benefits of offending. Recently, hooning or antisocial driving behaviours—such as illegal street racing, burnouts, donuts, drifting, unnecessary speed or acceleration (not necessarily beyond the speed limit), speed trials and even cruising—has become a new focus of concern. This 'nuisance' or 'loutish' behaviour has justified the introduction of what have been described by road safety experts as draconian penalties. Jurisdictions around Australia have engaged in a very specific type of law and order auction as they struggle to establish that they have the 'harshest [hooning] penalties in the country'. These penalties extend beyond the traditional fines and licence suspension to include the confiscation and possible forfeiture of the offending vehicles, even when the driver is not the registered owner. Harsh penalties are not restricted to drivers and vehicle owners: spectators and those seen to be encouraging this type of behaviour can be subjected to large fines and even imprisonment if they repeatedly participate in any group activity involving 'burnouts' (that is, for a second or third offence).

Following Bentham, these harsh punishments are justified by deterrence—general and specific—and rely on the prevention of future offences by example. The emphasis on example is based on a willingness to punish an individual according to the social consequences that would follow, and it can justify excessive punishment or the punishment of an innocent person if this would prevent future offending. In short, they are designed to 'send a clear message to the community that hoon behaviour is not acceptable and will not be tolerated' (Sharpe 2008). Road safety experts and others have expressed reservation, indicating that such responses are draconian, excessive and out of kilter with other law-enforcement sanctions. This is a reasonable concern. Nichols and Ross (1990) warn that the more severe the penalty administered, the more legal representations usually required. This can lead to delays in receiving punishment and even uncertainty about receiving any punishment at all. This challenge potentially compromises all other aspects of the deterrence threat. While harsh responses can be partly explained in terms of 'moral panic' (Fuller 2007), the governmental rationale of neoliberalism offers a broader account. Hooning is a behaviour that has been defined as an activity principally of not-so-deviant young men, as part of the mainstream young-driver 'problem' (Leal et al. 2007). In terms of liberal rule, the apparently harsh provisions of anti-hooning legislation are possible because they aim to restore neighbourhood peace not by changing the offender (rehabilitation), who in the normal course of development will acquire 'suitable habits of self government', but by removing (often temporarily) the offending vehicle, thereby altering and addressing a criminogenic situation.

11

The three Rs of the penological triangle

INTRODUCTION

This book has provided an overview of the ways that particular frameworks of thought, social institutions and practices have shaped punishment and sentencing in Australia. By sketching the historical and social context of Australian penality, the first chapter made it clear that while imprisonment has made, and continues to make, a significant contribution to the domain of criminal justice, there has always been much more to it. For example, the diversity of the convict experience itself is often obscured by a tendency to focus on the brutality of early penal settlements such as Port Arthur or Moreton Bay. In contrast, Finnane (1997) and others (Hirst 1983; Braithwaite 1999a; O'Toole 2006) describe an alternative version of the convict experience. The fate of the majority was assignment to work, which involved freedom to roam the countryside; good behaviour was rewarded with greater freedom offered by a ticket-of-leave and emancipation. Nevertheless, some convicts did die in chains and in conditions of relentless, savage confinement, at the scaffold, or on the voyage.

In the nineteenth century, the foundations of the physical infrastructure of Australia's prison system were laid. A significant commitment was made to prison building in this country between the 1850s and 1890s. By the end of the century, debates about the purpose of punishment introduced reform, and alternatives to prison were developed for specific populations, such as first offenders, delinquent youth, drunkards and mental 'defectives'. The reform process continued into the twentieth century; by the end of that century, the terrain of punishment had expanded considerably. Community corrections moved beyond diversion to medical institutions and supervision in the community to include a broad array of sentencing options for the management and treatment of offenders. This book shifted our focus into the twenty-first century, surveying a range of punishment options that are available in contemporary Australia. Its case-study approach explored why some offenders are considered so risky that incarceration is the only possibility, while others are seen as less problematic and suitable for a range of alternative punishments that do not involve prison.

RISK

Making up the first stage of this survey, the case studies in Part 2 (Risk) were, for example, concerned with offenders deemed to be too dangerous for release from custody: those subject to preventive detention that continued beyond time served for a criminal sentence or imposed without any criminal conviction at all. These forms of selective incapacitation are justified in relation to those offenders likely to pose a future threat to community safety. For instance, while the US sexual psychopath laws of the 1930s and 1940s were designed as an alternative to prison for offenders deemed too sick for punishment, recent legislation has aimed to extend the incarceration of convicted sex offenders deemed too dangerous for release from custody. This new generation of laws consists of a variety of provisions described in terms of enhanced sentencing for certain classes of violent or sex offenders, sexual predator laws, registration of sex offenders and community notification of sex offenders (Hinds and Daly 2001). With the exception of community notification, these types of laws have been introduced into Australian jurisdictions.

In relation to terrorism, an avalanche of recent legislative measures have introduced penalties for crimes such as engaging in a terrorist act and detonating an explosive device, while also criminalising and describing very heavy penalties for acts that fall short of the actual commission of such acts. These laws are used not merely to punish or deter specific conduct but to prevent it. Authorities are empowered to act pre-emptively by arresting people before they have formed a definite plan to commit the criminal act. Under new Australian powers granted to ASIO, a person who is not even suspected of any crime can be detained for longer than a suspect. Under new provisions in the criminal code, control and preventive detention orders can be imposed on a person. While control orders fall short of imprisonment, through various prohibitions, restrictions, reporting and electronic monitoring requirements, they can effectively provide a means for placing an individual under house arrest. Preventive detention orders involve the power to detain a person for forty-eight hours under federal laws and fourteen days under corresponding state laws to prevent terrorism or to preserve evidence. As McDonald and Williams (2007) point out, these orders challenge the traditional understandings of legal regulation: neither requires a finding of guilty or even a suspicion that a crime has been committed, yet both enable significant restrictions to be placed on individual liberty.

Both case studies provide an example of selective incapacitation that is justified in terms of community safety, rather than with regard to the culpability of the offender. Moreover, both responses are controversial. The incapacitation of sex offenders is based on assumptions consistently problematised by research: these offenders are predatory strangers driven by strong, deviant motivations that are untreatable, and there are high rates of crime-specific recidivism (Smallbone and Wortley 2000; 2001; Levenson and D'Amora 2007). Counterterrorism legislation—based on the precautionary principle—justifying detention without trial or the restriction of liberty without criminal conviction, is controversial because the right to personal liberty (that is, freedom from arbitrary detention) is considered the most fundamental and important common law right.

Both these responses are founded on the identification and management of dangerous groups; the focus is on the security of the population rather than disciplining and correcting offenders (Foucault 1991). They exemplify what Feeley and Simon (1992) call the 'new penology', which embraces an increased reliance on imprisonment and merges concerns for surveillance and custody, thereby moving away from a concern with punishing specific individuals to managing dangerous groups. In this context the language of probability and risk competes with that of clinical diagnosis and retributive judgment. The new penology is less concerned with responsibility, fault, moral sensibility, diagnosis or intervention and treatment of the individual offender. It is concerned with the techniques to identify, classify and manage groupings sorted by dangerousness: a task that is more managerial than transformative. From this perspective the criminal justice system pursues systemic rationality and efficiency. It seeks to sort and classify, to separate the less from the more dangerous, and to deploy control strategies rationally. The new penology is signalled by the development of more cost-effective forms of custody and control and new technologies to identify and classify risk. Among them are low-frills, no-service custodial centres; various forms of electronic monitoring systems that impose a form of custody without walls; and new statistical techniques for assessing risk and predicting dangerousness. These new forms of control are not anchored in aspirations to rehabilitate, reintegrate, retrain and provide employment, for example. They are justified in more blunt terms: variable detention depending on risk assessment.

But as Douglas (1992) points out, categorisation according to risk is not value-neutral. Political cultures work as filters, selecting problems for attention and suggesting images of threatening people and situations. In this way, risk is linked to Durkheim's idea of collective conscience. Laws act as an index of social phenomena and 'popular' opinion (Thompson 1988); the recent repressive developments in relation to sex offenders demonstrates a shift in the collective conscience and can easily be understood as reaffirming solidarity by taking vengeance on the offender. Elias's work on civilising and decivilising processes, however, helps us to better appreciate changing responses to this type of sexual offending. Moreover, it highlighted how bureaucratisation in Australia, a feature of the civilising process, worked against decivilising trends through the implementation of a national system of registration rather than one of public notification. In doing so, this perspective provides an explanation of why Megan's Law didn't make it to Australia; alternatively, in the case of terrorism, we can see at work the relationship between risk and fear of victimisation. The media play an important role in influencing and shaping public perceptions of crime risks and now the risk of terrorist attack. The amplification of certain issues by the media helps to set the agenda on a given issue. Following the political line, dominant media representations of radical Islam have been dehumanising and demonising, reinforcing a reductivist separation between good and evil. [Potential] offenders are cast as evil; they are suitable enemies for whom we should have no sympathy; they are deserving of punishment and in the interests of security they must be locked up! (Garland 1996).

REHABILITATION

In the second half of the book, we shifted attention to more familiar concerns of criminology. Part 3 described a range of responses that addressed offenders in need of correction rather than containment: those subject to the disciplinary control of the contemporary arm of Foucault's carceral archipelago made up by specialist courts. It explored case studies of problem-solving courts addressing three current areas of concern in Australia: reducing crime related to drug dependence, the over-representation of Indigenous offenders and the incidence of domestic violence (Makkai in Payne 2006). Such courts blur boundaries between sentencing, punishment and correction; they involve preventive partnerships (Garland 2001) with treatment service providers in the community; and (with the exception of a concern for safety in domestic violence courts) they are not so much concerned with victims or vulnerable situations but intensely focused on treating or changing the offender.

For example, drug courts explicitly aim to correct offenders by integrating treatment with criminal justice responses—they are based on the view that, when it comes to drug-dependent offenders, treatment is more effective than punishment as a means of changing behaviour (Murphy 2000). The court is conceived as a therapeutic domain, prosecution and defence lawyers swap their role as adversaries to become part of a multidisciplinary team, eligible offenders are provided access to a broad continuum of treatment and illicit drug use is routinely monitored, with non-compliance resulting in swift and certain sanctions by the court. A key difference with the traditional courtroom experience for (drug) offenders is ongoing judicial supervision and regular and personalised judicial interaction with each participant. These changes are founded on the principle of therapeutic jurisprudence—or the extent to which substantive rules, legal procedures and the roles of lawyers and judges produce therapeutic or anti-therapeutic consequences for individuals involved in the legal process (Wexler and Winick 1991).

The practice of therapeutic jurisprudence in drug courts is shaped by knowledge derived from social sciences. We have seen how the aspects that Foucault linked to the rise of the prison in the nineteenth century are evident in the drug court, where offenders, and their biography and capacity for correction and change, rather than the offence, are the focus of judgment. Drug court teams make decisions in relation to matters of health, social well-being and possible recidivism, explicitly illustrating expert intervention through the human sciences. More than this, as an alternative to prison, the court unambiguously functions as part of the carceral archipelago. The panoptic qualities of its services— regular judicial review, regular drug testing, restrictions on place of residence or movement, home visits by case managers and so on—ensure a continuum of surveillance and control (Costanzo 2003; Fischer 2003). While the potential for net widening, through a desire to get more people into treatment or more rigorous monitoring (which increases the potential for breaching an order), warrants critical consideration; as an alternative to prison, drug treatment courts can offer some redeeming possibilities. Remaining outside the 'total institution' allows offenders to avoid disculturation—the untraining that renders the inmate incapable of managing certain features of daily life on the outside following release from prison (Goffman 1957/1997). It also provides an opportunity to maintain connection with civil society and non-drug-using networks, which is an important factor in overcoming and developing future alternatives to drug-dependent (offending) behaviour.

Like drug courts, Indigenous courts and circle sentencing courts are concerned with the correction of offenders, and can and do attend to therapeutic outcomes though participation, coordination of service delivery and community involvement. The shaming and healing elements of Indigenous sentencing courts are similar to the desired elements of restorative justice conferences; however, Indigenous courts have a much broader agenda. They involve partnerships between state government and Aboriginal organisations; in particular, they rely on the participation of Indigenous elders or respected persons. Indigenous community representatives talk to defendants about their offending and assist judicial officers in sentencing. As we saw in Chapter 1, all the regulatory mechanisms of Aboriginal culture that might have assisted in the governance of the population were systematically dismantled by first the colonial and then the welfare state. The involvement of elders in these contemporary settings ideally works to frame rehabilitation in the context of Indigenous cultures. Through this move, Indigenous justice practices seek to reinstate Aboriginal cultural institutions of control and habits of regulation. They offer the potential for change not only at the individual level of the offender but also through innovative and active relationships with post-colonial institutions of justice. In short, these justice processes are focused on the rehabilitation not only of offenders but also of the institutions of the criminal justice system itself. They seek to reshape the relationship between Indigenous peoples and these institutions and disciplinary mechanisms of control.

The problem-solving response of domestic violence courts has been aligned with the principle of therapeutic jurisprudence (Goldberg 2005; Phelan 2003). However, the analysis above suggests that, like Indigenous courts, domestic violence courts (and the legal concept of battered women's syndrome) have a political dimension and seek change at both the individual and social structural levels. The practices they employ aim to locate the experience of domestic violence in its social, cultural and historical context. Domestic violence is often a course of behaviour rather than a single event. In the past, criminal justice agencies have failed to engage with this unpleasant reality. Chapter 8 described how some recent court innovations have tried to address this oversight. The legal concept of battered women's syndrome (BWS) was introduced as a feminist strategy to assist women charged with killing a violent partner in arguing self-defence by bringing their social context to the attention of the court (Stubbs and Tolmie 2008). Admittedly, this attempt to reshape self-defence law to better reflect the social context of battered women who kill has been fairly unsuccessful. Rather than explaining how the behaviour was reasonable in the circumstances, BWS has more commonly been used in a way that frames those circumstances subjectively rather than objectively. Programs responding to the more common occurrence of male offending also focus on the significance of the social context of violence against women. Perpetrator treatment programs delivered by the domestic violence courts in this country are developed from a socio-political perspective that focuses on the systemic nature of gender inequality and the tactics of power and control in relationships. These criminal justice responses aim to achieve an increased level of awareness of domestic violence within the community and agencies that respond to it. While it is clear that offender responsibility and victim safety are key considerations in the deliberations of domestic violence courts, prevention through offender programs addressing behavioural change is the core component of this type of response. As mentioned, treatment programs are delivered from a socio-political perspective. Like Indigenous justice initiatives, they are about change—challenging and changing community attitudes to violence against women and the violent behaviour of men.

The recent emergence of the types of programs described in Part 3 adds some weight to O'Malley's (2000) assessment that actuarial technologies of risk-based prediction in the Australian setting have not become a central consideration in sentencing processes. He suggests that while discourses of risk have permeated many aspects of criminal justice, the practices they represent are unchanged or virtually unchanged from those that have gone before. That is, there is no more than a slight translation into 'risk talk' of the traditional 'welfare sanction' work of developmental psychologists (p. 158). Even in parole contexts—where Pratt (1997) has suggested that actuarialism is most likely to become influential in Australasian settings—the model remains one of individual justice shaped around judicial consideration and the clinical expertise of the human sciences. Freiberg (2000) has argued that the Australian judiciary has deployed many effective defences against the encroachment of risk-based sentencing agendas. The uptake of justice innovations such as those described in Part 3 is an example of this. It has been facilitated and promoted by judicial activism and enthusiasm. For example, see the work of Michael King on drug courts and problem-solving courts published while he was a Western Australian magistrate, the work on Indigenous courts in New South Wales by Magistrate Doug Dick and references to the instrumental role of Chris Vass in South Australia (Daly et al. 2006). Internationally, see the website of the American National Association for Drug Court Professionals and the work of now retired Judge Peggy Hora (Nolan 2001).

This is not to deny that the welfare sanction has retreated and that the goal of rehabilitation has been downgraded to just one of a number of objectives: punishment, deterrence, protection or retribution. As we saw in Chapter 2, the ALRC in the late 1980s advised that while the Australian version of the just deserts approach had a 'primary emphasis on just deserts for the offender and reparation for the victim … Deterrence, rehabilitation and incapacitation should still be relevant but given a lesser priority' (ALRC 1987, p. 17 in Brown 1998, p. 383). Taking this tack accommodates rehabilitation in sentencing frameworks that emphasise proportionate sentences. According to Bottoms (1995), this is achieved through a rethinking of rehabilitation that moves from understanding it as a process of training or expert treatment of obedient subjects to one of persuading rational agents to (enter a guilty plea and) cooperate in their own longer-term interest.

RESTITUTION

In contrast to the case studies described in Parts 2 and 3, where offenders were positioned as abnormal in some way, in the final part of the book on restitution the offender is situated as a rational, opportunistic actor. The individual who is the subject of the interventions and responses is not the dangerous offender who must be locked up for the safety of all, or the poorly socialised misfit in need of assistance, rather an illicit, opportunistic consumer who lacks a strong moral compass or any effective internal controls, aside from a capacity for rational calculation and a will to pleasure (Garland 2001). Chapters 9 and 10 explored how interventions driven by the principle of restitution rely on the capacity of the offender to make 'the right' choices once made aware of the consequences of their behaviour and strategies that seek to govern crime though the manipulation of interests and the promotion of mechanisms of self-regulation. Here we saw how youth conferencing, fines and the recent provisions of anti-hooning legislation can be understood as exemplars of liberal approaches to crime (Bottoms 2003; Braithwaite 2000; Rose 2000), which largely govern by altering criminogenic situations rather than seeking to significantly change or retrain the offender.

Youth justice conferencing (YJC) is an example of restorative justice at work in the Australian criminal justice system. It is a meeting of two communities of care, in which offenders are asked to confront the consequences of the wrongdoing in the hope that they will take responsibility for their actions, experience remorse and offer restitution in the form of practical help and an apology to the victim and the community to right the wrong. We might wonder about the possibility of restorative justice in late modernity, which is defined in terms of the profound economic and cultural changes of the last few decades. Late modernity brought with it not only new freedoms, new levels of consumption and new possibilities for individual choice, but also new disorders and dislocations—and new levels of crime and insecurity (Garland 2001). These factors have caused a reconsideration of the ways we think about crime and punishment, and have been linked to the mutation of welfare capitalism into contemporary neoliberalism and the emergence of a preoccupation with the containment of risk (Garland and Sparks 2000; O'Malley 1999). On this horizon, restorative justice practices that are characterised by a localised focus, informal processes, lay participants and principles of communitarianism or interdependency seem inconsistent with new penological devices, such as risk assessment profiles; however, the appeal and growth of restorative justice are possible in this context for a number of reasons: it makes sense though its ability to address the victimological turn (referred to by Finnane); and to respond to the perceived deficiencies of the courts, demands for professional accountability and participatory decision-making, the decolonisation of justice and finally to the neoliberal privatisation of former state functions and insistence that individuals and groups take responsibility for their own welfare and security (Bottoms 2003).

The last of the case studies in Chapter 10 reviewed the penalties used to respond to traffic offences—until recently, treated as fairly mundane and often not considered 'real' crime. This perhaps accounts for the predominance of the administrative style of penalties that also rely on responsibilisation and the rational calculations of self-governing citizens and their ability to respond to graduated systems of penalties involving fines, point demerit schemes and licence suspension. These penalties rely on the utilitarian principle of deterrence. The key mechanism for behavioural modification is the driver's own rational calculation of the cost and benefits of offending. In Chapter 10, however, we also saw how the previously colloquial term *hoon* has crept into official vocabulary, and the behaviour associated with this label has been problematised and used to justify penalties such as confiscation and forfeiture of offending vehicles, even when the driver is not the registered owner. Such moves have been described by some as draconian. Indeed, this heavy-handed approach might have signalled that 'hooning' is out of place in this last section of the book; that it would be better considered under the risk heading of Part 2. But we should bear in mind that concerns about hooning are expressed more in terms of its 'nuisance' or 'loutish' qualities than the dangerousness of offenders themselves.

Given that liberalism (or neoliberalism) is a term used to describe the rationality of contemporary forms of government and regulation linked to the principle of not governing too much, or 'governing through freedom' (Rose 1999), many of the penalties described in recent anti-hooning legislation may seem out of place—that is, as very illiberal. However, they are understandable if we extend our consideration of liberal political reason. In the past, liberal political reason has been as much concerned with paternalistic rule over minors and adults judged to be incompetent as it has been with the government of autonomous individuals (Hindess 2001). Governmental action has been based on the assumption that although individuals may be naturally endowed with a capacity for self-regulation, this does not mean that the capacity will always be fully realised in practice. For example, Hindess describes three types of response to those identified as being less than fully autonomous. First, those who are considered incapable of developing a capacity for responsible autonomous action should be removed from society. Second, where there has been a relaxation of discipline and manners, it is necessary to break bad habits and establish better ones in their place. In these cases, self-regulation is developed through compulsion and the imposition of more or less extended periods of discipline. Third, in many cases, those who lack the capacities required do so because of external reasons, such as poor education. The regulation of these individuals is brought about with only limited resort to authoritarian means (Hindess 2001, pp. 100–1). We have seen how these responses have clear parallels with the penalties for traffic offences and hooning behaviour. The serious repeat offenders (particularly drink-drivers)—the hopeless cases—are cleared out of the way through the imprisonment or incapacitation of the offender. Those engaging in the bad habits and manners described as nuisance and loutish behaviour, such as hooning, are subjected to periods of discipline achieved through forfeiture and confiscation, through the incapacitation of the vehicle rather than the offender. Finally, those who speed or disregard traffic instructions are regulated with only limited resort to authoritarian means: individuals are mostly deterred through graduated sanctions of point demerit systems and fines that rely on calculated compliance.

From this perspective, hooning is an activity principally of not-so-deviant young men who will eventually mature to become responsible citizens. It is part of the mainstream young-driver 'problem' (Leal et al. 2007). So confiscation or forfeiture is not as illiberal as it might at first seem. The apparently harsh provisions of anti-hooning legislation are possible because they aim to restore neighbourhood peace not by changing (rehabilitating) or removing (incapacitating) the offender, who in the normal course of development will acquire 'suitable habits of self government', but by 'send[ing] a clear message to the community that hoon behaviour is not acceptable and will not be tolerated' (Sharpe 2008), and by removing (often temporarily) the offending vehicle, thereby altering and addressing a criminogenic situation.

PUNISHMENT AND SENTENCING: THE PRISON AND BEYOND

This overview of some recent trends and innovations in punishment and sentencing in Australia is not meant to be comprehensive. There is much more to it. For example, the risk section might usefully have considered youth curfews as an example of collective incapacitation—that is, the containment of particular categories of offenders. Youth curfews are government initiatives that prevent children or teenagers from being in public spaces during a certain time period. They may be imposed as a means of maintaining public order or to suppress targeted groups. Pratt (1998) describes them as an example of the decivilising of punishment. While curfews have a long history that goes back beyond the pre-modern as a means of enforcing control over local populations, provisions targeting particular groups such as young and Indigenous people appeared in the early nineteenth century. In Australia, curfews were used to exclude Indigenous people from city centres. For example, although they were 'allowed' into Brisbane Town during the day, from the early 1850s, Indigenous people were the targets of a curfew that was enforced after 4 p.m. and on Sundays (Kidd undated). Boundary Streets in West End and Spring Hill were named according to this practice. In the 1990s there was a resurgence of curfews in the United States, Britain, New Zealand and Australia, reflecting high levels of anxiety about public safety and a change in public perception about the permissibility of certain courses of action, such as curfews, as a legitimate means for responding to crime in modern societies. In 2003 the Northbridge Curfew was implemented in Perth to address the anti-social behaviour of young people in that precinct (Office of Crime Prevention 2003), and late in 2006 the Alice Springs Town Council unsuccessfully proposed similar measures for addressing security and youth issues. The idea was that 'unsupervised (not in the care of an appropriate adult) children under the age of 15, found on the streets or any other public places during the hours of 10 p.m. and 5 a.m., would be taken into protective care and custody' (Morris et al. 2007, p. 6). These are controversial measures of control, particularly as they are likely to impact more heavily on young Indigenous people and, given recommendations of the RCIADIC, aimed at keeping this group out of custody. More generally, they have been described as the indiscriminate and arbitrary containment of young people based on their age rather than any offending behaviour (White 1996; 2004). Young people are targeted as an aggregate, as members of a risky group. This point is made clear by a fifteen-year-old boy who won a landmark High Court ruling against the legality of Britain's child curfew zone. With regard to the coercive powers of the police he said, 'of course I have no problem with being stopped by the police if I've done something wrong. But they shouldn't be allowed to treat me like a criminal just because I'm under 16 years of age' (Morris et al. 2007, p. 9).

Part 3 might also have included a consideration of mental health courts. The concept of therapeutic jurisprudence was developed in the context of mental health law, and the term was first used by David Wexler and Bruce Winick in a paper delivered to the National Institute of Mental Health in 1987 (Wexler and Winick 1991). It was coopted in the late 1990s by the powerful American National Association for Drug Court Professionals as a juridical foundation for the development of treatment courts across that country and then in other parts of the world (Nolan 2001). While drug treatment courts provide a very distinct forum for the application of this principle (Hora et al. 1999; Senjo and Leip 2001), its expression varies across different criminal justice settings.

In Part 4 it would have been logical to include a case study on punishment and sentencing strategies that address corporate offenders. The long history of the regulatory state at work in the context of corporations and business would demonstrate that the use of managerialist techniques that has recently been highlighted in the domain of punishment is not as new or novel as we might think. The corporate sector has long been subject to government at a distance. Remarkably, the novelty in this arena is the recent trend for the individualisation of responsibility and criminalisation of specific company directors (Braithwaite 2003).

As part of being indicative, rather than exhaustively surveying the breadth and diversity of punishment and sentencing practices in Australia, the case studies included are often located at the extreme or the margins of the field of punishment and sentencing. Fortunately, offences warranting the extreme types of response described in the context of terrorist activity or serial sexual offending against children are fairly unusual or rare. In contrast, even though drug-related offending is frequent, domestic violence is a growing problem and Indigenous over-representation in prisons is seemingly intractable, the availability of the types of justice innovations described in Part 3 is decidedly restricted. Similarly, YJC and the confiscation or forfeiture of vehicles are more often the exception than the rule: not all victims are willing to participate in the conferencing process, and most traffic offenders are deterred by administrative penalties such as fines and demerit point schemes. The value of the examples in this book has been that these extreme, alternative or unusual (but not impossible) forms of punishment are able to provide clear or distinctive exemplars of the rationalities that shape punishment more broadly, as well as fairly straightforward opportunities for theoretical engagement. This is not to suggest mutual exclusivity; that there is a simple grid of this goes with that. Programs for the treatment of sex offenders clearly have rehabilitative potential, and as such could be understood in terms of discipline rather than security. In drug courts, risk assessment plays a part in determining an offender's eligibility to be involved in the program. Those facing charges of physical violence, sexual assault or drug trafficking are explicitly excluded from programs. At the initial appearance and as participants face termination hearings when they have breached an order, judicial officers frequently make judgments articulated in terms of community safety (Costanzo 2003). Moreover, illicit drug use is routinely monitored, with non-compliance resulting in swift and certain sanctions by the court—a clear marker of the use of deterrence in this rehabilitative context. Similarly, in Chapter 9 Table 9.1 described a range of objectives underpinning YJCs, including restorative, rehabilitative and just deserts principles.

So what have we learnt from thinking about punishment from the perspectives of risk, rehabilitation and restitution? First, from the diversity and breadth of the practices described in this book, the rationales and principles that underpin them and how we might interpret them from various sociological perspectives, it is clear that punishment is complex. This is why it is so difficult to define as a concept. There is so much more to it than the seven features identified at the beginning of Nigel Walker's (1991) useful little book *Why Punish?* However, he does provide a good starting place for thinking about punishment and sentencing. He begins by defining punishment as the intentional and justified infliction of something that is assumed to be unwelcome to the recipient by legitimate authorities for an action or omission that infringes law, where the person punished has played a voluntary part in the infringement (1991, pp. 1–3). He then goes on to discuss the justification of punishment by referring to principles of deterrence, education, incapacitation and correction. While penologically we can position various practices as more or less retributive, preventive or transformative, they may at the same time respond to the rise of managerialism and the three Es of economy, efficiency and effectiveness. This can include consumerist pressure for the effective delivery of individuals' entitlements, or for greater accountability and transparency or governmental strategies focused on security and community safety. Alternatively, thinking theoretically, punishment and sentencing can be understood in terms of broader more abstract concepts. We have seen how these practices can be interpreted as an emotional reaction, as a means of regulating populations (positively or negatively), as a means of shaping attitudes by reinforcing or contesting the collective conscience, or as a fundamentally political activity.

Second, punishment and sentencing are shaped by how we think about the persona of the offender. For example, the trend for incapacitation as a principle of punishment identified in Part 2 was based on the idea that offenders were risky or dangerous ungovernable subjects, with limited capacity (if any) for correction. In contrast, the problem-solving courts described in Part 3 focused on the participants' biography and, in particular, their capacity for change. These offenders can be rendered governable through the imposition of discipline. The practices of penality described in Part 4 rely on a perception of offenders as self-governing subjects, individuals with capacity for consequential thinking, who with the right information will 'naturally' behave as responsible citizens. This is a neat and convenient way of matching forms of punishment to offenders; however, individual behaviour and its relationship to identity are far more complex. As Foucault (1984) points out, the same individual can in some circumstances acquire the habits of thinking and capacities for being affected that are appropriate to apparently conflicting ways of comporting oneself. This is an appeal to the idea of the fragmented self, or multiple identities referred to by Braithwaite and Mugford. Accordingly, it is problematic to construct offenders in essentialised terms as simply dangerous, correctable or responsible. To do so sets a limit on the possibilities for the individuals concerned, as well as how we might respond to them.

Finally, the case studies provided applied examples of the distinctive questions that theoretical perspectives pose, highlighted major interpretive themes, and identified the kinds of insights that each theory has to offer for the understanding of particular examples of modern penality. Drawing on more than one perspective provided an opportunity for different theoretical interpretations to be brought into conversation with each other; for example, in the context of understanding how drug courts work, we saw how the analytical value of Foucault's ideas about the panopticon as the prototype of normalising discipline could be criticised, refined and augmented using the work of Cohen and Goffman. The enduring value of Durkheim's ideas, which were developed in the nineteenth century, was evident in Parts 2 and 4. Alternatively, the applied significance of theory in relation to punishment and public policy was clearly demonstrated by the influence and articulation of feminist perspectives, both in the formulation of the legal concept of BWS and the delivery of socio-politically oriented programs for perpetrators. The theoretical engagement throughout the book might have been more critical in places, but I aimed for a conversation rather than an argument or adversarial exchange. The field of social theory is not like that of the hard sciences, in which theories are falsified, disproved and then disregarded. As Garland (1997) explains, a range of theories has something to offer the analysis of punishment—where some fall short, it is often not because they are incorrect; rather they are not the whole story, or not able to explain everything. So we have seen how each way of thinking about punishment asks slightly different questions, pursues a different aspect, reveals different determinants and outlines different connections.

ABC Online (2006), 'Thomas to face retrial on terrorism charges', <www.abc.net.au/new/newsitems/200612/s/1815446.html>, accessed 29 November 2009.

Aboriginal Justice Advisory Council (undated), 'Aboriginal people and bail: Courts in NSW' (Sydney: Aboriginal Justice Advisory Council).

Aboriginal Justice Advisory Council and Debus, Bob (undated), 'Aboriginal justice agreement' (Sydney: NSW Attorney Generals Department).

Alcohol and Other Drugs Council of Australia (2000), '8.9 Diversion, drug policy 2000: A new agenda for harm reduction, June 2000' <www.adca.org.au/publications/Drug%20Policy%202000/89_diversion.htm>, accessed 16 July 2003.

Allen, F. (1981), *The Decline of the Rehabilitative Ideal: Penal Policy and Social Purpose* (New Haven: Yale University Press).

Altheide, David L. (2006), 'The mass media, crime and terrorism', *Journal of International Criminal Justice*, 4, 982–97.

Anglin, M. D., Longshore, D. and Turner, S. (1999), 'Treatment alternatives to street crime (TASC): An evaluation of five programs', *Criminal Justice and Behaviour*, 26 (2), 168–95.

Anthony, Thalia and Cunneen, Chris (2008), *The Critical Criminology Companion* (Sydney: Hawkins Press).

Armstrong, Kerry A. and Steinhardt, Dale A. (2006), 'Understanding street racing and "hoon" culture: An exploratory investigation of perceptions and experiences', *Journal of the Australasian College of Road Safety*, 17 (1), 38–44.

Ashworth, Andrew (2000), *Sentencing and Criminal Justice* (London: Butterworths).

Ashworth, Andrew (2005), *Sentencing and Criminal Justice* (Cambridge: Cambridge University Press).

Aungles, A. (1994), 'The prison and the home', *Monograph No. 5* (Sydney: Institute of Criminology).

Austin, J. and Coventry, G. (2001), 'Emerging issues on private prisons' (Washington DC: Bureau of Justice Assistance).

Austin, J. and Krisberg, B. (1981), 'Wider, stronger and different nets: The dialectics of criminal justice reform', *Journal of Research in Crime and Delinquency*, 18 (1), 165–96.

Australian Bureau of Statistics (2005), 'Personal safety survey Australia' (Canberra: ABS).

Australian Bureau of Statistics (2008a), 'Corrective services', cat. no. 4512.0 (Canberra: ABS).

Australian Bureau of Statistics (2008b), 'Prisoners in Australia', cat. no. 4517.0 (Canberra: ABS).

Australian Institute of Criminology (AIC) (2007), 'Is notification of sex offenders in local communities effective?', *AICrime Reduction Matters* (Canberra: Australian Institute of Criminology), no. 58, <www.aic.gov.au/publications/current%20series/crm/41-60/crm058.aspx>.

Australian Royal Commission into Aboriginal Deaths in Custody and Wootten, John
Halden (1989), 'Report of the inquiry into the death of Malcolm Charles Smith'
(Canberra: Australian Government Publishing Service).

Baregu, M. (2002), 'September 11: Structural causes and behavioral consequences
of international terrorism', in International Peace Academy (ed.), *Responding to
Terrorism: What Role for the United Nations?* (New York City: Chadbourne &
Parke), 40–4.

Beck, Ulrich (1992), *Risk Society: Towards a New Modernity* (London: Sage).

Beck, Ulrich (2001), 'The cosmopolitan state: Towards a realistic utopia', *Eurozine*.

Becker, Howard (1963), *Outsiders: Studies in the Sociology of Deviance* (New York:
Free Press).

Belenko, Steven (2000), 'The challenges of integrating drug treatment into the criminal
justice process', *Albany Law Review*, 63 (3), 833.

Bentham, Jeremy (ed.), (1843/1995), *Panopticon vs New South Wales*, ed. J Bowring
11 vols. (The Works of Jeremy Bentham, Bristol: Thoemmes Press) pp. 173–211.

Berliner, L. et al. (1995), 'A sentencing alternative for sex offenders: A study of
decision-making and recidivism', *Journal of Interpersonal Violence*, 10 (4),
487–502.

Biles, David and McDonald, David (1992), 'Deaths in custody Australia 1980–1989',
*Research Papers of the Criminology Unit of the Royal Commission into Aboriginal
Deaths in Custody* (Canberra: Australian Institute of Criminology).

Blagg, Harry (2008), *Crime, Aboriginality and the Decolonisation of Justice* (Sydney:
Hawkins Press).

Bograd, M (1988), 'Feminist perspectives on wife abuse: An introduction', in K. Yllo
and M. Bograd (eds), *Feminist Perspectives on Wife Abuse* (Newbury Park: Sage
Publications).

Bottoms, Anthony (1995), 'The philosophy and politics of punishment and sentencing',
in C. Clarkson and R. Morgan (eds), *The Politics of Sentencing Reform* (Oxford:
Clarendon Press).

Bottoms, Anthony (2003), 'Some sociological reflections on restorative justice', in
A. Von Hirsch et al. (eds), *Restorative Justice and Criminal Justice; Competing
or Reconcilable Paradigms?* (Oxford: Hart Publishing), 79–113.

Boulton, Phillip (2006), 'Counter-terrorism laws in practice', paper given at New South
Wales Public Defenders Office Conference Papers, Sydney.

Bradshaw, K. (1985), 'Twists, tricks, change and reform: Three eras in the
administration of community corrections in Queensland', M Pub. Administration
Thesis, University of Queensland, Brisbane.

Braithwaite, John (1989), *Crime, Shame and Reintegration* (Cambridge: Cambridge
University Press).

Braithwaite, John (1999a), 'Crime in a convict republic', *History of Crime, Policing and
Punishment Conference* (Canberra: Australian Institute of Criminology).

Braithwaite, John (1999b), 'Restorative justice: Assessing optimistic and pessimistic
accounts', in M. Tonry (ed.), *Crime and Justice: A Review of Research* (25;
Chicago: University of Chicago Press).

Braithwaite, John (2000), 'The new regulatory state and the transformation of criminology', *British Journal of Criminology*, 40 (222–38).

Braithwaite, John (2002), 'The fall and rise of restorative justice', *Restorative Justice and Responsive Regulation* (New York: Oxford University Press), 3–27.

Braithwaite, John (2003), 'What's wrong with the sociology of punishment?', *Theoretical Criminology*, 7(1), 5–28.

Braithwaite, John and Mugford, Stephen (1994), 'Conditions of successful reintegration ceremonies: Dealing with juvenile offenders', *British Journal of Criminology*, 34 (2), 139–71.

Broadhurst, Roderic (1987), 'Imprisonment of the Aborigine in Western Australia, 1957–85', in Kayleen Hazlehurst (ed.), *Ivory Scales: Black Australians and the Law* (Kensington: University of New South Wales Press).

Brown, David (1998), 'Penalty and imprisonment in Australia', in Robert P. Weiss and Nigel South (eds), *Comparing Prison Systems: Towards a Comparative and International Penology* (Amsterdam: Gordon and Breach Publisher).

Bull, Melissa (2003), 'Just treatment: A review of international programs for the diversion of drug-related offenders from the criminal justice system' (Brisbane: Queensland University of Technology).

Bull, Melissa (2005), 'A comparative review of best practice guidelines for the diversion of drug-related offenders', *International Journal of Drug Policy*, 16, 223–34.

Bull, Melissa (2007), 'Alcohol and drug problems in rural and regional Australia', in Elaine Barclay et al. (eds), *Crime in Rural Australia* (Sydney: Federation Press).

Bull, Melissa (2008), *Governing the Heroin Trade: From Treaties to Treatment* (Aldershot: Ashgate).

Bull, Melissa and Craig, Mark (2006), 'The problem of terrorism: Balancing risk between state and civil responsibility', *Current Issues in Criminal Justice*, 18 (2), 202–20.

Burchell, Graham, Gordon, Colin and Miller, Peter (1991), *The Foucault Effect: Studies in Governmentality* (Chicago: Chicago University Press).

Burdon, W. M. et al. (2001), 'Drug courts and contingency management', *Journal of Drug Issues*, 31 (1), 73–90.

Bureau of Justice Statistics (1997), 'Sex offenses and offenders: An analysis of data on rape and sexual assault' (Washington, DC: US Department of Justice).

Bureau of Justice Statistics (2000), 'Sexual assault of young children as reported to law enforcement: Victim, incident and offender characteristics' (Washington, DC: US Department of Justice).

Bureau of Justice Statistics (2002), 'Criminal victimisation' (Washington, DC: US Department of Justice).

Busch, Ruth (2002), 'Domestic violence and restorative justice: Who pays if we get it wrong', in Heather Strang and John Braithwaite (eds), *Restorative Justice and Family Violence* (Cambridge: Cambridge University Press), 223–48.

Carrington, Kerry (2008), 'Critical reflections on feminist criminologies', in Thalia Anthony and Chris Cunneen (eds), *The Critical Criminology Companion* (Sydney: Hawkins Press), 82–93.

Caven, Zoe (2003), 'Battered women syndrome' (Sydney: Australian Domestic and Family Violence Clearing House).

Chan, Janet (1992), *Doing Less Time: Penal Reform in Crisis* (Sydney: Institute of Criminology).

Chan, Janet and Zdenkowski, George (1986), 'Just alternatives: Part 1', *Australian and New Zealand Journal of Criminology*, 19 (2–3), 67–90, 131–62.

Chantrill, Paul (1998), 'Community justice in Indigenous communities in Queensland: Prospects for keeping young people out of detention', *Australian Indigenous Law Reporter*, 3 (2).

Christie, Nils (1977), 'Conflicts as property', *British Journal of Criminology*, 17 (1), 1–15.

Clark, M. (1980), *A Short History of Australia* (Winnipeg: Mentor).

Clarke, M. (2008), 'Report of the inquiry into the case of Dr Mohamed Haneef', (Canberra: Commonwealth of Australia).

Clear, T. and Cadora, E. (2001), 'Risk and community practice', in K. Stenson and R. Sullivan (eds), *Crime Risk and Justice* (Devon: Willan Publishing).

Coddington, D. (1997), *The Australian Paedophile and Sex Offender Index* (Sydney: Deborah Coddington).

Cohen, Stanley (1979), 'The punitive city: Notes on the dispersal of social control', *Contemporary Crises*, 3, 339–63.

Cohen, Stanley (1985), *Visions of Social Control, Cambridge* (Cambridge: Polity Press).

Collins, L. and Mouzos, J. (2001), 'Australian deaths in custody and custody—Related police operations 2000', *Trends and Issues in Crime and Criminal Justice* (Canberra: Australian Institute of Criminology), 217, 1–6.

Collins, S. (2008), 'Jack Thomas spared further jail time', The *Age*, 29/10/2008.

Commonwealth Department of Health and Ageing (2001), 'Illicit drug diversion initiative' <www.nationaldrugstrategy.gov.au/nids/diversion/index.htm>, accessed 16 September 2002.

Commonwealth of Australia (2004), 'Report on government services' (Melbourne: The Steering Committee for the Review of Government Service Provision).

Commonwealth of Australia (2005), 'Parliamentary debates, Senate Thursday 3 November 2005' (Canberra: Official Hansard, No 16), 43.

Commonwealth of Australia (2009), 'Report on government services' (Melbourne: The Steering Committee for the Review of Government Service Provision).

Cook, Bree, David, Fiona and Grant, Anna (2001), 'Sexual violence in Australia', *Australian Institute of Criminology Research and Public Policy Series* (Canberra: Australian Institute of Criminology), 36.

Costanzo, John (2003), 'Final report by the pilot program magistrate pursuant to section 46, *Drug Rehabilitation (Court Diversion) Act 2000*', *The Drug Court Magistrate's Final Report* (Brisbane: Queensland Department of Justice and Attorney-General).

Criminal Justice Commission (1999), 'Reported sexual offences in Queensland' (Brisbane: Research and Prevention Division).

Cullen, F. T. and Gilbert, K. E. (1982), *Reaffirming Rehabilitation* (Cincinnati: Anderson Publishing).

Cunneen, Chris (2001), *Conflict, Politics and Crime: Aboriginal Communities and the Police* (Chicago: Independent Publishers Group).

Cunneen, Chris (2007), 'Crime, justice and Indigenous people', in Elaine Barclay et al. (eds), *Crime in Rural Australia* (Sydney: Federation Press).

Cunneen, Chris and McDonald, David (1997), 'Keeping Aboriginal and Torres Strait Islander people out of custody' (Canberra: ATSIC).

Cunneen, Chris and White, Rob (2002), *Juvenile Justice: Youth and Crime in Australia* (Melbourne: Oxford University Press).

Daley, D. (2004), 'Australian community corrections, populations, trends and issues' in S. O'Toole and S. Eyland (eds), *Correctional Criminology* (Sydney: Federation Press).

Daly, Kathleen (2001), 'SAJJ Technical Report No. 2: Research instruments in year 2 (1999) and background notes' (Brisbane: School of Criminology and Criminal Justice, Griffith University).

Daly, Kathleen (2002a), 'Sexual assault and restorative justice', in Heather Strang and John Braithwaite (eds), *Restorative Justice and Family Violence* (Cambridge: Cambridge University Press), 62–88.

Daly, Kathleen (2002b), 'Restorative justice: The real story', *Punishment and Society*, 4 (1), 55–79.

Daly, Kathleen (2003), 'Mind the gap: Restorative justice in theory and practice', in A. von Hirsch et al. (eds), *Restorative Justice and Criminal Justice: Competing or Reconcilable Paradigms?* (Oxford: Hart Publishing).

Daly, Kathleen (2006), 'The limits of restorative justice', in Dennis Sullivan and Larry Tifft (eds), *Handbook of Restorative Justice* (London: Routledge), 134–45.

Daly, Kathleen et al. (1998), 'South Australian Juvenile Justice (SAJJ) research on conferencing, Technical Report No. 1: Project overview and research instruments' (Brisbane: School of Criminology and Criminal Justice, Griffith University).

Daly, Kathleen and Chesney-Lind, Meda (1988), 'Feminism and criminology', *Justice Quarterly*, 5 (4), 497–538.

Daly, Kathleen and Hayes, Hennessey (2001), 'Restorative justice and conferencing in Australia', *Trends and Issues In Crime and Criminal Justice* (Canberra: Australian Institute of Criminology), 186, 1–6.

Daly, Kathleen and Hayes, Hennessey (2002), 'Restorative justice and conferencing', in Adam Graycar and Peter Graboscky (eds), *Cambridge Handbook of Australian Criminology* (Cambridge: Cambridge University Press).

Daly, Kathleen, Hayes, Hennessey and Marchetti, Elena (2006), 'New visions of justice', in Andrew Goldsmith, Mark Israel and Kathleen Daly (eds), *Crime and Justice: A Guide to Criminology* (Sydney: Thompson Lawbook Co.), 439–64.

Daly, Kathleen and Stubbs, Julie (2006), 'Feminist engagement with restorative justice', *Theoretical Criminology*, 10, 9–28.

Dawes, John (2006), 'Prisons and imprisonment', in Andrew Goldsmith, Mark Israel and Kathleen Daly (eds), *Crime and Justice: A Guide to Criminology* (Sydney: Lawbook Co), 329–52.

Dean, Mitchel (1999), *Governmentality: Power and Rule in Modern Society* (London: Sage Publishing).

Department of Human Services (2007), 'Youth justice group conferencing', *Youth Justice Fact Sheet* (Victoria).

Department of Police and Emergency Management (2006), 'Police and the community' (Hobart, Tasmania), 1–30.

Dickinson, Alex (2008), 'Driver to face court as police impound bus', *Courier Mail*, 19 August, p. 11.

Dobash, R. E. and Dobash, R. P. (1997), 'Men's violence and programs focused on change', *Current Issues in Criminal Justice*, 8 (3), 243–62.

Dobash, R. E. et al. (2000), *Changing Violent Men* (Thousand Oaks: Sage Publications).

Douglas, Mary (1992), *Risk and Blame: Essays in Cultural Theory* (London: Routledge).

Durkheim, Emile (1893/1983), 'The division of labour in society', in Steven Lukes and Andrew Scull (eds), *Durkheim and the Law* (Oxford: Martin Robertson).

Durkheim, Emile (1901/1983), 'Two laws of penal evolution', in Steven Lukes and Andrew Scull (eds), *Durkheim and the Law* (Oxford: Martin Robertson).

Easteal, Patricia (1991), 'Battered women who kill: A plea of self-defence', in Patricia Easteal and Sandra McKillop (eds), *Women and the Law* (Canberra: Australian Institute of Criminology).

Edney, Richard (2002), 'Indigenous punishment in Australia: A jurisprudence of pain?' *International Journal of the Sociology of Law*, 30 (3), 219–34.

Elias, Norbert (1939/1979), *The Civilising Process, Volume 1: The History of Manners* (Oxford: Oxford University Press).

Elias, Norbert (1939/1982), *The Civilizing Process, Volume 2: State Formation Civilization* (Oxford: Oxford University Press).

Feeley, Malcolm and Simon, Jonathon (1992), 'The new penology: Notes on the emerging strategy of corrections and its implications', *Criminology*, 30 (4), 173–204.

Feeley, Malcolm and Simon, Jonathan (1994), 'Actuarial justice: The emerging new criminal law', in David Nelkin (ed.), *The Future of Criminology* (London: Sage), 173–200.

Feinblatt, J. and Denckla, D. (2001), 'What does it mean to be a good lawyer?' *Judicature*, 84 (4), 206–14.

Fergusson, D. M., Horwood, L. J. and Ridder E. M. (2005), 'Rejoinder', *Journal of Marriage and Family*, 67 (1), 1,131–1, 36.

Finnane, Mark (1997), *Punishment in Australian Society* (Melbourne: Oxford University Press).

Finnane, Mark and McGuire, John (2001), 'The uses of punishment and exile: Aborigines in colonial Australia', *Punishment and Society*, 3 (2), 279–98.

Finnane, Mark and Woodyatt, Tony (2002), '"Not the king's enemies": Prisoners and the rights in Australian history', in David Brown and Meredith Wilkie (eds), *Prisoners as Citizens: Human Rights in Australian Prisons* (Sydney: Federation Press), 81–101.

Fischer, B. (2003), 'Doing good with a vengeance: A critical assessment of the practices, effects and implications of drug treatment courts in North America', *Criminal Justice*, 3 (3), 227–48.

Fitch, K. (2006), Megan's Law: Does it protect children? (London: NSPCC).

Fletcher, J. (1997), *Violence and Civilisation* (Cambridge: Polity Press).

Folkman, Lisa-Marie (2005), 'Queensland's anti-hoon legislation and policing methods used to prevent hooning behaviour', paper given at Road Safety, Research, Policing and Education Conference Proceedings, Wellington, New Zealand, 14–16 November.

Foucault, Michel (1977), *Discipline and Punish: The Birth of the Prison*, trans. Alan Sheridan (London: Allen Lane).

Foucault, Michel (1984), 'What is an author?' in *The Foucault Reader*, Rabinow, Paul (ed.) (Harmondsworth: Penguin), 101–20.

Foucault, Michel (1990), 'The dangerous individual', in L. D. Kritzman (ed.), *Politics, Philosophy, Culture: Interview and Other Writings, 1977–1984* (New York: Routledge).

Foucault, Michel (1991), 'On governmentality', in Graham Burchell, Colin Gordon and Peter Miller (eds), *The Foucault Effect: Studies in Governmentality* (Chicago: University of Chicago Press).

Freiberg, Arie (1995), 'Sentencing reform in Victoria: A case study', in C. Clarkson and R. Morgan (eds), *The Politics of Sentencing Reform* (Oxford: Clarendon Press).

Freiberg, Arie (1997), 'Sentencing and punishment in Australia in the 1990s', in M. Tonry and K. Hatlestad (eds), *Sentencing Reform in Overcrowded Times* (New York: Oxford University Press), 156–63.

Freiberg, Arie (2002), 'Therapeutic jurisprudence in Australia: Paradigm shift or pragmatic incrementalism?', *Law in Context*, 20 (2), 6–23.

Fryer-Smith, Stephanie (2002), 'Aboriginal benchbook for Western Australian courts: AIJA model Indigenous benchbook project' (Carlton: Australian Institute of Judicial Administration Incorporated).

Fuller, Glen (2007), 'The hoon: Controlling the streets?' in Scott Poynting and George Morgan (eds), OUTRAGEOUS!: *Moral Panics in Australia* (Hobart: ACYS), 125–36.

Garfinkel, Harold (1956), 'Conditions of successful degradation ceremonies', *American Journal of Sociology*, 16, 420–4.

Garland, David (1985), *Punishment and Welfare: A History of Penal Strategies* (Aldershot: Gower).

Garland, David (1991), 'Sociological perspectives on punishment', in M. Tonry (ed.), *Crime and Justice: A Review of Research* (Chicago: University of Chicago Press).

Garland, David (1996), 'The limits of the sovereign state: Strategies in crime control in contemporary society', *British Journal of Criminology*, 36 (4), 445–71.

Garland, David (1997), '"Governmentality" and the problem of crime: Foucault, criminology, sociology', *Theoretical Criminology*, 1, 173–214.

Garland, David (2001), *The Culture of Control: Crime and Social Order in Contemporary Society* (Oxford: Oxford University Press).

Garland, David and Sparks, Richard (2000), 'Criminology, social theory and the challenge of our times', in David Garland and Richard Sparks (eds), *Criminology and Social Theory* (Oxford: Oxford University Press).

Garton, Stephen (1982), 'Bad or mad? Developments in incarceration in New South Wales 1880–1914', in Sydney Labour History Group (ed.), *What Rough Beast?: The State and Social Order in Australian History* (Sydney: Allen and Unwin).

Garton, Stephen (1986), 'The rise of the therapeutic state: Psychiatry and the system of criminal jurisdiction in New South Wales 1890–1940', *Australian Journal of Politics and History*, 32 (3), 378–88.

Garton, Stephen (1996), 'The convict taint: Australia and New Zealand', in Clive Emsley and Louis A. Knafla (eds), *Crime History and Histories of Crime: Studies in the Historiography of Crime and Criminal Justice in Modern History* (Contributions in Criminology and Penology, Number 48; Westport: Greenwood Press), 271–90.

Giddens, Anthony (1991), *Modernity and Self-identity: Self and Society in the Late Modern Age* (Oxford: Polity Press).

Gilbert, Kevin (1978), *Living Black* (Melbourne: Penguin).

Goffman, Erving (1957/1997), 'Characteristics of total institutions', in James W. Marquart and Jonathan R. Sorensen (eds), *Correctional Contexts: Contemporary and Classical Readings* (Los Angeles, California: Roxbury Publishing Company).

Goffman, Erving (1959), 'The moral career of a mental patient', *Psychiatry*, (22), 2.

Goffman, Erving (1961/1990), *Asylums: Essays on the Social Situation of Mental Patients and Other Inmates* (Harmondsworth: Penguin).

Goffman, Erving (1963), *Stigma* (Englewood Cliffs: Prentice Hall).

Goldberg, Susan (2005), 'Judging for the 21st century: A problem-solving approach' (Ottawa: National Judicial Institute).

Goldkamp, J. S. (1994), 'Miami's treatment drug court for felony defendants: Some implications of assessment findings', *The Prison Journal*, 73 (2), 110.

Goldsmith, Andrew (2006), 'Crimes across borders', in Andrew Goldsmith, Mark Israel and Kathleen Daly (eds), *Crime and Justice: A Guide to Criminology* (Sydney: Thompson Lawbook Co.), 219–42.

Gordon, Colin (1991), 'Governmental rationality: An introduction', in Graham Burchell, Colin Gordon and Peter Miller (eds), *The Foucault Effect: Studies in Governmentality* (Chicago: Chicago University Press).

Gottfredson, Michael R. and Hirschi, Travis (1990), *A General Theory of Crime* (Stanford, CA: Stanford University Press).

Government of South Australia (2008), 'Police nab 3000th hoon driver, 23 July 2008', *Action now for the future* <www.ministers.sa.gov.au/news.php?id=3471>, accessed 18 November 2009.

Gunaratna, R. (2002), 'Terrorism in the south before and after 9/11: An overlooked phenomenon', in International Peace Academy (ed.), *Responding to Terrorism: What Role for the United Nations?* (New York City: Chadbourne & Parke), 32–4.

Gutierrez, F. (2002), 'Terrorism and inequality', in International Peace Academy (ed.), *Responding to Terrorism: What Role for the United Nations?* (New York City: Chadbourne & Parke), 45–8.

Hacker, Fredrick J. and Frym, Marcel (1955), 'The sexual psychopath act in practise: A critical discussion', *California Law Review*, 43 (5), 766–80.

Hacking, Ian (2004), 'Between Michel Foucault and Erving Goffman: Between discourse in the abstract and face-to-face interaction', *Economy and Society*, 33 (3), 277–302.

Hales, J. et al. (2004), 'Evaluation of Queensland illicit drug diversion initiative (QIDDI) police diversion program' (Melbourne: Health Outcomes International Pty Ltd, Turning Point Alcohol and Drug Centre).

Hannam, Hilary (2003), 'Therapeutic justice', paper given at 21st Australian Institute of Judicial Administration Conference: New Challenges, Fresh Solutions, Fremantle, 19–21 September.

Hanson, R. K. (2002), 'Recidivism and age: Follow-up data from 4673 sexual offenders', *Journal of Interpersonal Violence*, 17 (10), 1046–62.

Hanson, R. K. and Bussiere, M. T. (1998), 'Predicting relapse: A meta-analysis of sexual offender recidivism studies', *Journal of Consulting and Clinical Psychology*, 66 (2), 348–62.

Hanson, R. K. and Morton-Bourgon, K. (2004), 'Predictors of sexual recidivism: An updated meta-analysis' (Ottawa: Public Works and Government Services).

Hanson, R. K. and Morton-Bourgon, K. (2005), 'The characteristics of persistent sexual offenders: A meta-analysis of recidivism studies', *Journal of Consulting and Clinical Psychology*, 73 (6), 1154–63.

Harris, A. J. R. and Hanson, R. K. (2004), 'Sex offender recidivism: A simple question' (Ottawa: Public Safety and Emergency Preparedness Canada).

Harris, M. (2004), 'From Australian courts to Aboriginal courts in Australia: Bridging the gap?' *Current Issues in Criminal Justice*, 16 (1), 26–41.

Hayes, Hennessey (2005), 'Assessing reoffending in restorative justice conferences', *Australian and New Zealand Journal of Criminology*, 38 (1), 77–101.

Hayes, Hennessey (2006), 'Apologies and accounts in youth justice conferencing: Reinterpreting research outcomes', *Contemporary Justice Review*, 9 (4), 369–85.

Hayes, Hennessey and Daly, Kathleen (2003), 'Youth justice conferencing and re-offending', *Justice Quarterly*, 20, 725–64.

Hayes, Hennessey and Daly, Kathleen (2004), 'Conferencing and re-offending in Queensland', *Australian and New Zealand Journal of Criminology*, 37, 167–91.

Hayward, K. and Morrison, W. (2002), 'Locating "Ground Zero": Caught between the narratives of crime and war', in J. Strawson (ed.), *Law After Ground Zero* (London: Glasshouse Press), 139–57.

Hazzard, M. (1984), *Punishment Short of Death: A History of the Penal Settlement at Norfolk Island* (Melbourne: Hyland House).

Head, M. (2003), 'Counter-terrorism laws: A threat to political freedom, civil liberties and constitutional rights', *Melbourne University Law Review*, 26 (3).

Healey, J. (2007), *Indigenous Australians and the Law* (Thirroul: Spinney Press).

Health Outcomes International (HOI) Pty Ltd (2003), *Evaluation of Council of Australian Governments' Initiatives on Illicit Drugs*, final report to Department of Finance and Administration, October 2002, Volume 2—Diversion Initiatives, (Canberra: Department of Finance and Administration).

Heidensohn, F. (1997), 'Gender and crime', in M. Maguire, R. Morgan and R. Reiner (eds), *The Oxford Handbook of Criminology* (Oxford: Clarenden Press).

Hindess, Barry (2001), 'The liberal government of unfreedom', *Alternatives* 26 (2), 93–111.

Hinds, Lyn and Daly, Kathleen (2001), 'The war on sex offenders: Community notification in perspective', *Australian and New Zealand Journal of Criminology*, 34 (3).

Hirst, John (1983), *Convict Society and Its Enemies: A History of Early New South Wales* (Sydney: Allen and Unwin).

Hirst, P. (1986), *Law Socialism and Democracy* (London: Collins).

Hogg, Russell (1999), 'Mandatory sentencing laws and the symbolic politics of law and order', *University of New South Wales Law Journal*, 22 (1).

Hogg, Russell (2001), 'Penality and modes of regulating Indigenous peoples in Australia', *Punishment and Society*, 3 (3), 355–79.

Hogg, Russell and Brown, David (1998), *Rethinking Law and Order* (Annandale: Pluto Press).

Hogg, Russell and Carrington, Kerry (1998), 'Crime, rurality and community', *Australian and New Zealand Journal of Criminology*, 31 (2), 160–81.

Hogg, Russell and Carrington, Kerry (2006), *Policing the Rural Crisis* (Sydney: Federation).

Holder, Robyn (2001), 'Domestic and family violence: Criminal justice interventions', *Issues Paper 3* (Sydney: Australian Domestic and Family Violence Clearinghouse).

Hora, P. F., Schma, W. G. and Rosenthal, J. (1999), 'Therapeutic jurisprudence and the drug treatment court movement: Revolutionising the criminal justice system's response to drug abuse and crime in America', *Notre Dame Law Review*, 74 (2), 439–527.

Huddleston, C. West (1998), 'Drug courts and jail-based treatment', *Corrections Today*, 60, 98–101.

Hudson, Barbara (2002), 'Gender issues in penal theory and penal policy', in Patricia Carlen (ed.), *Women and Punishment: The Struggle for Justice* (Cullompton: Willan Publishing), 21–46.

Hudson, Barbara (2003a), *Understanding Justice: An Introduction to Ideas, Perspectives and Controversies in Modern Penal Theory* (Buckingham: Open University Press).

Hudson, Barbara (2003b), *Justice in the Risk Society* (London: Sage).

Hughes, Caitlin and Ritter, Alison (2008), *A Summary of Diversion Programs for Drug and Drug-related Offenders in Australia* (Monograph 16; Sydney: Drug Policy Modelling Program, National Drug and Alcohol Research Centre).

Hughes, R. (1988), *The Fatal Shore* (London: Pan).

Ignatieff, Michael (1978), *A Just Measure of Pain: The Penitentiary in the Industrial Revolution, 1750–1850* (New York: Pantheon).

Ignatieff, Michael (1983), 'State, civil society and total institutions: A critique of recent social histories of punishment', in Stanley Cohen and Andrew Schull (eds), *Social Control and the State: Historical and Comparative Essays* (Oxford: Basil Blackwell), 75–105.

Ignatieff, Michael (2004), *The Lesser Evil: Political Ethics in an Age of Terror* (Edinburgh: Edinburgh University Press).

Indermaur, David and Roberts, Lynne (2003), 'Drug courts in Australia: The first generation', *Current Issues in Criminal Justice*, 15 (2), 136–54.

Innes, Martin (2001), 'Control creep', *Sociological Research Online*, 6 (3).

Ironside, Robyn (2008), 'Truck seized under anti-hooning laws', *Courier Mail*, 14 August, p. 7.

Israel, Mark (1999), 'Victims and justice', in R. Sarre and J. Tomaino (eds), *Exploring Criminal Justice: Contemporary Australian Themes* (Adelaide: South Australian Institute of Justice Studies Inc).

Jaffe, P. G. et al. (1993), 'The impact of police laying charges', in Z. Hilton (ed.), *Legal Responses to Wife Assault* (Newbury Park: Sage Publications).

Janus, E. S. (2000), 'Sexual predator commitment laws: Lessons for law and the behavioural sciences', *Behavioural Sciences and the Law*, 18 (1), 5–21.

Jarred, Wayne (2002), 'Police Powers and Responsibilities Act Amendment Bill 2002: Confronting bad and nuisance road behaviour', *Research Brief No. 2002/18* (Brisbane: Queensland Parliamentary Library).

Jenkins, A. (1990), *Invitations to Responsibility: The Therapeutic Engagement of Men Who Are Violent and Abusive* (Adelaide: Dulwich Centre Publications).

Johns, Rowena (2003), 'Child sexual offences: An update on initiatives in the criminal justice system', *Briefing Paper No 20/03* (Sydney: NSW Parliamentary Library Research Service).

Johnson, Michael P. (2005), 'Domestic violence: It's not about gender—or is it?' *Journal of Marriage and Family*, 67, 1, 126–1, 30.

Johnson, Michael P. and Ferraro, Kathleen J. (2000), 'Research on domestic violence in the 1990s: Making decisions', *Journal of Marriage and Family*, 62, 948–63.

Johnston, Elliott (1991), 'The Royal Commission into Aboriginal Deaths in Custody, National Report', volume 1 (Canberra: Australian Government Publishing Service).

Johnston, Les (2000), *Policing Britain: Risk, Security and Governance* (London: Longman).

Judicial Commission of New South Wales (2006), 'Equality before the law bench book' (Sydney).

Kamenka, E. and Tay, A. E. S. (1980), *Law and Social Control* (London: Edward Arnold).

Kemshall, Hazel (2003), *Understanding Risk in Criminal Justice* (Buckingham: Open University Press).

Kidd, Rosalind (undated), 'Aboriginal History of the Princess Alexandra Hospital Site', Brisbane, <www.linksdisk.com/roskidd/general/g2.htm>, accessed 3 March 2009.

Kidd, Rosalind (1997), *The Way We Civilise: Aboriginal Affairs, the Untold Story* (St Lucia: University of Queensland Press).

La Fond, J. Q. (1998), 'The costs of enacting sexual predator laws', *Psychology, Public Policy and Law*, 4 (1–2), 468–504.

Laing, Lesley (2002), 'Responding to men who perpetrate domestic violence: Controversies, interventions and challenges', *Issues Paper 7* (Sydney: Australian Domestic and Family Violence Clearinghouse).

Lawrence, R. and Fattore, T. (2002), 'Fatal assault of children and young people' (Sydney: Commission of Children and Young People).

Lawrence, R. and Freeman, K. (2002), 'Design and implementation of Australian's first drug court', *Australian and New Zealand Journal of Criminology*, 35 (1), 63–78.

Lawrie, R. (2002), 'Speak out strong: Researching the needs of Aboriginal women in custody' (Sydney: New South Wales Aboriginal Justice Advisory Council).

Leal, Nerida L., Watson, Barry C. and King, Mark (2007), 'Hooning offenders and offences: Who and what are we dealing with?', paper given at Australasian Road Safety Research, Policing and Education Conference, Melbourne, 17–19 October.

Leigh, Andrew (1996), 'Youth and street racing', *Current Issues in Criminal Justice*, 3, 388–93.

Levenson, Jill S. and D'Amora, David A. (2007), 'Social policies designed to prevent sexual violence: The emperor's new clothes?', *Criminal Justice Policy Review*, 18 (2), 168–99.

Levi, Ron (2000), 'The mutuality of risk and community: The adjudication of community notification statutes', *Economy and Society*, 29 (4), 578–601.

Lieb, R., Quinsey, V. and Berliner, L. (1998), 'Sexual predators and social policy', in M. Tonry (ed.), *Community Notification Laws: A Step Towards More Effective Solutions* (Crime and Justice: A Review of Research, 23), 43–114.

Lincoln, Robin and Wilson, Paul (2000), 'Aboriginal criminal justice: Background and foreground', in Duncan Chappell and Paul Wilson (eds), *Crime and the Criminal Justice System in Australia: 2000 and Beyond* (Sydney: Butterworths).

Lind, B. et al. (2002), 'New South Wales drug court evaluation: Cost-effectiveness' (Sydney: NSW Bureau of Crime Statistics and Research, Attorney General's Department).

Lipchik, E., Sirles, E. A. and Kubicki, A. D. (1997), 'Multifaceted approach in spouse abuse treatment', in R. Geffner, S. B. Sorenson and P. K. Lunberg-Love (eds), *Violence and Sexual Abuse at Home: Current Issues in Spousal Battering and Child Maltreatment* (Haworth Press Inc.), 131–48.

Luke, Garth and Lind, Bronwyn (2002), 'Reducing juvenile crime: Conferencing versus court', *Crime and Justice Bulletin, Contemporary Issues in Crime and Justice*, 69, 1–19.

Lupton, Deborah (1999), *Risk* (London: Routledge).

Lupton, Deborah (2000), *Risk and Sociocultural Theory* (Cambridge: Cambridge University Press).

Lynch, Andrew and Williams, George (2006), *What Price Security?: Taking Stock of Australia's Anti-Terror Laws* (Kensington: University of New South Wales Press).

Lynch, Mona (2005), 'Supermax meets death row: Legal struggles around the new punitiveness in the USA', in John Pratt et al. (eds), *The New Punitiveness: Trends, Theories, Perspectives* (Cullompton: Willan Publishing).

McAlinden, Anne-Marie (2006), 'Managing risk: From regulation to reintegration of sexual offenders', *Criminology and Criminal Justice*, 6 (2), 197–218.

McCulloch, J. (2006), 'Contemporary comments: Australia's anti-terrorism legislation and the Jack Thomas case', *Current Issues in Criminal Justice*, 18 (2), pp. 357–356.

McDonald, David (1992), 'National police custody survey, August 1988: National report', in David Biles and David McDonald (eds), *Deaths in Custody Australia, 1980–1989, Research Papers of the Criminology Unit of the Royal Commission into Aboriginal Deaths in Custody* (Canberra: Australian Institute of Criminology).

McDonald, Edwina and Williams, George (2007), 'Combating terrorism: Australia's criminal code since September 11 2001', *Griffith Law Review*, 16 (1), 27–54.

McGrath, Ann (1995), *Contested Ground: Australian Aborigines under the British Crown* (St Leonards: Allen and Unwin).

McGregor, R. (1997), *Imagined Destinies: Aboriginal Australians and the Doomed Race Theory, 1880–1939* (Melbourne: Melbourne University Press).

Makkai, T. (1999), 'Linking drugs and criminal activity: developing an integrated monitoring system', *Trends and Issues in Crime and Criminal Justice* (Canberra: Australian Institute of Criminology), no. 109, 1–6.

Makkai, T. and Payne, J. (2003), 'Key findings from the drug use careers of offenders (DUCO) study', *Trends and Issues in Crime and Criminal Justice* (Canberra: Australian Institute of Criminology), no. 267, 1–6.

Marchetti, Elena and Daly, Kathleen (2004), 'Indigenous courts and justice practices in Australia', *Trends and Issues in Crime and Criminal Justice* (Canberra: Australian Institute of Criminology), 277, 1–6.

Marchetti, Elena and Daly, Kathleen (2007), 'Indigenous sentencing courts: Towards a theoretical and jurisprudential model', *Sydney Law Review*, 29, 415–43.

Marshall-Beier, J. (2004), ''Beyond hegemonic statements of nature: Indigenous knowledge and the non-state possibilities in International Relations'' in Chowdhry, G. and Nair, S. (eds) *Postcolonialism and International Relations: Reading Race, Gender and Class* (London: Routledge).

Martinson, R. (1974), 'What Works? Questions and answers about prison reform', *The Public Interest*, 35, Spring, 22.

Mathews, Winsome (2002), 'Circle sentencing background and current NSW trial', paper given at Indigenous Governance Conference, Canberra, 3–5 April.

Maxwell, G. M. and Morris, A. (1993), *Family, Victims and Culture: Youth Justice in New Zealand* (Wellington: Institute of Criminology).

Maxwell, G. M. and Morris, A. (2001), 'Family group conferences and reoffending', in A. Morris and G. M. Maxwell (eds), *Restorative Justice for Juveniles: Conferencing Mediation and Circles* (Oxford: Hart Publishing), 243–63.

Melossi, D. and Pavarini, M. (1981), *The Prison and the Factory: Origins of the Penitentiary System*, trans. G. Cousins (New Jersey: Barnes & Noble).

Michandani, R. (2005), 'What's so special about specialised courts? The state and social change in Salt Lake City's domestic violence court', *Law and Society Review*, 39 (2), 379–417.

Mill, J. S. (1859/1974), *On Liberty* (Harmondsworth: Penguin).

Moore, D. and O'Connell, T. (1994), 'Family conferencing in Wagga Wagga: A communitarian model of justice', in Christine Alder and Joy Wundersitz (eds), *Family Conferencing and Juvenile Justice* (Canberra: Australian Institute of Criminology).

Morris, Sarah, Ryan, Claire and Alexander, Tara (2007), 'Youth curfew report', *Youth Minister's Round Table of Young Territorians* (Darwin: Northern Territory government).

Mouzos, J. (2001), 'Indigenous and non-Indigenous homicides in Australia', *Trends and Issues in Crime and Criminal Justice* (Canberra: Australian Institute of Criminology), 210, 1–6.

Mouzos, J. (2005), 'Homicide in Australia: 2003–2004 National Homicide Monitoring Program (NHMP) annual report', *Research and Public Policy Series*, No. 66 (Canberra: Australian Institute of Australia).

Mouzos, J. and Rushforth, C. (2003), 'Family homicide in Australia', *Trends and Issues in Crime and Criminal Justice*, 255, 1–6.

Mouzos, J. and Smith, L. (2007), 'Partner violence among a sample of police detainees', *Trends and Issues in Crime and Criminal Justice* (Canberra: Australian Institute of Criminology), 337, 1–6.

Moyle, Paul (2000), *Profiting from Punishment: Private Prisons in Australia: Reform or Regression?* (Sydney: Pluto Press).

Murphy, T. (2000), 'Coercing offenders into treatment: A comprehensive state-wide diversion strategy', paper given at Society for the Study of Addiction Annual Symposium, Leeds, United Kingdom, October.

Mythen, Gabe and Walklate, Sandra (2006), 'Communicating the terrorist risk: Harnessing a culture of fear?', *Media, Culture and Crime*, 2 (2), 123–42.

New South Wales Legislative Council Standing Committee on Law and Justice (2006), 'Community-based sentencing options for rural and remote areas and disadvantaged populations' (Sydney: New South Wales Parliament).

Nichols, J. L. and Ross, H. L. (1990), 'The effectiveness of legal sanctions in dealing with drinking drivers', *Alcohol, Drugs and Driving*, 6 (2), 33–60.

Nolan, J. L. (2001), *Reinventing Justice: The American Drug Court Movement* (Princeton: Princeton University Press).

O'Connor, Ian (1997), 'Models of juvenile justice', in A. Borowski and I. O'Connor (eds), *Juvenile Crime, Justice and Corrections* (Melbourne: Longman), 229–53.

Office of Crime Prevention (2003), *Young People in Northbridge Policy* (Perth: Government of Western Australian).

O'Malley, Patrick (1992), 'Risk, power and crime prevention', *Economy and Society*, 21, 252–75.

O'Malley, Patrick (1999), 'Volatile and contradictory punishment', *Theoretical Criminology*, 3 (2), 175–96.

O'Malley, Patrick (2000), 'Criminologies of catastrophe? Understanding criminal justice on the edge of the new millennium', *Australian and New Zealand Journal of Criminology*, 33, 153–67.

O'Malley, Patrick (2001), 'Risk, crime and prudentialism revisited', in K. Stenson and R. R. Sullivan (eds), *Crime, Risk and Justice: The Politics of Crime Control in Liberal Democracies* (Cullompton: Willan Publishing).

O'Neill, W. G. (2002a), 'Beyond the slogans: How can the UN respond to terrorism?' in International Peace Academy (ed.), *Responding to Terrorism: What Role for the United Nations?* (New York City: Chadbourne & Parke), 5–17.

O'Neill, W. G. (2002b), 'Conference report', in International Peace Academy (ed.), *Responding to Terrorism: What Role for the United Nations?* (New York City: Chadbourne & Parke), 18–26.

O'Toole, Sean (2006), *The History of Australian Corrections* (Sydney: University of New South Wales Press).

Parliament of Australia (2002), 'Terrorism and the law in Australia: Legislation, commentary and constraints' (Canberra: Parliamentary Library).

Pashukanis, E. B. (1924/1978), *Law and Marxism: A General Theory*, ed. C. Arthur, trans. B Einhorn (London: Ink Links).

Pasquino, E. B. (1991), 'Criminology: The birth of a special knowledge', in Graham Burchell, Colin Gordon and Peter Miller (eds), *The Foucault Effect: Studies in Governmentality* (Hemel Hempstead: Harvester Wheatsheaf).

Pawson, R. (2006), *Evidence-based Policy: A Realist Perspective* (London: Sage).

Payne, Jason (2005), 'Final report on the North Queensland drug court', *Technical and Background Paper No. 17* (Canberra: Australian Institute of Criminology).

Payne, Jason (2006), 'Specialty courts: Current issues and future prospects', *Trends and Issues in Crime and Criminal Justice* (Canberra: Australian Institute of Criminology), 317, 1–6.

Petrucci, Carrie (2002), 'Respect as a component in the judge–defendant interaction in a specialized domestic violence court that utilizes therapeutic jurisprudence', *Criminal Law Bulletin*, 38 (2), 263–95.

Phelan, A. (2003), 'Solving human problems or deciding cases? Problem-solving courts', paper given at INNOVATION: Promising Practices for Victims and Witnesses in the Criminal Justice System Conference, Canberra, 23–24, October.

Polk, Kenneth et al. (2003), 'Early intervention: Diversion and youth conferencing: A national profile and review of current approaches to diverting juveniles from the criminal justice system' (Canberra: Commonwealth of Australia).

Potas, Ivan et al. (2003), *Circle Sentencing in New South Wales: A Review and Evaluation* (Sydney: Judicial Commission of New South Wales, Aboriginal Justice Advisory Council), 1–64.

Poynting, S. (2004), *Bin Laden in the Suburbs: Criminalising the Arab Other* (Sydney: Institute of Criminology).

Pratt, John (1991), 'Punishment, history, empire', *Australian and New Zealand Journal of Criminology*, 24 (2), 118–38.

Pratt, John (1995), 'Dangerousness, risk and technologies of power', *Australian and New Zealand Journal of Criminology*, 29 (1), 3–30.

Pratt, John (1997), *Governing the Dangerous* (Sydney: Federation Press).

Pratt, John (1998), 'Towards the "decivilising" of punishment', *Social and Legal Studies*, 7 (4), 487–515.

Pratt, John (2000), 'Civilisation and punishment', *Australian and New Zealand Journal of Criminology*, 33 (2), 183–201.

Pratt, John (2005), 'Elias, punishment and decivilisation', in John Pratt et al. (eds), *The New Punitiveness* (London: Willan Publishing), 256–71.

Pratt, John and Brown, Mark (2000), *Dangerous Offenders: Punishment and Social Order* (London: Routledge).

Pratt, John et al. (2005), *The New Punitiveness: Trends, Theories, Perspectives* (Cullompton: Willan Publishing).

Queensland Department of Justice and Attorney General (undated), 'Issues for Counselling' (Brisbane: South East Queensland Drug Court).

R v Thomas (2006), VSCA 165 <www.austlii.edu.au/au/cases/vic/VSCA/2006/165.html>, accessed 18 August 2006.

R v Thomas (No. 2) (2006), VSCA 166 <www.austlii.edu.au/au/cases/vic/VSCA/2006/166.html>, accessed 18 August 2006.

Rajaee, F. (2002), 'The challenges of the rage of empowered dispossessed: The case of the Muslim world', in International Peace Academy (ed.), *Responding to Terrorism: What Role for the United Nations?* (New York City: Chadbourne & Parke), 35–9.

Renwick, J. (2007), 'Counter-terrorism and Australian law', *Security Challenges*, 3 (3), 67–77.

Roberts, Adam (2005), 'The "war on terror" in historical perspective', *Survival*, 47 (2), 101–30.

Roberts, Lynne and Indermaur, David (2006), 'Timely intervention or trapping minnows? The potential for a range of net-widening effects in Australian drug diversion initiatives', *Psychiatry, Psychology and Law*, 13 (2), 220–31.

Robertson, Boni (2000), *Aboriginal and Torres Strait Islander Women's Task Force on Violence Report*, Section 3, pp. 86–104 (Brisbane: Queensland Government Department of Aboriginal and Torres Strait Islander Policy and Development).

Ronken, Carol and Johnston, Hetty (2006), 'Community notification of sex offenders', *Position Paper* (Brisbane: Bravehearts Inc.).

Ronken, Carol and Lincoln, Robin (2001), 'Deborah's Law: The effects of naming and shaming on sex offenders in Australia', *Australian and New Zealand Journal of Criminology*, 34 (3), 235–55.

Rose, Nicolas (1996), 'Governing "advanced" liberal democracies' in Andrew Barry, Thomas Osborne and Nicolas Rose (eds), *Foucault and Political Reason: Liberalism, Neoliberalism and Rationalities of Government* (UCL Press Limited).

Rose, Nicolas (1999), *Powers of Freedom: Reframing Political Thought* (Cambridge: Cambridge University Press).

Rose, Nicolas (2000), 'Government and control', in David Garland and Richard Sparks (eds), *Criminology and Social Theory* (Oxford: Oxford University Press), 183–208.

Rose, Nicolas and Miller, Peter (1992), 'Political power beyond the state: Problematics of government', *British Journal of Criminology*, 43, 173–205.

Ross, H. L. (1991), 'Licence deprivation as a drunk-driver sanction', *Alcohol, Drugs and Driving*, 7 (1), 63–9.

Rowse, Tim (1998), *White Flour, White Power: From Rations to Citizenship in Central Australia* (Melbourne: Cambridge University Press).

Rudin, J. (2005), 'Aboriginal justice and restorative justice', in E. Elliott and R. M. Gordon (eds), *New Directions in Restorative Justice: Issues, Practice, Evaluation* (Cullompton: Willan Publishing), 89–114.

Rusche, G. and Kirchheimer, O. (1939/1968), *Punishment and Social Structure* (New York: Russell and Russell).

Schneider, E. (2000), *Battered Women and Feminist Lawmaking* (New Haven: Yale University Press).

Schull, Andrew (1977), *Decarceration, Community Treatment and the Deviant: A Radical View* (Englewood Cliffs: Prentice Hall).

Schur, E. M. (1973), *Radical Non-Intervention* (Englewood Cliffs: Prentice Hall).

Senjo, S. and Leip, L. (2001), 'Testing therapeutic jurisprudence theory: An empirical assessment of the drug court process', *Western Criminology Review*, 3 (1).

Seymour, J. (1988), *Dealing with Juvenile Offenders* (North Ryde: Law Book Company).

Sharpe, Penny (2008), 'Legislative Council 2R Speech, Road Transport Legislation Amendment (Car Hoons) Bill 2008 NSW—5/03/2008' (Sydney: New South Wales Parliament, Hansard).

Shearing, Clifford (2001), 'Punishment and the changing face of the governance', *Punishment and Society*, 3 (2), 2003–220.

Sherman, L. and Strang, H. (1997), 'Restorative justice and deterring crime', *RISE Working Papers*, 4, April 1997 (Canberra: Australian National University).

Sherman, L., Strang, H. and Woods, D. (2000), 'Recidivism patterns in the Canberra Reintegrative Shaming Experiments (RISE)' (Canberra: Centre for Restorative Justice, Research School of Social Sciences, Australian National University).

Simon, Jonathan (1988), 'The ideological effects of actuarial practices', *Law and Society Review*, 22 (4), 772–800.

Simon, L. and Zgoba, K. (2006) 'Sex crimes against children: Legislation, prevention and investigation' in R. Wortley and S. Smallbone (eds), *Situational Prevention of Child Sexual Abuse, Crime Prevention Studies* Vol. 19 (Monsey, NY: Criminal Justice Press), pp. 65–100.

Smallbone, Stephen and Ransley, Janet (2005), 'Legal and psychological controversies in the preventive incapacitation of sexual offenders', *University of New South Wales Law Journal*, 11 (1), 299–305.

Smallbone, Stephen and Wortley, Richard (2000), 'Child sexual abuse in Queensland: Offender characteristics and modus operandi' (Brisbane: Queensland Crime Commission).

Smallbone, Stephen and Wortley, Richard (2001), 'Child sexual abuse: Offender characteristics and modus operandi', *Trends and Issues in Crime and Criminal Justice* (Canberra: Australian Institute of Criminology), 193, 1–6.

Sparks, Richard (2000), 'Perspectives on risk and penal politics', in Tim Hope and Richard Sparks (eds), *Crime, Risk and Insecurity* (London: Routledge).

Spooner, Catherine, Hall, Wayne and Mattick, Richard P. (2001), 'An overview of diversion strategies for Australian drug-related offenders', *Drug and Alcohol Review*, 20, 281.

Staysafe 35 (1997), 'The Traffic Amendment (Street and Illegal Drag Racing) Act 1996: Report relating to the sunset provision' (Sydney: New South Wales Parliament).

Steinman, M. (1990), 'Lowering recidivism among men who batter women', *Journal of Police Science and Administration*, 17, 124–33.

Stewart, Julie (2005), 'Specialist domestic/family violence courts within the Australian context', *Issues Paper 10* (Sydney: Australian Domestic and Family Violence Clearinghouse).

Strang, Heather (2002), *Repair or Revenge: Victims and Restorative Justice* (Oxford: Clarendon Press).

Strang, Heather and Braithwaite, John (2002), *Restorative Justice and Family Violence* (Cambridge: Cambridge University Press).

Strang, H. et al. (1999), 'Experiments in restorative policing: A progress report on the Canberra reintegrative shaming experiments' (Canberra: Australian National University).

Stubbs, Julie (2002), 'Domestic violence and women's safety: Feminist challenges to restorative justice', in Heather Stang and John Braithwaite (eds), *Restorative Justice and Family Violence* (Cambridge: Cambridge University Press), 42–61.

Stubbs, Julie and Tolmie, Julia (2005), 'Defending battered women on charges of homicide: The structural and system versus the personal and particular', in W. Chan, D. E. Chunn and R. Menzies (eds), *Women and Mental Disorder and the Law* (London: Glasshouse), 191–210.

Stubbs, Julie and Tolmie, Julia (2008), 'Battered women charged with homicide: Advancing the interests of Indigenous women', *Australian and New Zealand Journal of Criminology*, 41 (1), 138–61.

Sutherland, E. H. (1950), 'The diffusion of sexual psychopath laws', *American Journal of Sociology*, 50, 142–8.

Swain, M. (1999), 'The illicit drug problem: Drug courts and other alternative approaches', *Briefing Paper* (Sydney: NSW Parliamentary Library Research Service).

Syers, M. and Edleson, J. L. (1992), 'The combined effects of coordinated criminal justice intervention in woman abuse', *Journal of Interpersonal Violence*, 7 (4), 490–501.

Tapin, S. (2002), 'The New South Wales drug court evaluation: A process evaluation, New South Wales drug court evaluation: Cost-effectiveness' (Sydney: NSW Bureau of Crime Statistics and Research, Attorney General's Department).

Tasmania Police (2008), 'Anti-hooning—law empowers police to confiscate cars' <www.police.tas.gov.au/road_safety/anti-hooning_law>, accessed 12 November 2008.

Tauber, J. (1999), *Drug Courts: A Revolution in Criminal Justice* (Washington, DC: Drug Strategies).

Tauri, Juan (1999), 'Explaining recent innovations in New Zealand's criminal justice system: Empowering Māori or biculturalising the state?', *Australian and New Zealand Journal of Criminology*, 32 (2), 153–67.

Tavuchis, N. (1991), *Mea Culpa: A Sociology of Apology and Reconciliation* (Stanford CA: Stanford University Press).

Telfer, Jonathon R. (2003), *A Brief History of Correctional Practices in South Australia* (Adelaide: South Australian Institute of Justice Studies Inc).

Tench, W. (2006), *Settlement at Port Jackson*, eBooks@Adelaide <http://ebooks .adelaide.edu.au/t/tench/watkin/settlement/>, accessed 9 May 2009.

Territory Roads (2004), *Annual Report 2003–2004* (Darwin: Department of Infrastructure, Planning and Environment) 73–7.

Thompson, Kenneth (1988), *Emile Durkheim*, ed. Peter Hamilton (Key Sociologists; London: Routledge).

Tomaino, J. (1999), 'Punishment practice', in R. Sarre and J. Tomaino (eds), *Exploring Criminal Justice: Contemporary Australian Issues* (Adelaide: South Australian Institute of Justice Studies Inc.).

Ullathorne, W. B. (1941), *From Cabin-boy to Archbishop: The Autobiography of Archbishop Ullathorne* (London: Burns Oates).

United States Department of Justice (1997), 'Final Guidelines for *Megan's Law* and *the Jacob Wetterling Crimes Against Children and Sexually Violent Offender Registration Act*' (Washington, DC).

Van de Veen, S. L. (2004), 'Some Canadian problem-solving court processes', *The Canadian Bar Review*, 83, 91.

van Ness, D. (1993), 'New wine and old wineskins: Four challenges of restorative justice', *Criminal Justice Law Forum*, 4, 251–76.

von Hirsch, Andrew and Ashworth, Andrew (1998), *Principled Sentencing: Readings on Theory and Policy* (Oxford: Hart Publishing).

Walker, J. (2001), 'International experience of drug courts' (Edinburgh: The Scottish Executive Central Research Unit).

Walker, Nigel (1991), *Why Punish? Theories of Punishment Reassessed* (Oxford: Oxford University Press).

Wallace, A. (1986), 'Homicide: The social reality' (Sydney: New South Wales Bureau of Crime Statistics and Research).

Ward, Jeff, Mattick, Richard and Hall, Wayne (1992), *Key Issues in Methadone Maintenance Treatment* (Kensington: New South Wales University Press).

Washington Institute for Public Policy (1996), 'Washington's sexually violent predator law: Legislative history and comparisons with other states' (Olympia: Washington).

Wexler, David (2004), 'Therapeutic jurisprudence: It's not just for problem-solving courts and calendars anymore', in C. Flange et al. (eds), *Future Trends in State Courts 2004* (Williamsburg: National Center for State Courts), 86–9.

Wexler, David and Winick, Bruce (1991), 'Therapeutic jurisprudence as a new approach to mental health law policy analysis and research', *University of Miami Law Review*, 979.

White, Michael (1989), 'The conjoint therapy of men who are violent and the women with whom they live', *Selected Papers* (Adelaide: Dulwich Centre Publications).

White, M. and Epston, D. (1989), 'Literate means to therapeutic ends' (Adelaide: Dulwich Centre Publications).

White, Rob (1996), 'Ten arguments against youth curfews', *Youth Studies Australia*, 15 (4), 28–30.

White, Rob (2004), 'Police and community responses to youth gangs', *Trends and Issues in Crime and Criminal Justice* (Canberra: Australian Institute of Criminology), no. 274, 1–6.

Williams, George (2005), 'Balancing national security and human rights: Lessons from Australia', *Borderlands*, 4 (1).

Williams, John M. (2006), 'Law and order: No end in sight', *Trends and Issues 2006 Update* (Adelaide: Australian Institute for Social Research).

Williams, Paul (2001), 'Deaths in custody: 10 years on from the Royal Commission', *Trends and Issues in Crime and Criminal Justice* (Canberra: Australian Institute of Criminology), 203, 1–6.

Worsley, Peter (1991), *The New Modern Sociology Readings* (London: Penguin).

Wortley, Richard and Smallbone, Stephen (2006), *Situational Prevention of Child Sexual Abuse* (Monsey, New York: Criminal Justice Press).

Wundersitz, Joy (1996), 'Juvenile justice', in Kayleen Hazlehurst (ed.), *Crime and Justice: An Australian Textbook in Criminology* (North Ryde: Law Book Company), 113–49.

Young, Jock (1999), *The Exclusive Society: Social Exclusion, Crime and Difference in Late Modernity* (London: Sage).

Zaal, Dominic (1994), 'Traffic law enforcement: A review of the literature', (Melbourne: Accident Research Centre, Monash University), 1–200.

Zdenkowski, George (2000), 'Sentencing trends: Past, present and prospective', in Duncan Chappell and Paul Wilson (eds), *Crime and Criminal Justice System in Australia: 2000 and Beyond* (Sydney: Butterworths), 161–202.

Aboriginal community courts (WA) 143
Aboriginal Justice Advisory Council
      (NSW) 146, 157
Aboriginal and Torres Strait Islander
      Women's Task Force on Violence 159
Aborigines Act Amendment Act 1939
      (SA) 14
Aborigines and Torres Strait Islanders
   community justice groups 140–2
   corporal punishment and restraints 13
   in criminal justice system 130–3
   curfews 230
   deaths in custody 129, 130
   decolonisation of justice 147–50
   development of Indigenous justice 146
   exemption certificates and access to
      citizens rights 14–15
   Indigenous courts and circle sentencing
      courts 142–5, 148–9
   Indigenous justice programs 139–42
   institutional surveillance and control 14
   nature of crimes committed by
      offenders 133
   overrepresentation in prisons 40,
      129–33, 148
   overrepresentation as victims and
      offenders 132–3
   overrepresentation of women in intimate
      homicides 156–7, 158–9
   protection and segregation policies 13,
      14, 147–8
   see also Royal Commission into
      Aboriginal Deaths in Custody
      (RCIADIC)
actuarialism 56, 80, 226
Adelaide Central Violence Intervention
      Program (CVIP) 160
administrative sanctions 35–6
aggregative tendencies of managerialism
      36–7, 57, 79
al Qaeda 87
American National Association for Drug
      Court Professionals 230
American War of Independence 4
anti-hooning laws
   in ACT 207
   and deterrence 213–15, 228
   evaluation 218

   in NSW 206, 209–10
   objective of 199
   police powers 206–10, 214
   in Queensland 207–8
   reasons for 200–1
   in South Australia 208, 210–11
   in Tasmania 208
   in Victoria 207, 208
anti-hooning offences 207–8, 209, 211
anti-hooning penalties
   draconian nature 199, 206, 213, 215–18
   imprisonment 207
   licence suspension 209, 212
   toughening of 209
   vehicle confiscation and impoundment
      206–9, 212
Anti-Terrorism Act (No.2) 2005 (Cwlth) 88
anti-terrorism laws *see* counter-
      terrorism laws
antisocial driving behaviour
   identification of perpetrators 217–18
   nature of 215
   nuisance factor 215–16
   perceived dangerousness 215–16
   see also hooning
Armadale Family Violence Court 161
attendance centres, introduction 16
Australian Bureau of Criminal Intelligence
      (ABCI), sex offender register 72
Australian Capital Territory Family Violence
      Intervention Program 160
Australian Federal Police (AFP), sex offender
      register 72
Australian Law Reform Commission 167
Australian National Child Offender Register
      (ANCOR) 74, 76
*Australian Paedophile and Sex Offender
      Index* 75
Australian Security Intelligence Organisation
      (ASIO), new counter-terrorism powers
      88, 91–2
*Australian Security Intelligence Organisation
      Legislation Amendment (Terrorism) Act
      2003 (Cwlth)* 88, 92

back-end net widening 124
Ballarat Family Violence Court 161
Bathurst Prison, riots 32

battered women's syndrome (BWS) 158–9

Beck, Ulrich, and the 'risk society' 55

Bentham, Jeremy
  on exemplary punishment and
      deterrence 23, 24, 43–4, 212–13
  opposition to transportation 24–6, 43
  panopticon 25, 53, 121
  Panopticon v New South Wales 25
  penal theory 24
  principle of utilitarianism 23, 24, 43–4

Bigge, John Thomas 7

Borallon prison (Qld) 10

'boy racer' laws (NZ) 199

Braithwaite, John
  concept of reintegrative shaming of
      offenders 179, 191–3
  Crime, Shame and Reintegration
      39, 179, 191
  on rise of restorative justice 195–6

Brisbane, Thomas (Governor) 8

British criminal justice system
  dominance of penitentiaries as
      punishment 9
  penal settlements as punishment 7–9
  reform in late eighteenth and early
      nineteenth century 25–6, 27
  see also transportation

bureaucratic administrative law 194

burnouts (hooning) 201, 209

Campbelltown Domestic Violence
      Court 161

carceral archipelago 10–12, 53

Child, Joseph 9

*Child Protection (Offender Reporting) Act
      2004* (Qld) 73

*Child Protection (Offender Reporting and
      Registration) Act 2004* (NT) 73

*Child Protection (Offenders Registration) Act
      2000* (NSW) 73

child saving movement 177

child sex offender laws
  community notification 74–7
  enhanced sentencing 70–1
  registration of sexual offenders 72–4
  sexual predator laws 70, 71–2

*Child Sex Offender Registration Act
      2006* (SA) 73

child sex offenders
  characteristics 67–8, 79
  recidivism rates 66
  treatment 65–6
  vigilantism against 76, 80

child sex offending
  assumptions underpinning penal
      policy 79–80
  Australian responses 70–7
  and civilising vengeance 80–2
  control model versus sexual deviance
      model 68, 79–80
  criminal justice responses
      68, 69–70
  difficulty of researching 66
  Durkheimian analysis of penal
      policy 81
  Eliasian analysis of penal policy 82
  Foucauldian analysis of penal
      policy 80
  as a multidimensional and
      multidetermined phenomenon 66

child sexual abuse, increased public
      awareness 65

*Children, Young Persons and their Families
      Act 1989* (NZ) 178

Children Youth and Families Act 2005
      (Vic.) 187–8

Children's Court (NSW) 12

children's court system *see* juvenile
      justice system

circle sentencing courts 142–5

citizen alert programs 18

'civilised sensibilities' 58

civilising process
  and penal trends 60–1
  and 'privatisation' 59–60

Cohen, Stanley, *Visions of Social
      Control* 54, 123

Collingwood Neighbourhood Justice Centre
      (NJC) (Vic.) 42, 43

colonisation, post-colonial
      perspectives 51–2

*Commerce, Justice, and State, the Judiciary
      and Related Agencies Appropriations
      Act 1998* (US) 75

Commonwealth Criminal Code Act,
      terrorism offences 89–91

communitarianism
  and reintegrative shaming of
    offenders 191
  and restorative justice 37–40
community conferencing 18, 179
community corrections 54, 123
community custodial facilities 10
community justice groups (CJGs)
  for ATSI communities 140–2
  Local Justice Initiatives Program
    (Qld) 140–1
  NSW Aboriginal Justice
    Agreement 141–2
  roles and responsibilities 141, 142
community justice mechanisms 18
community justice panels 142
community notification of sex offenders 70,
  74–7, 78, 82
Community Protection Act 1990
  (Vic.) 71–2
Community Protection Act 1994 (NSW) 72
Community Protection Act 2004 (WA) 73
Community Protection Act
  (Washington, US) 74
community service orders
  criticism 32
  introduction 16
  in rural and remote areas 132
Community Services Legislation Amendment
  Act 2002 (Qld) 141
community-based intervention
  compatibility with neoliberalism 17
  contemporary options 17–18
  underlying principles 17
community-based sanctions,
  development 15–16
community-based sentencing options 132
conditional release 12
'conscience collective' 46–8
consequentialism
  approaches to punishment 26
  defined 23
control orders 94, 96
convict system
  assignment, tickets-of-leave and land
    grants 6–7
  brutality 5, 8–9
  chain-gang system 7

early working conditions and rights of
  convicts 5–6
hard labour and secondary punishment
  in remote settlements 7
place in history of punishment in
  Australia 3, 4–5
treatment of young offenders 176
convict transportation *see* transportation
corporal punishment 5–6, 13
corporate offenders 230–1
Council of Australian Governments
  (COAG), national illicit drug
  strategy 114
Council of Civil Liberties 213
counter-terrorism laws
  in Australia 88–92
  control orders 93, 94, 96
  conviction of Jack Thomas 98–100
  detection and prevention 91–2
  pre-emptive policy 93–7, 100–2
  preventative detention orders 93, 94–5
  prohibited contact orders 95
  provisions 85, 92
  rationale for 88–91
counter-terrorist operations, key assets 96–7
counter-terrorist response
  and discourse of insecurity 104–5
  Durkheimian analysis 102–3
  expressive punitivism and essentialised
    difference 105–6
  media role in shaping public perceptions
    of risk 105
  risk and relation to fear and
    victimisation 103
  risk and relationship between discourse
    and practice 103–4
  risk and retaliation 102–6
  underlying principles of punishment
    and sentencing 100–2
CREDIT (Court Referral and Evaluation for
  Drug Intervention and Treatment) 114
crime control, modes of regulation
  employed in contemporary
  programs 19–20
Crimes (Child Sex Offenders) Act 2005
  (ACT) 74
Crimes (Confiscation of Proceeds of Crime)
  Act 1988 (Vic.) 207

Crimes (Restorative Justice) Act 2004
   (ACT) 187–8
Crimes (Sentencing Procedure) Act 1999
   (NSW) 71
Crimes (Sentencing Procedure) Amendment
   (Standard Minimum Sentencing) Act
   2002 (NSW) 71
Criminal Code Amendment (Offences Against
   Australians) Act 2002 (Cwlth) 89
Criminal Code Amendment (Suppression
   of Terrorist Bombings) Act 2002
   (Cwlth) 89
Criminal Code Amendment (Terrorism) Act
   2003 (Cwlth) 89
criminal law, as a reflection of moral values
   of society 47–8
Criminal Law Amendment Act 1945
   (Qld) 70, 72
Criminal Law (Sex Offenders Reporting)
   Bill 72
criminology, emergence 53
CrimTrac agency 74
critical theory
   and criminology 49–52
   nature and focus 48–9
curfews 229–30

Dangerous Prisoners (Sexual Offenders) Act
   2003 (Qld) 30, 72
Darling, Ralph (Governor) 7, 8
David, Garry 72
death penalty 25, 26
decivilising process
   nature of 59–60
   and responses to child sex offending 82
delinquency, creation of 53–4
deterrence
   and anti-hooning laws 212–15
   making an 'example' of offenders
     24, 25, 26
   versus reform or rehabilitation 11, 27
deterrence-based sentencing 26
domestic violence
   battered women's syndrome (BWS) 158–9
   characteristics of offenders 164
   gendered experience of interpersonal
     violence 154–5
   intimate partner homicide 155, 156

   intimate partner violence in criminal
     justice populations 155–6
   and principles of punishment and
     protection 167–70
   responding to women as offenders 156–9
   responding to women as victims 160–6
   role of feminism in recognising and
     addressing 170–1
   socio-political perspective 165
   systemic theories of patterns of
     interaction 164–5
domestic violence courts
   assessing eligibility/suitability for
     programs 164
   core components of programs 160–2
   gender-based cognitive behaviour
     groups 166
   introduction 153, 160–2
   objectives 167–8
   perpetrator treatment programs 164–5
   as problem-solving courts 169
   protection orders 163
   rationale behind establishment 162–3
   and restorative justice 168–70
   sentence discounting 163
   sentencing options 163
   sentencing process 163–4
   and therapeutic jurisprudence 168
   victim-focused nature 162–3, 168
Douglas, Mary
   political cultures as filters for risk 57–8,
     80–1, 102–3, 107
   Risk and Blame 57
drifting (hooning) 201
drivers' licence suspension 204, 209, 212
Drug Court Act 1998 (NSW) 115, 116
drug courts
   evaluation 42
   introduction 41, 112
   see also drug treatment courts
Drug Rehabilitation (Court Diversion)
   Act 2000 (Qld) 115, 121
drug testing 121–2
drug treatment courts
   changes to traditional adjudication
     process 119–20
   and crime reduction 119
   design and implementation 120

differences between diversion programs
and carceral alternative 125–7
incentives for offenders to participate in
treatment 114
introduction 113, 118–19
just treatment or preventive
punishment? 118–20
key components 113
and net widening 123–5
options for offenders 113
panoptic techniques 121–2
primary goals 113, 126
primary objective 119, 125
and principle of therapeutic
jurisprudence 119, 224–5
sanctions for failure to comply 114, 123–4
drug treatment courts in Australia
court diversion programs 114–15
differences between NSW court and US
courts 115–16
duration of programs (sentences)
118, 124
eligibility criteria for referral to NSW
court 116
failure to meet needs of certain
population groups 117
operation of NSW court 115–16
phases of treatment programs 116–17
positive and negative aspects of
treatment programs 117–18
types of treatment programs 116
drug-dependent offenders
differences between diversion programs
and carceral alternative 125–7
diversion programs in Australia 114–18
diversionary approaches 112–14
early identification and access to
treatment 113
incentives to participate in
treatment 114
sanctions for failure to comply with
programs 114, 123–4
self-identification of issues for
counselling 126–7
drug-related offences
reduction 119
zero tolerance response and arrest
statistics 112, 126

Durkheim, Emile
assumptions underpinning functionalist
theory 48
The Division of Labor in Society 46
functionalist approach to social
change 46
on law and punishment as indicators of
social evolution 46–8
on symbolic nature of punishment 191

Elias, Norbert, The Civilising Process 58–9
Elizabeth Northern Violence Intervention
Program (NVIP) 160
Engels, Friedrich 49
enhanced sentencing 70–1
exclusion 53–4
expressive punitivism, and essentialised
difference 105–6

family group conferencing 18, 178
family homicides 155
Family Violence Court (Vic.) 161
family violence courts, and therapeutic
jurisprudence 42
Fardon v Attorney General (Qld) 93
feminism
role in gaining recognition for problem
of domestic violence 170–1
role in highlighting significance of
social context in domestic violence
157–9, 171
socio-political perspective on domestic
violence 165
feminist criminology
contemporary perspectives and
assumptions 50
early criticism of male bias in
criminology 49–50
later deconstructionist approaches 50
practical and theoretical components 50
filicide 155
fines, and managerialism 212
The First Offenders Act 1894 11
fixed amount fines 203, 212
flogging 5–6, 13
Foucault, Michel 52–4
Discipline and Punish: The Birth of the
Prison 10–11, 19, 52–4, 120

Foucault, Michel (cont.)
   on distinction between discipline and
      security 56, 80
   on 'governmentality' 52, 55–6, 80
   on power–knowledge principles
      52–4, 120–1
Fremantle Family Violence Court 161
front-end net widening 123–4
functionalism
   approach to social change 46
   underlying assumptions 48

Garton, Stephen 11
gemeinschaft law 194
gender-based cognitive behaviour
      groups 166
general deterrence 26
Geraldton (Family Violence) Court 161
gescellschaft law 194
Goffman, Erving
   on power relationships 54
   on total institutions 125–7
governmentality, and law 55–6

The Habitual Criminal Act 1905
   (NSW) 12, 30
habitual offender legislation 30
Haneef, Mohamed 96
hegemony 49
Heidelberg Family Violence Court 161
history of punishment in Australia
   adoption of 'just deserts' 33–4
   Australia's carceral archipelago 10–12
   brutality and harsh disciplinary regime
      in mid-nineteenth century 27
   contemporary alternatives to prison
      15–18
   deterrence versus rehabilitation 11, 27
   development of community-based
      sanctions 15–16
   prison building 1850–1880 9, 19
   reforms aimed at diverting certain
      groups away from prison 11–12, 19
   remote penal settlements as first
      prisons 7–9
   rise of privately-run prisons 10
   risk, rehabilitation, restitution and
      recidivism 20

state responsibility 10
transportation and penal settlements
   4–7, 18–19
treatment of young offenders 176–8
Hobart, Robert (Lord) 8
home detention 132
homicide 155, 156
hooning
   definition 200
   media portrayal 216
   problem of 200–1, 216
   see also anti-hooning laws
hoons
   demographic characteristics
      201, 217–18
   preferred car models 202
   punishing 204–6
human sciences, and adjudication of
      correction 120–2

ideology 49
illegal street racing see anti-hooning laws;
      hooning; hoons
illicit drug strategy
   in Australia 114–18
   in US 112–14
illicit drug use
   and imprisonment rates 111
   punitive responses 111
   relationship to crime 111
imprisonment, as a form of punishment
   3–4, 9, 10–11, 52, 120–1
incapacitation
   and anti-hooning laws 214–15
   and consequentialist utilitarian
      philosophy 29–30
   and pre-emptive prevention 100–1
   sentencing and punishment 30–2
   utility of 77–80
   see also selective incapacitation
indefinite incarceration 31
The Indeterminate Sentences Act 1907
   (Vic.) 30
indeterminate sentencing 12, 30
Indigenous courts and circle sentencing
      courts
   availability 143
   degree of Indigenous involvement 143–5

distinctions between different
models 144–5
key characteristics 143
laws and procedures employed 143–5
objectives 146
political dimension 146
range of courts established 142–3, 149
Indigenous customary law 143
Indigenous justice
activism driving development 146
advantages and limitations 41
and decolonisation of justice 147–50
development 40, 146
links to therapeutic jurisprudence and
restorative justice 145–6
practices and control over
process 40–1
rehabilitation of offenders and criminal
justice system 149–50, 225
Indigenous justice programs 139–42
Indigenous peoples
over-representation in criminal justice
system 40
post-colonial perspectives 51–2
see also Aborigines and Torres Strait
Islanders
individual deterrence 26
industrial schools 177
The Inebriates Act 1901 12
infringement notices 36, 212
insecurity, prevailing discourse 105
interpersonal violence, gendered
experience 154–5
intimate partner violence
blurring of boundaries between victim
and offender 157–9
in criminal justice populations 155–6
homicide 155, 156
perpetrator treatment
programs 164–5
socio-political perspective 165

*Jacob Wetterling Crimes Against Children
and Sexually Violent Offender
Registration Act 1994* 74–5
Joondalup Family Violence Court 161
just deserts theory, and retributive
philosophy 32–4

just deserts-based sentencing
aims 34, 167
associated problems 35
support for 32–3
justice, decolonisation of 147–50
The Justice Fines Act 1899 12
Juvenile Justice Act 1992 (Qld) 187–8
juvenile justice system 12, 177
juvenile reformatories 12, 27, 177

Kable, Gregory 72
Kanka, Megan 75
King, Philip Gidley (Lieutenant) 8
Koori Court (Vic.) 143, 145, 146

labelling theory 192–3
lapping (hooning) 201
law
Durkheim's functionalist
perspective 46–8
types of 194–5
'learned helplessness' 158
lex talionis 32, 34
Local Justice Initiative Funds (Qld) 148
Local Justice Initiatives Program
(Qld) 140–1
London terrorist bombings 93

MacDonald, John 179
Maconochie, Alexander (Capt.) 9
Macquarie, Lachlan (Governor) 6, 7
Magistrates' Court (Koori Court) Act 2002
(Vic.) 144, 145
managerialism
actuarial dimension 37
and administrative sanctions 35–6
aggregative tendencies 36–7
consumerist dimension 37
deterrence and incapacitation in
anti-hooning laws 211–15, 216
effect on Australian criminal justice
system 35
influence on punishment and
sentencing 118–19
and introduction of drug
courts 118–19
and restorative justice 194–6
rise of 35, 211–12

managerialism (cont.)
    systemic dimensions 36–7
    and use of fines 212
    and use of infringement notices 36, 212
Māori people, and restorative justice 178
Marx, Karl 49
Marxist accounts of punishment *see* neo-
    Marxist theories of punishment
Megan's Law 75, 76, 82
mens rea 34
mental disorder, and sexual deviance 69
mental health courts 42, 230
mental health law 230
MERIT (Magistrates Early Referral into
    Treatment) 114
Midland Family Violence Court 161
Moreton Bay penal settlement 7
Movement Against Kindred Offenders
    (MAKO) 65, 74, 75–6
Murri courts (Qld) 143

national offender registration system 65
*National Security Information (Criminal and
    Civil Proceedings) Act 2001*
    (Cwlth) 89
Native Welfare Act 130
Neitenstein, Frederick (Capt.) 11
neo-Marxist theories of punishment 49
neoliberalism
    approaches to crime 175
    and community-based interventions 17
    and introduction of anti-hooning
        legislation 216–18, 228–9
net widening
    and criminal justice reforms 123–5
    and social control 123
new penology 223
new terrorism 85, 87
non-custodial management of offenders
    bureaucratisation and codification 16–17
    justification of alternatives to
        incarceration 17
    sentencing options during twentieth
        century 17
non-custodial orders, as punishment 4
Norfolk Island penal settlement 7, 8–9
Northbridge Curfew 230
NSW Aboriginal Justice Agreement 141–2

NSW Child Protection Register 73
NSW circle sentencing court 144
NSW *Equality Before the Law Bench* 148
NSW Legislative Council Standing
    Committee on Law and Justice 132
Nunga Court (SA) 143, 144–5

offenders
    as broken machines 26–9
    construction of 232
    making an 'example' of 24–6
    methods for reforming 28, 175
    as opportunistic 175
*The Offenders Probation and Parole Act
    1959* (Qld) 16
on-the-spot fines 36
organic solidarity 46–8

*Pam Lychner Sexual Offender Tracking and
    Identification Act 1996* (US) 75
panoptic techniques 121
panopticon 25, 53, 121
parole, introduction 12, 16
penal reforms
    in the 1960s and 1970s 32–3
    aimed at diverting certain groups away
        from prison 11–12, 19
    driving forces at end of nineteenth
        century 27
penal settlements
    brutality of convict system 5, 8–9
    early working conditions and rights of
        convicts 5–6
    encouragement of marriage 7
    governors' objectives for convict
        population 6
    hard labour and chain-gangs 7
    as punishment 7–9
    reduction of living standards of
        convicts 7–9
    reform strategy 6–7
    secondary punishment in remote penal
        settlements 7–9
Penalties and Sentences Act 1992
    (Qld) 70, 141
penalty
    and civilising and decivilising
        processes 60–1

and modern sensibilities 58–9

and risk 57

penitentiaries *see* prisons

penological principles

anti-hooning laws: managerialism, deterrence and incapacitation 211–15

counter-terrorism: pre-emptive prevention 100–2

domestic violence courts: punishment and protection 167–70

drug courts: treatment or preventive punishment? 118–20

Indigenous justice: the politics of partnership 145–6

sex offending: utility of incapacitation 77–80

youth justice conferencing: restoration or restitution? 184–91

periodic detention

availability in rural and remote areas 132

and child sex offences 71

introduction 16

periodic detention centres 10

Perth Family Violence Court 161

Phillip, Arthur (Governor) 8

point demerit schemes 203, 212

Police Offences Amendment Bill 2004 (Tas.) 208

Police Powers and Responsibilities Act 2000 (Qld) 207–8, 215

political cultures, as filters for risk 80–1, 102–3

Port Arthur penal settlement 7

post-colonialism, perspectives on punishment 51–2, 147

post-prison orders, as punishment 4

power, and punishment 49, 52–4

power–knowledge principles 52–4, 120–1

pre-emptive prevention, and counter-terrorist laws 100–2

preventive detention, and protective orders 30–1

preventive detention orders 94–5, 96

Price, John 9

prison action groups 32

prison farms, establishment 27

prison riots 32

prison system in Australia

extensive program of construction from 1980s 10

foundation in mid-nineteenth century 9, 27

introduction of privately-run prisons 10

range of types of 'corrective' institutions 28

reform at end of nineteenth century 27–8

responsibility of the state 10

see also names of prisons

The Prisoners Detention Act 1908 12

Prisoners' Parole Act 1937 (Qld) 16

Prisoners' Parole Act 1943 (Qld) 16

prisons

purpose in eighteenth century 26–7

rise as dominant form of punishment in nineteenth century 9, 10–11, 52, 120

as total institutions 125–7

see also prison system in Australia

'privatisation'

and civilising process 59

and function of prisons 59

probation, introduction 11, 12, 16

problem-solving courts

domestic violence courts 169

and therapeutic jurisprudence 41–2

procedural rights, and restorative justice 38

prohibited contact orders 95

protection orders 161–2, 163

protective orders 30–1

punishment

consequentialist approaches 26

and construction of offenders 232

definition 3, 231–2

Durkheimian perspective 46–8, 191

as 'example'/deterrence to others 24–5

feminist perspectives 49–50

to foster reform of character 25

Foucauldian perspective 52–4

functionalist perspective 46–8

neo-Marxist perspectives 49

post-colonial perspectives 51–2, 147

and rehabilitation 26–9

risk, rehabilitation and restitution 231–3

Queensland Crime Commission 72

recidivism, problem of 20
reformatories 12, 27, 177
reforming offenders *see* rehabilitation
registration of sex offenders 70, 72–4
rehabilitation
    declining support for 32–3
    and definition of who should be in
        prison 29–30
    domestic violence courts, punishment
        and protection 167–70, 225–6
    drug court programs as just treatment or
        preventive punishment 118–20, 224
    of offenders and criminal justice system
        under Indigenous justice 149–50, 225
    and systems of classification of
        prisoners 30
    and treatment of sex offenders
        69, 77–8, 83
    versus deterrence 11, 27
rehabilitation programs
    methods for reforming offenders 28
    view of offenders 20, 21, 26–9
rehabilitative-based sentencing
    objective of 118
    problems 29
reintegrative shaming of offenders
    179, 191–3
release-on-licence system 12
restitution
    and anti-hooning laws 199, 228–9
    and youth justice conferencing
        184–5, 227–8
restitution strategies
    positioning of offender as opportunistic
        20, 21–2
    significance of saying 'sorry' in
        YJCs 191–4
restorative justice
    and communitarianism 37–40
    definition 39, 184
    and domestic violence courts 169–70
    false dichotomy with retributive justice
        176, 184
    limitations 39–40
    and managerialism 194–6
    promotion by 'First Nation' groups 39

    proponents and programs 38–9
    and the regulatory state 194–6
    rise of 195–6
    and role of victims 18, 169
    see also youth justice conferencing (YJC)
retributive justice, false dichotomy with
    restorative justice 176, 184
retributive penal systems 32
retributive perspectives, on
    punishment 23, 32
RISE (ReIntegrative Shaming Experiments)
    181–2, 183
risk
    counter-terrorism and pre-emptive
        prevention 100–2, 222
    and relationship between discourse and
        practice 103–4
    and its relationship to fear and
        victimisation 103
    and retaliation 102–6
    sex offending and the utility of
        incapacitation 77–80, 221–2
    as a social product 102–3
risk assessment, view of offenders 20, 22
risk control 57
risk identification, and political culture
    80–1, 102–3, 223
risk management
    actuarial techniques 56
    defined 57
    influence on criminal justice system
        56–7, 223
'risk society' 55–8
risk-reduction techniques, aggregative
    focus 57
road blockades (hooning) 201
Road Safety Act 1986 (Vic.) 208
*Road Traffic Amendment (Impounding and
    Confiscation of Vehicles) Act 2004*
    (WA) 208
Road Transport (General) Act 1999
    (NSW) 207
*Road Transport (Safety and Management)
    Act 1999* (NSW) 207
*Road Transport (Safety and Traffic
    Management) Act 1999* (ACT) 207
Rockingham Family Violence Court 161
Rottnest Island Aboriginal prison 13

Royal Commission into Aboriginal Deaths
    in Custody (RCIADIC)
    catalyst for 129, 134
    findings 134–5
    implementation of findings 40, 129, 139
    individual death report of Malcolm
        Smith 136–8
    recommendations 139
rural and remote areas, absence of
        community-based sentencing
        options 132–3

Security Legislation Amendment (Terrorism)
    Act 2002 (Cwlth) 89
selective incapacitation
    appeal of 30, 31–2
    associated problems 30–1, 32
    justification for 222
    nature of 30–1
    without imprisonment 31
sentence discounting 163
sentencing, defined 3
The Sentencing Act 1989 (NSW) 33
September 11 terrorist attacks 85, 89, 100
Serious Sex Offenders Monitoring Act
    2005 (Vic.) 73
sex offences, as a separate category
    of crime 69
sex offender laws
    community notification of offenders
        70, 74–7, 78
    introduction of sexual psychopath
        laws 69
    registration of offenders 70, 72–4
    sentencing enhancement 70–1
    sexual predator laws 70, 71–2, 77–8
sex offenders, definition 72
Sex Offenders Registration Act 2004
    (Tas.) 74
Sex Offenders Registration Act 2004
    (Vic.) 73
Sex Offenders Registration (Amendment) Act
    2005 (Vic.) 73
sexual deviance, and mental disorder 69
Sexual Offenders (Protection of Children)
    Amendment Act 2003 (Qld) 73
sexual predator laws 70, 71–2, 77–8
Sexual Psychopath Act (Calif., US) 69, 81

Sexually Violent Persons Commitment Act
    1993 (Wisconsin, US) 74
shaming 191–2
    see also reintegrative shaming of
        offenders
social control, and net widening 123–5
sociology of punishment
    civilising process and sensibilities 58–61
    focus on prisons 19
    modes of regulation in contemporary
        programs of crime control 19–20
    theoretical interpretations of systems of
        punishment 45–6
South Australia Juvenile Justice (SAJJ)
    project 182
Statute Amendment (Misuse of Motor
    Vehicle Act) 2004 (SA) 208
Staysafe Parliamentary Committee
    (NSW) 206
street racing 201
Stuart, Robert Pringle 9
summary offences, and suspended
    sentences for first offenders 11–12
Suppression of the Financing of Terrorism
    Act 2002 (Cwlth) 89
surveillance arrangements
    and power–knowledge principle 53, 54
    in total institutions 125

Telecommunications Interception
    Legislation Amendment Act 2002
    (Cwlth) 89
terrorism
    Australia's response 88
    causes and responses 87–8
    definition 86
    history of 85, 87
    problem of 86–7
    see also counter-terrorism laws
terrorist acts, definition 87, 89, 95
therapeutic jurisprudence
    advantages and limitations 42
    application in Australia 42
    definition 41–2
    and domestic violence courts
        168, 225–6
    and drug courts 119, 224–5
    introduction 41

Thomas, Jack 98–100
total institutions
    dispossession of property 126
    effect on identity of inmates 125–6
    key characteristic 125
    prisons as total institutions 125–7
    and surveillance 125
*Traffic Amendment (Street and Illegal Drag
    Racing) Act 1996* (NSW) 206
traffic offence penalties
    confiscation of vehicles 204, 206, 212
    fixed amount fines 203, 212
    imprisonment 204, 207
    licence suspension 204, 212
    options 202–3
    point demerit schemes 203, 212
    vehicle defect notices 204–6, 212
transportation
    and colonial objectives 9
    duration of practice 5
    end of practice 5, 9, 23, 24–6
    and imperial objectives 5, 8, 9
    number of convicts transported to
        Australia 5
    objectives of British criminal justice
        system 7
    as punishment 4–5, 6, 7
twenty-four-hour court cell complexes 10

Ullathorne, William (Rev.) 8–9
UN *Declaration on the Basic Principles of
    Justice for Victims of Crime and Abuse
    of Power* 38
utilitarian theory of punishment
    basis of principles 23, 43
    deterrence 24–6
    and the end of transportation 24–6, 43
    incapacitation 29–32, 77–80
    rehabilitation 26–9
utilitarianism, defined 23

vehicle confiscation and impoundment
    204, 206–7, 212
vehicle defect notices 204–6, 212
vengeance, and child sex offending 81–2
victim impact statements 38
victims' movement 38–9

victims' rights and needs
    participation in response to crime 18
    recognising and meeting 37–9, 195
    see also restorative justice
Victorian Aboriginal Justice Agreement 146
Victorian Parliament Crime Prevention
    Committee 72
vigilantism, and child sex offenders 76, 80

Wagga Wagga Domestic Violence
    Court 161
Walker, Nigel, *Why Punish?* 231–2
'war on drugs', strategies 112–14, 127
'war on terror' 85, 97, 101, 107
welfare model of justice 177–8
welfare services, and restorative
    justice 38
women offenders
    battered women's syndrome
        (BWS) 158–9
    domestic violence and social
        context 154–8
women prisoners
    parole conditions 12
    restrictions on punishment 5
    treatment as children 27
women's prisons, establishment 27
Wood Royal Commission (NSW) 72
work release, introduction 16

young offenders, history of responses
    to 176–8
Young Offenders Act 1993 (SA) 187–8
Young Offenders Act 1994 (WA) 185–6
Young Offenders Act 1997 (NSW) 187–8
Youth Affair Network of Queensland 213
youth curfews 229–30
Youth Justice Act 1997 (Tas.) 185–6
Youth Justice Act 2005 (NT) 185–6
youth justice conferencing (YJC)
    apology process 189–90, 193–4
    benefits for offenders 180–1
    effective participation 190–1
    expectations of victims 189
    introduction in Australia and
        New Zealand 178–9
    and labelling theory 192–3

outcomes, fairness and offending
181–4, 190–1
principles and objectives
180–1, 185–9
process and procedures 180
and the regulatory state 194–6
reintegrative shaming of offenders
179, 191–3
and reoffending and reduction of
crime 183–4
restoration or restitution
184–91, 227–8

and restorative justice principles
175–6, 190–1
RISE (ReIntegrative Shaming
Experiments) 181–2, 183
as rituals of responsibilisation 191–6
significance of apology 191–4
treatment of offenders 181
variations in practical characteristics
across jurisdictions 179
youth justice system 177–8

zero tolerance response, to drug offences 112